Global Powers

Michael Mann is a central figure in contemporary sociology. His analysis of how the four sources of social power – ideological, economic, military and political – have shaped world history is a major contribution to social science. In this volume, distinguished scholars assess Mann's work, focusing on his final two volumes of *Sources of Social Power* which deal with the twentieth and twenty-first centuries. They tackle some of the major themes in Mann's work including globalization, American empire and the recent financial crisis. They also question his stance on some perennial topics in sociology: is the trajectory of American society 'exceptional'? How is military power different from other sources of power? What is the role of agency and ideology in social change? How do the relations between states affect domestic social development? *Global Powers* will provoke debate among all those interested in understanding the next phase of globalization.

Ralph Schroeder is a professor at the Oxford Internet Institute, University of Oxford.

Global Powers

Michael Mann's Anatomy of the Twentieth Century and Beyond

Edited by Ralph Schroeder
University of Oxford

CAMBRIDGE
UNIVERSITY PRESS

CAMBRIDGE
UNIVERSITY PRESS

University Printing House, Cambridge CB2 8BS, United Kingdom

One Liberty Plaza, 20th Floor, New York, NY 10006, USA

477 Williamstown Road, Port Melbourne, VIC 3207, Australia

314-321, 3rd Floor, Plot 3, Splendor Forum, Jasola District Centre, New Delhi - 110025, India

79 Anson Road, #06-04/06, Singapore 079906

Cambridge University Press is part of the University of Cambridge.

It furthers the University's mission by disseminating knowledge in the pursuit of education, learning and research at the highest international levels of excellence.

www.cambridge.org
Information on this title: www.cambridge.org/9781107450561

© Cambridge University Press 2016

First published 2016

A catalogue record for this publication is available from the British Library

Library of Congress Cataloging in Publication data
Schroeder, Ralph, editor.
Global powers : Michael Mann's anatomy of the twentieth century and beyond / edited by Ralph Schroeder.
Cambridge ; New York : Cambridge University Press, 2016. | Includes index.
LCCN 2015041406 | ISBN 9781107086142 (hardback) |
ISBN 9781107450561 (paperback)
LCSH: Mann, Michael, 1942– Sources of power. | Social history. | Historical sociology. | Power (Social sciences) | Political sociology. | Sociology – Philosophy.
LCC HN8 .M284 2016 | DDC 306.09–dc23
LC record available at http://lccn.loc.gov/2015041406

ISBN 978-1-107-08614-2 Hardback
ISBN 978-1-107-45056-1 Paperback

Contents

List of contributors   *page* vii

1   Introduction
    RALPH SCHROEDER   1

Part I Theory and history   9

2   The evolution of the sources of social power, and some
    extensions
    RISTO HEISKALA   11

3   The return of big historical sociology
    DENNIS SMITH   38

4   Taming the chief: from evolutionary theory to political
    ideology
    GEORGI DERLUGUIAN, TIMOTHY EARLE, AND WILL RENO   62

Part II Political, economic, military and ideological
questions   87

5   On political decency
    JOHN A. HALL   89

6   Mann on neoliberalism
    MONICA PRASAD   107

7   Nationalism and military power in the twentieth century
    and beyond
    SINIŠA MALEŠEVIĆ   117

8   History, historical sociology and the problem of ideology:
    the cases of communism and neoliberalism
    DAVID PRIESTLAND   143

  9 Mann's globalizations and their limits
     RALPH SCHROEDER   164

Part III American exceptionalism   183

 10 Ethnicity, class and the social sources of US
     exceptionalism
     LILIANA RIGA   185

 11 Mann's big picture of US social citizenship: "Road to
     World Empire" with Bob Hope
     EDWIN AMENTA   209

Part IV Empire   227

 12 Mann and the problem of empire
     JOHN DARWIN   229

 13 Hegemonic power during the Cold War and beyond
     ODD ARNE WESTAD   246

 14 The last empire? American power, liberalism, and world
     order
     G. JOHN IKENBERRY   256

Part V Response   279

 15 Response to the critics
     MICHAEL MANN   281

     Index   323

Contributors

EDWIN AMENTA is Professor of Sociology and Political Science at the University of California, Irvine.

JOHN DARWIN is Professor of Global and Imperial History at the University of Oxford.

GEORGI DERLUGUIAN is Professor of Social Research and Public Policy at New York University, Abu Dhabi.

TIMOTHY EARLE is Professor Emeritus in the Department of Anthropology at Northwestern University.

JOHN A. HALL is the James McGill Professor of Comparative Historical Sociology at McGill University.

RISTO HEISKALA is Professor and Director of the Institute for Advanced Social Research at the University of Tampere.

G. JOHN IKENBERRY is the Albert G. Milbank Professor of Politics and International Affairs at Princeton University.

SINIŠA MALEŠEVIĆ is Professor of Sociology at University College Dublin.

MICHAEL MANN is Professor of Sociology at the University of California, Los Angeles.

MONICA PRASAD is Professor of Sociology and Faculty Fellow at the Institute for Policy Research at Northwestern University.

DAVID PRIESTLAND is Professor of Modern History at the University of Oxford.

WILL RENO is Professor in the Department of Political Science at Northwestern University.

LILIANA RIGA is Lecturer in the Department of Sociology at the University of Edinburgh.

RALPH SCHROEDER is Professor at the Oxford Internet Institute at the University of Oxford.

DENNIS SMITH is Emeritus Professor of Sociology at the University of Loughborough.

ODD ARNE WESTAD is ST Lee Professor of US–Asian Relations at Harvard University.

1   Introduction

Ralph Schroeder

This volume brings together critical assessments of Michael Mann's sociology. It focuses on Volumes 3 and 4 of his major work, *The Sources of Social Power*, which cover the late nineteenth century to the present day. It is a follow-up to an earlier volume, *An Anatomy of Power: The Social Theory of Michael Mann* (co-edited by John A. Hall; 2006), which was put together before Mann's Volumes 3 and 4 had been published. The earlier volume was therefore in a sense premature. In this one, it has become possible to take stock of Mann's 'Sources', though he is now working on a fifth volume where he will reflect on his project. But apart from these further reflections, we can now examine his project as a whole and his analysis of our present condition in particular.

Mann's work does not need much by way of introduction. There are already several overviews of his work. Smith's essay (Chapter 3) puts Mann's 'Sources' into the context of similar macro-historical projects, and I have also provided an introduction to his sociology (Schroeder 2007). Further, there are essays on Mann's background (Hall 2006) and interviews with Mann which add some of the biographical and academic contexts to his work (Mann 2011; and the video and text of an interview with Alan McFarlane at www.alanmacfarlane.com/ancestors/ mann.htm; last accessed 20 October 2014). Mann (2013) has himself described how 'Sources' developed over the course of time. Chapter 2, by Heiskala, also gives an excellent account of how Mann's project has progressed from the first volume to the fourth. Here, it can be added that Mann reflects on the fact that, unlike in Volume 2, where he pulled together much data, especially about changes in state expenditure, this is not needed for his two volumes about the twentieth century: there is such an abundance of data as we get closer to the present that the main task is rather to make sense of these data.

Various themes and criticisms emerged in the 'Anatomy' volume that are worth briefly recapitulating here by way of setting the scene for this volume. One is the relative neglect of ideological power. In the 'Anatomy' volume, this criticism was made in relation to early

Christianity (by Joseph Bryant), to the role played by religion in the rise of the modern state (by Phil Gorski) and to Islamist fundamentalism and other ideologically or normatively driven movements (Jack Snyder). There is a also a different aspect to the neglect of ideology which was highlighted by Jack Goldstone, which is the absence of scientific knowledge as a factor in the rise of the West (a criticism that I repeat here). But it is also possible to overplay this criticism: Mann has always resisted the temptation to invoke free-floating ideology, ideology without the backing of organizational capabilities, as a factor in social change. His position in this respect goes against the grain of much contemporary sociological analysis that focuses on culture and identity, but Mann's position is also a useful brake on seeing short-term cultural and ideological shifts – which tend to wax and wane – as indications of larger important changes.

One shortcoming of the 'Anatomy' volume that has already been mentioned was that it could only deal with history up to the First World War, even though two books outside the 'Sources' sequence, *Fascists* (2004) and *The Dark Side of Democracy: Explaining Ethnic Cleansing* (2005), had been published. Only one essay in the 'Anatomy' volume, Laitin's, directly engaged with Mann mainly on a predominantly twentieth-century topic, and he criticized Mann's association between democracy and ethnic cleansing citing counter-examples. Critical assessment of Mann's work on 'Fascists' is also a gap in the current volume. Further, there is still little engagement (apart from Malesevic's essay in this volume) with military power, which is often left to other disciplines like international relations and war or strategic studies. Yet these disciplines treat war in isolation from underlying social changes. This is also true for historians of militarism (van Creveld 2008), who treat war and the preparation for war as a separate topic without integrating it with broader social changes. Mann is therefore among the few sociologists who has given us an account of how the two world wars in particular caused major changes, such as the extension (and sometimes a regress in the extension) of citizenship rights and the economic rise and decline of nations. Still, the interplay between economic and military fortunes is covered in many chapters of 'Sources', including chapters on the First and Second World War (Chapters 5 and 14) in Volume 3.

The global purview of Mann's analysis was still missing in the first two volumes which focused on the 'great powers'. Nowadays, global history has become a major focus of historians, particularly in synoptic works about the long nineteenth century by Bayly (2003) and Osterhammel (2014). But such a global purview is still missing among historians of the twentieth and twenty-first centuries. Yet scholars from any discipline who are interested in the shape of the twentieth century and in understanding the present in a longer-term perspective will now need to engage with his work. This is particularly so since the weakness of other sociological works about globalization is their thinness concerning longer-term patterns (Walby 2009; Martell 2010). Other treatments of globalization tend to be highly theoretical without being grounded in history (Giddens 1990). Mann has resisted the label 'theory', and, apart from adopting a comparative historical approach, he does not practice a particular method (but see Lange 2013 for a state-of-the-art overview). Whether historical sociology is currently due for a revival is still open to question (Lachmann 2013). Mann's reflections in the concluding chapter of Volume 4 about how history enables us to recognize the constraints and possibilities we face are revealing, even if he also notes the limits of social scientific knowledge in this respect.

With this, we can turn to the present volume, which is organized as follows: Part I contains assessments of Mann's 'big picture' and also locates him in the landscape of contemporary historical sociology. Part II considers each of the four sources of power in turn, and then my own essay then interrogates how Mann sees the relation between the four powers, particularly in the recent trajectory of globalization. Part III tackles the question of American exceptionalism, which echoes the discussion of European exceptionalism that was a major theme in the 'Anatomy of Power' volume: both are important in different ways for the question of whether there was – and is – a 'Western' model of social development. The final part of the book contains three essays on empire, which Mann himself regards as one of the three master processes governing the twentieth century, alongside the rise and growing dominance of the nation-state and capitalism. The three essays in Part IV can also be read as reflections on how American empire is in keeping with how empires have functioned throughout large swathes of history – or if the American empire is exceptional.

Against this background, we can turn to the individual contributions: Part I, 'History and Theory', contains three chapters that put Mann's work into context and provides overall assessments. Chapter 2, by Risto Heiskala, not only summarizes and offers a commentary on all four volumes, but also urges Mann to engage with other contemporary theorists of power such as Michel Foucault and Bruno Latour. Heiskala also wants Mann to expand his ideas about gender, identity and nature and the environment which would bring his work into dialogue with a wider array of contemporary sociological thinking. Chapter 3, by Dennis Smith, contextualizes Mann's work differently, situating him in the tradition of the macro-historical sociology of Skocpol, Moore and Tilly and others (see also Collins 1999). Smith also counter-poses Mann's ideas with those of Marxist world-systems theory, particularly as expounded by Wallerstein, which is arguably the main rival project to Mann's on the left, as well as with Gary Runciman's evolutionist theory, another theoretical tradition which has recently been revived.

Chapter 4, by Derlugian, Earle and Reno, also provides a long-term evolutionary perspective on Mann's work, though in this case an anthropological one (instead of Runciman's socio-biological approach). The authors argue that leading strata (or 'chiefs') have always been able to evade the strictures of lesser powers throughout the course of history and especially so in the twentieth century with great increases in the strength of bureaucracies and information technologies. They point out that even if these chiefs have always been 'personalistic', they will in the future be counteracted by the drive towards greater egalitarianism which has, during long-term social development, continued to gain strength as an ideological impulse 'from below'.

Part II takes a different approach, interrogating Mann's project through the lens of the different types of power. John Hall (Chapter 5) begins with politics. He has engaged with Mann's project from the beginning and in his own work developed a comparative historical sociology that presents a liberal alternative to Mann's more radical views. As Hall points out, there is often more agreement than disagreement between them, but in my view this makes his chapter all the more interesting as it highlights their somewhat different viewpoints on contemporary social democracies and the prospects of more and less liberal regimes. Liberalism, or rather economic neo liberalism, is also at the centre of Chapter 6, by Monica Prasad, which challenges Mann's account of neo liberalism and the financial crisis of 2008: what, she asks, can Mann's general theory of power and his macro-approach contribute to our understanding of a specific event that a more economics-based explanation of just this event or turning point cannot? Not much, she answers, and she proceeds to show how Mann does not really depart from the specific explanations of the crisis by economists, including neoliberal ones, whose explanations we might expect to differ quite substantially from Mann's.

One of the unique contributions of Mann's sociology is that he treats military power on par with economic, political and ideological power. Since Volumes 3 and 4 cover two world wars and the major revolutions of the twentieth century, he can explain better than most social scientists why wars and militarism have been such a decisive influence on social change. Siniša Malešević (Chapter 7) thinks that Mann's account of this macro-role of military power leaves out the solidarity of small units among soldiers on the one hand and the role of military ideology in everyday life outside of times of war on the other. He also points to the rise of technocracy and surveillance in the twentieth century, which plays a minor role in Mann's writings.

David Priestland (Chapter 8) levels a different charge against Mann, and one that has been made before (in the 'Anatomy' volume), which is that he downplays the role of ideology or culture at various turning points covered in Volumes 3 and 4. Among Priestland's examples are the different elite factions during the final years of the Soviet Union, as well as how financiers and economic experts advocated different responses to the financial crisis of 2008, including a right-wing interpretation of the crisis which has remained intact in the several years since it took place. Chapter 9, by Ralph Schroeder, then gives an account of one of the main themes of Volumes 3 and 4, globalization, in order to challenge him on the absence of science and technology as a separate source of power (this is also done in Heiskala's Chapter 2) and about how globalization reinforces or goes against the overlap between the four (or, in my view, three) sources of social power.

A number of commentators have pointed out that approximately a third of Mann's last two volumes are concerned with the United States, domestically and abroad. In Part III, 'American Exceptionalism', two papers confront Mann's version of this. Liliana Riga (Chapter 10) revisits an argument that has been made a number of times: that the reasons for America's 'Sonderweg' are the strong divisions by ethnic groups that outweighed the formation of strong economic class identities. Riga develops a new position in this debate, since she asks how ethnic immigrants were 'americanized' by the authorities and how their immigration status for the most part prevented them from union participation and participation in elections, denying them citizenship rights. Mann's account of the period in question, the late nineteenth century up to the New Deal, largely leaves out ethnicity, focusing instead on class compromises, a serious omission in Riga's view.

Edwin Amenta (Chapter 11) picks up this argument for the New Deal, which is often seen as the crux of the exceptionalism debate. Here, Mann argues that the United States did, in fact, achieve the build-up of a welfare state at this time that compares well with others. This nascent American welfare state only shrank for different reasons later, including that the economy picked up strongly during the Second World War and that the high unemployment rates of the 1930s were reversed (weakening pressures 'from below'). Amenta argues instead that the reasons for the development of the American welfare state are more to do with policy elites and the political opportunities they had at the time, which allowed these elites to shape the domestic agenda despite opposition. However, they could only do so episodically and slowly within a political system as fragmented as the American one, unlike in the more centralized political systems in Europe. The different implications of these views for the contemporary possibilities to strengthen American welfare – notably President Obama's push for greater health care coverage – are in plain view in this debate about America's past (as are, perhaps more obliquely, the implications of Chapter 10 for the current debate about immigration).

Part IV, finally, is devoted to the role of empire, which is a shift in Volumes 3 and 4, because empire is much more central than in the first two volumes. This shift entails that Mann must revisit, in Volume 3, the period covered in 'Sources' Volume 2 (pre–First World War) to go back to the origins of (particularly British and American) empire in the late nineteenth century. Mann's view of history at the most macro-level, including in Volumes 1 and 2, charted the rise and decline of great powers. Yet his focus on external forces is quite different from conventional comparative historical sociology, which traditionally compares and contrasts the status of 'great power' nation-states (not empires) as units. Yet John Darwin (Chapter 12) wants to further amend Mann's account of empires by noticing the connections between imperial centres and their subject populations, including in terms of ideologies which travelled in both directions. In doing this, he also raises the question of whether the label empire can be applied to the contemporary United States at all, particularly as the American ideology has often been an anti-colonial one.

Mann, uniquely for a sociologist, sees American empire not as driven by economic forces, but rather primarily by military and ideological ones. This controversial view is challenged by Arne Westad and John Ikenberry in different ways: Westad (Chapter 13) argues that even if the Soviets and their empire turned out to be, post facto, less of a threat than the United States made it out to be (as Mann also argues), this does not mean that the threat was not a real one. The competition for control between the Cold War imperial powers for Westad was less one-sided than on Mann's view, with implications for the terrible human costs to the client regimes which the two Cold War sides supported. Perhaps, the balance sheet of American empire – if such it is – is still too early to tally. Chapter 14, by Ikenberry, presents the case for a positive balance sheet. He argues for the benefits of American empire in preserving and extending the liberal international order, while Mann's weighing of the costs and benefits goes in the other direction. Westad and Ikenberry therefore also disagree with Mann on the rivalry between the American empire and its current main rival, China: Westad thinks that China is now on a capitalist path (Mann thinks it is only half-capitalist), but he also suggests that there are opportunities for the Chinese state to pursue a course that departs from Anglo-American capitalism. According to Ikenberry, in contrast, the

United States can continue to shape the world order in a positive way through its liberal norms, whatever the case may be for the competition between American and other (including Chinese) variants of capitalist economy.

As will be evident from this short overview, Mann's 'Sources' will be a central point of departure for any discussions of the social order in the twenty-first century. This volume does not cover all the major powers or topics in Mann's Volumes 3 and 4. There is little on Japanese empire, for example, to which Mann devotes one and a half chapters in Volume 3. Yet the chapters here have focused on what will arguably be the most controversial topics for some time to come: the shape of history during the 'short' twentieth century and its legacies, the changing role of the United States, the nexus between empire and globalization and questions of capitalism and politics.

It remains for me to get out of the way of what I hope the reader will find a series of stimulating debates. I can only add my thanks to the contributors for their incisive contributions to these debates, and to Mann for a thorough and generous response. Finally, I have been fortunate in having a very astute reader at Cambridge University Press, who had a number of suggestions that improved the volume. Thanks also go to John Haslam and Carrie Parkinson at Cambridge University Press who did a great job in shepherding the project at various points.

References

Bayly, Christopher Alan. 2003. *The Birth of the Modern World 1780–1914*. Oxford: Blackwell.

Collins, Randall. 1999. 'Maturation of the State-Centred Theory of Revolution and Ideology', in his *Macro-Sociology: Essays in Sociology of the Long Run*. Stanford: Stanford University Press, pp. 19–36.

Giddens, Anthony. 1990. *The Consequences of Modernity*. Cambridge: Polity Press.

Hall, John A. 2006. 'Political Questions', in John A. Hall and Ralph Schroeder (eds), *An Anatomy of Power: The Social Theory of Michael Mann*. Cambridge: Cambridge University Press, pp. 33–55.

Hall, John A. and Ralph Schroeder (eds) 2006. *An Anatomy of Power: The Social Theory of Michael Mann*. Cambridge: Cambridge University Press.

Lachmann, Richard. 2013. *What Is Historical Sociology?* Cambridge: Polity Press.

Lange, Matthew. 2013. *Comparative-Historical Methods*. London: Sage.

Mann, M. 2004. *Fascists*. Cambridge: Cambridge University Press.

    2005. *The Dark Side of Democracy: Explaining Ethnic Cleansing*. Cambridge: Cambridge University Press.

    2011. *Power in the 21st Century. Conversations with John A Hall*, Cambridge: Polity Press.

2013. 'The Sources of My Sources', *Contemporary Sociology: A Journal of Reviews*, 42: 499–502.

Martell, Luke. 2010. *The Sociology of Globalization*. Cambridge: Polity Press.

Osterhammel, Juergen. 2014. *The Transformation of the World: A Global History of the Nineteenth Century*. Princeton: Princeton University Press.

Schroeder, Ralph. 2007. 'Michael Mann', in Rob Stones (ed), *Key Sociological Thinkers*, Basingstoke: Palgrave Macmillan, pp. 338–354.

Van Creveld, Martin. 2008. *The Changing Face of War*. New York: Ballantine Books.

Walby, Sylvia. 2009. *Globalization and Inequalities: Complexity and Contested Modernities*. London: Sage.

Part I

Theory and history

2   The evolution of the sources of social power, and some extensions

Risto Heiskala

Historical sociology is, according to the famous characterization of Reinhard Bendix, a chimera of research programmes, most of which took many of their questions from Marx and most answers from Weber. Provided that creativity is allowed in formulating both questions and answers, this characterization fits well with the possibly greatest of living historical sociologists, Michael Mann, who has recently completed his five millennium-long journey from the emergence of the state to our time, with two new volumes in *The Sources of Social Power* series.

In what follows I will first briefly describe what is specific in Mann's neo-Weberian approach to historical development and particularly in his approach to power. I will then highlight some of the historical narrations in each of the four volumes. My focus will be on the two recent volumes, but the two earlier volumes cannot be completely neglected because they provide the context for the two new books and their analysis also shows that Mann's model of analysing power and particularly the way he uses it has gone through some transformation in the course of writing the series. Finally, I will recall the theoretical aspects of Mann's work and make two interventions. I will ask, first, whether his theoretical approach could be made more systematic and developed further, and, second, whether his classification of power sources is the most suitable one for the purposes of the analysis of our time or whether it could be adjusted in one way or another. The interventions include discussion on the relationship of Mann's approach to Foucault's analytics of power and an attempt to expand Mann's most important theoretical tool, the IEMP model (ideological, economic, military and political power sources), to a NACEMP model (natural, artefactual, cultural, economic, military and political power sources) with an even broader scope.

What is power and how does the IEMP model work?

Mann is not a grand theorist. He finds it difficult to understand the use of theory that has not emerged in the context of empirical social research. Therefore, his concepts tend to be methodological ideal types in nature and oriented towards a middle-range type of interpretation of social processes. Yet he cannot avoid social ontology completely, even if he tries to keep his commitments on that level few, abstract and open to reinterpretation.

Here is what he says. Human beings are purposeful creatures who reach for various ends. In their actions they both purposefully and unwittingly create social networks in which their actions are embedded. Those networks give birth to different forms of institutional organization and these provide actors with power resources (i.e. means to control their environment to achieve desired ends). How exactly this happens in each time and place is for empirical social research to reveal, but conceptual tools can be developed which are useful for study in varying historical contexts.

The most important of such concepts is that of power. In its conceptualization, Mann (1986) accompanies Giddens (1995) as both of them swim against the currents of time and discipline and find Parsons' understanding of power useful in some senses. The most established forms of power analysis (such as Mills 1956 and Dahl 1957) tend to understand power as a scarce resource that is subject to competition in a zero-sum game where every increase of the power of actor A simultaneously is a loss in the power of actor B, and vice versa. Mann admits the importance of such a form of power analysis (departing here from Parsons, who never quite got the point of Mills' *The Power Elite*, as is evident from Parsons 1960) but continues (following Parsons) that this form of power, which Mann calls 'distributive power', is just one side of the phenomenon. The other side is the analysis of 'collective power' by which he refers to cases in which A and B, acting together, can enhance their joint power over third parties or over nature. A great part of Mann's historical narration of our civilization concentrates on changes taking place in the amount of collective power due to technological development (such as agricultural, industrial and military revolutions or printing) or new forms of social organization (such as the Roman legions, bureaucratic organization or democracy). He maintains that such leaps in the amount of available power resources are central to our understanding of the course of history, and, therefore, in his studies he concentrates on the 'leading edges' or such historical episodes that result in enhancement of the collective power resources of actors. To the relief of those to whom such an account sounds far too Parsonian (even if Mann does not commit himself to Parsons' linear evolutionism) it may be noted that Mann always connects his analysis of increasing collective power to an analysis of distributive power games in which some actors win and some lose due to the very innovations that cause the enhancement of collective power. The general part of Mann's analysis also includes two other distinctions: extensive vs. intensive and authoritative vs. diffused power. If we cross-tabulate these we get an army command structure as an example of the authoritative-intensive form of power and market exchange as an example of the extensive-diffused form. The intermediate cases of extensive-authoritative and intensive-diffused forms are exemplified by a militaristic empire and a general strike.

The forms of people's purposeful actions are various, and Mann believes that it is not possible or even useful to try to develop a conceptualization that covers all forms without exception. Yet he also believes that we need some kind of general conception of different forms of power that can be used in an empirical study of the contexts. To find such a conception he turns to Weber, who transformed Marx's binary conceptualization of base and superstructure to a triad consisting of the economic, cultural (or status-related) and political (or institutional–organizational) spheres. Weber also loosened Marx's expectations of causal determination, which, according to Marx, in the end always went from the economic base structure to the ideological and legal superstructure, by saying that the study of causal links is a matter of empirical study: sometimes it goes exactly as Marx expected, but sometimes it goes exactly the opposite way. Mann accepts all that in Weber but interprets Weber's spheres as forms of social power and divides (mainly due to the influence of Herbert Spencer, to mention another classical, to some extent unjustly unpopular, figure in addition to Parsons) Weber's political sphere into two different forms of power: 'political power' and 'military power'. This is a move justified by several empirical analyses in different volumes of Mann's book series, showing that political and military forms of control of the environment often take different paths in cases such as the Roman Empire or Western Europe and Japan after the Second World War. He also changes the term 'cultural' to 'ideological'. That is how we end up with his IEMP model.

Ideological power in the model refers to 'the human need to find ultimate meaning in life, to share norms and values, and to participate in aesthetic and ritual practices. ... Religions provide most examples ... with secular ideologies like liberalism, socialism and nationalism.' Diffusion of ideological power takes two principal forms: 'It may be sociospatially "transcendent." That is, an ideology may diffuse trough the boundaries of economic, military, and political organizations. Second, ideological power may solidify an existing power organization, developing its "immanent morale"' (Mann 1993:7). Despite the definition that puts emphasis mainly on ritually affirmed value commitments, Mann has dealt under the title 'ideology' also with cognitive cultural categorization throughout his career. Thus he emphasized already in Volume 1 the role of world religions in general and Christianity in particular after the collapse of the Roman Empire in Europe as a shared world view and context of action. In the more recent volumes, written well after the 'cultural turn', cultural cognition tends to affect also the definition of ideological power so that Mann (2012:7) adds a third type, 'institutionalized ideologies', such as patriarchy, to this power source and therefore comes close to replacing the term 'ideological power' with that of 'cultural power'. However, for the sake of continuity and some other factors to be discussed in the closing section of this chapter, he keeps on speaking about the IEMP model instead of the CEMP model (where the letters would refer to the cultural, economic, military and political power).

Economic power for Mann includes market exchange but is not restricted to it. Instead, it derives 'from the need to extract, transform, distribute and consume resources of nature' (Mann 1993:7). The meaning of 'economic' then clearly goes beyond the neo-classical canon and resembles more the way the term was used by Karl Polanyi and political economists from Smith to Marx. All these theorists were, in addition to their concern with market exchange, interested in the reproduction of the societal whole and relations between classes, thus departing from current neo-classical economics. In Volume 1, which came out in 1986, Mann emphasized this in using the term 'circuits of praxis' in referring to economic organization. But fashions change as time goes by and he dropped this semi-Marxist terminology in Volume 2 in 1993. However, the definition of the economic form of power has remained the same throughout all the four volumes even if Mann's actual empirical analyses do not pay much attention to the development of productive forces after Volume 1.

Military power is the social organization of physical force, and *political power* 'derives from the usefulness of territorial and centralized regulation. ... Domestically, it is "territorially centralized"; externally, it involves geopolitics' (Mann 1993:9). Here, Mann differs from Weber in two senses. First, he makes a distinction between military and **political power**, referring to historical cases in which it is obvious that military and political power have not been, contrary to Weber's understanding, integrated. Here it suffices to refer to the current European Union (EU) and Mark Eyskens, who in 1991, when he was the foreign minister of Belgium, famously said, just before Operation Desert Storm was launched, that 'Europe is an economic giant, a political dwarf and a military worm' (The New York Times, January 25, 1991) working under the US military shield. Second, while Weber's analysis of political domination (*Herrschaft*) included all kinds of institutional organizations. Mann wants to reserve the term 'political power' for the analysis of states (i.e. territorially centralized power organizations). The third relevant factor in this context is that in the course of writing his book series Mann made a slight change in his definition of military power. While in Volume 1 he was quite ready to follow Spencer and include all forms of *corvee* labour (enforced labour based on tradition from that which built the pyramids or the Roman network of highways to that which provided the European nobility with its affluence compared to the populace) under the title of organized physical force, from Volume 3 onwards he starts to put more emphasis on the lethal nature of military power and underlines that its message everywhere is 'if you resist, you die' (Mann 2012:11).

It is important to understand that Mann considers his IEMP model as an analytical tool and not a structural description of society. After the emergence of the state, all societies probably have had some forms of all four power sources, but it is a matter of empirical study to detect which forms of power are institutionalized – and also to what extent in a certain society – and which forms are living in the interstices of others and waiting for the possibility to flourish. Therefore, the status of the IEMP model for Mann is quite different from the base/superstructure model for Marx or the AGIL scheme (adaptation, goal-attainment, integration and latent pattern-maintenance) for Parsons or the System/Lifeworld scheme for Habermas. He emphasizes that 'societies are much *messier* than our theories of them' (Mann 1986:4) and understands his concepts as analytical tools to 'cope with the patterned mess that is human society' (Mann 1993:4). Therefore, he says,

My IEMP model is not one of a social system, divided into four "subsystems", "levels", "dimensions", or any other of the geometric terms favoured by social theorists. Rather, it forms an analytical point of entry for dealing with mess. The four power sources offer distinct, potentially powerful organizational means to humans pursuing their goals. But which means are chosen, and in which combinations, will depend on continuous interaction between what power configurations are historically given and what emerges within and among them. (Mann 1993:10)

The first two volumes

Volume 1 is subtitled 'A History of Power from the Beginning to A.D. 1760'. It starts from the emergence of first states and closes with the collapse of the last European non-territorial state. In effect, it covers the period of agrarian societies preceding the modern state and industrialization. The volume is a story of human innovation or development of the leading edges of enhancement of available power resources. The reverse side is a story of how human beings are, at the same time, slowly but firmly being 'caged' within power organizations which have increasing resources for surveillance, control, taxation and adjustment of behaviour.

There is no way of giving even a telegraphic summary of the volume but some highlights may be telling.

Did the rulers of traditional empires possess such an absolute power over their territories as is reflected in the ideological codifications of their regimes? No, they did not. Simple logistical calculations show that traditional military powers were unable to move their troops from one centre to another faster than the maximum speed of 30 kilometres per day. Even that needed to be carefully planned because maintaining a marching army was a difficult business and the maximum period a self-supplied army could survive was three days, in which it could not cover more than 90 kilometres. If successfully implemented, conquering a rebelling centre was possible, but even then the conquering army usually lost its contact with the centre from which it had departed. Moreover, it was more difficult to maintain a standing army than a marching army and therefore troops of the central power often eroded or merged into the local population unless they moved on to maintain themselves. Hence the astonishing speed at which armies such as Alexander the Great's moved during their campaigns. Territorial control or caging of populations then is a difficult business that requires developed communication channels, transportation routes and organizational capabilities, and it was not very effective before modern times.

Why then did the Inca Empire surrender to the attack of 160 Spanish warriors, 60 of whom were mounted on horses, who came in three ships? On the surface, this encounter looks like a confrontation between two traditional empires. Yet the one with significantly less manpower and far from home won. Why? The answer can be found in the division of power resources between the parties. Compared to the Incas, the Spanish Empire had several powerful technological benefits at its disposal. It had means of transportation in the form of ships and skill in navigation. It had better arms and knights mounted on horses, and it had better military organization. Naturally, also, the diseases brought unintentionally by the Europeans contributed to the result (a factor not mentioned by Mann but emphasized by Diamond 1997) but obviously the difference in available power resources is a major part of the solution to the riddle.

Why did the centre of power in Europe move from the Mediterranean to northern Europe and England? The solution to the problem is based on the nature of the agricultural revolution that over several centuries transformed the European economy and created the base for the Industrial

Revolution by liberating part of the population from agricultural production. One of the important inventions in this long process was the new type of plough dragged by draft animals such as horses and oxen, enabling the cultivation of the central- and north-European soil irrigated by rain-water. Yet all the power sources and natural features of Europe (such as long sea- and river coasts and deep, rich soil) contributed to the transition.

Did Marx and Engels get it right when they said that all history is the history of class struggle? No, they did not. Class struggle requires symmetrical and politically organized classes. Such a condition has indeed existed in modern times, but this is a special case accompanied only by some rare historical constellations such as the struggle between debtors and lenders in ancient Greece and Rome. What has been the normal case in history has been an arrangement in which the ruling class has been organized but other classes have been latent at the most. Hence, the endless succession of unsuccessful revolts motivated by famine in the course of the history of agrarian societies.

These highlights show that the enthusiasm with which Mann's first volume was received was to a great extent based on his ability to tell informative, condensed and often surprising historical stories. A great part of the attraction was that often in these stories technological innovations and new forms of social organization were entangled together, and this interlink provided the solution to the question, 'why did the direction of history change'?

Volume 2 is subtitled 'The rise of classes and nation-states, 1760–1914'. It takes the form of five interlinked case studies: studies of France, Great Britain, Habsburg Austria, Prussia-Germany and the United States as the North American offshoot of Europe. The selection of cases is justified by an attempt to cover relevant variation and limit the cases to a representative set of 'leading edges'.

Volume 1 showed that the enlargement of state took huge leaps in Europe due to the military revolution and constant waging of war between the European states over several centuries preceding the Industrial Revolution. These resulted in a huge increase of tax collection and recruitment of men to armies. This again made the state a significant factor within societies and turned everybody's attention to the state. The new architectonics of power was codified in the bourgeoisie's demands to have a say in the use of state power and Lenin's maxim, according to which political struggle is nothing if it is not struggle of state power – both strikingly new ideas in a world that had been accustomed to live like Robin Hood with attempts to avoid the reach of the state on a routine basis instead of trying to conquer it.

The rising importance of the state was now accompanied by the Industrial Revolution, causing a significant increase of material resources, on the one hand, and great suffering of most of the working population, on the other. The bourgeois demands of equal participation in political power were thus quickly followed by similar demands coming from other social strata. The demands of bourgeois men were therefore soon accompanied by analogous demands from the men of the rising working class and both bourgeois and working women. This is the hidden history behind the continuing universal demands for equality and democracy in modern times.

The rise of classes other than the nobility and clergy was accompanied by a cultural revolution in the form of the rise of nationalism. It too was a new phenomenon creating, for the first time in history, mass-scale populations that loved the state bureaucracy caging them so much that they were soon ready to march to their deaths to protect that bureaucracy and its elites in the First and Second World Wars. The extension of educational institutions and development of mass media were an important condition for this development. The most important carrier strata though were the state-dependent strata such as military personnel, civil servants and their family members.

According to Mann, the respective rises of classes and of nation-states were new and thoroughly interlinked processes. The form of linkage, however, varied. In Germany, France and England, one enforced the other and created a relatively integrated nation-state. In Austria-Hungary, the new movements eroded the empire. The United States was somewhere in between and also different in the sense that as a conquered land it did not have the European abundance of past traditions for the new movements to fight with. It was also virtually an island and thus did not have to constantly prepare for war. All the cases were different but in their own ways all of them brought us to the modern architectonics of power we have today.

A terrifying feature of the process of modernization was that the increase of economic and military resources was coupled with increasing complexity of the international system. The concluding chapter of the volume in which Mann analyses the process leading to the First World War exemplifies this. He joins that current of scholars who believe that the war was an accident brought about by a group of 'sleepwalkers', and reading his analysis quite convinces the reader that the responsible parties actually did not know what they were doing.

Volume 3: Global Empires and Revolution, 1890–1945

As already mentioned, Volume 2 was different from Volume 1 in the sense that even if it dealt with the time of great industrialization it did not pay much attention to the development of productive forces in addition to mentioning the fact. The two new volumes are, if possible, even further from the infrastructural base of social development. The IEMP model is used, of course, and particularly in the case of military and economic power it makes it impossible to completely avoid the material aspects of power. Yet the focus of Mann's work in the new volumes is mainly on the level of reality that one could describe as political history. Another difference from the previous volumes is that the new volumes are much more opinionated than the previous ones. They are political history written from a standpoint of defending freedom, equality and environmental sustainability, and the author of the historical narrations in Volumes 3 and 4 does not conceal his views concerning the question of who in each case has been for and who against his values. As a professional historian and a good Weberian, however, Mann always writes in a way that makes it possible to tell apart his values and his factual statements. Therefore, the fact that he lets his standpoint show does not destroy the value of his text as academic historical writing but just makes his diagnosis of the era more interesting to read.

Temporally, the third volume does not start exactly from where the second ended (i.e. from the beginning of the First World War). This is so because in addition to continuing the story of the deepening capitalist–industrial transformation of the economy and strengthening of the nation-state that was started in Volume 2, Volume 3 also tells the story of the rise and fall of European empires, a story which needs to be started from the end of the nineteenth century at the latest.

In Volume 2 Mann based his account of the booming increase of the powers of the state on the curious European pattern of the states to constantly wage war with each other. In Volume 3 he puts even more emphasis on this European curiosity and says that even if it may not be true that men are from Mars and women from Venus, it seems to be the case that Europeans are from Mars since for almost a millennium they had been waging war on each other. At the end of that millennium, European empires had become so strong that they were able to transfer that pattern from Europe to all other continents of the world. This is how they, for a short period of time, conquered almost the entire globe. Mann calls that period the time of sectorial globalization, thus emphasizing the two crucial features of the era: first, a genuine increase of inter- and transnational connectedness under the control of the European powers, and, second, the fact that that form of globalization was restricted to within the sectors controlled by the different European empires.

In addition to the sectorial nature of colonialist globalization, Mann's account of colonialism emphasizes the extremely violent nature of European power in the colonies and its political and military nature, which leaves economic factors in a somewhat marginal position. According to Mann, most of the time, most colonial powers did not profit economically from the colonies but ended, in the final count, putting more resources into their conquests than what could be gained. This makes theories such as Wallerstein's world-system analysis doubtful because the economic centre-periphery model does not seem to work in the way expected in the theory. Rather, colonialism seems to be a continuation of the European age-long pattern of politically and militaristically motivated conquests.

The Second World War, of course, brought European colonialism crashing down. It meant the end of all European empires. According to Mann, this was a new world-era, starting less violently than the previous one run by European imperialism. It began in the European continent and then spread around the globe. The new start was sealed by the establishment of the forerunner of the EU, the European Coal and Steel Union, which made it impossible for any European state to monopolize access to the two products necessary for waging a modern war. Outside Europe, the gradual process of decolonization sealed the process.

However, the route to the new world order with fewer inter-state wars and consolidation of the capitalist–industrial nation-state system was not a smooth process. It involved two European wars that, owing to colonialism, extended across half the globe and caused a death toll of tens of millions of people. The First World War was analysed in Volume 2 and was found to have been a consequence of an unfortunate somnambulism of the, at the time, still very hierarchical and aggressively expansive European empires that were unable to coordinate their joint actions and therefore ended with a war that nobody wanted. The unfortunate peace treaty of the First World War and the rise of the fascist alternative to the capitalist–democratic modernization caused the Second World War. As Mann presents more thoroughly elsewhere (Mann 2004) and summarizes here, Nazism was an ideologically coordinated movement that captured, first, hegemony and then the German state with a skilful combination of the use of paramilitary troops and propaganda. The geopolitical programme of the movement was suicidal and without prospects of long-term success from the beginning. However, the extremely intensive nature of the movement become evident at the end of the war when

Nazi troops often fought to the bitter end in battles that clearly were already lost, a phenomenon rarely seen in wars. Japanese colonialism during the Second World War also benefited from the intensive ideological power and the use of paramilitary troops to affect the state, but it was also enforced by the strong hold of the military elite on the state machinery before the war and the general (and realist) Japanese understanding that colonialism on the Asian mainland was the only solution to the serious lack of resources of the Japanese islands. These aggressive–expansive forms of colonialist imperialism should not be confused with more peaceful forms of internally oriented corporatism under hierarchical rule backed by ideological power and the use of paramilitary troops, such as Italian fascism. Fascists there too were not nice guys but the death toll of the Italian fascist revolution was still counted only in tens of thousands, a moderate figure compared to the number of victims of German Nazis or Japanese colonialists.

In addition to fascism there was, of course, another alternative to the capitalist–industrial modernization, the socialist revolution. Such a revolution took place in the Russian cities and slowly spread from there to the countryside, finally consolidating the Soviet power in a hierarchical and authoritarian form in Russia before the outbreak of the Second World War. Other attempts at socialist revolution in Europe were rare and weak and failed soon in the wake of the German attempt, which meant that the plans for world revolution were soon replaced by the pragmatic policy of the Comintern, oriented towards the national interests and survival of the Soviet Union. Revolutions in general, according to Mann, occur rarely because people often have also something else to lose other than their chains and are, therefore, driven to such a risky form of action only in desperate situations. Attempts at revolution are also rarely successful because challenging the powers that be is so difficult and problems of coordination are so hard to solve even if the first battles are won. Moreover, even if revolutions succeed, people do not usually get what they were striving for, as is evident from the examples of the French and Russian revolutions.

In addition to the urban proletarian revolution outlined by Marx and Lenin, there was also a second variant of anti-capitalist revolution. This type was exemplified by the successful agrarian revolution in China. Because of certain bad experiences with the Kuomintang in the urban areas, its most important leader and ideologist Mao Zedong outlined a completely new strategy based on the idea of the Long March through agrarian areas with a revolution that only in its last phase entered city centres. This strategy was, in the main, successful (despite being severely traumatic and for many people a lethal experience, such as the Cultural

Revolution under the regime of Mao) and became a model for several other coup attempts in the Third World.

In general, the world after the Second World War witnessed the victory of the capitalist–industrial economy and nation-state with the collapse of fascism and all the European empires as well as the Japanese empire. The existing capitalist–industrial nation-states, of course, varied according to the degree of affluence, democracy, ability of the state to structure people's lives in their area and benefits provided to their population. The strongest in this sense were soon to be those mostly Western countries that came to be called the OEEC/OECD group (a group established in 1948 as the Organisation for European Economic Cooperation to administer the Marshall Plan to support the European reconstruction after the war and made permanent in 1961 by the name Organisation for Economic Cooperation and Development), with the rest of the world not coping as well – a curious result because the war had been caused by these areas and they had also suffered the worst damage during it. In addition, there were also some such state-socialist enclaves as the Soviet Union and China, which for some time managed to convince the world that there was a struggle between two alternative world-systems going on. This illusion, however, was soon to be revealed as false.

Volume 4: Globalizations, 1945–2011

The title of Mann's Volume 4 is 'Globalizations'. The plural is there to underline the view included in the IEMP model that we are not dealing with a single process but several interlinked processes in the fields of ideology, economy, the military sector and politics. Some of these phenomena push certain forms of internationalization or transnationalization forward and some have an exactly opposite impact. The phenomena must, therefore, be studied empirically. This is so when we speak about the period after the Second World War in general. However, it is particularly important in the study of the period from the late 1970s onwards when the current intensive globalization wave set in due to new policy solutions by states in general and the Thatcher and Reagan administrations in particular, which tackled the decline of the long post-war economic boom. Space does not allow covering the whole volume, which is rich in subject matter, and I can do no more than just touch superficially on some of the themes analysed in the volume. They are the nature of the United States as the only remaining empire, the development and variations of the welfare state, neoliberalism and the forthcoming environmental crisis.

As the victor of the war, the United States was in the leading role when the new world order for the era succeeding the Second World

War was drafted. Keynes' plans for creating a genuine global currency and central bank were side-tracked at the Bretton-Woods Conference when the economic institutions of the UN, such as the International Monetary Fund (IMF) and World Bank, were established. Instead, the United States made the US dollar, then backed by the gold standard, into a virtual world currency, thus replacing the pound sterling and the United Kingdom in the global system of currencies. This move was later sealed by the US support of the economies and currencies of the losing states, Germany and Japan.

That economic strategy was in congruence with the general policy of the United States. After the destruction of all European empires and the Japanese empire in the war, the rising US empire was the only one in the world. However, it was different from the previous ones, 'an incoherent empire' as the title of a separate book on the topic published by Mann (2003) says. The previous empires were based on military invasion, and the heavy and long-standing presence of the colonialists also often mixed with the local population and they were extremely cruel in their conquests and when dealing with cases of revolt. The US empire, too, has sent troops around the world but it has been wary of keeping them anywhere for long periods. Under public pressure on the home front it has desperately tried to minimize its own casualties and has in all ways tried to prevent any closer contact between its troops and the local population. According to Mann, this just is not how empires are genuinely run. There is no doubt of the fact that the US military machinery, which today controls one half of the entire military resources of the world, is invincible. Yet the way its use is restricted within the limits described earlier channels US imperialism towards other forms of power and, therefore, it is the economy that has been its principal tool.

Yet there is no doubt that the US economic hegemony, crystallized in the central role of the US dollar in the international system, has been backed by ideological, political and military means. Owing to the strong position of the US cultural industry from Hollywood onwards, US culture has become familiar and loaded with positive connotations everywhere in the world. Politically and whenever needed militarily, the United States has been and still is backing friendly governments and parties everywhere and has not hesitated to defend its interests and access to resources, such as oil, with explicit threats, such as the following statement made by President Carter in 1980 as a response to Soviet pressure in Afghanistan: 'Let our position be absolutely clear. An attempt by outside force to gain control of the Persian Gulf region will be regarded as an assault on the vital interests of the United States of America. And such an assault will be repelled by any means necessary, including military force'

(Mann 2013:124). In its front yard, at home and in Western Europe, this has usually also meant promoting democracy and freedom. In all other parts of the world, the US ideological canon crystallized from Carter's administration onwards to the slogan of 'human rights'. Yet this is a deceptive facade which conceals the back stage on which the United States has cynically supported whatever paramilitaries or despotic governments have promoted its interests in the part of the world in question. Such a policy was crystallized already in the 1930s by the US secretary of state Cordell Hull who famously said of a Latin American dictator: 'he may be a son-of-a-bitch but he's our son-of-a-bitch' (Mann 2013:105).

During the Cold War, of course, it was not so obvious that the United States was the only remaining empire in the world. The Soviet party too had a say in the world order, at least in the sense that it could, in a hostile relationship with the United States, together create a situation that researchers of international relations call 'mutually assured destruction' or MAD. The expression, of course, refers to the fact that both of the two superpowers had the capability to destroy all life on the entire globe with their nuclear warheads and were related to each other in the way that a complete global destruction sometimes seemed to be the most realist scenario – as people such as myself well remember who spent their youth watching films like Kubrick's *Dr. Strangelove* and fearing the worst. According to Mann, the problem was solved, or the situation at least eased considerably, when Reagan and Gorbachev signed a nuclear arms reduction treaty at the Reykjavik Summit in 1986 after a closely avoided catastrophe that scared both parties, in which a NATO military exercise almost launched an automatic Russian lethal counter-strike system. The collapse of the Soviet Union in the early 1990s further reduced the threat and left the United States the only remaining empire on the world scene.

According to Mann, it is still too early to predict how successfully the United States will be able to defend its position as an incoherent empire against the currents moving to shift the balance of power resources to Asia, even if he seems to think that the US position is stronger and its influence on firmer ground than is usually thought. What we already know, however, is that one of the positive features that came with the end of the Second World War was that it put an end to the European Martian pattern of expansionist inter-state wars that had burdened Europe for almost one millennium and the rest of the globe for several hundred years. What followed was a still ongoing era of significantly reduced inter-state violence, even if it has been overshadowed by an increasing risk of ethnic cleansing in existing and emerging nation-states in which the effort to create culturally homogenous nationalities often takes violent forms as 'the dark side of democracy', as in the title of Mann's (2005) separate book on the topic.

In addition to new aspects, Mann's interpretation of the development of the welfare state includes many conventional factors. Thus, he builds on Marshall's (1949/1963) classification of the forms of citizenship, Polanyi (1944/1957) on the rise of the market society and Esping-Andersen (1990) on the distinction between three types of welfare regimes. Yet he is also faithful to his style and tailors the sources used for his own purposes, for example, in naming the three welfare models as Anglos, Euros and Nordics. Over and above innovative naming and adjustment of the classifications of others, there are also some more original features in his analyses. Probably the most important one is the new interpretation of the development of the US welfare model.

It is conventionally believed that the US welfare model has constantly lagged behind those of the European welfare states. Mann agrees that this indeed is the current situation but qualifies the conception and the process leading to the current situation in several ways. First, contrary to common belief, there actually exists a full-blown welfare state in the United States. The only problem is that it is restricted to the military sector, which provides extensive healthcare benefits, social security and possibilities for education to its personnel. Second, outside the military sector, too, if we focus our attention on the level of total investment in welfare and not on whether it is channelled through the public or the private sector, we find that the total investment in welfare in the United States is at the top level compared to other OECD countries. The high level of total investment in welfare, however, does not make the great inequality in the allocation of resources within population vanish. People are divided into those upper-class, middle-class and prosperous working class families that can secure their well-being through private insurance, often based on terms negotiated by their employers, and those who are marginalized and left almost completely without protection. Third, even the obvious lagging behind of the United States in the treatment of the marginalized today is not an age-old pattern but something new that happened during the Cold War and then again due to neoliberalism from the late 1970s onwards. Before that point in time, the US system had been moving toward the centre-left type of a welfare regime that is relatively normal among the OECD countries. Neoliberalism, however, changed its route.

Another new factor is the analysis of the process in which the Anglo model with its lower level of benefits (in the United States) and ongoing reduction of existing systems (in the United Kingdom) seems today to be moving further away from the two other regimes. This was already included in the above analysis of the US scene but is a new feature in the United Kingdom which, in the tradition of Beveridge Plan, used to be a relatively equal system rewarding all social strata for their sacrifices in the Second World War. In that sense, in the early phases of welfare state construction, it was often seen as a model country also among the North-European countries, all of which today are much more equal and treat their marginalized people better than the United Kingdom.

The change in the United States and in the United Kingdom is, of course, part of the process called the rise of neoliberalism. What exactly neoliberalism is, is a tricky question according to Mann. On the surface, we are dealing with the rise of market fundamentalism and a related invasion of free market thinking into every sector of society. However, if we study what has actually happened in different societies under the neoliberal movement, it turns out that in the financial sector indeed something that can be called removing obstacles to free market actions has taken place. In all other sectors, the situation is more complex. In the United States, the neoliberal political movement was implemented with carrier strata, many of which were not liberal in any sense but conservatives. The neoliberal turn then reallocated resources from investment in welfare to the military and other forms of security maintenance systems such as jails and the police, which was the reason why neither the Reagan administration nor the Thatcher administration actually managed to cut state expenses even though they both successfully increased inequality among citizens. Deregulation advanced in the financial sector, and market thinking entered the public sector in the form of new public management that considered the state as a firm to be run along the lines of business doctrines. These developments, however, were coupled to an emergence of an abundance of new forms of regulation that increased public surveillance, inspection and accounting, which all was quite against the official neoliberal dogma but in accordance with the agenda of the conservative values that were carried by the groups promoting the change.

What Mann calls the Great Neoliberal Recession that started in 2007 was caused by the deregulation of the financial sector. It has caused tremendous trouble around the world. Yet the curing of the problems has been to a great extent left to the same interest groups that originally caused the trouble. Measures taken in the United States have resulted in a modest potential for new recovery, but the EU, which has had a far less developed regulative toolbox at its disposal than the US federal state, has been merely causing itself more trouble with its restrictive austerity policies. The recession is all but over, and it remains to be seen how the OECD countries and the rest of the world are going to cope with it in the future.

Mann thinks that problems with the recession may be big in the future but he also says that the biggest threat we are facing now and will face in the future is not recession but the environmental crisis. Based on his studies, he is not a complete pessimist but not very optimistic either. Creating effective policy solutions to deal with environmental threats requires an ability to coordinate the actions of different nations and interest groups on a global scale. Can we do that?

There are at least five cases, all of which took place in the twentieth century, which can be studied if we wish to learn something of our abilities to prevent the worst. There are attempts to prevent the two World Wars, attempts to tackle the Great Depression of the 1930s as well as comparable attempts to cure the still ongoing great Neoliberal Recession that started in 2007, and finally, there are the attempts to prevent MAD. Studying these cases does not make one an optimist. Nobody wanted the First World War but it was still fought, mainly due to the problems caused by the shocking inability of the parties involved to understand each other, negotiate and coordinate their mutual actions. Hitler did want the Second World War, and he got what he wanted because other parties, once again, were shockingly unable to coordinate their joint actions. Curing the Great Depression was first delayed by the austerity politics of Hoover, then somewhat eased by Roosevelt's New Deal, but a genuine recovery finally took place only due to the Second World War. The case of the 2007 recession may be even worse. Opinions are divided between the austerity policy camp and the Keynesians, and responsibility for resolving the situation is to a great extent given to those who caused the problem. It seems then that the answer is 'no we cannot' on four counts to the question 'can we coordinate the policies of nation-states and interest groups to reach vital policy targets', and the environmental challenge is even more demanding because it is genuinely global. Yet Mann sees some hope in the prevention of MAD by the nuclear arms reduction treaty in Reykjavik. It is a great achievement and encourages some optimism indeed, but I think that there is no reason for exaggerated enthusiasm in relation to this case either. First, it was an easy case in the sense that even if there were organized interest groups such as the military-industrial complex involved, it was in essence a treaty between only two nation-states and was therefore easier to reach than a genuinely global treaty. Second, can we be sure that the treaty actually cured the problem? Even if the number of nuclear weapons has been significantly reduced, there are still enough nuclear warheads around to destroy all human life on the entire globe. In addition, the technology to build nuclear arms is widely spread and has not disappeared anywhere. Therefore, also if we remember Mann's point that even if innovations can be copied not all actors can copy all innovations, it is realistic to predict that there may be many more political actors who possess nuclear arms in the future. That means that perhaps even the fifth of our test cases of tackling difficult coordination problems has not yet been solved! Without being a prophet of doom, these considerations make it easy to agree with Mann when he says that attempts to find solutions to environmental problems are among the most important topics of research in the social sciences now and for the foreseeable future.

Intervention 1: toward theoretical integration?

I have tried to give the reader a feel for the type of analyses included in Mann's book series. This has had to be in a telegraphic form of just outlining some highlights because it is simply not possible to cover a book series of more than 2,000 pages in one chapter. Yet I hope that what has been said will encourage some readers to pick up one or all of the books themselves. Be that as it may, in the rest of the chapter I will make two interventions and deal with two issues: could the theoretical approach be made more coherent, and should something possibly be added to it?

To start with, there are some themes one would have wanted Mann to discuss more thoroughly.

One is the future of capitalism. Mann has great confidence in the endurance and resilience of capitalism in the future. He has defended this view against Wallerstein, Collins and others elsewhere (see Wallerstein et al. 2013) and does not hesitate to do the same here. Yet he also mentions several times, particularly in Volume 4, that there are many varieties of capitalism, and, over much of the globe, we are going to face one or the other form of political capitalism instead of market capitalism pure and simple. This is nicely in line with Weber but quite abstract. Some kind of classification of the possible forms of political capitalism would have been illuminating. It would also have answered demarcation questions such as is it really correct to describe China today as a capitalist society or should we rather speak about a developmental state, including some market elements but largely based on slave labour and run by the political elites of the central government in tandem with the, to some degree, autonomous local political elites? A somewhat similar question can be asked about Russia. Is it a capitalist country now?

Another open question is the relationship between class politics and identity politics. Throughout Volume 4, Mann flirts with the conception that the current neoliberal reduction of worker rights and benefits, along with the rise of inequality and the change in the balance of power for the benefit of those who have, is caused by the shift from class politics to identity politics. Given the legitimate demands of ethnic groups, women and gays, and the fact that Mann's political orientation is that of a North-European social democrat born and educated in the United Kingdom who then moved to California to study the current leading edge of power, he does not quite have the courage to say so. Yet he describes in an illuminating way the rise of identity politics, taking the US civil rights movement against institutionalized racism as a point of departure, and then showing how the political pattern of interest articulation of identity spreads from ethnicity to other fields such as gender and sexual orientation. He also points out the strange phenomenon that while there would have been every reason for class politics to strengthen everywhere during the neoliberal invasion, this has not happened in the West (in the United States the union membership rate is now approaching 10 per cent of the labour force and is going down less radically in all other OECD countries as well). Instead, at a time of diminishing expectations people seem to have lost their interest in class politics and are focusing on questions of cultural identity. Why exactly this happens is relatively clear in the case of the US civil rights movement but not elsewhere. Moreover, why class politics has been replaced by identity politics instead of being supplemented with it is a good question but remains unanswered in Volume 4.

One could go on with pointing out topics lacking and themes not covered in full, but that would be both fruitless and unjust. Mann is an encyclopaedist who has covered an astonishing number of topics in his four volumes and related books, and quite justly he says in the introduction to Volume 4 that one man cannot do everything. Therefore, it is more relevant to ask whether we are dealing with not just a series of brilliant books written by one man but a research programme that can also be followed by others.

The answer to this question depends on whether we think that in addition to illuminating stories on the constellation of power relations in different times and places, Mann's book series also includes a relatively coherent and distinctive theoretical view on social reality. The author himself seems to think so because he is currently engaged in writing a fifth and final volume to the series, including a systematic account of his social theory and methodology.

I, too, think so. Even if Mann has done almost all that can be done to downplay the status of his theoretical vocabulary, he actually has quite an extensive toolbox of theoretical concepts. These include the distinction between collective and distributive power, supplemented by the two other distinctions between extensive vs. intensive and authoritative vs. diffused power. In addition, just to mention some more, there is the important concept of caging, the IEMP model with the idea of historically contingent patterns of causation, and the way of embedding the model into the social totality through the concepts of purposive action, institutions and networks, as well as the idea of an interstitial emergence of new forms of power whenever leading edges arise. Closer to specific topics, each of the volumes also includes many conceptual schemes such as the (somewhat dubious) idea of historical dialectics between eras controlled by an empire and the erosion of empires to a multi-actor civilization, as well as distinctions between different forms of empire, class articulation, factors intersecting class articulation or types of welfare states. No doubt there is a need to explicate this conception and develop it further in the form of an independent book.

I look forward to reading Mann's theoretical volume and do not want to anticipate its content too much, but one comment can be made now. Mann has thus far avoided an explicit discussion with another currently popular approach to power, Michel Foucault's power analysis. This has probably been due to the different intellectual styles. Mann writes admirably clear British sentences that formulate their message in ways that seldom leave the reader confused about the meaning intended. He is also an empirical historian who is proud of that fact and has so far downplayed the theoretical element of his work. Foucault is something quite different. He is a philosophically oriented critical theorist who, as a French intellectual, uses empirical material merely as an illustration of his ideas. Yet there are at least two reasons for Mann to discuss with Foucault explicitly.

First, Mann and Foucault share a distrust of grand theory. Weber was a methodological individualist because he was worried about not letting the concepts of the social scientist such as the state, Protestant faith or capitalist economy become reified and self-sufficient structures to which researchers would mistakenly attribute causal powers. He therefore considered concepts such as the state only as the social scientist's shorthand that the scientist must always be able to deconstruct when needed into single acts of specified actors in certain specified situations. Curiously enough, the same reason led Foucault, who was approaching the same problem from the structuralist direction, to replace the concept of structure with another because he believed (mistakenly, see Heiskala 2014) that the concept of structure cannot be defined in any other way than one in which it is reified from actual events. That was the reason why Foucault (1978) replaced the concept of structure with that of *dispositive*, the idea that a dispositive only exists when actual events can be seen as tactical encounters implementing the strategic pattern of the dispositive. I believe this all should be very familiar to Mann who always aims for such middle-range types of theoretical account that are empirically grounded and says that 'my power sources are distinct in not being abstract but embodied in real networks of people' (Mann 2006:343).

Second, both Mann and Foucault are among those rare thinkers who have put an emphasis on the positive and productive nature of power. One of the implications of such an approach is that not only the actions, ends and means of the actors become relative to the situation of the action at hand but also the identities of actors can and may transform in the course of the processes studied. Foucault has been very explicit on this point, and it is probably the most important single reason why his conception of biopower is so popular today. He also has appropriate conceptual means to deal with this phenomenon because his conception is explicitly relational and thus immediately open to problems of identity transformation. Mann's theory, again, is a Parsonian resource theory of power. On the surface, it would seem that it is not fit to deal with transforming identities but presupposes solid identities. Yet when reading Mann's volumes, it immediately becomes obvious that his analyses of leading edges and transforming forms of caging often also include the element of transformation of the identities of the parties involved. Theoretically, too, there are ways to build up mediation between the resource theoretical and the relational approach in general, and Mann's and Foucault's approaches in particular (see Heiskala 2001).

What does Mann's project get if the above points are taken into account? First, integrating Foucault's relational approach to power provides some tools currently lacking to specify descriptions of caging and identity transformation. Second, Foucault's historical descriptions of the genealogy of biopower are worth exploring. They are, of course, full of lacunae, idiosyncratic, and sometimes completely mistaken, as is fitting for a pioneer understanding himself as a critical intellectual rather than a historian. Yet the intuition and vision are strong and all the rest can be provided by other theorists (such as Dean 1999 and Miller & Rose 2008) and the efforts of careful empirical historians many of whom have already started their work. Such work is excellent material for such second-order macro narrations in historical sociology as Mann's.

Intervention 2: toward the NACEMP model?

It has been suggested by Schroeder (2007) that science should possibly be considered an independent modern social structure due to the great impact it has had on the enhancement of the power resources available for humankind during the series of industrial revolutions that have taken place under the expansion of the capitalist–industrial modernization (see also Goldstone 2006). In Schroeder's conception, science is accompanied by two other structures, market capitalism and the state, but in relation to the IEMP model the question is, should science be integrated into it as the fifth source of power? Mann thinks that it should not. He admits that science and its impacts, especially the second industrial revolution, are important and he should have paid more attention to them. Yet he maintains that scientists themselves just try to create knowledge and rarely try to command our obedience. Science has indeed had 'emergent properties in increasing the collective powers of human groups, but it has very little distributive power, for it places itself in the service of those who wield other sources of social power' (Mann 2012:8; see also Mann 2006:375–378).

But let us see what happens if we extend the definition of the proposed fifth power source and call it, instead of science, artefactual power (A)? Such power includes science as an institution but it also includes tools, technologies and other artefacts as well as all infrastructures. This suggestion brings us to a conception, which is in congruence with the 'material turn' and analysis of *agencement*, through which social and material factors are interlinked as a new direction for social analysis proposed by actor-network theorists such as Latour (1987, 2005). There are no doubt plenty of gimmicks and somewhat reckless essayistic position-taking in their writings. Yet they also have a sincere point to make: maybe it is time to finally drop the Durkheimian maxim (also shared by Weber in his definition of social action as the object of sociological analysis) according to which it is important to always explain social facts by other social facts (Durkheim 1895/1982; Weber 1922/1968). Maybe it is time to once again take material structures seriously and pick up, in a new form, the idea of historical materialism according to which productive technologies and other material factors have a vital role in the explanation of the development of human societies. This idea was, without a genuine theoretical conceptualization, though, included in the logistical analyses and analyses of technological innovations in Mann's Volume 1. It was also one of the main factors explaining the great enthusiasm this volume evoked. Somehow, however, Mann lost this perspective in the later volumes, which are without doubt insightful books in many senses but do not build on this idea in any way.

There are two possible counter-arguments to making the above addition. One was already presented in the context of science above: even if the element of collective power is obviously present if we start to speak about artefactual power, can we also detect the element of distributive power? I think that we can because material structures such as highways and the Internet provide great advantages to those who have proper means such as cars and computers to use the structures but marginalize others. The same is true of other infrastructures, as was discovered by many German people in front of the Berlin wall before it was taken down, and as many immigrants can today discover in front of the emerging walls on the southern borders of the United States and the European Union.

Another counter-argument has to do with Mann's Weberian pattern of always accompanying the analysis of power sources with the analysis of carrier strata that organize the use of power in some institutional way. Therefore, he says, for example, that 'I prefer the term "ideology" to "culture" and "discourse" because the other two terms are too all-encompassing, covering the communication of beliefs, values and norms, even sometimes all "ideas" about anything'. Yet 'ideas can't *do* anything unless they are organized ... ideas are not free-floating' (Mann 2006: 345–347). The analysis of carrier strata or, to put it in Bourdieu's terms, cultural intermediaries such as teachers, journalists or priests, is without doubt a reasonable thing to do when analysing the ideological/cultural power source. However, the point of the 'cultural turn' in sociology has been exactly the discovery that in the age of highly efficient technological transmission of cultural messages, cultural categorizations have also and above the influence of the carrier strata, some autonomous power independent of any human intermediaries (Heiskala 1993, 2003). Therefore, I defend the extension of the ideological to cultural power source (C). In a similar vein, artefactual instalments of all kinds have in addition to their undeniable purposive use in the service of ideological, military, economic and political ends some autonomous power independent of any human intermediaries. That is why artefactual power could and, as I try to show below with two examples, should be considered a source of power of its own.

Before we go to the examples, let us briefly discuss the possibility of adding one more source of power. Here I am proposing adding the sixth power source called natural power (N) to the model. This suggestion is even more contestable than the previous one because it involves considering one of the power sources as a natural structure and a set of potentialities that exist and are what they are without any human intervention. The reason to add this factor has to do with the fact that the human species has biologically developed to become a certain kind of an animal with certain kinds of faculties and qualities, and the globe as the environment in which that species lives also has a specifiable structure. Both of these dimensions include both variation and the limits in which that variation can take place. Going over the limits means that a point is reached where human life is no longer possible. Within the limits, however, some environments are more favourable to certain forms of agriculture and other productive technologies than others, and different people vary according to strength, endurance and intelligence. Such variation favours some people and groups living in certain environments over others. It explains, for example, why almost all early high cultures emerged in river valleys where agriculture could be cultivated with irrigation systems, as Mann shows in his Volume 1, or why the dissemination of agricultural innovations was more successful in Eurasia than in other continents, as shown by Diamond (1997) and McNeill and McNeill (2003) who both emphasize the fact that unlike the Americas and Africa, which extend from north to south, the whole of Eurasia is located on roughly the same latitudes that enable transmission of plants and cultivation technologies from one area to another. The variation, therefore, provides power resources and also causes differences in the distribution of such resources. Note that one implication of adding natural power to the model is that the evolutionary topics dealt with in sociobiology and cognitive psychology must be taken seriously (see Laland & Brown 2011). That, of course, should be done with great caution because in the case of the human species, the other five power sources that can be developed through innovations greatly modify the impact of our evolution based on biological structures, and this has not always been taken into account to a sufficient degree in the existing sociobiological literature (Richerson & Boyd 2005).

This is how we end up with an extension of the original IEMP model, to be called the NACEMP model. Let us now see whether there are any benefits from adopting the new model. This examination takes the form of a discussion of two exemplary cases, both extensively dealt with but under-theorized in Mann's new volumes, the gender issue and the impending environmental crisis.

Mann was accused of omitting the analysis of gender in the two first volumes of his book series. This is an omission he has corrected in the two new volumes. I do not have any disagreement with his analyses that competently point out the importance of the spread of the ideology of equality after the rise of bourgeoisie, the increasing role of women in the workforce, and the variation caused by different welfare models. Yet it seems that, to a great extent, he conducts his analyses of gender not based on his conceptual toolbox but in spite of it. As an alternative, I would suggest that we start the analysis of the modern change of the gender system with the biological differences between men and women and the range of gendered opportunity structures open to men and women in different societies. The less affluent a society is, the shorter the life expectancy is, and the larger the number of children the women have during their life, the more important the factors associated with natural power (N) pure and simple in the determination of gender differences. In addition, cultural power (C) always has a significant role, but communities that stretch too far the limitations set by natural power are less likely to prosper than others that are less radical. In modern times, this is all gradually changing due to political (P) and economic (E) factors but not without the mediating role of artefactual power (A), creating a possibility to distance more and more parts of the gender system from nature by the development of contraceptive technologies, mother's milk substitutes, sex-change technologies, the possibility to create human beings in the future in hatcheries outside the female body and the like. This is how we end up with the current world where gender, for the first time in history, is largely a cultural style (Heiskala 2009).

Another example deals with environmental problems. Mann (2012: 6) writes:

The increasing productivity of agriculture and industry enabled a fourfold world population growth, from 1.6 billion in 1900 to almost 7 billion in 2010, with the average person being taller, heavier, living twice as long, and becoming twice as likely to be literate. These increases are rightly regarded as tremendous human achievements. Yet ironically, the increased extraction of resources from nature has also had a dark side of environmental consequences, which might even threaten human life on Earth. What hubris that would be: our greatest triumph becomes our ultimate defeat!

With this quotation I can rest my case: if the forthcoming environmental crisis is our biggest challenge as Mann convincingly argues, surely we need concepts such as natural (N) and artefactual (A) power in addition to the other four power sources both to describe the current situation and the process that led to it and to attempt to come up with alternatives and policy solutions!

Let us be clear about what I suggest. With the preceding ideas and examples I am not trying to make the original IEMP model redundant. There are obviously several cases in which it is perfectly sufficient for the purposes at hand, as shown by Mann's brilliant book series on social power. Therefore, I am just providing the NACEMP model as an additional theoretical tool for the purposes to which it is suited better than the original. The new model, of course, is not a model for studying just *social* power because natural power is also included. However, if dropping the sociological canon of always explaining the social only by the social and opening the discipline up to influences from other disciplines is what it takes to make an effective analysis of the forthcoming environmental crisis, I can live with the redefinition of the discipline.

References

Dahl, Robert A. (1957) The concept of power. *Behavioral Science* 2, 3:201–215.
Dean, Michell (1999) *Governmentality. Power and Rule in Modern Society.* London: Sage.

Diamond, Jared (1997) *Guns, Germs and Steel. A Short History of Everybody for the Last 13,000 Years*. London: Vintage.

Durkheim, Émile (1895/1982) *The Rules of Sociological Method*. New York: The Free Press.

Esping-Andersen, Goesta (1990) *The Three Worlds of Welfare Capitalism*. Cambridge: Cambridge University Press.

Foucault, Michel (1978) *The History of Sexuality. Volume I: An Introduction*. Suffolk: Pelican Books.

Giddens, Anthony (1995) Power in the writings of Talcott Parsons. In Giddens: *Politics, Sociology and Social Theory: Encounters with Classical and Contemporary Social Thought*. Cambridge: Polity.

Goldstone, Jack A. (2006) A historical, not comparative, method: breakthroughs and limitations in the theory and methodology of Michael Mann's analysis of power. In Hall, John A. & Schroeder, Ralph (esd): *An Anatomy of Power. The Social Theory of Michael Mann*. Cambridge: Cambridge University Press, pp. 263–282.

Heiskala, Risto (1993) Modernity and the intersemiotic condition. *Social Science Information* 32, 4:581–604.

(2001) Theorizing power. Weber, Parsons, Foucault and neostructuralism. *Social Science Information* 40, 2:241–264.

(2003) *Society as Semiosis. Neostructuralist Theory of Culture and Society*. Frankfurt am Main and New York: Peter Lang.

(2009) Modernity and the articulation of the gender system: Order, conflict, and chaos. *Semiotica* 173, 1/4: 215–231.

(2014) Toward semiotic sociology. A synthesis of semiology, semiotics and phenomenological sociology. *Social Science Information* 53, 1: 35–53.

Laland, Kevin N. & Brown, Gillian (2011) *Sense and Nonsense: Evolutionary Perspective on Human Behaviour*. Oxford: Oxford University Press.

Latour, Bruno (1987) *Science in Action. How to Follow Scientists and Engineers through Society*. Cambridge, Mass.: Harvard University Press.

(2005) *Reassembling the Social. An Introduction to the Actor-Network Theory*. Oxford: Oxford University Press.

Mann, Michael (1986) *The Sources of Social Power: Volume 1, A History of Power from the Beginning to A.D. 1760*. Cambridge: Cambridge University Press.

(1993) *The Sources of Social Power: Volume 2, The Rise of Classes and Nation-States, 1760–1914*. Cambridge: Cambridge University Press.

(2003) *Incoherent Empire*. London: Verso.

(2004) *Facists*. Cambridge: Cambridge University Press.

(2005) *The Dark Side of Democracy. Explaining Ethnic Cleansing*. Cambridge: Cambridge University Press.

(2006) The sources of social power revisited: a response to criticism. In Hall, John A. & Schroeder, Ralph (esd): *An Anatomy of Power. The Social Theory of Michael Mann*. Cambridge: Cambridge University Press, pp. 343–399.

(2012) *The Sources of Social Power: Volume 3, Global Empires and Revolution, 1890–1945*. Cambridge: Cambridge University Press.

(2013) *The Sources of Social Power: Volume 4, Globalizations, 1945–2011*. Cambridge: Cambridge University Press.

Marshall, T.H. (1949/1963) Citizenship and social class. In Marshall: *Sociology at Crossroads and Other Essays*. London: Heinemann.

McNeill, J.R. & McNeill, William (2003) *The Human Web. A Bird's Eye View of World History*. New York: Norton.

Miller, Peter & Rose, Nikolas (2008) *Governing the Present: Administering Economic, Social and Personal Life*. Cambridge: Polity.

Mills, C. Wright (1956) *The Power Elite*. London: Oxford University Press.

Parsons, T. (1960) The distribution of power in American society. In Parsons: *Structure and Process in Modern Societies*, pp. 199–225. Glencoe, Illinois: The Free Press.

Polanyi, Karl (1944/1957) *The Great Transformation. The Political and Economic Origins of Our Time*. Boston: Beacon Press.

Richerson, Peter J. & Boyd, Robert (2005) *Not By Genes Alone. How Culture Transformed Human Evolution*. Chicago: Chicago University Press.

Schroeder, Ralph (2007) *Rethinking Science, Technology and Social Change*. Stanford: Stanford University Press.

Wallerstein, Immanuel, Collins, Randall, Mann, Michael, Derluguian, Georgi & Calhoun, Craig (2013) *Does Capitalism Have a Future?* Oxford: Oxford University Press.

Weber, Max (1922/1968) *Economy and Society. An Outline of Interpretive Sociology, Volume I*. Ed. by Guenther Roth and Claus Wittich. Berkeley: University of California Press.

3   The return of big historical sociology

Dennis Smith

Introduction

The publication of Michael Mann's two recent volumes in his *The Sources of Social Power* (Mann 1986–2013; henceforth *Sources*) after a gap of more than two decades gives a welcome boost to the practice of large-scale comparative historical sociology. Immanuel Wallerstein's world-system series (Wallerstein 1974–2011) also burst back into life recently after a similarly extended hibernation.[1]

Three decades ago when I published *The Rise of Historical Sociology* (Smith 1991) 'big' historical sociology was a crowded field. Its leading figures included, for example, Charles Tilly, Perry Anderson, Gary Runciman, Theda Skocpol, Anthony Giddens, Barrington Moore, Eric Hobsbawm, Michael Burawoy, and Immanuel Wallerstein, while the memory of Fernand Braudel, recently deceased, lived on in the centre at Binghampton University, and the work of Norbert Elias, still alive and writing in his nineties, was being introduced to a new young audience.[2]

In fact, despite fluctuations, the flow of work has never stopped, and it has been enriched by the recent output of (for example) Christopher Bayley, Jürgen Osterhammel, Victor Lieberman, Dominic Lieven and Geoffrey Parker.[3] However, the completion of Mann's project is especially welcome because of the great scope and strenuous austerity of his approach, which reminds me of the combination of intellectual ambition and self-contained independence of mind that Barrington Moore provided in his books.[4] Like Moore, Mann is neither a disciple nor a guru and is not propagating a specific grand theory of the world.

---

[1] Mann 2012, 2013; Wallerstein 1974a; 1980; 1989. See also Mann 1986, 1993; Wallerstein 1974, 19809, 1989.
[2] See, for example, Anderson 1974a, 1974b; Braudel 1972, 1981–4; Burawoy 1985, 2009; Elias 1983, 1994; Giddens 1981, 1985; Hobsbawm 1987; Moore 1969, Runciman 1966, 1970, 1983, 1989a, 1989b; Skocpol 1979; Tilly 1989, 1990. See also Smith 1982, 1983, 1991.
[3] See Bayly 2004; Lieberman 2009; Lieven 2001; Osterhammel 2014; Parker 2013.
[4] See Moore 1969, 1978; Smith 1983, 1984.

Mann's four volumes are so full of closely worked empirical analysis that it will take a long time to absorb them fully and respond adequately. However, I begin with a highly preliminary assessment. Then I ask how Mann and his work fit in to the broader field of historical sociology. Pursuing that issue, I return to a discussion I began in *The Rise of Historical Sociology* and especially to two suggestions I made. The first was that the approaches taken by writers in this field might be influenced, although not 'determined', by whether they came from the 'insider' or 'outsider' position in terms of their social origins. The second was that distinctions might be drawn between four approaches to historical sociology: those of, respectively, the advocate, the scientist, the partisan expert witness and the examining magistrate. At this point, I will contrast Mann with other writers, notably Immanuel Wallerstein and Gary Runciman. Michael Burawoy also makes an appearance in the argument.

The sources of social power[5]

For the non-specialist reader, including undergraduates, the first volume of *The Sources of Social Power* (Mann 1986) is the most immediately rewarding to read. Mann shows us his basic analytical tools, relating to the universal modalities of power, which find expression in intertwining networks that enact the potential of political, military, economic and ideological resources. From the interstices of this dynamically morphing cat's cradle have emerged modern states, modern nations and modern capitalism.

Volume 1 ranges from early humankind to 1760. Mann uses his power tools to gather and organize vast stretches of time and space. Confronted with so much material, Mann gives prominence to ambitious and stimulating empirical generalizations such as the distinction between multi-power actor civilizations (e.g. ancient Greece) and empires of domination (e.g. ancient Persia). It is exciting stuff, sometimes reaching Verdi-like sweep and drama.

By contrast, the second volume (Mann 1993) is a more strenuous read. It is less a visit to the opera, more a trip to the operating theatre. Its main topic is the rise of classes and nation-states between 1760 and 1914. Within its pages five leading nation-states are dragged onto the dissecting slab. Mainly European but including the United States, they are taken apart with determination and precision, displaying Mann's talent for précis and tight narrative. If there is a central message, it is that economic,

[5] Some passages in this section draw upon passages from my review article in *The Sociological Review*, here substantially updated, edited and revised. See Smith 2014c.

military and, increasingly, political power 'generated emergent, interpenetrating collective actors – classes, nations and modern states' (737). The collective power of these nation-states expanded rapidly, over nature and other nations, a process bringing unpredictable results, which included the First World War.

The second volume provides a library of analytical reports. These theorize the modern state and compare national experiences of class- and nation formation. It is a virtual 'boxed set' of monographs. They focus, in turn, on the modern state's infrastructure, liberalism's revolutionary origins, the geopolitics of international capitalism and the dynamics of class struggle in Europe and the United States. In each segment, the reader finds an analysis that densely weaves together empirical data and theoretically charged categorizations. Their attraction is their eminent usefulness to scholars with many divergent approaches and interests. Conveniently, they have not been loaded into the blunderbuss of a pre-ordained 'big theory'.

Global Empires and Revolution, 1890–1945 (Mann 2011), Mann's third volume, takes us back into the wide world. Mann gives full weight, unlike in Volume 2, to the fact that many of Europe's capitals were the headquarters of empires, some of them stretching across Asia and Africa. Dynamism is added to his comparative analyses by focusing on the contest between capitalist democracy, state socialism and fascism, reaching crisis points during two major wars and a great depression whose impact was global. The presentation is more integrated than in the previous volume. One reason is that he is able to tell a story that has a clear endpoint in 1945 when Japan's defeat ended the Second World War. The other reason is that Mann manages to maintain a delicate balance between contingency, structural tensions and system breakdowns as they played their parts within complex, interacting historical processes.

Volume 3 is a masterpiece, although absorbing it is a challenging task. Mann begins by surveying the colonial empires of Britain, the United States and Japan with a side glance at China. Following this, the First World War is summarized in a breathtaking six pages although analysed over many more, leading towards a discussion of the Russian revolution and proletarian revolutions more generally. Moving forward to the interwar period, Mann explains the onset of the Great Depression, followed by the New Deal. Again, he broadens the argument, exploring how social citizenship developed in other capitalist democracies. The following chapters examine the alternative forms of national polities that developed between the wars in Germany, Italy, Russia, Japan and, finally, China, leading on towards the Chinese revolution and, finally, the Second World War.[6] This volume is crammed with tightly packed intellectual structures, beautifully made. They sit side by side like ornate villas in a world city. Readers, like tourists in Venice, have to find their way through some dense and crowded passages. The best approach is to start with Mann's concluding chapter, which draws the argument together.

Globalizations, 1945–2011 (Mann 2013), the final volume, begins with the transition from a declining British empire to a US-dominated global order; analyses class conflicts, civil rights and identity struggles in post-war United States; traces US imperialism and hegemony across Eurasia and the Americas; and delineates the 'rise and faltering' (129) of neo-liberalism. There is then a brief shift of emphasis as Mann turns to the collapse of the Soviet Union and the economic reforms in China, and inserts a theory of revolution (179–267). Then we return to America and the world America has made: its empire at the turn of the twenty-first century (268–321), the 'great neoliberal recession' (322–360), and the global crisis of climate change (361–399).

The work as a whole is a great achievement. That fact is not diminished in any way by two observations I would like to make. The first flows from the way that Mann has pursued his strategy of following power's 'leading edge' (Mann 186, 31). I was a little disappointed that, in the last third of his first volume, Mann turns away from the stimulating global conspectus that makes the first two-thirds of the book so interesting. He suddenly narrows the focus and puts his energies almost entirely into investigating 'The European dynamic' (Mann 1986, 373) from 800 AD onwards. The reader has to abandon the prospect of vineyards, rice fields and silk markets and instead follow Mann along the muddy furrows that lead to the brute, provincial court of Charlemagne.

But where were the most cultivated intellectuals, the most influential powerbrokers, and, more generally, the world's brightest and best in 800 AD? Not in little Aachen. They were to be found in the magnificent imperial capitals of Constantinople (Byzantium), Ch'ang-an (China) and Baghdad (the Abbasid Caliphate). In the ninth century, Baghdad was the leading centre for Islamic science and one of the world's biggest cities. These cities in China, Mesopotamia and Turkey may have become medium-term losers, for a few centuries at least. However, they have always been in the game and are now making a notable comeback, despite the fact that Baghdad was recently wrecked fairly comprehensively by a US-led invasion.

---

[6] A personal recommendation: for added technicolour, read these chapters alongside Piers Brendon's *The Dark Valley* (Brendon 2001).

Why did Mann neglect these cities and civilizations, comparatively speaking, in Volume 1 The answer is, in fact, very clear. It is because North-West Europe was the future, and would become dominant globally, even if few people in AD 800 foresaw the rise of the West. Mann followed the leading edge of power. However, and perhaps this is only a matter of personal preference, I missed not seeing what was happening on the road not taken. Travelling more than one road simultaneously might have been a viable option. A few years after that volume was published, Charles Tilly in *Coercion, Capital and European States, AD 990–1990* (Tilly 1993) followed an ultimately defeated socio-political option, the city-state, as it made its way alongside an alternative, the national state, which would eventually become dominant. By doing this, insights were gained into how the balance of power and influence swung towards the latter within the wider geopolitical context, and we could assess what was gained, and what was lost.

It is evident that Mann's approach brought analytical advantages from his perspective. But then I ask why does Mann not adopt the same strategy in the later volumes? After all, it is widely expected that China will overtake the United States as power's 'leading edge' in the foreseeable future, say, during the next half-century. Japan and India also have to be reckoned with, especially if they find ways to live comfortably alongside a strong China. Given this strong expectation, why not give equivalent attention in Volumes 3 and 4 to 'the Asian dynamic', the rise of South and South-East Asia, especially since 1945?[7] In fact, in Volume 3, subtitled *Global Empires and Revolution, 1890–1945*, no more than a fifth of the text is devoted to China, Japan and India. Those same three countries take up no more than one-sixth of the pages in the final volume.[8]

My second observation is that Mann's analysis might well have benefited from factoring in more systematically certain dynamics within social relationships that he mentions only briefly. There are occasional references to factors such as 'emotional fears for status and security' (34) and the 'relevant emotions that enter into decisions – [e.g.] not losing face, not backing down' (137). These are indirect references to the part played by the threat of humiliation in human affairs at many points. As I have come to understand it, humiliation is a form of forced displacement, part of the larger theme of displacement and response. The dynamics of

---

[7] It should be added that what seems 'obvious' in 2014 may seen a misguided expectation when looking back from 2114. For further comments see this chapter's conclusion.

[8] This relative neglect is partially remedied in *Power in the 21st Century* (Mann 2011), a series of edited conversations with his long-time associate, John A Hall. On the 'capitalist party-state' in China see pages 21–4 and 89–93.

displacement have identifiable mechanisms – of withdrawal, challenge, escape, revenge and resistance, actions driven by fear, anger and sorrow – and these patterns are well worth noticing and taking into account within our social science.[9]

The dynamics of humiliation operate at all levels of the socio-political order and may be seen at work, for example, in colonialism, anti-colonial resistance and the pursuit of liberation; in the run up to the First World War and the revenge-seeking conditions of the post-war Versailles Treaty in 1918–19; in the rhetorical appeals of Hitler to the German people and the bombing of Dresden; at Suez in 1956 and in the Tet offensive of 1968; in the shock of 9/11; and in the very logic of the market that creates 'losers', imposes the Washington Consensus and sends economic migrants into scenes of degradation and despair. This comment hardly amounts to a major criticism since Mann's four volumes are already very densely packed, and he covers some of this ground in his books entitled *Fascists* (Mann 2004) and *The Dark Side of Democracy* (Mann 2005).

Mann in context

My next task is to locate Mann and his approach within a broader conspectus of transatlantic historical sociology, specifically through comparisons with Gary Runciman, author of *A Treatise on Social Theory* (Runciman 1983; Runciman 1989a); Runciman 1997), and Immanuel Wallerstein, author of *The Modern World-System* (Wallerstein 1974; Wallerstein 1980; Wallerstein 1989; Wallerstein 2011).

Mann: dedicated empiricist

Mann, Runciman and Wallerstein started in different places and have been moving in different directions. To begin with Michael Mann, he was a salesman's son who went to Manchester Grammar School, then Oxford. Like Michael Burawoy, who came from a family that 'lived a lower-middle class life on the south side of Manchester' (Burawoy 2005, 30), Mann was an 'outsider' who 'made it', as did Burawoy, through a combination of stamina, determination, luck and great talent.[10] Mann's doctoral research was decidedly empirical and local, based on factory work and industrial life in Banbury. However, very soon afterwards, Mann, by then at Cambridge, was operating within an internationally

---

[9] On the dynamics of forced social displacement, including humiliation, see, for example, Smith 2006, 2010, 2012, 2013a, 2013b, 2014a, 2014b.

[10] See Burawoy 2005 and the interview with Michael Mann by Alan Mcfarlane summarized at www.alanmacfarlane.com/DO/filmshow/mann_fast.htm

comparative research context and looking for an answer to the following question, both theoretical and political: 'Is the working class still a force for revolutionary change in the West?' (Mann 1972, 9).

In *Consciousness and Action among the Western Working Class* (Mann 1972; henceforth *Consciousness and Action*), Mann takes note of the turbulence engendered by the unrest of 1968 and tries to identify the underlying dynamic processes those events expressed. Mann was, in part, exploring the question, notoriously posed by Sherlock Holmes, of the dog that did not bark in the night or, more specifically, in this case, the working class revolution that did not occur in 1968. This short book is a virtuoso display of clarity and compression. It takes Mann little more than sixty pages to drag the issue of the working class out of the hands of Touraine, Althusser and Gorz and pull it onto terrain being marked out by sociologists such as Barrington Moore: historical, comparative, engaged but dispassionate, and determined to identify all the alternatives structurally available, both in principle and in practice, in a range of empirical situations.

Mann sketches the anatomy of hegemonic capitalism in segmented industrial societies and the dualistic forms of working class consciousness that shaped industrial and political action within such societies. In *Consciousness and Action*, the agenda of *The Sources of Social Power* (Mann 1986–2013; henceforth *Sources*) is already being put together as he notes 'the considerable historical scholarship' (Mann 1973, 17) required to pursue his questions in depth, the significance of the distinction between collective and distributive modes of action (21), the explanatory importance of 'non-capitalist elements of society' (39), the role of 'rural influences ... [and] ... pre-industrial political influences' (40), and the 'immense' issue of 'religious, philosophical and scientific influences' (43).

Mann found that available Marxist scripts, whether old or new, did not narrate any story actually unfolding in the real world. They did not provide reliable guidance or convincing explanations that applied to the dynamic socio-historical processes in which he was interested. Nor did the alternative depiction of social trends contained in the 'end-of-ideology' thesis.[11] In response, Mann set out to construct his own depiction of, to put it crudely, the 'workings' of the world, focusing on the characteristics of the human and technological relationships within which power capacities are created, managed and put into effect within organizations, communities and human terrains of many kinds.

---

[11] See Mann 1973, 9–11. See also, for background, Hall and Schroeder 2006.

As we have noticed, Mann has paid most attention to the political, economic, ideological and military manifestations of these bonds, mechanisms and processes. An important consideration is that his approach provides him with a range of sensitizing concepts that are not far removed from the mental 'working tools' actually employed by actors on the field of play. That includes men and women trying to make things happen in households and communities, in trading houses, on the front line of battle and in the streets, people such as bureaucrats, merchants, rulers, revolutionaries, and others, ancient, medieval and modern. They all have a highly practical interest in, for example, the distinctions between collective and distributive power, authoritative and diffused expressions of power, intensive and extensive applications of force and immanent and transcendent forms of ideology.

Like Mann, front line operators and investigators are interested in how things can be made to work in practice and keen to measure their own successes and failures. This compatibility of interest enhances the usefulness to Mann of records left by such people, including, for example, tax returns.[12] Mann is able to generate empirical data based on such records that provide the basis for comparisons and generalizations, for example, about likely causes and consequences. This approach gives Mann great flexibility since he has not burdened himself with the need to make the results of his investigations fit into the intellectual structure of a specific pre-ordained theory. Mann's theories, typically based upon accumulated empirical generalizations, emerge from comparative and historical analyses generated from within his heuristic typology.

Runciman: reluctant theorist[13]

The challenges posed by debates between Marxian theorists and their opponents drove Mann towards an ever-deepening engagement with empirical data in a comparative framework that became global in extent and a historical context that stretched back to early humankind. By contrast, Gary Runciman found himself moving in the opposite direction towards a deeper engagement with theory, following the publication of *Relative Deprivation and Social Justice* (Runciman 1966; henceforth *Relative Deprivation*).

Relative Deprivation included an extensive foray into large-scale empirical measurement of the changing attitudes of people in England to social

---

[12] See, for example, Mann's paper entitled 'State and Society, 1130–1815: an Analysis of English State Finances' that is to be found in Mann 1988, 73–123.
[13] See Runciman 1989b.

inequality during the twentieth century. This book continued a debate taken up earlier by T. H. Marshall about the discontent generated in British society by social stratification. However, Runciman paid more attention than Marshall to the subjective experience of relative deprivation and the criteria of social justice being applied. Like E. P. Thompson and Barrington Moore, Runciman wanted to know about stratification's subjective consequences, what people had a right to expect and the moral and political implications of those findings.[14] The effect of such work was to undermine the conservative assumption that social order in capitalist democracies and elsewhere was built upon the supposed fact that people spontaneously acquiesced in the society's ruling norms, finding them self-evident and justified.

Relative Deprivation was one of a clutch of books in the early and mid 1960s that helped to release debates about power and moral evaluation, and the discussion of coercion and exploitation, from the cage in which they had been trapped by the followers of Talcott Parsons. This change of atmosphere fed the climate of protest and rebellion that found expression on both sides of the Atlantic in the late 1960s and early 1970s.

Despite the topicality and success of *Relative Deprivation*, Runciman was left with a sense of having failed to achieve what he had been aiming for when 'shuffling and tabulating my stack of IBM cards in the approved Columbia style' (Runciman 1989, 3). He had thought he was 'discovering something', relating his findings to reference group theory and John Rawls's theory of justice. However, he gradually realized that 'precisely because I did not have a well-formulated theory which I was putting to the test, I hadn't succeeded in explaining anything in more than a very limited and tentative sense' (4). In his eyes, being quantitative no longer seemed to guarantee the scientific value of a sociologist's endeavours.

Runciman found inspiration for his subsequent theoretical work in the evolutionary approaches of Charles Darwin, who emphasized processes of natural selection, and Carl Linnaeus, who created a scheme of systematic classification for plants, animals and minerals. At the centre of Runciman's 'Darwinian' typology of socio-political orders is the state that has clearly differentiated systems or modes of production, persuasion and coercion through which a usable surplus of power resources may be institutionally distributed and applied in a reliable and effective way. This full-fledged form is distinguishable from 'protostates' (not quite states, so to speak), as it is from cases where power is obstructed, shared or dissipated, and from situations of generalized reciprocity where there is no surplus of power resources.

[14] See Moore 1969; Thompson 1963. On Marshall see, for example, Smith 1991, 27–33.

Runciman's typology is refined further by identifying various sub-modes within his three basic modes of societal power: the modes of production, persuasion and coercion. These sub-modes are identified with particular role complexes such as those found in serfdom or debtor–creditor relations (in the mode of production); in the hereditary status of kings, nobles and commoners or hierarchies of caste relations (in the mode of persuasion); and in the military monopolies of warrior aristocracies or the bureaucratic authority of professionalized administrators (in the mode of coercion).[15]

Where is the dynamic? Runciman's answer is competitive selection. What is being selected and how? Selection is part of a continuing struggle for power advantages, and it is the wider context of this power struggle that determines which characteristics are especially advantageous. In fact, it is only after each particular struggle has taken place in a specific environment that anyone can analyse which decisive strengths and weaknesses settled the outcome, favouring one competitor over another. The crucial factor is always the practices embedded in the key roles involved, whether they are in the mode of production (e.g. the introduction of steam power), the modes of persuasion (e.g. the spread of television) or the mode of coercion (e.g. the invention of the machine gun).

In *The Theory of Cultural and Social Selection* (Runciman 2009), Runciman refined his approach by making distinctions between the following: *natural selection*, which operates via evoked responses that are innately human such as fear, anger, sexual desire and rhythmic awareness; *cultural selection*, which triggers acquired responses learned through, say, religious socialization or sustained exposure to commercial advertising or political propaganda; and, finally, *social selection*, which works through imposed responses backed up with various sanctions such as those wielded by employers and governments.

To oversimplify, confronted with the vast array of societies in the world, past and present, Runciman designates the following strategy for imposing intellectual order and making sense of the rich diversity on display. There are four steps. First, for each society, identify its core institutional order (e.g. capitalist political economy or feudal structures of landholding and government) with its distinctive role clusters cultural patterns (or memes) and social practices. Second, locate each society within a comparative historical typology, say from hunter-gatherers to industrializing nation-states.

---

[15] The examples given are illustrative. Runciman sets out many more such examples. See Runciman 1989a.

Third, using focused comparative and historical analysis, trace shifts in social practices and cultural responses that give new power advantages to the occupants of specific roles and then identify the relevant causal selective pressures in the environment that produced this outcome. Fourth, by implication at least, accumulate sufficient case studies to identify comparative differences and historical patterns. Perry Anderson may have caught the spirit of Runciman's approach to sociological theory when he commented that his ideal seemed to be a classification in which every single known society would have 'its own "Linnaean" polynomial and its own "Darwinian" niche' (Anderson 1990, 57).

Like Mann, Runciman has found it useful to focus upon power as a key dimension of 'the social'. However, in his *Treatise of Social Theory* (Runciman 1983–97; henceforth *Treatise*), Runciman turns to the actual dynamics of power only after he has, so to speak, 'drawn in', for each type of society, the architecture of three basic power modes (production, persuasion and coercion) within which all the action occurring within the relevant role clusters will be structurally contained. The game is to be played on a pitch he has already marked out.

By contrast, Mann's analytical approach leads him first to the pervasive 'ground-level' articulations of power – manifesting itself as collective, distributive, extensive, intensive and so on – and then to the functions that the exercise of power fulfils within and between societies as they take shape, expand, diversify, contract, undergo conflict and so on. It is at this point that Mann discerns the economic, political, ideological and military expressions of power coming into play. These distinctions between types of power network are as pragmatic as Runciman's specification of particular role clusters as the core institutional order in this or that type of society. In both cases, it just seems obvious to the writers concerned.

Runciman is concerned with the ways that power dynamics alter the internal arrangements of his three power 'modes': production, persuasion, and coercion. Mann, for his part, is more interested in how the pragmatic workings of power lead to the creation of dynamic and often rather flexible power networks. These include the outward-facing mechanisms of war-making and military might, a distinctive expression of power operating through an identifiable network. This military power network is liable to produce outcomes that impact decisively, and with independent causal force, on the economic, political and ideological conditions of socio-political life.

Runciman is clearly aware of the significance of relations established across and beyond the boundaries of entities such as nation-states, feudal kingdoms and city-states, for example, through the activities of traders and soldiers. He argues, for example, that Athens and Sparta failed to achieve, respectively, the dominant position of Venice in Mediterranean trade or the imperial might of Rome. This was mainly because both those Greek *poleis* had customs and institutions that were too democratic to allow the central accumulation of power resources within the state that this would have required.[16] However, Runciman's theoretical focus is primarily upon explaining changes in relevant practices inside key role clusters within particular core institutional orders and only secondarily with examining the intrinsic dynamics of the inter-societal 'environment'.

Wallerstein: global adventurer

Immanuel Wallerstein's home ground has become the very arena Runciman largely leaves aside: the systematic aspects of economic and socio-political processes that bind countries and ruling elites across the world into unequal relationships with each other. Like Mann and Runciman, Wallerstein took a little time to settle on his central project. After completing his undergraduate schooling at Columbia University in 1951, Wallerstein spent about two decades travelling to, from and across, Africa. He was equipped with five valuable assets: institutional backing, including funding, the ability to speak French, profound sympathy for movements seeking liberation from European colonial rule, a high level of curiosity about how capitalism worked and a great deal of self-confidence.

By his own calculation, Wallerstein travelled to about three-quarters of Africa's separate states. His network extended to several people who held 'important positions in their countries' political arenas'.[17] Four of his first five books were on African politics. The other, significantly, was on the political implications of the unrest among university staff and students in 1968 and the following few years.[18] Wallerstein was very active in the local struggles within the United States, and he came to attach a greater importance to 'the world-revolution of 1968' (Wallerstein 2014, 28) than did either Mann or Runciman. The year 1968 was a way station on his shift from being an African specialist to an analyst of the rise and 'future demise' of the world capitalist system (Wallerstein 1974b).

Four volumes of *The Modern World-System* (Wallerstein 1974–2011) have so far been published, setting out Wallerstein's historical analysis of the unfolding politico-economic logic that, in his view, explains the persistent division of an increasing proportion of the world's territory

[16] See Runciman 1989a, 81–96.
[17] For this quotation and more generally for this paragraph and the previous one, see www.iwallerstein.com/intellectual-itinerary
[18] See Wallerstein 1961, 1964, 1967, 1969, 1972. See also Wallerstein 1998, 2003.

since the sixteenth century into what he designates as core, peripheral and semi-peripheral zones. As a result of Wallerstein's propagation of these ideas from prominent positions such as the presidency of the International Sociological Association (1994–98), the main themes are too well known to require a detailed exposition here.[19] A recent highly accessible summary of the central ideas and their contemporary relevance may be found in his contribution to the book *Does Capitalism Have a Future?* (Wallerstein, Collins, Mann, Derluguian and Calhoun 2014). Here are the main points.

The capitalist world-system, like all systems, has a life: it was born, has persisted for half a millennium and will pass away. Its central activity is the search for endless capital accumulation, which triggers repeated cycles that take the system first away from its point of equilibrium in phase A of each cycle, then back towards equilibrium without fully restoring it in phase B. The precondition of substantial and continuous capital accumulation is the backing of a powerful state, which enables the creation of quasi-monopoly conditions for the manufacture and sale of new and innovative products within an expanding market. Maintaining the monopoly in the hands of capitalists while avoiding complete expropriation of the profits by generals and politicians means having more than one state in the capitalist system so that businesses have rival state powers to which they may turn if the most powerful state, the hegemonic power, becomes too oppressive.

Two cycles may be identified. The 'hegemonic cycle' (Wallerstein 2014, 11) is the longest, being punctuated by struggles, typically lasting a few decades, between would-be successor states as each incumbent hegemon (e.g. the British Empire after the 1870s or 1880s) gradually loses its capacity to maintain its own dominance. There are also shorter economic (Krondatieff) cycles whose drivers include the search for cheaper labour followed by a willingness to buy off worker discontent with higher wages. This is, in turn, followed by a decrease in profit margins as new competitors enter the field, typically leading to a shift of capital into purely financial operations entailing the widespread creation, then exploitation, of indebtedness to generate income.

According to Wallerstein, the decades since 1945 have witnessed, first, the coming together of the two cycles with the rise and decline of both American political hegemony and economic dominance, and second, the arrival of the existing capitalist world-system at a point of such extreme disequilibrium that it cannot return to equilibrium. This condition has been exacerbated by the insurgency of 1968, which marked

---

[19] For one attempt at summary, see Smith 1991, 95–102.

the widespread mobilization of new anti-systemic movements championing the rights of aggrieved minorities and submerged interests alongside longer-established nationalist and socialist movements. They have undermined the dominance of the American state and challenged global capital, the main victim being the soft left/moderate right consensus around 'centrist liberalism' (see Wallerstein 2011). The result has been polarization and division on all fronts. The existing system is coming to an end, a fate hastened by the recent recession. The future is impossible to predict. It will be shaped by the cumulative impact made by the interacting behaviour of citizens, movements, businesses and states everywhere.

In the medium term, Wallerstein's major achievement, perhaps, has been to help carve out a safe space on the US mainland for deeply critical analyses of global capitalism. The Fernand Braudel Center at Binghampton University has done for the unequal and exploitative world order what the Chicago School between the two world wars did for the unequal and exploitative city. Each enabled academics and other intellectuals in America to shoot stinging barbs deep into capitalism's head and heart and yet survive, and even prosper, professionally. Both ventures avoided the deadly epithet of being 'un-American' by making their formal object of attention either smaller than the American nation-state (the city) or greater (the capitalist world-economy). Like Chicago, Binghamton has been a broad church. It has allowed wide variation within and around the main world-system thesis, encouraging debate and permitting creativity. There is even a family resemblance between Wallerstein's assumption, following Ilya Prigogine, that social systems, like systems in nature, have a life cycle[20] and the Chicago School's explorations of the 'natural history' of social institutions such as the gang and the newspaper, drawing on ideas from natural ecology.[21]

Two heretical insiders

Wallerstein and Runciman are both nonconformists. In other words, they have adopted intellectual approaches seen as potentially threatening by some leaders of, respectively, the American and British university establishments. Wallerstein is an avowed opponent of capitalism.[22] Runciman has brought Darwin into sociology, a move that brings anxiety to opponents of 'sociobiology' with its possible links to ultra-conservative

---

[20] See Prigogine 1996. For background on Park's intellectual genealogy, see Gross 2004.
[21] An earlier version of this paragraph may be found in Smith 2014c. See also Smith 1988.
[22] 'Wallerstein *hates* capitalism', according to Runciman. Runciman 1999, 62. Emphasis in original.

politics.[23] Wallerstein and Runciman have both shown dogged determination in their chosen paths. However, those paths have been made easier by the fact that they both became recognized members of those same establishments early in their careers. This brought them support and protection.

Runciman, educated at Eton, senior research fellow at Trinity College, Cambridge, and one-time president of the British Academy, was born into what Noel Annan has labelled the British 'intellectual aristocracy', whose interlocking kinship links may be traced back at least to the early nineteenth century.[24] Wallerstein, unlike Runciman, does not have an aristocratic title but his parents resided on the Grand Concourse in the West Bronx, an address that in the 1920s and 1930s was 'the ultimate in prestige' for upwardly mobile New York Jews.[25] By the time Wallerstein finished his undergraduate degree at nearby Columbia University in 1951, the world was becoming his oyster. The imperial baton had been wrenched from British hands and seized by the new dominant global super power. Its business headquarters were in Wall Street, not far from the new UN headquarters under construction in Manhattan. New York had become the world's powerhouse and meeting place. What is more, academically, 'Columbia sociology in the 1950s was the center of the world' (Williams 2013, 207), as Wallerstein recalled in an interview published in 2013.

By spending a large part of two decades in Africa soon after the defeat of Hitler at a time when the United States was still renowned as humankind's great liberator, Wallerstein was acting in America's noblest tradition. He was undertaking a mission analogous with the risk-laden journeys into India made during the mid nineteenth century by enlightened British students of Jeremy Bentham and James Mill who wished to rescue the indigenous population from the oppressive irrationalities from which they suffered. In both cases, in mid nineteenth century India and mid twentieth century Africa, the object of these adventurers was to discover the socio-political workings of a complex continent and become involved with the process of emancipation, as they understood it.[26]

---

[23] See, for example, 'Science confronts the beast within' by Tom Wilkie, *Independent* 17th July 1995 at www.independent.co.uk/news/science-confronts-the-beast-within-1591801.html

[24] See Annan 2000, 314.

[25] The quotation is from Constance Rosenblum, 'What's Grand about the Grand Concourse in the Bronx' at http://historynewsnetwork.org/article/120374#sthash.Vsju CR5V.dpuf See also 'Immanuel Wallerstein's Planet' by Robert Fitch at www.oocities .org/zed_chaotics/english/iwp.htm

[26] For historical background on British India in that period, see James 1997, part three, Chapter 2 entitled 'Utility and Beneficence: British Visions and Indian Realities.

Africa had been French and British and was coming under increasing American influence. Wallerstein's research was a part of this broader transition. His graduate teachers at Columbia 'looked upon this interest with a bemused eye. Why not? they seemed to imply. One more geographical zone for the Columbia sociology department to conquer' (Wallerstein 2012, 6). Later, when Wallerstein and Terence Hopkins took a radical position during the 1968 crisis, a colleague described them as 'His Majesty's loyal opposition' (Wallerstein in Williams 2013, 207); in other words, fractious insiders, but insiders nevertheless. There has never been the slightest doubt about Wallerstein's intense commitment to America's highest ideals.[27] Runciman's own strong attachment to his native land is shown in another way, in the leading empirical object upon which he deploys his theory. At the end of 2015 Runciman published his third book-length study of English society (Runciman 2015), the previous works on this theme being *Relative Deprivation and Social Justice* (Runciman 1966) and the final volume of his *Treatise* entitled *Applied Sociology* (Runciman 1997).

Mann's response to Wallerstein and Runciman

In a paper on social evolution presented at University College Dublin in August 2014[28] but as yet unpublished as far I know, Mann argued, *inter alia* that Runciman's theoretical approach of social change amounts to little more than discovering which group had gained an advantageous position because its power resources were best adapted to the prevailing environment. In Mann's view, this is little better than tautology, a matter of identifying winners and losers after the event and then finding reasons for the outcome. This procedure, in Mann's view, was unlikely to generate useful empirical generalizations since key cases such as the so-called European/English industrial miracle were ad hoc and specific, not clearly linked to other cases either comparatively or historically. On this matter, Mann agrees with Giddens who described adaptation as a concept that had become 'so vague that it is useless as a means of explaining anything at all' (Giddens 1984: 235).[29]

Mann is less dismissive of Wallerstein, whose historical scholarship he appreciates even though he disagrees with many of Wallerstein's

---

[27] As Wallerstein declared in an address soon after 9/11, 'I am not someone who denigrates American ideals. I find them quite wonderful, even refreshing. I cherish them, I invoke them, I further them.' See http://essays.ssrc.org/sept11/essays/wallerstein.htm

[28] Mann's paper was given as part of a historical sociology workshop. I was asked to respond to his paper.

[29] In this passage, Giddens was not specifically referring to Runciman's work.

assumptions. Put quite simply, Mann notes that the various sources of social power Wallerstein identifies have diverging cycles, each with its separate point of equilibrium and may not be reduced to a single world-system. This disagreement is evident in Mann's own contribution (Mann 2014) to *Does Capitalism Have a Future?* (Wallerstein et al 2014). Mann suggests that the prospects for continued US hegemony and future socialist revolution are both pretty dim. The death knell for American hegemony is bound to follow when, as he expects, the US dollar ceases to be the world's main reserve currency at some point during the next few decades. For their part, revolutionaries prosper best in the extreme socio-political conditions engendered by war, as in France after 1789, Russia in 1917 and China during the 1930s and 1940s, but such major wars are becoming less likely, in Mann's view.

Mann argues that capitalism itself is far more likely to survive, although its future character is impossible to predict: perhaps it will develop an even more severely unequal form, perhaps it will become subject to greater state control, perhaps lower growth expectations will become normal and so on. In any case, all bets would be off if the world were to be confronted with the consequences of a nuclear war or an escalating ecological crisis. Avoiding these dangers, especially the second, might bring heavy costs. That is because, as Mann reminds us, our environmental challenge has been caused by 'the three great triumphs of the modern period – capitalism, the nation-state and citizen rights' (Mann 2014, 95).

It is already clear that Mann, Wallerstein and Runciman stand far apart from each other on key matters. But how do they each fit into the firmament of historical sociology? That is our final question.

Scientists, advocates, partisan expert witnesses and examining magistrates

In an earlier work (Smith 1991), I suggested that there were four ways – all valuable and desirable – in which scholars in the social sciences, broadly understood, could handle the tension between two factors. One of these factors is our capacity and tendency to empathize with and evoke the feelings and perceptions of participants in specific situations, a disposition that enables us to understand, or at least think we understand, their motivations and predicaments. The other, countervailing, factor is the desirability of preventing our capacity for objectivity from being overwhelmed by feeling, and this may lead us to discount and suppress, partially at least, our emotional, moral and political responses to the processes and relationships of which we become aware in the course of our research. To put it another way, we seek to balance involvement and detachment in a way that we find appropriate. This is a rather challenging task.

Four approaches to this challenge may be discerned. The first approach is that of the *'partisan expert witness'*, an individual who derives a sense of certainty from a prior commitment, however arrived at, to specific beliefs and perceptions relating to human relationships and the socio-political world including, for example, how key mechanisms and processes operate, how they should operate ideally and the types and directions of change that are possible and likely to occur. Within that perceptual and ideological context, he or she searches for and deploys the most persuasive and relevant data, which are presented in a confident matter-of-fact tone with rigorous conformity to canons of objectivity, maintaining high standards of accuracy and relevance.

Next, the *'scientist'* prioritizes objective detachment over involvement although he or she may well be capable of, and value, both. This approach prizes above all the sophistication of the concepts and techniques that can be brought into play, judging the value of this intellectual apparatus in terms of the range of empirical evidence it is capable of categorizing and assessing without built-in bias of any kind towards or against any particular view about how the world does or should work.

Third, the *'advocate'* operates within a framework of objectives and motivations shaped by engagement with, and commitment to, the chosen subject of his or her inquiries and concern. The primary objective is to express as effectively and fully as possible the content, strength and legitimacy of the needs and demands relating to that chosen subject in order to be able to give them effective voice. Doing this requires a capacity for detached inquiry in order to identify accurately the content of those needs and demands, combined with the rhetorical ability to evoke them effectively in the minds of others who may thereby be led to empathize with the cause and the people for whom the advocate speaks.

Finally, the main concern of the *'examining magistrate'* is to discover all potentially relevant evidence and make it available in a way that allows it to be perceived and assessed accurately in the interests of precise and comprehensive reportage. This will enable alternative explanations to be tested through critical dialogue and self-questioning backed up, where appropriate, by further inquiry of a similar kind. The relevant evidence gives full weight to insights obtained by the inquiring scholar through empathetic imagination, intuiting the situational challenges and responses likely to be in play in the situations studied while ensuring that such involvement does not overcome the capacity to maintain self-reflexive distance.

If we think of these four approaches as points of magnetic attraction, we may ask in which directions the historical sociologists that have been discussed here have been drawn. It may not be unreasonable to suggest that Immanuel Wallerstein, whose work combines formidable historical scholarship, a strong vision of the dynamics of systems and a highly sophisticated version of Marxian analysis, is located in the category of 'partisan expert witness', clear in his commitments and dedicated to presenting the most scholarly case possible.

Turning to Gary Runciman, his fourfold division of social theory's tasks into reportage, description, explanation and evaluation indicates where his main strength and interest lie[30]: in fashioning a robust and elegant methodological instrument for carrying out research and deploying its findings. Whereas Mann often soaks us in empirical data, Runciman relishes another form of therapeutic immersion: in conceptual mechanisms for capturing and classifying the dynamic social world. The main product of his *Treatise* and his *The Theory of Social and Cultural Selection* is a laboratory of categories and concepts and a large collection of illustrative instances. This is definitely the zone of the historical sociologist as 'scientist'. The latest deployment of this intellectual apparatus may be found in Runciman's recent book entitled *Very Different, But Much the Same; The Evolution of British Society since 1714* (Runciman 2015), which unfortunately appeared too late to be considered here.

For his part, Michael Mann has been edging, slowly but surely, into the zone of the historical sociologist as 'examining magistrate'. His potential capacity to fulfil this challenging role was made evident early on, in *Consciousness and Action among the Western Working Class* (Mann 1973) where subtle links were made between the dualistic consciousness of workers and the segmented structures of capitalist societies. In *The Sources of Social Power*, Mann never succumbed to the temptation to see human beings *en masse* as mere raw material used up by industry and war. In his work, he has created for himself opportunities to express political passions, as in *Incoherent Empire* (Mann 2003), to explore the cultural and experiential roots of fascist ideology (Mann 2004), and, most impressive of all, take intellectual hold of the phenomenon of ethnic cleansing in *The Dark Side of Democracy* (Mann 2005). This trilogy, which appeared between the second and third volumes of *The Sources of Social Power*, reinforces Mann's claim to stand alongside Marc Bloch, Fernand Braudel and Barrington Moore.

This leaves unfilled the category of historical sociologist as advocate. Here we may, perhaps, locate Michael Burawoy, the other 'successful

[30] See Runciman 1983.

outsider' from Manchester. Burawoy has, according to his own testimony, conducted a sustained inquiry into 'postcolonialism, the organization of consent to capitalism, the peculiar forms of class consciousness and work organization in state socialism and ... the dilemmas of transition from socialism to capitalism', especially from perspectives that arise from the intellectual dialogue between Marxism and sociology.[31] Like the three sociologists already discussed, Burawoy has been keen to identify and explain patterns of continuity and difference across historical time and geopolitical space.

Burawoy's main object has been to engage the understanding, empathy and support of educated elites for embattled groups who experience deprivation, exploitation and manipulation due to their near-poverty and relative powerlessness. Burawoy concentrates on drawing attention to the local structural and cultural conditions that shape the balance of advantage in the struggles for a better deal in which workers and subaltern groups of all kinds are engaging worldwide. His object is to give added prominence to the experiences and perceptions of those in struggle. He also wishes to educate workers, subaltern groups and those who might help them about the wider significance, politically and sociologically, of these socio-political conflicts. In all those respects, public sociology is about intelligent advocacy.[32]

Conclusion: foresight and hindsight

When this chapter was first envisaged, its author did not anticipate this neat denouement, with everything slotting into place. As these words are being written, this outcome feels like a pleasant surprise, but after a while it may come to seem obvious and inevitable. This is a small example of a larger phenomenon, often noticed: our capacity to predict the past once it has happened.

Compared to predicting the past, predicting the future is much more difficult, and arguably impossible. Gary Runciman has fully accepted this fact and built it explicitly into his methodology, which makes full use of hindsight. Michael Mann has been prepared to undertake a limited degree of controlled forward speculation, for example, drawing evidence from crises in the past and present in order to consider possible futures.[33] Immanuel Wallerstein has his own handle on the future based on his

---

[31] The quotations are taken from Burawoy's personal website at http://burawoy.berke ley.edu

[32] For critiques of Burawaoy, see Smith 1990, 2008.

[33] See Mann's chapter in Wallerstein 2014 which is entitled 'The End May Be Nigh, But For Whom?'

certainty that capitalism's systemic character guarantees it will experience a future demise even if the date cannot be known in advance. For his part, Michael Burawoy's approach implies a determination to help 'make' the future through a combination of analysis, persuasion and action in the spirit of solidarity. All of these positions command respect, but it is impossible to predict which of them will prove in hindsight to have been the most fruitful.

References

Anderson, P, 1974a, *Passages from Antiquity to Feudalism*, London: Verso.
 1974b, *Lineages of the Absolutist State*, London: Verso.
Annan, N, 2000, *The Dons. Mentors, Eccentrics and Geniuses*, London: HarperCollins.
Bayly, C, 2004, *The Birth of the Modern World 1780–1914*, Oxford: Blackwell.
Braudel, F, 1972, *The Mediterranean and the Mediterranean World in the Age of Philip II* (2 vols), London: Fontana.
 1981–4, *Civilization and Capitalism 15th–18th Centuries* (3 vols), London: Weidenfeld and Nicolson.
Brendon, P, 2001, *The Dark Valley. A Panorama of the 1930s*, London: Pimlico.
Burawoy, M, 1985, *The Politics of Production. Factory Regimes under Capitalism and Socialism*, London: Verso.
 2005, 'Antinomian Marxist' in Sica, A and Turner, S (eds), *The Disobedient Generation. Social Theorists of the Sixties*, Chicago, IL: University of Chicago Press, 48–71.
 2009, *The Extended Case Method*, Berkeley, CA: University of California Press.
Elias, N, 1983, *The Court Society*, Oxford: Blackwell.
 1994, *The Civilizing Process*, Oxford: Blackwell.
Giddens, A, 1981, *A Contemporary Critique of Historical Materialism*, London: Macmillan.
 1984 *The Constitution of Society. Outline of the Theory of Structuration*. Berkeley & Los Angeles: University of California Press.
 1985, *The Nation-State and Violence*, Cambridge: Polity.
Gross, M, 2004, 'Human Geography and Ecological Sociology: The Unfolding of a Human Ecology, 1890 to 1930–and Beyond, in *Social Science History*, 28, 4, 575.
Hall, J A and Schroeder, R (eds), 2006, *An Anatomy of Power. The Social Theory of Michael Mann*, Cambridge: Cambridge University Press.
Hobsbawm, E, 1987, *The Age of Empire 1870–1914*, London: Abacus.
James, L, 1997, *Raj. The Making and Unmaking of British India*, London: Abacus.
Lieberman, V, 2009, *Strange Parallels. Southeast Asia in Global Context, c 800–1830* (2 vols), Cambridge: Cambridge University Press.
Lieven, D, 2001, *Empire: The Russian Empire and Its Rivals*, New Haven, CT: Yale University Press.
Mann, M, 1973, *Consciousness and Action among the Western Working Class*, London: Macmillan.

1986, *The Sources of Social Power, Volume 1: A History of Power from the Beginning to AD 1760*, Cambridge: Cambridge University Press.

1988, *States, War and Capitalism. Studies in Political Sociology*, Oxford: Blackwell.

1993, *The Sources of Social Power, Volume 2: The Rise of Classes and Nation-States, 1760–1914*, Cambridge: Cambridge University Press.

2003, *Incoherent Empire*, London: Verso.

2004, *Fascists*, Cambridge: Cambridge University Press.

2005, *The Dark Side of Democracy. Explaining Ethnic Cleansing*, Cambridge: Cambridge University Press.

2011, *Power in the 21st Century. Conversations with John A Hall*, Cambridge: Polity Press.

2012, *The Sources of Social Power, Volume 3: Global Empires and Revolution, 1890–1945*, Cambridge: Cambridge University Press.

2013, *The Sources of Social Power, Volume 4: Globalizations, 1945–2011*, Cambridge: Cambridge University Press.

Moore, B, 1969, *Social Origins of Democracy and Dictatorship. Lord and Peasant in the Making of the Modern World*, London: Penguin.

1978, *Injustice. The Social Bases of Obedience and Revolt*, London: Macmillan Press.

Osterhammel, J, 2014, *The Transformation of the World. A Global History of the Nineteenth Century*, Princeton, NJ: Princeton University Press.

Parker, G, 2013, *Global Crisis. War, Climate Change and Catastrophe in the Seventeenth Century*, London: Yale University Press.

Prigogine, I, 1996, *The End of Certainty*, New York: Free Press.

Runciman, W G, 1966, *Relative Deprivation and Social Justice*, London: Routledge.

1970, *Sociology in Its Place and Other Essays*, Cambridge: Cambridge University Press.

1983, *A Treatise on Social Theory. Vol One: The Methodology of Social Theory*, Cambridge: Cambridge University Press.

1989a, *A Treatise on Social Theory. Vol Two: Substantive Social Theory*, Cambridge: Cambridge University Press.

1989b, *Confessions of a Reluctant Theorist*, London: Harvester Wheatsheaf.

1997, *A Treatise on Social Theory. Vol Three: Applied Social Theory*, Cambridge: Cambridge University Press.

1999, *The Social Animal*, London: Fontana.

2009, *The Theory of Cultural and Social Selection*, Cambridge: Cambridge University Press.

2015, *Very Different, but Much the Same. The Evolution of British Society since 1714*, Cambridge: Cambridge University Press.

Skocpol, T, 1979, *States and Social Revolutions*, Cambridge: Cambridge University Press.

Smith, D, 1982, *Conflict and Compromise. Class Formation in English Society 1830–1914. A Comparative Study of Birmingham and Sheffield*, London: Routledge.

1983, *Barrington Moore. Violence, Morality and Political Change*, London: Macmillan.

1984, 'Morality and Method in the Work of Barrington Moore' in *Theory and Society*, 13, 151–76.

1988, *The Chicago School. A Liberal Critique of Capitalism*, London: Macmillan.

1990 'Organization and Class: Burawoy in Birmingham' in Clegg, S R (ed), *Organization Theory and Class Analysis. New Approaches and New Issues*, New York, NY: Walter de Gruyter, 367–87.

1991, *The Rise of Historical Sociology*, Cambridge: Polity.

2006, *Globalization: The Hidden Agenda*, Cambridge: Polity.

2008, 'Globalization, Degradation and the Dynamics of Humiliation' in *Current Sociology* 56, 371–79.

2010, 'Social fluidity and social displacement' in *Sociological Review*, 58, 4, 680–98.

2012, 'Dimensions of world-making: thoughts from the Caspian Sea' in D. Kalekin-Fishman and A. Denis (eds), *The Shape of Sociology for the Twenty-First Century*, London: Sage, 113–33.

2013a, 'Inside stories: Oscar Wilde, Jean Améry, Nelson Mandela and Aung San Suu Kyi' in N. Demertzis (ed) *Emotions in Politics: The Affect Dimension in Political Tension*, London: Palgrave-Macmillan, 60–83.

2013b, 'Prisoners' dilemmas and humiliation theory: how avant-garde writers and radical politicians have confronted the challenge of incarceration' in A. C. Sparkes (ed), *Auto/Biography Yearbook 2012*, Durham: British Sociological Association.

2014a 'When the *peloton* hit the mud: displacement struggles and the EU crisis' in J. E. Fossum and A. J. Menendez (eds), *Europe in Crisis, Europe as Crisis*, Oslo: ARENA, Oslo University.

2014b, 'Coping with the Threat of Humiliation: Contrasting Responses to the Eurozone Crisis in Greece and Ireland' in N. Petropoulos (ed) *The Debt Crisis in the Eurozone: Social Impacts*, Proceedings of Disaster, Conflict and Social Crisis Research Network Conference, September 2012, Newcastle: CSP.

2014c, 'The Return of Historical Sociology' in *The Sociological Review*, 62, 206–16.

Thompson, E P, 1963, *The Making of the English Working Class*, London: Penguin.

Tilly, C, 1989, *Big Structures, Large Processes, Huge Comparisons*, New York: Russell Sage Foundation.

1990, *Capital, Coercion and European States AD 990–1990*, Oxford: Blackwell.

Wallerstein, I, 1961, *Africa, The Politics of Independence*, New York: Vintage.

1964, *The Road to Independence: Ghana and the Ivory Coast*, Paris: Mouton.

1967, *Africa: The Politics of Unity*, New York: Random House.

1969, *University in Turmoil: The Politics of Change*, New York: Atheneum.

(with Jones Rich, E), 1972, *Africa: Tradition and Change*, New York: Random House.

1974a, *The Modern World-System: Capitalist Agriculture and the Origins of the European World-Economy in the Sixteenth Century*, New York: Academic Press, 2011.

1974b, 'The Rise and Future Demise of the World Capitalist System: Concepts for Comparative Analysis' in *Comparative Studies of Society and History*, 16, 4, 387–415.

1980, *The Modern World-System II: Mercantilism and the Consolidation of the European World-Economy, 1600–1750*, New York: Academic Press.

1989, *The Modern World-System III: The Second Era of Great Expansion of the Capitalist World-Economy, 1730–1840s*, New York: Academic Press.

1998, *Utopistics or Historical Choices of the Twenty-First Century*, New York: The New Press.

2003, *The Decline of American Power*, New York: The New Press.

2011, *The Modern World-System IV: Centrist Liberalism Triumphant 1789–1914*, Berkeley: University of California Press.

2012, 'Reflections on an Intellectual Adventure' in *Contemporary Sociology*, 41, 1, 6–9.

Wallerstein, I, Collins, R, Mann, M, Derluguian, G, Calhoun, C, 2014, *Does Capitalism Have a Future?*, Oxford: Oxford University Press.

Williams, G, 2013 'Interview with Immanuel Wallerstein' in *Journal of World-Systems Research*, 19, 2, 202–10.

4 Taming the chief: from evolutionary theory to political ideology

Georgi Derluguian, Timothy Earle, and Will Reno

Michael Mann and Immanuel Wallerstein, our two greatest macrohistorical scholars, delivered on their long-standing promise to explain the origins of our times. We do have now a much clearer and broader vision of the past, if one cares to notice. The world in the meantime looks as complex and contradictory as ever. Many people despair that it would ever get better. Will it? Our tribute to the life achievement of Michael Mann goes in two steps. We heavily draw on his theories, and we must also draw on his own irreverence for we are going to disagree with Mann's rejection of social evolution. It is far from scholastic disputation. The evolutionary logic is not merely an academic construct but rather a matter of ideological and political power to change other sources of power in the coming decades.

Knowledge on power

After 1945, the world reconstruction boosted mightily the modern intellectual ambition to explain scientifically the patterns of human societies from the beginnings of history and into the future. The departure point was perhaps in the new grave awareness of the threats to life on earth, from the fascist exterminationism in the recent past to the looming future possibilities of nuclear war and global environmental disasters. The fears, however, were outweighed by tremendous optimism and the "can do" spirit of the age. The universal expectation of renewed progress was supported by victory over fascism, the postwar economic growth and welfare expansion, the end of terror and the beginnings of democratization in the communist Eastern Europe, and the independence of former colonies and their resolve to "develop." Not in the least, worldwide expansion of university education and rapid accumulation of research led to a renewed hope in the abilities of modern science. The key collective actors of the post-1945 transformations were national states and the popular movements aspiring to become national states. Hence the

62

centrality of states, state-directed development, movements, revolutions, and their ideologies for the research agenda of what became called (arguably too narrowly) historical sociology.

In the 1970s and the 1980s, historical sociology experienced its "Golden Age" prepared by the accumulation of social science research across many countries and academic disciplines.[1] The theoretical formulations reconsidering the canonical topics of social science arrived in rapid succession. This "unthinking" of the nineteenth-century paradigms cleared a lot of underbrush.[2] It also left a lot to be filled in, tested, reconnected, and, remembering the public origins of social science, eventually returned to the non-academic, accessible discourses. In short, we have much work to do.

Michael Mann enters the field in the 1980s at the point when historical sociology was reaching maturation. Typical of successful "insider outsiders" in the networks of intellectual creativity, Mann became a serious and erudite critic of the ideas then at the focus of attention.[3] He proved splendid in the chosen role. (In his own way, Pierre Bourdieu claimed a structurally analogous position in the French intellectual arena.) The founding theories of historical transformation were mostly telescopic in their macro-vision culminating in the world-systems analysis of Immanuel Wallerstein. Once the parameters of the new paradigm were established, the focus of research logically moved to the more microscopic studies even if their subjects were still as big as state-formation, elites, revolutions, demographics or commodity chains. The key innovation of Michael Mann was then in offering a kaleidoscopic vision. He argued and demonstrated empirically that shifting lenses could be better attuned to discerning the crystallizations of the four distinct modalities of social power across the whole span of recorded history. At each juncture, Mann carefully took apart the existing theoretical explanations, scrutinized their elements through the four lenses and then reassembled the arguments in the way he considered more robust to the extent of available knowledge. Mann's explanations in turn could be questioned, but one could hardly wish for a more productive critique.

The dialectical move, from macroscopic to microscopic and then to kaleidoscopic, sought to overcome theoretical controversies of the time emerging along the axis of macro- and microstructural determination and contingency, symbolic and political versus the economic and structural. Mann also added another controversy by insisting on the autonomous role of military force in human history. Such insistence provoked or downright scandalized Mann's readers because it undermined the loftier

---

[1] Collins (1999).   [2] Wallerstein (2001).   [3] Collins (2000).

imagery of the modern liberal state and evidently because many among the contemporary social scientists had formative experiences in the anti-war movements and dissidence of the sixties.

Our questions to Mann would be different. We take the four kinds of social power as heuristic tools in the analysis of historical record, but we also ask whether the four are always as "orthogonally" autonomous, as in Mann's theoretical statements. The attentive readers, however, notice that in his empirical–historical reconstructions, Michael Mann – and this is much to his credit – might contradict his own theoretical statements.[4]

Mann launched his project at the time when many social thinkers put their hopes for a better future in the autonomous power of politics and ideological imagination (but certainly not the military). Unfortunately, such optimism is rarely borne by historical evidence. The crassly material factors of political economy and armed force typically dominated for long periods of time, as actually shown in Mann's empirical narrative. Still there also were the moments when ideologies prevailed. Such moments typically arrived with the breakdown of political economies due to military defeats, fiscal strains, relative overpopulation (especially among the elites), and whatever is now established as the usual causes of revolutions.[5] The question therefore should be not the abstract "whether" but rather the more theoretical–empirical "when" and under what conditions does human agency prevail in ideological vision and political action that reshape the inherited "sticky" structures of economy and geopolitics. It would be ironic then though hardly unprecedented if the next dialectical move in the development of our knowledge regarding human societies brings us to a renewed version of Marxian theories with their main weight put on the political economy and their hopeful vision of change vested in the construction of a cultural counter-hegemony. In fact, Michael Mann's analysis of past ideological movements in terms of "organizational materialism" clarifies in major ways how ideology, culture, and now the modern knowledge of scientists could become sources of power.

In their "Golden Age" of the 1970s and 1980s, the new generation of macrohistorical theories encountered two different kinds of opposition, both typically emerging in moments of heightened intellectual creativity. One was the rear-guard defensive action coming from the established schools. In this case, it was the orthodox "party-line" Marxism, while it lasted, and the liberal modernization theory reincarnated in the globalization enthusiasm of the 1990s. Neoclassical economics in the meantime essentially withdrew into the formidable protection of its

---

[4] Chibber (2013).   [5] Hanson (2010).

institutional ramparts where the mainstream economists could continue in splendid isolation. The other critique was avantgardistic. It called for an even newer wave of intellectual innovations incorporating the sensibilities of identity or the latest tools of mathematical modeling. In the following decades, however, the avant-garde manifestos did not translate into fundamental books of the caliber produced in the "Golden Age" of historical sociology. This failure of promise is very sad or worse.

Can we abandon evolutionism?

The interest in historical sociology and its allied intellectual projects in anthropology, history, and developmental economics dramatically receded around the turning point of 1989. The lightning conversion to neoliberal orthodoxy of East European dissidents together with the defecting elements of communist nomenklatura, motivated by their internal political logics, helped to seal the change in global intellectual climate. Whatever the inconsistencies in the formulations of Francis Fukuyama and Samuel Huntington, these became the self-fulfilling prophecies channeling public expectations toward the normalcy of market liberalism or the nationalist fundamentalisms taken for "civilizations." We see the consequences in the impasse of popular revolts seeking greater egalitarianism in the West, the Arab countries, in Russia, Ukraine, and all over the world. The social energies are evidently there. What is missing is a reliable map of existing social realities and the compass directing the energies to act on emerging possibilities. Mann comes closest to public engagement in the three single-topic books published between his main volumes: on fascism, genocides, and imperial hubris.[6] These were not merely extended footnotes but rather warnings regarding the conditions and contingencies opening ways to much darker possibilities. Even Immanuel Wallerstein during the times of political extinctions in the 1990s tempered his earlier optimism and now gives only a 50/50 chance to the successful transformation of the world-system into something more egalitarian. Indeed, a useful map must carry warnings alongside the directions to better destinations. Still, what could be better destinations? Can they be predicted on the basis of what we have now learned about the changing patterns of human societies?

Let us briefly explain what we mean by social evolution and how we reason about it. Social evolution has at least two distinct yet dialectically meshing movers. The original mover corresponds to Michael Mann's notion of collective power. We call it productive intensification, meaning

---

[6] Mann (2003, 2004, 2005).

the cumulative changes in technology, knowledge and social organization that enabled humans to expand in numbers and overcome the environmental constraints on populations. Two evolutionary streams could be further distinguished under this rubric. The first strategy of survival followed what biologists call "adaptive radiation," here meaning the spread of human groups into new productive environments, from the shallow littorals with their abundance of seafood to the tundra where big mammals once roamed. This is, of course, the old staple of anthropology. The textbooks of archaeology and history traditionally dwell on the divergent evolutionary stream where we find sustained growth in the size and complexity of human societies. Around ten to eight thousand years ago our ancestors occupied some of the most productive environments where, once the post-glaciation climate had stabilized, it made eminent sense to intensify production through the extensive agriculture.[7]

While these human groups were domesticating plants and animals, the aggrandizing individuals among them had also been learning how to "domesticate" other humans and turn them into beasts of burden.[8] The aggrandizers could establish themselves due to what Michael Mann pithily called the "caging effect" of sedentary economies.[9] Caging effects could irregularly coalesce in the groups of foragers extraordinarily endowed by nature perhaps as early as the Upper Paleolithic. But the considerable investments of labor in agriculture (especially irrigated agriculture) and its enlarged surpluses created the self-reinforcing combination of caging and ratchet effects driving up social complexity in the agrarian populations. This included the new institutions of warfare because it now made sense not merely to raid but also conquer and enslave the productive neighbors. The growth of social complexity meant evolutionary progress but along its winding paths we encounter the novel specialized tools like the swords shaped solely to disembowel humans and the increasingly imposing temples where humans might be sacrificed to dramatize the new ideological spectacle of power.

Chieftaincy imposes itself upon the collective powers of humans. Its coercive and entrepreneurial aspects become the second mover of social evolution. Chieftaincy corresponds to Mann's notion of despotic power, in turn relying on three pillars: economic, military and ideological controls. We suggest calling them elemental powers. Political power comes later in history with the new state institutions. States greatly intensified the pace of historical transformations reaching in recent centuries revolutionary proportions. The question for us now, as in fact it stood already

---

[7] Ristvet (2007).   [8] Flannery and Marcus (2012).   [9] Mann (1986).

before the first evolutionary thinkers of the late nineteenth century, is where might this progression go next?

Logically, there are three possibilities. The social evolution overreaching beyond the humanity's ecological and social conditions could always produce extinction, as we know it did to many human populations in the past. Mann himself warns of the threats of environmental degradation and the ultimate self-extermination with atomic weapons. The second possibility is stasis at the pinnacle of achievement. Indeed this is the long-standing modern hope of progressive liberals and some conservatives. The analytical problem with this expectation is the lack of a clearly defined mechanism (except moralistic sermon) by which social evolution slows down to a comfortable halt in a society still characterized by class and ethnic inequities. The third logical possibility then is the continuation of social evolution. But what can we meaningfully say about this possibility if our recent past and present are without historical precedent?

Michael Mann warns that there can be no comparative historical sociology because the empirical examples available for comparison are too few or none at all. Only in careful historical reconstructions might we glean some logic in the kaleidoscopic succession of "power crystallizations." Immanuel Wallerstein, the other grandmaster of macrohistorical reconstructions, sounded a little more confident in reminding us that the astronomers do not seem deterred by the fact that they can observe only one universe. A common doubt in the theories of social evolution points to the problematic applicability of Darwinian principles beyond biology. But must all evolution be Darwinian? The key mechanisms of cultural change do seem more Lamarckian than Darwinian: the inheritance of knowledge through learning, the purposeful amalgamation and anastomosis of different traditions.[10] In the past couple centuries, the very period Mann sees as revolution in social change, science has hugely enhanced and directed these two mechanisms of knowledge change.

Is knowledge power? It is arguably a core component in any kind of power identified by Mann though perhaps not a source of power on its own. The production and use of knowledge depend on the conditions flowing from the main sources of social power. Yet Mann consistently shows that social change emerges interstitially. Modern universities were created in the nineteenth and twentieth centuries out of the administrative, military, and industrial concerns of states and ruling elites. After 1945, the universities have vastly expanded their enrollments and spread around the world on the newly added concern of incorporating the rising lower social strata and dominated groups that had been politically

---

[10] Gould (1996).

empowered by the effects of world wars and the subsequent revolutions, reforms and decolonizations. Despite the neoliberal policies of economization, universities proved overall remarkably resilient. They were defended by the prestige and collective powers of the professoriate (who in fact became the newest variety of labor aristocracy) but in the main because higher education was now part of the middle-class life cycle and hopeful destination for increasing numbers of new arrivals into middle-class positions. In effect, the universities did turn into a major site of class and identity contention.

The interstitial situation of universities, their extensive organization and the positional interests of their numerous inhabitants, both permanent (staff) and temporary (students), together create the potential for advancing political claims that could change the existing distribution of powers. To put it in Mann's terms, the collective power achieved by humanity could yet become less monopolistic and more collectively distributional. If this reminds you of rebellious 1968 hopes, it is not coincidental. The period between 1956 and 1989 (which also witnessed, far from coincidentally, the rise of historical sociology) registered the first waves of contention by educated specialists against the "System." Their failure, followed by the lasting period of reaction, was fundamentally a failure of ideological vision. The educated dissidents in advanced industrial society, guided by pre-rational aversion more than good reason, did not take the path of erstwhile revolutionaries epitomized by the Jacobins and the Bolsheviks. This route led to totalitarian dictatorship and war. Instead, the dissidents earnestly embraced the dominant reformist ideologies of their states demanding socialism or liberal capitalism "with a human face." The Historical sociology arrived a little too late to spread its newly gained insights into the ideology and politics of practical social change toward greater egalitarianism. Will we be late again?

We extend on the more optimistic insights of Michael Mann. Accepting some of his critical arguments, we also argue that Mann goes too far in rejecting the idea of social evolution. One can hardly disagree with Mann that recent centuries were marked by revolutionary change in the collective powers of humans, first in the West and now probably spreading to the rest. Social power is a tricky thing, and the collective powers are especially hard to keep in monopoly for too long. Let us think through the two concepts that have produced most enthusiasm and controversy around Mann's theories; that is, the autonomy of states and the growth of their infrastructural reach at the expense of despotic arbitrariness.

The sketch of our evolutionary argument starts in prehistory and thus even earlier than the time frame of Mann's four volumes. But we will bring our sketch to the present age of globalization where, we argue, the elemental powers of personal chieftaincy are still operating above, between and within the institutions of modern bureaucracy, both state and private. These are the warlords, the mafia dons, the religious and secular ideological entrepreneurs, and above them all, the corrupt politicians and corporate bosses. We see the key contradiction of our time in this juxtaposition of chiefly despotic power, which is by nature private, and the public infrastructural power, which tends to be collective because of its extent and complexity. Chiefly powers effectively corrupt public power, turning institutional regulation and resource flows to benefit the few. In the same contradiction, we see the possibility for a political agenda that could bring our social evolution to a more egalitarian turn. The situations when social powers are monopolized in the hands of chiefs or "bosses" might yet prove to be only an episode – an episode lasting several thousand years, but still, an episode in the evolution of human societies. This is our main thesis and, if you wish, ideological message from the positions of social science.

Chiefs, chiefs all the way up

Once upon a time, all graves were created equal. Typically, these burials were also collective. They began appearing in archaeological record as small groups of humans acquired permanent stakes in their productive ecologies. These could be particularly rich hunting, fishing and gathering grounds or some sort of rudimentary gardens. Past attempts to tie the stages in social evolution to particular technologies were proved inadequate.[11] What rather seemed to matter was the size of human groups that could be maintained in a given ecological niche using the available productive techniques. The varied and increasingly sophisticated data on the very long span of prehistory indicate that the egalitarian collective power of human groups had long predated vertical social power over the human collectivities. Evidently, the collective powers had also kept in check the social powers of aspiring individuals. In recent decades, portraying the nastier of chimpanzee behaviors as modeling human individualism produced a stream of bestsellers advocating an overtly ideological line. The knowledge obtained by social science, however, can help to evaluate the relative claims of ideologies, too.

The professional observations of primatologists demonstrated that between the different behaviors of modern apes, such as gorillas, chimps and bonobos, none directly applies to humans.[12] Our range of behaviors

[11] Johnson and Earle (2000).   [12] Boehm (2001).

is much wider than among other species, evidently because human motivations are mainly cultural and situational. Outside the context of vicious inter-group violence (which is also a very human behavior, but it had to be rare in the earlier sparser populations), humans are demonstrably more cooperative and altruistic than any other social primates.[13] As primatologist Frans de Waal puts it, we are the species in which individual weakness is not immediately lethal.[14] After all, humans rather than apes are now found on all continents and in the possession of such improbable acquired abilities as fishing with hooks, hunting with the deliberately designed missiles, or, later in history, milking cows and mounting horses. Individual aggrandizers, both male and female, are widely found among humans. The anthropologists, however, documented a range of countering social behaviors, from ridicule and shaming to the threat of expulsion and killing to simply ignoring demands, which limit and channel the entrepreneurial energies of aggrandizers toward collective goals.[15] This is a fundamentally important baseline that we want to establish.

Yet at some point rich tombs began appearing, to the delight of the curators and patrons of modern museums. Who were these exceptional individuals staring at us from their lavish burials, typically looted long ago by enterprising contemporaries? They were the archaic aggrandizers who succeeded in establishing chokepoints on the networks of group conflict, collective belief, or material exchange. *Chokepoint* is the keyword here, and such controlling devices become possible only after the networks of social interaction expanded beyond the collective abilities of a cozy small kin group and good neighbors. In other words, intensification created the resource structures, which made possible control, protection, and spiritual sanction. Hence came the emergence in history of the Warrior, the Priest, and the Trader. But not yet the Great Ruler, because in prehistory the aggrandizers could hardly support the logistics of building states.

The archaic aggrandizers, or simply chiefs, were too busy anyway. If you decide to become a great chief yourself, which of the elemental powers would be your prime choice: warrior might, economic wealth, or ideological belief? This is a tricky question. If you prove naïve enough to make a choice, as prospective chief, then you failed the test. Long before Machiavelli or, for that matter, the Japanese videogame "Pokemon," the chiefly maxim was *Gotta catch 'em all!* Elemental powers have no trump card. Nobody would fight for a destitute chief (wealth calls for force protection); and few would be convinced to pray and sacrifice at your

---

[13] Turchin et al. (forthcoming).   [14] de Waal (2006).   [15] Cashdan (1980).

self-styled temple unless you can invest in impressive decorations and ritual spectacles while policing against the detractor prophets and other such heretics.

The sources of social power are not free-standing abstractions. Power is the never-ending challenging process of grabbing and braiding together the strings of human interactions within the social networks that look separate only in our scholarly analyses. But not all powers are equally important or accessible at different times, social settings and geographical locations. In some epochs armed conquest takes the lead. In other times conquest may prove unfeasible, especially over longer distances. Trade might then bring better profits. Both wealth and might may better be secured by the cults and monuments venerating their wielders that, in turn, create further possibilities for trade, tribute, and gathering warriors. Such crafty calculations and contingent possibilities are mainly responsible for the motley and seemingly aimless historical succession of what Mann dubbed "power crystallizations."

This conclusion has been the stumbling block for many evolutionary theories too straightforwardly derived from empirical generalizations. Power is indeed elemental – like water, fire, and wind. Chieftaincy is then the human-made node, a gathering of chokepoints on social networks, always imperfect and never long lasting, which allows individuals to pursue and enjoy their aggrandizement efforts as chiefs. Chiefs come in many historical guises. They were tribal leaders and champion warriors, traders and kings, sometimes even emperors. They were high priests and insurgent prophets (but only the successful ones pass the threshold, which means they had to do more than merely claim to hear voices). Chiefs dominated in human history since the invention of the village in the Neolithic if not earlier. They are found, to stress a main point, wherever the extent of social networks created a potential for establishing chokepoints.

Chieftaincy, the particular "braiding" of three elemental powers, carries all the advantages of a handmade tool. It is custom-fitted to the specific circumstances and could be refitted. In fact, it must be continuously refitted apace with ever-changing circumstances. Crucially, each chieftaincy snugly fits the hand of its principal maker and owner. As an utterly personal and highly adaptive process of domination, chieftaincy must be arbitrary and despotic, within the constraints of the governed. Chieftaincy is made, after all, to stay in the same chiefly line – provided that they have strong and expert hands because rarely is there any safe retirement for the chiefs, either in the archaic past or in the present-day Arab "presidencies for life" and in Putin's Russia. To its masters, chieftaincy offers numerous crucial advantages which ensured the survival of this old social design well into our present day. It is the exercise of despotic will over subordinates, the multi-tasking adaptability, insulation from popular claims, and, of course, the sweet fruits of power along with the accoutrements and energizing sense of exclusive status.

The downside of chieftaincy, however, flows from the same advantages of despotic power concentrated in the human chief. Personal domination is unavoidably constrained in space and time. The simple chiefs (i.e. those either before states or operating in the margins of states as the mafia dons and warlords) could personally know, bark commands, and bestow the personally obligating rewards to at most a few hundred retainers undergirding the chieftaincy's control over upward to several thousand subjects in a realm that could be crossed in a couple days. Chieftaincy is confined to the physical limits of direct interpersonal exchange and communication. Moreover, the chief's commands would be obeyed only insofar as he himself appears fit and capable of enforcing the commands. Senility and disease are the merciless nemesis of all successful chiefs who had once survived the necessarily ferocious and dirty struggles for ascendancy. Succession is therefore the inevitable moment of highest danger and fragility precisely because all chieftaincies come custom-made to fit a personal ruler.

It is then not too difficult to see why the archaic aggrandizers sought to establish states and also why they have been failing repeatedly. States are essentially machines that, like all machines, extend human abilities beyond the humanly possible. State power is more extensive than what any individual chief could ever organize and supervise. In a strikingly consequential dialectic, however, state power, in order to stay extensive, must also become intensive. Many great chiefs in world history approached the threshold of state power but fewer have crossed it and stayed alive for long or ensured the longevity of their dynasties once on this new level of power. This is because the techniques of social intensification – literacy, bureaucracy, the market commercialization of life – remained rudimentary until the high points achieved by the Roman empire, Han China, and especially the modern capitalistic West. The premodern chieftaincies, whatever their greatly varied shape, size, and coloring, were limited to the elementary morphology of the syphon. They simply sucked upward, often as mercilessly as in raiding and slaving, the resources that could be detached and sucked from the elementary production units of peasant and pastoralist households. In their own manner, Karl Polanyi's "redistributive economy," Charles Tilly's feudal "racketeering," and Mancur Olson's "roaming bandits" refer to largely the same reality. The limitation was not in the despotic power to extract but rather in what could be effectively extracted and deployed for the purposes of state-building.

The power to rule them all

States presented the most ambitious chiefs with irresistible allure precisely because states promised so much more wealth and power. For several millennia, however, states had to remain crude and despotic. What else could one expect from conquering the rudimentary agrarian societies? Richard Lachmann wryly observes regarding the famous dictum of Julius Caesar *Veni, vidi, vici* that any ancient general could have accurately added to this "I plundered, I left."[16] Continued control and tribute extraction from the territories beyond immediate purview remained problematic. Large armies staying too long in the same area threatened with starvation first the locals and next themselves. Michael Mann's insistence on the limiting role of logistics in premodern warfare is much to the point. Ancient empires had to be coercive and tenuous confederations of elemental chiefdoms.

How did the early states solve their principal/agent dilemma? They experimented with all sorts of personalistic arrangements such as breeding in royal harems many sons (who then often killed each other), or elevating slaves to administrative positions, employing eunuchs, promoting ethnic aliens as mercenaries and mamelukes and shuffling the "friends" and other such *amici* as did Roman emperors. No arrangement, however, proved satisfactory in the longer run because, as Mann explains in his Volume 1, all clients dispatched to the provinces tended to disappear into the local "civil societies" or, we would say, start their own chieftaincies. Another solution was the fostering of civilizations or, more precisely, the shared elite patterns of conspicuous consumption, religious ritual, language, and literacy, and what Mann calls the "immanent morale" of the ruling class. But, again, the cohesion of elites in imperial civilizations depended on the expectations of material career rewards from conquests and booty or, once there remained little to conquer profitably, in the elite trade and collective defense. All civilizations inescapably generated along their outliers the various "barbarian" chieftaincies fed by trade and military raiding across the imperial boundaries.

This is, roughly described, what propelled the familiar rhythm of intermittently rising empires irregularly but inevitably collapsing into the "feudal" ages. Yet the periods of reverting to smaller, more autonomous and thus typically quarrelsome chieftaincies had been progressively acquiring lesser degrees of "darkness." During such periods of fragmentations, the techniques of empires were spread and recycled with the important additions of various barbarian innovations.[17] There are not

---

[16] Lachmann (2010).

[17] 'Feudal synthesis' remains a key insight established by Perry Anderson's (1974).

very many but still not too few empirical examples of the progressing alternation between empires and feudalisms that we call evolutionary.[18] Mann more cautiously prefers to call it dialectic.

The "Rise of the West" is the canonical example of evolutionary breakthrough. There surely were other examples of such synthesis wherever the previously barbarian tribesmen from the outliers could pick up and inventively recombine the valuable pieces of central empires such as the Arab Caliphate or medieval Japan. The classical Greek polis, for that matter, was a major earlier example of similar synthesis. On close scrutiny the West might appear unique in lots of respects, from its rich Roman inheritance to its lucky geography (that also brought disaster to native Americans). Yet placing the Western developments in a larger perspective suggests that at some point it had to click somewhere across Eurasia and launch the capitalist dynamic. The barriers were many but there were also many movers going in the same direction.[19]

Capitalism grew the market dynamics going back many centuries and broadly diffused across Eurasia.[20] Capitalism obtained its historical breakthrough in the far western cluster of warring feudal coalitions that, in their medieval form, were more chieftaincies than states. It remains the task for future generations of scholars to formulate a synthetic theory of capitalist transition but its elements now seem well established – and they are materialist. Even the old (and largely ideological) controversy regarding the role of Christianity is largely settled now, with much credit to Michael Mann, by shifting the focus on the material aspects of ecclesiastic organizational infrastructure and the elite conflicts over the appropriation of church assets and authority.[21]

The main factor, however, is as brutally materialist as military geopolitics. The lasting situation where many warring monarchs had to attract mobile cosmopolitan capital in order to support their military and state aggrandizing permitted the capitalists to collectively lower their protection costs.[22] In turn, capitalism offered to state aggrandizers a qualitatively different kind of power "metabolism." Where the archaic aggrandizers had to rely on crude staple finance, the modern state aggrandizers had at their disposal the much more versatile and quicker wealth finance (of which they could never have enough).

The effects cascaded all over. Wealth finance afforded the still relatively small European rulers much bigger military forces than the staple tribute could have ever supported and, even more importantly, the new

---

[18] Lieberman (2003 and 2009) recently added a whole cluster of previously ignored histories.
[19] Collins (1999).   [20] Abu-Lughod (1989).   [21] Lachmann (2000).
[22] Arrighi (2010).

fabulously expensive hardware of guns and ocean-going ships. Truly world conquest became possible for the first time in history. The perennially fractured West, however, extended several colonialisms whose rivalries carried the seeds of their eventual undoing. Military employment and colonization maintained wages relatively high, at least in countries like England, which made worthwhile technological innovation.[23] Amidst all of this, the states had to and could finally afford to grow bureaucratic.

Taking the state by tentacles

We need not go to any length relating what subsequently happens to social power in the West because this story, in rich variation, is among the best established in the new historical sociology. States operating in capitalist environments acquired extensive infrastructural powers and grew an array of "tentacles" (in Mann's own expression) deeply penetrating into society. But the same process of infrastructural buildup created its backflow effects, allowing societies to lay claims on the state. This new possibility fostered two rival ideologies of citizenship: nationalism and socialism. The ideological response of elites was mainly gradualist liberalism.[24] Citizens now increasingly mattered to their state rulers as compliant taxpayers, skilled labor, loyal (and preferably healthy) military recruits. Otherwise the citizens could organize themselves using the new techniques of literacy and communication all the way to staging mass protests and revolutions.[25] What made the citizen claims effective was, ultimately, the continuing geopolitical rivalries of states. Successful strikes, revolutions, decolonizations, and welfare reforms cluster in the wake of difficult or downright lost wars.[26]

The historical high point of citizens taking on their states arrived in the wake of 1945. This brings us back to the beginning of our arguments. The moment of unprecedented progressive political change and social advances fostered the optimism that ran strongly through the 1950s and the 1960s. These were still the decades of state rivalry which, as many feared, were now fraught with nuclear extermination. But the nondestructive Cold War proved to be exceptionally good for economic growth, welfare reforms, development projects, and, let us not forget, the generous funding of science. The Cold War period also brought an enormous expansion of state powers worldwide. No other period in history witnessed the creation of so many ministries of education, health, and planning. Even the various guerrillas armies in Latin America, Asia, and Africa now

---

[23] Allen (2011).   [24] Wallerstein (2011).   [25] Tilly (1990).   [26] Silver (2003).

hastened to start their own schools, clinics, and the departments of women's affairs which became required for international and domestic legitimacy. In the same period, public order has also reached its highest point in many places, including notorious Palermo, Odessa, Shanghai, and Chicago.[27]

All this meant the taming of chiefs by the states and popular movements putting pressure on states. In fact, taming the chiefs has been the central story in the formation of modern states that have been eliminating or incorporating chieftaincies as their internal organs. Most explicitly, this was the story of modern militaries passing from feudal retinues to the aristocratic war commanders of absolutist monarchies and finally into the professional officer corps. The military leaders who are not interchangeable and cannot be reassigned to other units today are called warlords or gangsters. In their precarious lives they enjoy limited (though still despotic) power and little legitimacy, let alone the prospect of honorable discharge from duties. Another route led former aristocracies and gentries to become provincial notables and then elected politicians or elite commercial professionals exploiting the symbolic capital of their good manners and connections (provided their ancestors could avoid the blades of revolution). The fate of those wielding ideological power in modern times was not too different. Priests and religious hierarchies were gradually brought to bureaucratic conformity and nationalized within their states and to the exclusion of self-styled mystics. The voices of modern ideologies would become the propagandists for parties and movements, creative intellectuals or professors of social science.

The historical trend of taming the chiefs, however, went through a disastrous lapse in the wake of the First World War. The grievous disorganization of defeated empires and their ruling classes opened the way to the seizure of state power by revolutionary socialists and counter-revolutionary fascist nationalists. Extending on the wartime mobilization techniques, these movements built the frighteningly effective totalitarian dictatorships that fused the infrastructural reach of the modern bureaucratic state with the despotic power of new revolutionary emperors whose prototype was Napoleon Bonaparte. Fascist totalitarianism was eliminated in war, and it is scarcely imaginable how it could have ended in anything but war. Communist totalitarianism, which was nowhere as apocalyptic as its fascist enemies, had longer and varied trajectories. Let us note that in all communist states the leaders were eventually tamed from within by their own bureaucratic elites and intelligentsia much preferring liberal reforms rather than the vagaries of continued revolutionary

[27] Derluguian (1996).

militaristic mobilization. The Soviet *nomenklatura*, however, never figured out how to escape from the institutional shell of their own heavily industrialized and multiethnic state. In the end, they broke it into pieces. In the meantime, the communist cadres in China successfully rebuilt their institutionally much simpler apparatus to make it the latest expanded edition of the East Asian developmental state. Communism, in the end, was neither destined to supersede capitalism nor was it doomed to collapse.[28]

Totalitarianism must not be regarded as past historical calamity. Its causes were not in any particular ideology but rather in the unprecedented capacities of the modern state. The state is a machine for generating and directing social power. Like any machine it can have different uses, from sheltering and provisioning its citizens to spying on them or even exterminating whole populations. The darker side of modern states, as Michael Mann warns us, is there and could reemerge in future crises. The conditions are roughly known: panicking elites, ideological polarization, paramilitaries emerging from the political fringes and from within the disorganized state. The professional private security forces and advanced means of electronic surveillance add new danger. Even if we offer some optimistic predictions arising from our theory of social evolution, we see hefty reasons to stay vigilant. Totalitarian lapses will remain an ongoing possibility as long as we live with states and cannot rule out big sudden crises.

The capitalist flight into globalization

One special kind of modern chief was never fully tamed by states. These were, of course, capitalists. The capitalists operating in the modern world-system could survive and mostly get their way in bargaining with state rulers by threatening to withhold their investments and organizational expertise. Some states could expel and exterminate their capitalists, as the communists did. Others attempted to expropriate through nationalizations the certain "unpatriotic" categories among the capitalists. This never worked in the long run and often provoked economic disasters in the shorter run, too. The anticapitalist states of the twentieth century resorted to crude military-style substitutes, and moreover the commanding heights of the world economy remained privately controlled by the biggest capitalists anyway.

The capitalists, however, were never entirely averse to state power as their typical class ideology would make us believe. Capitalism evolved and spread around the world apace with the modern states because states

---

[28] Derluguain (2013).

were making social environments safe and profitable for capitalism while capitalism was supporting (rarely without profit) the wealth-finance metabolism of the states. But, as in any complex system, the environment has been irreversibly changing over time. Capitalism emerged originally into the predominantly agrarian world where its main profits were in long-distance trade and banking while the costs went overwhelmingly toward military protection. Peasant households, as ever before, continued to bear the costs of social reproduction, supplying towns and markets with labor, while the only thing that mattered about natural resources was getting them. Still, from the outset, it made eminent sense to internalize the protection costs of business by merging the interests of the state and capitalist elites. As states became more capitalist and thus more modern, the capitalists acquired stakes in becoming more national. Nonetheless, the truly big capitalists always maintained their elite cosmopolitan networks for the purposes of business, pleasure, prestige, marriage and, if came to that, escape.

As time went by, capitalism faced further needs to internalize its costs. The Industrial Revolution essentially meant a huge advance in internalizing the costs of production. The new social classes of the industrial age and their protest movements pressed to internalize the costs of social reproduction at least in the Western countries. The market upheavals of the nineteenth century elicited the internalization of transaction costs in the sectorial cartels and, eventually, corporations. The Great Depression of the 1930s was finally overcome by involving state regulation and investment on a truly massive scale. Amidst the world wars, fascism, and communism, all this looked to many contemporary capitalists as the price of survival.

In fact, the costs paid before 1945 secured the three extraordinary postwar decades of prosperity, peace, and legitimacy. This period culminated in the protest movements demanding actually more of the same – peace, well-being, ethical politics – but now minus the paternalism of Big Bosses. For all the polemical commentaries, the 1968 world wave of protests remains poorly understood and largely ignored by scholars. Charles Tilly in his impressive catalog of European revolutions over the past five centuries puzzlingly omits some of the most serious events of his lifetime. Michael Mann gives them a short shrift, too. Immanuel Wallerstein, exceptionally, equates 1968 in importance with the revolutions of 1848 that had institutionalized the Old Left. But even Wallerstein only vaguely indicates what caused 1968 and what it had actually institutionalized. The following decades of neoliberalistic reaction are still awaiting good explanation, too. At least we have now a good starting point in the nuanced empirical investigations of Monica Prasad and Richard

Lachmann who relate the internal politics of hegemonic America to the world context.[29]

Globalization in its current form is not merely a structural extension of previously local processes or stages of progress. It is the political and economic strategy devised by a specific set of powerful actors that at the time went under the rubric of multinational corporations. They were motivated by the perception of acute crisis threatening the hegemonic position of the United States and the existence of capitalism itself in the wake of political turmoil generally associated with the 1968 protest wave. This wave, initially provoked by the unexpected humiliation of the US military and political establishment in the Vietnam war, rapidly spread and connected to many other sources of discontent. Internationally, the reverberations of protest continued for more than a decade resulting, due to largely local reasons, in the overthrow of American allies in Iran and Nicaragua, and the student-led rebellions in South Korea and the Philippines. In several countries of Southern Europe, communists suddenly seemed on the verge of taking power through popular elections. The picture will be critically incomplete without recalling the veritable panic in the face of economic and technological prowess displayed by Japan and West Germany. We must be reminded today of how differently the world situation looked in the 1970s and early 1980s to appreciate the sense of grave urgency felt by the US elites.

Their search for solutions led to the abandonment of compromises observed since the Great Depression and the First World War. Globalization along with deregulation became the big escape of primarily American big business from the constraints of national borders where, they now feared, political demands could corner them and force them into making intolerable concessions. In a major historical contingency, these actors were helped by the unexpected emergence and failure of Gorbachev's *perestroika* ending in the collapse of Soviet Union. Had Gorbachev or a more realist Kremlin leader succeeded in converting the Soviet superpower position into an honorable invitation to rejoin the capitalist economic networks of Europe, there would be no neoliberal Washington Consensus. Instead, a more regulated market might have formed along the axis of Paris, Berlin and Moscow. Globalization could then have assumed a different shape and character. But this possibility did not come to pass. Another contingency was the equally surprising opening of communist China for business. East Asia became a major destination for the new business strategy of outsourcing, or what David Harvey dubbed the "spatial fix."[30]

---

[29] Prasad (2006); Lachmann (2014).   [30] Harvey (2005).

The protest wave of 1968, to which we must add the 1989 wave in communist countries, marked a culmination in the modern-era trend toward greater egalitarianism in human societies, starting earlier and becoming more pronounced in the West but very rapidly, if also unevenly, spreading to world regions. Just compare the distance from 1968 to the situation in European societies around 1868 and 1768. A new social class asserted itself in 1968 and in Eastern Europe in 1989: the institutionally employed wage earners with university degrees. They are variously called professionals, intelligentsia, specialists or simply working middle classes but these are largely misnomers because all these labels originally belonged to quite different social groups and in other historical contexts. The fundamental realities of this social class (to which we might belong ourselves) are the dependence on regular wages during adult life, which makes us akin to proletarians. But the new wage earners also carry considerable amounts of sophisticated knowledge (call it professional or symbolic capital) accumulated during lengthy periods of learning in schools and universities. Another difference with the situation of Western proletarians in the age of Karl Marx is that the educated specialists today are overwhelmingly dependent for their employment and life conditions on large impersonal institutions, whether state agencies or private corporations.

The combination of considerable symbolic capital, high self-esteem, massive numbers, and extensive interconnectedness (yes, the Internet, however ephemeral it might be) and, at the same time, the drudgery of routine and relatively ill-paying office labor, when it is available, result in a very contradictory class consciousness. On the one hand, it is prone to anarchism as protest against the impersonal bureaucratic "System." This could be seen in the counter-culture movements of the sixties and seventies and the symbolic rejections of communist officialdom in the eighties. On the other hand, the same inchoate attitudes of self-affirmation against the dominating institutions could find shape and purpose in fad consumerism; infatuations with "knowledge economy," "creative class," "independent start-ups," and all the way to market libertarianism. Religious fundamentalism and New Age mysticism are still other and possibly meshing ideological possibilities. Should we then wonder that this new class, once its early anti-systemic stirrings went nowhere, could be hitched to the neoliberal project? We doubt, however, that after nearly a generation this situation could last much longer.

In a consequential irony, the inherent contradiction between legitimacy and profits made the capitalists betray their new-found political supporters among the educated middle classes. The enthusiasm for globalization and computer technology founders on the realization that both the "spatial fix" and "technological fix" restore the profitability of businesses by displacing middle-class specialist jobs.[31] The pride and prejudices of specialists are bound to be hurt by the realization that they must seek help from states held captive to big businesses and public budgets critically depleted by the bail-outs of major capitalist groups after the 2008 Great Recession. In the absence of a positive political alternative, this coming realization could create more ugliness than hopeful solutions. Hence the urgency of restarting the intellectual enterprise of historical sociology, developmental economics and evolutionary theory and making their insights relevant in today's context.

The chiefs must be tamed, after all

We began by promising to show reasons for optimism regarding the evolutionary future of humanity, and we intend to hold the promise. Perhaps after all that has been said about states, it may sound counter-intuitive that we place hope in bureaucratic power. But let us explain. We started from the very early prehistory to establish an important baseline. Humans differ from chimpanzees precisely in their patterns of group behavior. The most successful adaptation of our ancestors apparently was in greater egalitarianism and altruism. We are very inquisitive coop-erative creatures strongly averse to inequality and violence. This unu-sually positive statement regarding human nature increasingly finds evidence in primatology, anthropology, and the microsociology of indivi-dual interactions.[32] But things would change with the arrival of agricul-ture and much denser populations where a minority became ferocious beasts while the majority were reduced to beasts of burden.

Social inequality and warfare appeared and became institutionalized in those human groups that had acquired fixed assets, mainly the staple surpluses and various kinds of symbolic wealth that could be in turn controlled and manipulated by individual aggrandizers. Those political economies with a variety of chokepoints, depending on the geographical and historical context, then turned mere aggrandizers into chiefs. Wearing intermittently the hats of the Warriors, the Priest, and Trader (these were often in fact spectacular headdresses), our chiefs braided and strengthened combinations of elemental powers going to and beyond the threshold of statehood. The social inequality in such societies became glaring and brutal and included slavery, mass torture and human sacrifices.

States have evolved along this long difficult history. Limiting and undermining them were the inherent structural weaknesses that even

---

[31] Collins (2013).   [32] Collins (2008).

the most formidable ancient empires like Rome and Han China could never overcome. It is, however, demonstrable that states had been growing in size and complexity. This progression alternated with the periods of "dark ages" when more elemental chieftaincies burst free from the hold of state power. The periods of failed empires and active chieftaincies were surely destructive but sometimes also innovative. During such periods the democratic Greek polis or the medieval city communes could take shape, and the diffuse "feudal synthesis" helped to invent and accomplish what the imperial civilizations somehow did not.

Some scholars put special emphasis on the evolution in religion, especially on what, following the modernist theologian Karl Jaspers, they call the "Axial Age." We doubt the usefulness of this concept both empirically and theoretically. It should not be surprising that alternative spiritual ideologies emerged among the disparate populations facing the harsh realities of living within ancient empires. Such spiritual movements were egalitarian reactions in their prophetic and insurgent phases. But only those that had been eventually incorporated into the officialdom of empires survive to our day as world religions. So what explain the lag of nearly two thousand years between the Axial Age and modern democratization?

The great historical reversal in social inequality originated, paradoxically, in the rapidly changing political economy of the modern West. It is indeed a paradox because there was not much particularly democratic about early capitalism let alone the European geopolitics of chronic warfare. Capitalism produced and eventually endowed with mobilization resources its own democratic insurgents, if not exactly its gravediggers. The states in the meantime fostered the national political arenas and citizenries who came to be in a position to demand rights from their rulers. Needless to say, it has been a very contentious process.

The rulers themselves have changed dramatically. They could no longer afford to be the self-serving and capricious chiefly aristocracies. Such antiquated personages would perish in modern interstate warfare and revolutionary upheavals. The ruling classes had to recast themselves as bureaucratic public servants, whether civilian or professional military or the service clergy and secular intelligentsia. The chiefs tamed themselves and each other by entering state service, where their descendants could further be tamed by the growing democratic claims over the behavior and usefulness of state offices. The paradox then is that the states, originally designed as war machine and tax-extracting apparatuses, could not escape issuing guarantees against themselves and acquiring such wonderfully "unnatural" new functions as market regulation and social provision.

Modern democratization was achieved and consolidated under the threat of wars and revolutions, and then still very unevenly. Frightening major relapses occurred during the 1920s and the 1930s. Only after 1945, which marked, of course, the end of the biggest war in human history, was democratization finally consolidated in the West and began rapidly spreading to other world regions. At the level of specific histories, this all seems very contingent. But at the level of world historical generalization, this appears evolutionary because the ratchet effect of social complexity prevented backsliding and procrastination by eliminating anomalies mainly through lost wars and successful revolutions.

Viewed under this angle, the recent neoliberal decades appear an evolutionary anomaly. Their origins of neoliberal reaction were contingent and the practices it fostered are self-destructive. It became possible because capitalists, and especially hegemonic big business in the United States, had preserved considerable autonomous power compared to other elite fractions. In other words, the capitalists remained personalistic chiefs. This actually shows who are the true dominant elite of our age. The observation that they preside over private corporate bureaucracies does not contradict the fact that, at the top, corporations are chieftaincies. The greatest test and perk of one's power in a modern bureaucratic institution is the ability to exempt oneself from the strictures of bureaucratic routine (do we need to cite Carl Schmitt again?). When in the 1970s, the capitalist chiefs perceived the danger of additional regulations and taxation (i.e. the prospect of being tamed and incorporated in states as merely economic managers), they counter-reacted vigorously and broke loose into the under-regulated abode of globalization.

The self-destructiveness of neoliberal reaction is to undermine the legitimacy and capacity of the very states that used to protect them. That evidently includes protection against the self-serving destruction of the natural environment. But while this frightening prospect looms on a distant horizon of several decades, the more immediate effects are seen all around. In recent years, many lesser chieftaincies have gone untamed and quite predatory. They go by many different names including "wild" speculators, oligarchs, corrupt politicos, gangsters, traffickers, warlords, religious fanatics, and terrorists. For all their differences, these personages share in common a crucial trait: they are entrepreneurs beyond public control.

We feel reasonably confident that this anomaly will eventually be finished in the re-imposition of states. Fortunately, too much in our recent history and institutions (that are, let us recall, "sticky") militates against a different outcome. Perhaps not everything is bad in the current "dark age." A large majority of states remain intact while quite a few in

Latin America and East Asia continue to consolidate. Extinct is the Marxist–Leninist orthodoxy that purported to become the latter-day Christianity. The ideological field lost much of its polarizing tension and seems more open for innovation. American hegemony is still flailing in the Middle East, but it is now obviously in decline. There is no geopolitical rival of equal destructiveness and no rising hegemonic power anywhere on the horizon. The world might yet become more peaceful, and large parts of it are already more peaceful than at any time in recent centuries. The demographic dynamics appear stabilizing in most world regions (perhaps with the sole exception of Sub-Saharan Africa). Technological and economic growth continues even if not at the same pace as in the post-1945 decades.

In short, there is little reason to expect that neoliberalism might end in a colossal war or ferocious revolution. More likely, it will peter out in a protracted recession centered on the United States. The chiefs will be re-tamed, this time almost certainly including the economic variety. Then humanity may continue its long evolutionary return to egalitarianism because the infrastructural power of states is amenable to public control and democratization while personalistic chieftaincy is by definition des-potic. We might, however, think in advance about substitutes for the inventive entrepreneurialism of prospective chiefs. Bureaucrats are not reputed to be particularly inventive. Who knows, maybe the anarchistic dreams of cooperatively creative communities could become more realis-tic in a world with tame geopolitics and markets? This does not mean paradise because we would still face big challenges like environmental degradation or poverty. We would also face many personal-level pro-blems like old age in rapidly aging populations without the support of extended (and, let us not omit, patriarchal) families. But we might become better equipped to deal with our problems. This is what seems to us eminently worth debating today.

References

Abu-Lughod Janet L. *Before European Hegemony: the World System A.D. 1250–1350.* New York: Oxford University Press, 1989.
Allen Robert C. *Global Economic History: A Very Short Introduction.* New York: Oxford University Press, 2011.
Anderson, Perry. *Passages from Antiquity to Feudalism,* London: New Left Books, 1974.
Arrighi Giovanni. *The Long Twentieth Century: Money, Power, and the Making of Our Times.* 2nd edn. London: Verso, 2010.
Boehm Christopher. *Hierarchy in the forest: The evolution of egalitarian behavior.* Cambridge, MA: Harvard University Press, 2001.

Cashdan Elizabeth. "Egalitarianism among Hunters and Gatherers," *American Anthropologist* 82: 116–120 (1980).

Chibber Vivek. "The Ghost of Theories Past," *European Journal of Sociology*, Vol. 54:3, December 2013, pp 439–449

Collins Randall. "A Buddhist Road to Capitalism," in: *Macro-History: Essays in Sociology of the Long Run*. Stanford: Stanford University Press, 1999.

Collins Randall. "The End of Middle-Class Work: No More Escapes," pp. 37–70 in: Immanuel Wallerstein, Randall Collins, Michael Mann, Craig Calhoun, and Georgi Derluguian (eds.) *Does Capitalism Have a Future?* New York: Oxford University Press, 2013.

Collins Randall. "The European Sociological Tradition and Twenty-First-Century World Sociology," pp. 26–42 in: Janet L. Lughod (ed.) *Sociology for the Twenty-First Century*. Chicago: University of Chicago Press, 1999.

Collins Randall. *The Sociology of Philosophies: A Global Theory of Intellectual Change*. Cambridge, MA: Harvard University Press, 2000.

Collins Randall. *Violence: A Micro-sociological Theory*. Princeton, NJ: Princeton University Press, 2008.

de Waal Frans. *Our Inner Ape*. New York: Riverhead, 2006.

Derluguain Georgi. "What Communism Was," pp. 99–130 in: Immanuel Wallerstein, Randall Collins, Michael Mann, Craig Calhoun, and Georgi Derluguian, *Does Capitalism Have a Future?* New York: Oxford University Press, 2013.

Derluguian Georgi. "Social Cohesion of the States and Popular Challenges," in: Terence K. Hopkins and Immanuel Wallerstein (coord.) *The Age of Transition. Trajectory of the World-System, 1945–2025*. London: Zed Books, 1996.

Flannery Kent and Joyce Marcus, *The Creation of Inequality: How Our Prehistoric Ancestors Set the Stage for Monarchy, Slavery, and Empire*. Cambridge, MA: Harvard University Press, 2012.

Gould Stephen Jay. "An Epilog on Human Culture," pp. 217–230 in: *Full House: The Spread of Excellence from Plato to Darwin*. New York: Three Rivers Press, 1996.

Hanson Stephen. *Post-Imperial Democracies: Ideology and Party Formation in Third Republic France, Weimar Germany, and Post-Soviet Russia*. New York: Cambridge University Press, 2010.

Harvey David. *A Brief History of Neoliberalism*. New York: Oxford University Press, 2005.

Johnson Allen W. and Timothy Earle. *The Evolution of Human Societies: from Foraging Group to Agrarian State*. (2nd edn), Stanford: Stanford University Press, 2000.

Lachmann Richard. "From Consensus to Paralysis in the United States, 1960–2010," pp. 195–233 in: Richard Lachmann (ed.) *The United States in Decline. Political Power and Social Theory* 26, Emerald Publishing, 2014.

Lachmann Richard. *Capitalists In Spite of Themselves: Elite Conflict and Economic Transitions in Early Modern Europe*, New York: Oxford University Press, 2000.

Lachmann Richard. *States and Power*. Cambridge: Polity Press, 2010.

Lieberman Viktor. *Strange Parallels: Southeast Asia in Global Context, c. 800–1830.* 2 volumes. New York: Cambridge University Press, 2003 and 2009.

Mann Michael. *The Dark Side of Democracy: Explaining Ethnic Cleansing,* New York: Cambridge University Press, 2005.

Mann Michael. *Fascists,* New York: Cambridge University Press, 2004

Mann Michael. *Incoherent Empire,* London: Verso, 2003

Mann Michael. *The Sources of Social Power, vol. I: A History of Power from the Beginning to 1760 AD.* New York: Cambridge University Press, 1986.

Prasad Monica. *The Politics of Free Markets: The Rise of Neoliberal Economic Policies in Britain, France, Germany, and the United States.* Chicago, IL: University of Chicago Press, 2006.

Ristvet Lauren. *In the Beginning: World History from Human Evolution to the First States.* New York: McGraw-Hill, 2007.

Silver Beverly. *Forces of Labor: Workers' Movements and Globalization Since 1870.* New York: Cambridge University Press, 2003.

Tilly Charles. *Coercion, Capital, and European States, AD 990–1990.* New York: Oxford: Blackwell, 1990.

Turchin Peter, Thomas Currie, and Harvey Whitehouse, "Understanding the Dynamics of Inequality over the Long Term: A Cultural Evolution Approach" (forthcoming).

Wallerstein Immanuel. *The Modern World-System, Volume IV: Centrist Liberalism Triumphant, 1789–1914.* Berkeley: University of California Press, 2011.

Wallerstein Immanuel. *Unthinking Social Science: Limits of the Nineteenth-Century Paradigms.* (New edition) Philadelphia: Temple University Press, 2001.

Part II

Political, economic, military and ideological
questions

5   On political decency

John A. Hall

> No sociological enterprise of this magnitude has ever been undertaken
> that was not animated by some – tacit or implicit – political passion. One
> waits absorbed to see what that will prove to be.
>
> (Anderson 1986: 176)

Although Michael Mann may yet give us another volume on social theory,
the completion of the philosophical history allows attention to be given to
Perry Anderson's question.[1] A large part of the answer seems to me to be
simply that of a passionate desire to understand how the world works, the
intellectual drive of a great scholar. Moreover, this attitude has much to
recommend it: we did not make the world, and the extent to which we are
responsible for it can easily be overdone – thereby so often allowing hope
to replace analysis. Still my concern here is with normative matters. What
can we hope for given the constraints imposed by history? What should we
value and how should we act? Mann does have views here, and I have
great sympathy for them. Still, examining them may push him a little
further – perhaps to add something, perhaps to say that I am mistaken.

An initial consideration is necessary. One of the pleasures of my life has
been that of witnessing the unfolding of this great book. Accordingly, I
have seen many twists and turns over thirty years. A very substantial one
concerns ideological power. In the 1980s, Mann once told me that
ideology would not play much role in the volumes that were to follow
the first one, which had taken the historical account to 1760, at least in
part because territorial consolidation had taken place within Europe. It is
very much to his credit that intellectual discovery made him change his
mind. For the massive ideological power that changed the modern world
has been at the center of much of his work in the past fifteen years. Mann
has been especially perceptive – as David Priestland notes in this volume –
when dealing with fascism and ethnic cleansing and has done so in a

---

[1] This is my second set of reflections on the moral import of Mann's work, having made use
of Anderson's comment in the earlier piece as well (Hall 2006). There is some overlap, but
the earlier piece had a different focus, namely Mann's social and intellectual background.

wholly admirable way. Sociologists need to reconstruct the meanings at the back of the minds of actors, and this requires putting oneself into the shoes of those whom one might loath for moral reasons. It may well be that a title, *The Dark Side of Democracy*, was too provocative, with some of its theses perhaps mistaken, but the insistence that cleansing could be popular, could be done by people like us, seems to me to be wholly admirable, a brave foray into human behavior.[2] So moralities can be evil, and the forces of "civil society" passionate and reactionary.

With this at the back of his mind, Mann suggests that our chances in life depend on a loose package made up of several elements. Transcendental ideologies are very dangerous largely because they join together all of his four sources of social power in attempts at total social engineering; immanent ideologies can have the same effect. It is better if power sources are in separate hands for standard liberal reasons – to allow the blocking of total visions and to enhance what might be termed social and political space within social life. It is important to note that his last volumes have considered ideologies beyond bolshevism and fascism, paying attention both to some within the advanced world (neoliberalism, American imperialism, Christian fundamentalism) as well as to others in the non-European world (most notably, revivalist versions of Islam, Judaism, and Hinduism). One injunction here is that of respect: "[W]e should allow other civilizations their own ideologies, however deviant and repugnant they might seem to us – and so should they allow us our choices ... this would largely prevent ideology from overwhelming the pragmatism and compromise, which more appropriately govern the economic, military and political realms of human societies" (Mann 2013: 406). But there is another firm demand. Liberalism has concentrated nearly all its attention on balancing political power. Just as important for Mann, however, is the need to counteract the centralization of power in the other sources with which he has been concerned. Particular attention is needed to deal with concentrations of capital that seek to overwhelm the choices available to some of the citizens of the advanced world, especially those in the United States and Great Britain. Finally, there is a firm insistence that history is not so organized as to ensure moral progress. Life expectancy and literacy have increased massively, of course, but there have been reversals in moral standards and, most recently, the loss of support for social democracy in some parts of the advanced world. We must struggle to maintain our lot as well as seeking to improve it.

---

[2] I am reminded here of Ernest Gellner's late work seeking to understand the bloodiest periods of Soviet history. That the heroic romanticism of collectivization caused enormous suffering was seen as necessary and excusable; decline set in when stagnation took over (Hall 2011: 354).

It may be useful to lightly characterize these views. They are a plea for decency, based bluntly on an extreme dislike for organizations and movements that kill large numbers of people – as did white settlers overseas, fascists, communist revolutionaries, and empires as a whole. There seem to me to be links to the independent liberal world from which he came, to that strand of British thought that distrusted empire, as well as to the left wing of British Labour Party politics concerned with increasing social equality. As this attractive set of values results from his long excursus into history, it deserves evaluation. To that end I begin by saying something about ideologies, the area in which he has most changed his mind, and then follow it with and link it to a discussion of the origins of political decency, together with an analysis of forces that maintain it and of those that threaten it.

Ideologies

Classifications are never perfect, never the recognition of Platonic essences. Rather, they are more or less useful. With this in mind let me go a little against his views of modern ideology. His division between transcendant and immanent ideologies on the one hand, capable of diverting the course of history, and more stable and taken-for-granted cultural belonging on the other seems to me sensible and useful. But one can be a little uneasy about the lumping together of "total" ideologies, offering a complete way of life, and newer belief systems essentially based on a single issue, as is largely true of environmentalism. It is good to recognize the never-ending creation and impact of what might be termed middle-range ideologies, but there is something to be said for a different classification.

Bluntly, there are three and only three metatheoretical ideological options in the modern world (Hall 2013). We can approach the first one by remembering Mann's criticism of Daniel Bell's claim, much amplified by Francis Fukuyama, that we have reached an end of ideology (Mann 2013: 404). Of course the critique is accurate, as the emergence of neoliberal and environmental thought shows. But in one way it is the wrong critique. Bell had presumed that his own position was not ideological, but that is not at all so. For the first position of interest is the world of civility, understood in generic enlightenment terms. Respect for reason and science is in many ways strange. Doubt is privileged rather than certainty, essentially on the grounds that not filling out the world with belief allows for progress, for the correction of mistakes. Then there is the certain fact, well known in the eighteenth century to Hume and Kant, that we have no fundamental reason to believe that the world can be split into separate pieces nor that it is orderly – merely the discovery that these beliefs seems to ensure an ever increasing body of sustained knowledge. This is a cold world in Weberian terms because it does not provide a complete set of answers for every eventuality in life. But one need not accept the tone of cultural pessimism that pervades Weber's thought. The implicit suggestion that lives were warmer in the past, before secularization took place, can surely be challenged: lives were often poor and miserable, cursed by high mortality rates. The achievements of modern science have for many made the modern world the warmest in the historical record. The background assumption here is that normal people can manage their own lives, deal with the dramas of families and identities. Of course, a corollary of this is that of the acceptance of a great deal of relativism given that human beings get up to all sorts of ridiculous things, but that is combined with the crucial element of universalism insisting that difference takes place within an agreement on minimal liberal values. The single thinker who sums all of this up best is, at least for me, Montesquieu – at once aware of the variety of human behavior and the universalist insisting that every human being can feel pain and that liberalism must seek to diminish it.

There is an elective affinity that must be noted between this metatheory and a rather particular set of institutions. Our societies are attractive as long as they are both liberal and democratic: differently put, the formal rights of a *Rechtsstaat* need to be subject to control, whilst democracy is attractive only if those rights exist so as to allow contest rather any sort of forced unanimity or any mere acclamation of power. But how strange is this! Conflict is allowed but it has to be followed by acceptance by those who have lost – which means, of course, that it takes place within narrow bounds and most easily within a strongly shared national culture. Beyond this description of liberal democracy stands one of Mann's most powerful insights: that exclusion politicizes and inclusion tames – allowing us to reform rather than having to mount barricades.

The second ideological option can neatly be introduced by noting that its greatest thinker, Rousseau, began his career with an attack on Montesquieu, who had rejected the tradition of civic virtue in favor of an acceptance of the complexities and confusions of the modern world. Rousseau was horrified by this attitude: moral complexity and division can only bring psychic discomfort. There is a certain oddity here. The apostle of individualism bases everything he says on the weakness of human beings, their need for social support – and quite possibly religious meaning as well. We cannot manage by ourselves, as unrestricted individualism will inevitably lead to chaos and unhappiness. These sentiments led Rousseau to admire Sparta, and he accordingly felt that virtue should be the business of the state.[3] This is the tradition of belonging. This theme gained enormous prominence after the eighteenth century, which is not surprising given the disruptive social changes brought by the coming of industrial society. Marx's thought for instance stresses the need to remove "splitting," to restore moral unity to mankind: an end to alienation means that human beings can again be creators in many different spheres rather than dull specialists in one. There is, of course, a measure of confidence in the individual in Marx that is wholly lacking in Durkheim, who was so deeply influenced by Rousseau: the sociologist believed he had shown that individuals bereft of social support were prone to kill themselves. These views are all-too-present in modern social thought, and they certainly inform some versions of socialism and of nationalism. There is a "malaise to modernity," as the Canadian philosopher Charles Taylor puts it, such that happiness can only be found through fraternity, through being embedded within a rich cultural tradition, very often of a nation and a religion (1991). It is not at all clear to me how a rich and shared sense of belonging is compatible with the division of labor which stands at the back of the riches that we have become used to, and which we most certainly do not wish to give up.

The view of man in the first tradition, especially in Montesquieu and the Scottish moralists, is naturalistic. Human beings are driven by passions of varied character, a view disliked by the second tradition, which sees us in more elevated terms, as spiritual beings. The third tradition, exemplified by Nietzsche and Freud, differs from both. It has no time at all for the elevated moral tone of communitarianism, regarding this as a dreadful escape from truly knowing ourselves. Those who are brave and face reality should of course have a measure of power or influence over their more passive fellows, a view that we can see at work in the view of democracy that Max Weber famously ascribed to General Ludendorff in the middle of the First World War. The naturalism this describes differs from that of the first tradition. The passions are seen, so to speak, in the light of Darwin. Smith's benign view of human behavior is one based on jealousy, of wanting to attain what others have. But there is also envy. When God told a Russian peasant that he could have whatever he wanted as long as his neighbor had twice as much, his reply was simple: "Take out an eye." Of course, envy is but a perverted element of the more general "will to power" that is central to this view. And one should stress perversion. The third tradition makes much of the certain fact that our instincts are devious and half-hidden from us, placing rationality at something of a

---

[3] The expression, derived from Xenophon, is used by used by Adam Ferguson (1969: 267) – whose position stands *opposed* to that of Rousseau.

discount. But the crucial, deeply worrying contribution of this tradition that remains for me is its awareness that the exercise of power can be pleasurable.

It is easy to see how these elements can interact. Replacing the emptiness of the first option seems to have worked best when blood was joined to belonging. When Raymond Aron returned from Germany, he remarked to Leon Brunschvicg that the Nuremburg rallies were religion accordingly to Durkheim, society worshipping itself. This combination was attractive to many intellectuals, and it proved to be terribly dangerous. Maynard Keynes realized this and sought to save liberalism by reviving its economic base when it was faced with power systems blessed with ideological fervor. It is largely because of this that my preference is for the first tradition, despite some cogent points made by the two other positions.[4] In negative terms, one can insist that it is the least bad alternative. But a more positive note is possible. We are or ought to be grown up. Down with enthusiasm. Let us end the search for warmth and unity! For Kantian reasons, let us be masters of our own souls!

I think this account adds a little to what Mann has said. He tends to see ideologies as solutions that arise to meet social stress, with great emphasis on the way in which the interwar period bred ideological responses. That is a little too simple. The late nineteenth century was a period of ideological ferment, in which many of the stakes of conflict were becoming apparent – not least to Jews, some of them well aware that the rise of ethnonationalism would be at their expense. So a minimal but certain negative critique is that ideologies have a history, that they do not always become available at the drop of a hat, and that the mainstream of European thought had entirely comprehensible and utterly repulsive ideological options on offer. I wobble when considering a maximal critique. This would involve saying that the new ideological options so fired up social movements in the nineteenth century as to cause the collapse of empires. I agree with Mann that this is not wholly so and am as reluctant as he is to move toward such generalized idealism. After all, there are plenty of nasty ideologies in the marketplace, thankfully ignored given peace and prosperity. More importantly, the First World War was caused in part for traditional reasons, above all those centering on Anglo–German rivalry. Further, most nationalist movements sought autonomy rather than secession, with Jews as a particular group facing the new intellectual dilemma posed by ethnonationalism by a deepening of

---

[4] It may be useful to highlight a disagreement with Charles Taylor's *A Secular Age* (2007). It is indeed true that the first tradition is an ideology, but that does not mean for a second that all of these ideologies deserve equal respect. Relativism is fine, but only within strict limits.

patriotism. Differently put, most new nation-states were born, as he says, in the aftermath of defeat when imperial regimes lost their capacity to repress. But a wobble is in order. Serbian nationalism mattered, and so too did the nationalist elements inside Germany. Further, one empire did collapse as a result of nationalist pressure: the Oldenburg imperial monarchy was felled because of the intransigence of the nationalist liberals in Copenhagen (Jensen and Hall 2014).[5]

Origins

The origins of political decency are complex, diverse and worthy of more sustained analysis than they have received. There is much to be said in favor of the view, when considering the historical record as a whole, that agrarian empires, lacking real infrastructural power, often allowed much social life to continue untouched by state power, with self-help organizations doing more to ensure order than the metropole. Still, one can romanticize these entities in the light of what followed, thereby forgetting their obscurantism, dogmatism, and occasional bursts of viciousness – deliberate exercises in violence designed to deter any movement of similar kind. In any case, decency inside modern states, blessed with infrastructural capacities, is a very different matter. I continue to believe that one deep background condition allowing for political decency within Europe was the fact that power was not unified but rather in several sets of hands, thereby allowing for the emergence of those tags of canon law – "what concerns all must be agreed by all" and "no taxation without representation" – that formed the basis of European liberties (Hall 2013: chapter 1).[6] But I recognize, too, what matters greatly for Mann when speaking about the decencies of social democracy. Class struggles from below established citizenship rights, thereby cementing the institutional pluralism of parts of NW Europe, with a firmer base in Scandinavia thanks to alliances between free peasants and industrial workers. Such struggles had ideological elements to them, but one feels both lucky and worried at this point: the transcendence involved was limited, the bitter legacy of which is that loyalty to the ideals involved at times lacks passionate intensity. These

[5] History is not black and white; there is room for argument here. The loss of Norway in 1815 unbalanced the ethnic composition of the Oldenburg realms; to that extent defeat in war is part of this case too.

[6] This view is now, so to speak, conventional, as is its corollary – that state-building then emerged as the result of intense interactions between states and their societies resulting from multipolar geopolitical competition. It is a pleasure to note that Deborah Boucoyannis will soon present a fundamental challenge to this view.

are the societies portrayed in the map in Mann's *Fascists*, able, at times with difficulties, to escape the appeal of fascism.

One thing that can be added to this account is the recognition of occasions on which middle-class elements have pushed for progressive change (Hall 1988). There is something to social evolutionary views suggesting that late industrial society depends on freedom of movement, increasing technical skills and openness to world markets such that new middle-class elements can push against authoritarian regimes. This seems to have been true in Korea, and one notes the role of TUSIAD in Turkey now, clamoring for admission to the European Union. I do not wish to exaggerate this. For one thing, change of this sort very much depends on political leaders endorsing technical change, recognizing that the prosperity it would bring might allow them to hang on to the reins of power. Putin is not such a leader. For another, middle classes do not take in the ideas of John Stuart Mill with their mothers' milk. They can and do often prefer order to change, thereby accommodating themselves to existing circumstances. I do not place great hopes for decency here, and so tend to mild pessimism in general – as must Mann, given the loss of centrality of labor in modern political economies.

But there is another consideration that deserves attention. Comparative historical sociologists characteristically look to explain continuities and change with reference to social structural conditions. As it happens, a novelty in Mann's last two volumes is occasional talk of "irrationality" and "folly" – slightly dangerous talk in my view as it might mean a step away from his superlative abilities, already noted, to place himself in the minds of actors whom he deeply dislikes. Nonetheless, something can be said about the style in which politics is conducted. Political leaders need skill. Gorbachov lacked such skill at the moment he decided, in the midst of *glasnost*, to put a mild brake on nationalist feelings by short repressions in Georgia and the Baltics. He thereby demonstrated Tocqueville's fully worked out point about revolution: if decompression places a regime in danger disaster surely follows if reversal takes place in the middle of the process. Similarly, Tony Blair did much harm to his wholly meritorious efforts to decentralize the British state by saying that the powers of the Scottish Assembly were minimal and nothing to worry about. The particular addition I have in mind is slightly different, more about the mental change that can follow from exhaustion, but it too draws on the process and style of political life rather than on structural conditions.

Let me begin with an example and then seek to generalize on its base. An early period of extreme viciousness within European history was that marked by religious war. The principle of *cujus regio, ejus religio*, enshrined in 1555 at the Treaty of Augsburg, seemingly allowed for diversity and difference, at least between states. But the principle was not really accepted and internalized, as the brutality of the Thirty Years War so massively demonstrated. The Westphalian settlement of 1648 is a better marker of development in European attitudes since it went beyond the principle established at Augsburg to the attempt to take religion out of public life altogether, one mechanism toward which end was the insistence that existing religious groups be allowed to worship as they saw fit. What had happened? The long religious wars of Europe could not be won by either side, for the forces of pluralism were always sufficient to defeat any drive to political–religious unification. Sustained Caesaropapism failed. Facing an endlessly destructive stalemate, an extraordinary change in attitudes slowly took place: if agreement on detailed matters of belief could neither be reached nor imposed, a background consensus to tolerate religious differences was a viable alternative. If toleration was at first accepted as a "sour grapes" philosophy – that is, one imposed by circumstances beyond one's control – it came to be positively valued. In the spirit of Marx, one can say that decency "in itself" in which negative resisting power was great, became "decency for itself" – a world in which the principle of toleration was not just accepted but positively embraced, thereby leading to depoliticizing political passions. The general point that follows from this is that stalemate is a condition that has mattered elsewhere, one to which we can pay systematic attention. It has helped decompression and liberalization in our time in Southern Europe, Latin America and in the Soviet Bloc, and it accordingly features quite heavily in the "transitions to democracy" literature. There is some room for hope here.

Two cautionary notes are in order. First, learning experiences of this kind may well not last for long. Kant realized this in his famous essay on perpetual peace when he insisted that the continuing presence of war was not altogether a bad thing – for it would remind people of the benefits of peace. Clearly, the memory of ideological fissure through religion did not prevent the bitter ideological wars both of the revolutionary period as well as of twentieth-century Europe. Second, Mann has put at the center of our attention something that we knew but placed to one side.[7] Human beings can hold at one and the same time contradictory views. British people are proud of their ability to be civil, but this did not stop most of them from endorsing the British Empire. Some people were of course

---

[7] I am certainly indebted to him and should have made much more of European imperial behavior to counteract what praise that I gave for political decencies within Europe (Hall 2013).

consistent, arguing firmly against imperial rule, stressing correctly that it was not really necessary for the economic health of the country. Others were blatant racists. It may be that the majority of the population paid little attention to the empire (Porter 2006). Though elites have often been responsible for designing horrors, especially in imperial terms, the laziness of decent people is far from reassuring.

Conditions

Let me turn toward conditions that maintain decent political life, paying attention in staccato fashion to three factors. The first factor, capitalism, is the most complex, and it will also require going backward to origins – and a little later to the consideration of a danger that threatens our life chances.

Capitalism has not been considered to this point, but it played a significant role in the emergence of the first metatheoretical option discussed above. Commercial society, as Smith had it, helped to establish a culture of political decency in England. Soft political rule was certainly not always present there: to the contrary, it was an historical achievement. Seventeenth-century England had been a prey to civil war, treason trials, regicide and the sundering of families. The very sudden move to political stability between 1675 and 1725 seems to be best explained by such traumatic experience. In a condition of continuing stalemate, in which neither side was capable of outright victory, it suddenly began to make sense, as it had to those divided by religion in early modern Europe, to try to live together – the successful accomplishment of which then fostered a politics of decency. Though the political achievement was genuinely autonomous, it was nonetheless aided by economic factors. For one thing, the stalemate resulted from negative resisting power being widely spread. For another, the acceptance of party alternation in government was eased by the presence of a growing economy that provided sources of remuneration other than those derived from the possession of political power (Plumb 1967). Very similar points can be made about the emergence of parties in the early United States and more generally about the collapse of communism – with the Hungarian elite realizing that the market rather than the party was a better avenue to ascendancy well before the final collapse of the system (Hofstader 1970: Szakolczai and Horvath 1992). There is a deal of room for skillful policy of this type in our world, demonstrating to varied "bunkers" that they can survive political decompression – both because of different means to maintain ascendancy and because that will de-radicalize the people.

Behind all this is something more general. Samuel Johnson famously declared that "a man is never so innocently employed as when he is making money," thereby neatly encapsulating the view that commerce was a softer passion than political power, capable in the eyes of Keynes, the great inheritor of this tradition, of undermining – not always, but at times – power systems and thereby of maintaining liberal rule. But an interesting distinction can be drawn here between the view of Smith and Keynes, the former deeply concerned – as has been Thomas Piketty more recently – to equalize social conditions, the latter leaving much more to the technical skills of the political elite (Boucoyannis 2013). Still, the extent to which decent political rule has depended on economic growth is great, making Mann's worry about the costs of growth truly terrifying.

The second factor to be considered is that of constitutional design. There is something to the claim, at the back of Ernest Gellner's theory of nationalism, that societies that are relatively culturally homogeneous, whether through forced assimilation, the benefits of time or from prior horrors, seem to find it easier to maintain high standards of welfare provision as well as to move flexibly within capitalist society (Patsiurko, Campbell and Hall 2013). One particular problem that results from this is the fact that such societies – and more particularly the less mobile within them – are resistant to the immigration that their low fertility rates make necessary. But the more serious consideration comes from the fact that many countries in the world are not homogeneous, with many new states being deeply divided in ethnic terms. In his last years, Gellner was forced by events to move from analyzing nationalism to offering prescriptions as to how it could be handled. It has to be said that his characteristically witty comments favoring cultural pluralism within a system of order, something of a replay of Austro-Hungary, offered little guidance. But the theorists of constitutional design have made some progress by going beyond Gellner to creating schemes for power sharing in deeply divided societies. Very detailed plans have emerged of mixes of consociationalism and federalism, often bound together by ingenious voting procedures. The Good Friday agreement is one such measure that has done much to defuse a quarter century of violence in Northern Ireland. A sociological viewpoint is needed, and sophisticated political scientists are now moving in that direction. For instance, McGarry and O'Leary (2005) suggest that there are five conditions that facilitate but do not guarantee successful multinational federations. First, a *Staatsvolk* is needed because the security that comes from being so central to the state can allow it to be generous to minorities. Second, a federation's national communities should not only have self-government, but also consociational powers at the center. Third, authentic (democratic) multinational federations are more likely to succeed than pseudo (undemocratic) federations. Fourth, voluntarily holding together multinational federations are more likely to endure under democratic conditions than those that are coercively constructed after modern social mobilizations. Finally, prosperity helps. Of course, these were such demanding conditions that it is not at all surprising that many federal schemes failed, most obviously in countries that had been colonized or that formed part of the socialist bloc. Recent developments in India, often touted as the crucial example of successful political design, are more worrying. The skill with which regions and languages have been managed stands deeply opposed to the continuing fall in socioeconomic status of Muslims. Might the great achievements of that subcontinent yet be undermined by Hindu revivalism (Anderson 2010)? Further, a background sociological element in Northern Ireland was the realization by Protestants that their majority status was being undermined by the greater fertility of the Catholic community. One wonders what Mann thinks of the attempts of constitutional designers to create and maintain political decency. What other factors can be added to create a more general account?

Finally, let us consider a central claim of international relations theory, namely that changing political economies can cause geopolitical crisis – although there is little agreement as to whether trouble results from rising powers seeking their "place in the sun" or from the resistance of established powers to reasonably accommodating them. This claim does cast light on the disasters of the twentieth century even if it does not capture all the factors at work. Hence, a real source of optimism in the contemporary world is the possibility that circumstances have changed in such a way as to diminish the chances of a repeat of early twentieth-century history. Two background conditions need to be borne in mind. The first is the fundamental sea change in world affairs caused by the nuclear revolution. War is no longer a rational means for political gains, making it much less likely that great powers will choose to escalate geopolitical tensions to the point of major war. The second is the continuing structural power of the North within the world economy; that is, the presence of continuing prosperity that means that the ascent of the South need not be seen in zero-sum terms.

With these factors in mind, four points suggest that rising powers will not disrupt the world polity in the near future. A first skeptical consideration concerns the nature of threat itself. It takes but a moment to realize that the height of threat comes when one wishes to assail a genuine enemy, either because one has something superior to offer or because the very presence of the enemy makes one's own existence precarious. The vital consideration that follows from this is that threats in the contemporary world are nothing like as great as they were in the immediate postwar period. The threat from the Soviet Union has disappeared, above all in ideological terms. A similar story can be told of China. Some of the extreme statements of Mao were viciously oppositional in character, hoping that popular movements would destroy states altogether and even contemplating nuclear war on the grounds that China would survive, blessed as it was by its huge population. But the 1970s witnessed the end of this radicalism, as Mann notes, first in coming to terms with the United States and then in moving away from economic autarky to trading with the rest of the world. China may not be happy with the current ordering of the world polity, but it is seeking to change it rather than to destroy it. All of this can be summarized in the simplest way. War is no longer a preferred option, not least as there is much more awareness of the costs that the most recent military revolutions impose.

A second reason for skepticism, already partly noted, is that a sea change has taken place in economic affairs (Brooks 2005). Military conquest is no longer seen as a prerequisite for growth and development – a recognition that gives the rising powers a measure of confidence that they can be part of a world polity that no longer threatens them. The costs of holding territory in the face of nationalist movements typically far outweigh the benefits. Just as important, however, is the realization that the advanced powers can gain much of what they need in the world economy through different means. Foreign direct investment, the mobility of knowledge and capital, interfirm alliances and joint ventures can bring crucial benefits through cooperation. Attempting to capture these benefits by occupying territory is likely not only to be expensive but to fail.

Third, rising powers have some reason for confidence in the world polity. On the one hand, the norm of nonintervention together with great reluctances to change territorial boundaries gives a measure of security lacking before 1945. On the other hand, the world economy is not so closed that the newly rising powers have no chance of entering into it. In this regard, it is very important to note that there is a web of institutions into which rising powers can be and have been introduced – at times with assistance from the powers of the North. Of course, some seats at the table have greater centrality than others, above all in the UN Security Council, but one again observes struggles to change rules – to have the next head of the International Monetary Fund (IMF), for example, come from the South rather than from Europe – rather than to disrupt the existing system as a whole. Still the embrace of institutions like the World Trade Organization (WTO) or the G20 has the capacity to de-radicalize rising powers. Furthermore, not everything goes in one direction. Brazilian agribusiness was able to mount a successful challenge against the subsidies given to sugar and cotton by the EU and the United States, respectively, using the tools created by the North against them (Hopewell 2013).

The final factor concerns the changing nature of elites within a more integrated world. In the late nineteenth century, elites often sought to advance by modernizing their societies through state- and nation-building, a practice that often involved visions of territorial conquest. An alternative is now open to some elements of elites in the South – to leave their societies behind and join the action elsewhere, at times with the intent of staying abroad, at times with that of returning home. Immigration of elites from the South to the North to become better educated and to facilitate business deals is becoming more commonplace. In 2012, nine of the top ten countries from which most immigrants left were in the South, and seven of the top ten countries to which they moved were in the North.

One should not be naively optimistic. Against these favorable developments stands a measure of social dynamite. Nationalism within rising powers can destabilize an international order. This was true for Wilhelmine Germany in the years just preceding 1914 (Chickering 1984). It may yet be true today. Consider the joke that appeared when the United States bombed the Chinese embassy in Belgrade: on the first day, protests were held against the United States, and this happened again on the second day, but on the third day, protests turned against the government – for being too bound by international rules, not nationalist enough. As it happens, this case has been the subject of a brilliant recent article (Weiss 2013), arguing that the party controlled the demonstrations, not least so as to signal to others the pressures that it was facing. But that may not last, as it did not in Imperial Germany.

Dangers

Just as there are conditions that favor political decency, so too are there factors that threaten it. One has already been mentioned. In an early but little known essay, Mann noted that the importance of intellectuals had faded over the historical record. Once they were clerks with real power because of their privileged access to literacy, then they relied on patrons and now, all too often, they live either in universities or in the interstices of the marketplace (Mann 1975). It is not surprising that theories of alienation and anomie have resulted: they reflect their own position for sure, and perhaps not that of normal people in society. I have already sided with Mann in opposing any facile idealism so would not want to play up the danger of new intellectual ideas. Still, terrible intellectual ideas are all over the place. At a purely theoretical level, a very great deal could be said against the outpourings of a Zizek and endless search of thinkers such as

Badiou for some crystallizing "event." At the practical level, the malign impact of intellectuals can be seen as well. The experience of "the charter of values" in the last Quebec election was, for instance, deeply disturbing – a cynical and xenophobic attempt to pass a law sure to be blocked by the Canadian Supreme Court, thereby allowing a separatist referendum to have a decent chance of success – on the grounds that "the rest of Canada" scorned Quebec. More important is the role of intellectuals in the foreign policy of the United States, discussed below.

Hints have been dropped about a second danger. I am at one with Mann in noting the impact of increasing social inequality – in the case of the United States now equaling that of the 1890s. It is hard to talk of decency when one sees increasing numbers sleeping on the streets and a massive proportion of young African American men incarcerated. By and large, British society has not really become more efficient despite an obvious increase in the sheer hardness of life facing very many. And there is a certain horror here. The result may well not be mass mobilization, just inequality with viciousness. It is worth remembering in this regard an important article written in the early years of Mrs Thatcher's period as Prime Minister. If the state takes care to provide programs of various sorts for the young, increasing unemployment may well not lead to social change – for the loss of union cards for older workers, indeed the decline of unions more generally, may lead rather to passivity, a sense that nothing can be done (Bradley and Gelb 1980).

One of the central principles of Mann's sociology is that social movements gain their character as a result of the nature of the regimes with which they interact. More particularly, his claim, as noted, is that exclusion creates political consciousness, whilst inclusion allows reform, at the cost of diminishing radicalism. What can be said here about the behavior of elites? It may be worth noting a resemblance here with Raymond Aron. In a late piece looking back at late nineteenth- and early twentieth-century Europe, the great French sociologist blamed the folly of elites for not opening their political systems so as to ensure stability (Aron 1979). I wonder if Mann shares this view? In our own world, elites have the opportunity of softening political rule, thereby retaining their predominance. But this route is not always taken. Furthermore, sometimes elites are strong enough to completely crush opposition. More often radicalization is encouraged, not least in the classical heartland of the Muslim world, by political exclusion.[8] There is plenty of revolutionary material around, all too capable of upsetting our expectations.

---

[8] One needs now to note as well the peculiarities of this part of the world that have been brilliantly expounded by Mabry (2015).

A fourth and final point concerns the role of the United States in the world polity. One can argue that the United States did provide a benign frame that allowed, at least for the North, for security and prosperity in the immediate postwar world. But I agree with Mann that this is no longer so. The North suffers from the global imbalances that result from the United States living beyond its means, whilst some part of the instability of the South follows from American imperialism. In regard to the latter, it is horrifying now to be able to read detailed accounts of various actions in Afghanistan – the stuff of medals for Americans and death for innocent Afghans (Gopal 2014). This is not to say that I think his views about American decline are correct. Retreat from imperial ventures may yet be possible, as after Vietnam, whilst I am very reluctant to believe that the burden of the military is undermining the power of the United States – as can be seen in the amazing and unexpected fact that the dollar has strengthened in recent years, in the midst of economic and political catastrophe (Campbell and Hall 2015: chapter 6)! But there is slim comfort at present in the thought of the resurgence of American power, perhaps through new forms of seigniorage and certainly because of the "fracking revolution" that will increase the global warming which so terrifies Mann at the end of his book.

Conclusion

That Mann has given us a philosophical history helps us in characterizing his work. Roughly speaking, there are two types of philosophical history. Marx exemplifies the first type: he gives us a determinist theory applicable to all societies, in his case blessed with an account of the mechanism driving the process forward to something like salvation, in that we will leave the realm of necessity and enter that of freedom. The second type might well be called that of fortuitous openings. Adam Smith's account of the accidental rise of commercial society in the third book of *The Wealth of Nations* exemplifies this position and so does Max Weber's account of "rise of bourgeois rational capitalism in the West."

Mann's history is thankfully of the latter type. World wars led to the rise of communism and fascism, and more recently to the rise of Communist China. There was no necessity for such wars, nor was their outcome determined. If Imperial Germany had not started the submarine campaign against the United States, it would have dominated Europe – for the defeat of Imperial Russia meant that it was faced with war on a single front. The result of the Second World War was just as consequential, and contemporary historians seem to suggest that the result was far closer than was previously imagined. So we can end with a single thought. It is wonderful that humans have room to act, but to try to control our destiny means, as Mann rightly concludes, that we must struggle.

References

Anderson, P. 1986. "Those in Authority," *Times Literary Supplement*, 12 December.

Aron, R. 1979. "On Liberalization," *Government and Opposition*, 14.

Boucoyannis, D. 2013. "The Equalizing Hand: Why Adam Smith Thought the Market Should Produce Wealth without Steep Inequality," *Perspectives on Politics*.

Bradley, K. and A. Gelb, 1980. "The Radical Potential of Cash Nexus Breaks," *British Journal of Sociology*, 31.

Brooks, S.G. 2005. *Producing Security*, Princeton, Princeton University Press.

Campbell, J.L. and J.A. Hall. 2015. *The World of States*, London, Bloomsbury.

Chickering, R. 1984. *We Men Who Feel Most German: A Cultural Study of the Pan-German League, 1886–1914*, London, George Allen and Unwin.

Ferguson, A. [1773] 1969. *An Essay on the History of Civil Society*, 4th edn, rev. and corrected, Hants, Farnborough.

Gopal, A. 2014. *No Good Men Among the Living: America, the Taliban, and the War through Afghan Eyes*, New York, Henry Holt.

Hall, J.A. 1988. "Classes and Elites, Wars and Social Evolution: A Comment on Mann," *Sociology*, 22.

2006. "Political Questions," in J.A. Hall and R. Schroeder, eds, *An Anatomy of Power: The Social theory of Michael Mann*, Cambridge: Cambridge University Press.

2011. *Ernest Gellner: An Intellectual Biography*, London, Verso.

2013. *The Importance of Being Civil: The Struggle for Political Decency*, Princeton, Princeton University Press.

Hofstader, R. 1970. *The Idea of a Party System: The Rise of Legitimate Opposition in the United States, 1780–1840*, Berkeley, University of California Press.

Hopewell, K. 2013. "New Protagonists in Global Economic Governance: Brazilian Agribusiness at the WTO," *New Political Economy*, 18(4): 603–623.

Jensen, J. and J.A. Hall. 2014. "The decomposition of the Danish imperial monarchy," *Nations and Nationalism*, 20.

Mabry, T. 2015. *Language, Nationalism and Islam*, Philadelphia, University of Pennsylvania Press.

Mann, M. 1975. "The Ideology of Intellectuals and Other People in the Development of Capitalism," in L. Lindberg, R. Alford, C. Crouch and C. Offe, eds, *Stress and Contradiction in Modern Capitalism*, Lexington, MA, D.C. Heath.

2013. *The Sources of Social Power. Volume Four: Globalizations, 1945–2011*, Cambridge, Cambridge University Press.

McGarry, J. and B. O'Leary. 2005. "Federation as a Method of Ethnic Conflict Regulation," in S. Noel, ed., *From Power Sharing to Democracy: Post-Conflict Institutions in Ethnically Divided Societies*, Montreal and Kingston, McGill/Queens.

Patsiurko, N., J.L. Campbell and J.A. Hall. 2013. "Nation-State Size, Ethnic Diversity and Economic Performance in the Advanced Capitalist Countries," *New Political Economy*, 18.

Plumb, J.H. 1967. *The Growth of Political Stability in England, 1675–1725*, London, Penguin.

Porter, B. 2006. *The Absent-Minded Imperialists: Empire, Society and Culture in Britain*, Oxford, Oxford University Press.

Szakolczai, A. and A. Horwath. 1992. *The Dissolution of Communist Power: The Case of Hungary*, London, Routledge.

Taylor, C. 1991. *The Malaise of Modernity*, Toronto, Anansi.

2007. *A Secular Age*, Cambridge, MA, Harvard University Press.

Weiss, J.C. 2013. "Authoritarian Signaling, Mass Audiences and Nationalist Protest in China," *International Organization*, 67.

6   Mann on neoliberalism

Monica Prasad

What is the value of global histories like this one? Most other academic disciplines, including the disciplines closest to sociology such as political science and history, have long abandoned the attempt to write encompassing histories of the world in favor of precise renderings of narrow events. Even most of sociology follows the advice to specialize. Given the explosion of data in our contemporary world, it seems hard enough to get even one small thing right – can anyone really get the history of the world right? Comparative historical sociology is perhaps the last holdout against academic specialization, the last space within academia where one can attempt projects of this nature, and it is good to ask ourselves periodically if the attempt is producing anything of value.

Michael Mann is one of the most talented practitioners of this kind of big think comparative historical sociology, so a close reading of his efforts should tell us something important about whether comparative historical sociology is itself worthwhile. I propose that for comparative historical sociology of this sort to be worthwhile, it should tell us more than we can learn from reading a series of separate in-depth examinations of particular episodes. It should allow us to reach new insight into historical events or identify important patterns that could not be seen by looking at a single event. As an example, Theda Skocpol's comparative analysis of revolutions demonstrated among many other things that close examination of single episodes is a method biased toward explanations that highlight agency, whereas comparative examination of multiple episodes can show that what seems like agency is in fact highly structured. Similarly, any good comparative analysis should be able to provide a different perspective than can be gleaned from reading a series of isolated in-depth studies of particular cases or events; if it does not, one would be well-advised to read a series of books by specialists instead, who will surely provide narratives with more nuance and attention to context.

This chapter therefore subjects parts of Mann's Volume 4 – specifically, his examination of neoliberalism and financialization – to this high bar:

does his meta-analysis tell us something about these episodes that we could not have gleaned from the specialist literature? Does it cast the specialist literature in a new light, as Skocpol did? Or does his reading of these episodes in the light of world history help him to develop new theories or new perspectives about politics, economics, or history, telling us something that we did not know before about the world?

Mann's overarching accomplishment in prior volumes of this work is not in doubt. Although he personally wishes to avoid getting bogged down in sterile debates over structure and agency and contingency, what is remarkable about Mann's project is that he has in fact put forward a new and *useful* theory of structure, agency, and contingency. Building on Talcott Parsons's ideas on power, Mann develops the concept of infrastructural power, "the power to actually penetrate society and to implement logistically political decisions" (Volume 1, 170), distinguishing it from despotic power, "the range of actions that the ruler and his staff are empowered to attempt to implement without routine, institutionalized negotiation with civil society groups" (169–170). He notes that despots throughout history have been infrastructurally weak.

In previous volumes of this work, Mann's achievement was to show that the development of infrastructural power, a structural transformation, can put into the hands of human agents the capacity to do enormous good or harm. These agents are not individuals; they are more likely to be collectivities, such as parliaments. This means that the development of infrastructural power changes the pattern of history and makes history *more* volatile and unpredictable rather than less because the coordination of decisions across large groups is an unpredictable process, and those unpredictable decisions can now have worldwide consequences.

This perspective was used to enlightening effect in the earlier volumes of this project to explain the arrival of the First World War, as in this memorable passage from Volume 2: "On the one hand, the diplomacy of modern statesmen and the professionalism of modern militaries were systematic in their consequences because they commanded ... massive power infrastructures ... Regimes and Powers were toppled, economies devastated, millions killed or maimed – by their decisions to risk war .... on the other hand, the structures whereby 'sovereign' states made 'their' decisions were disorderly ... The modern state was unitary in its consequences but polymorphous and factionalized in its structure" (796). Mann neatly explains how actors could be both powerful and powerless, forcefully moving in a direction that they did not choose. The mirror opposite of the infrastructurally weak despot is the infrastructurally strong leader of the modern state accountable to, and often beholden to, multiple constituencies whose cacophony marches the nation over the cliff.

In Volumes 1 and 2, Mann also advanced the ideology, economic, military and political power sources (IEMP) model, but I have never found this model to be as interesting or useful as the distinction between infrastructural and despotic power. I know many other scholars are fans of IEMP, but it's hard to see how this model helps us understand history. It's one thing to argue that single-factored theories of history are unconvincing. But it does not seem much of an advance to say that historical changes are caused by changes in ideology, and/or by changes in economics, and/or by changes in military power, and/or by changes in political power and that examining which source of power was operating in a particular instance requires in-depth historical study. This seems the same as not having a theory at all.

If this were the extent of Mann's contribution, a reasonable conclusion would be that Mann's volumes present a supremely well-informed *history* of power rather than a *historical sociology* of power and that the urge to reach strong theoretical conclusions about history is misguided. Indeed, if this were the only kind of thing that comparative historical sociology gave us, we would conclude that the whole enterprise is not worthwhile because any casual observer of history already knows that these four sources of power are important at different times in different ways. Luckily, this is not the extent of Mann's contribution: the distinction between infrastructural and despotic power does suggest that it is possible to construct useful theoretical frameworks with which to analyze history. I hope that in his response Mann will defend the usefulness of the IEMP model, as it may be helpful for historical sociology to have a general discussion of the meanings and purposes of historical sociological explanation.

Volumes 3 and 4 attempt to explain the twentieth century. The perspective remains non-reductionist and nonsystemic and avoids making assumptions about the rationality of actors. A large part of Volume 4 focuses on the phenomena of neoliberalism, the attempt to reduce the role of the state and its intervention into markets, and financialization, the rising role of financial services in developed economies. Examining how Mann explains neoliberalism and financialization allows us to examine whether his framework, which was so powerful and convincing when mobilized to explain phenomena such as the rise of the state, is equally compelling when turned to the question of the retreat of the state that has been the dominant element of political economy across the world over the past thirty years.

Mann's analysis of neoliberalism is multifactored. Although he is not Marxist, in practice he draws on the analysis of Marxists and other economic determinists to make sense of the fall of Keynesianism, for example, "There was a sharp fall in the rate of profit, especially in the international manufacturing sector, which induced a slowdown in growth and an overaccumulation of capital, which was now placed more into financial instruments than manufacturing investment" and "Stagflation intensified class conflict in the North. Since capital and labor were both suffering, each strove to retain its economic returns amid a stagnant economy" (146). Mann also sees the technological revolution as a key trigger because it destroyed middle-class jobs, leaving the workforce composed of "well-educated workers in offices, especially in financial services, and low-level, often casual workers in the personal service sector" (155). This weakened unions. On the other hand, Mann notes "Polling data for twenty developed countries reveal no decline in support for leftist economic programs, but greater salience of conservative moralist and nationalist rhetoric . . . Overall, the correlation between class and voting did not decline . . . but rightist populism strengthened, and Left parties moved into the center, making further progressive taxes or welfare programs unlikely" (155–156). So we have ideological forces at play as well.

Mann's argument for financialization is mostly focused on one source of power, economic. He argues, drawing on the work of Greta Krippner, Robert Brenner, and others, that financialization was ultimately caused by a crisis of manufacturing and was worsened by growing inequality in the United States: "Overcapacity, overproduction, falling profits became general, and capitalist corporations were not able to find major new industries that were able to compensate for that. So capital shunned manufacturing and went instead into finance. The subsequent financial crisis therefore ultimately depended on the weakness of manufacturing, especially in the United States and Britain, but in other countries too" (325). Inequality also mattered because "Since the neoliberal offensive had kept wages low and reduced welfare and other public spending, demand and investment were reduced, and so private debt became the supposed way to restore profitability" (328). Mann thus pauses to consider carefully the rise of inequality in the US, tracing it to three sources: the confluence of the crisis of manufacturing and demographic changes, which put pressure on the welfare state (a factor common to all the rich countries); the collapse of the working class, which made governments less able to resist the pressures on the welfare state, along with rising pay for executives (factors common to the Anglo countries); and contingent factors such as the skill of Republican leaders, which have made the trend more extreme in the United States than other countries (331–344).

Mann then ably summarizes the triggers of the recent economic crisis, moving through the roles of the mathematical modelers who ran their models only on post-1998 data and the failure of rating agencies and regulators. A political factor is mentioned in passing when Mann mentions the orthodox explanation that Alan Greenspan's low interest rates during the early 2000s led to a real-estate bubble (344). And he also (amusingly and accurately) points to a source of ideological power in the episode: "Mathematical economists had developed models so abstruse as to be beyond ordinary human understanding, a form of ideological power like that of priests or sorcerers who alone know how to communicate with the spirits. In reality, it all depended what you put into the equations" (345). Mann writes: "Since it was a financial crisis fueled by inequality and deregulation, I call it the Great Neoliberal Recession" (347).

Before turning to critique, it is worth pausing to appreciate what Mann has pulled off: without being a specialist in either neoliberalism or financialization, he has written a narrative that captures the essence of both. He may have missed nuances within the debates, but he gets the main lines exactly right. So there is little to fault with the explanation.

But there is also little that we have not seen elsewhere, for example, in Greta Krippner's *Capitalizing on Crisis* or Raghuram Rajan's *Fault Lines* or in the countless articles in newspapers and magazines dissecting the recent crisis. The IEMP model and the meta-analysis do not contribute any new insight. Mann repeats and synthesizes what others have said before him. There are some differences of emphasis – for example, Mann emphasizes that neoliberalism has different roots from traditional conservatism – but there is no dramatic Skocpolian recasting of the scholarship. Mann does narrate the events in terms of the IEMP model, so fitting the events to the model is not the problem; rather, the problem is that this narration does not shed new light on the events or otherwise teach us things that we did not know before. It leads to the question of why we want to build a larger model or conduct a big picture analysis at all.

What has gone wrong? Why does Mann's framework, which produced such an interesting new analysis of the cataclysms of the early part of the twentieth century, not have much new to say about the unraveling of the state and the rise of a new form of extreme capitalism that is perhaps the most characteristic feature of the end of the twentieth century?

There are three possible reasons. The first is that the inability to shed new light on recent events points to some more general problem with Mann's work. The second is that Mann's approach and concepts are better at explaining the origins and organization of power than at explaining its dissolution, or better at explaining some kinds of power than others. And the third is that although the concepts do hold within them the potential to shed new light on neoliberalism and financialization, Mann himself has not been able to realize that potential, perhaps because he is simply too close in space and time to these events to develop an objective view of them. I think there is something to be said for each of these arguments, but I will argue that the third is most convincing.

First, the question of whether there is some more general problem with the work. Surely the most surprising aspect of the four-volume work for any reader is the disconnect between the radical premise that launched the work and the fairly traditional execution of it. On the first page of Volume 1, Mann opened with an exciting manifesto: "Societies are not unitary. They are not social systems (closed or open); they are not totalities. We can never find a single bounded society in geographical or social space . . . ." (1, 1). He suggested instead that we conceptualize societies as networks of power. But, as other readers have noticed, as he has moved closer to the present day, Mann has increasingly fallen into the grooves of narrating history from the point of view of the nation-state. Of course, his warrant for this is that he is studying the "leading edge" of power, and it is the nation-state and capitalism that have been the most important sources of power in recent centuries. Indeed in Volume 4, there is much more attention to the United States than to any other part of the world, as the most powerful nation of the twentieth century. But if there does seem to be some coherent social process roughly analogous to the "society" called "the United States" that exerts this "leading edge" of power, then one can be forgiven for thinking that Mann's radical critique of prior scholarship was exaggerated. Alternatively, if one is committed to the radical critique, then what we would have wished to see was a history organized around, say, circuits of high finance, or religious networks, or diasporas. Either Mann fails to fulfill the potential of his own radical premises, or those premises were not suited to studying the history of power to begin with.

I think this argument has something to it, but I also find Mann's groping through this issue to be quite honest. He has not resolved this question, but he does not shy away from either the need to imagine history beyond the nation-state or the difficulty of actually doing so. We are now about twenty years into the attempt to write history beyond the nation-state, and surely we all accept, at this point, the need for transnational histories that place the idea of the nation itself in context. But it does seem that if we want to understand some of the most important events of our world, writing histories of diasporas is not always going to get us there. Certainly, there are global elements in the history of neoliberalism, as analysts have always noted (and as Mann also notes), but it is impossible to write a history of neoliberalism that does not place the nation-state squarely at its center, precisely because the rise of neoliberalism was only made possible by the concentrated exercise of state power – for example, in the breaking of labor unions under both Reagan and Thatcher (and even more starkly in other cases, e.g. Chiu, Ho, and Lui 2012). In this it is hard to fault Mann for either his appreciation that history needs to go beyond nation-states or for his accurate rendering of the importance of state action when examining particular episodes. He is simply encapsulating the difficulties of an entire generation of historically oriented scholars.

A second possibility for why the book has nothing new to say about neoliberalism is that Mann's tools may be better suited to explaining the rise of power than its demise. The idea of infrastructural power seems particularly useful for making sense of how states grew in the nineteenth and twentieth centuries, when bureaucratic organization and growth did not always match the concentration of formal power. But neoliberalism, which is an attempt to restrain the growth of both infrastructural and despotic power, may not gain much from this distinction. Moreover, there are many debates about the origins of neoliberalism, but all scholars seem to agree that it was triggered by the economic crisis of the 1970s. And one way to interpret this economic crisis is that it showed the underlying *weakness* of the infrastructure of capitalism. If we remain at the mercies of global economic forces that we little understand and even less control, can we really boast that history has been an upward march of progress in infrastructural power? Perhaps Mann's concepts are best applied to the literal infrastructure of armies, roads and telecommunications, rather than to the global infrastructure of capitalism, which remains fragile and prone to crisis. And perhaps an attempt to dismantle both infrastructural and despotic power, triggered by the weaknesses of the infrastructure of capitalism, is simply beyond Mann's framework.

Again, there does seem to be something to this second explanation, but there is at least one area where the idea of infrastructural power remains useful, the issue of climate change. In one of the last chapters in Volume 4, Mann explains the slow-motion catastrophe of global warming as the inability to exert despotic control over our overdeveloped infrastructure, "generated by our own supposed mastery over nature, humanity's peak of collective power" (362). Just as the unpredictability of despotically weak regimes combined with the sheer reach of infrastructural power to tip nations into the First World War at the start of the twentieth century, at century's end the same pattern – extensive and sophisticated exploitation of nature to satisfy human needs and wants but an inability to corral this system and make it heed coherent commands – is leading to the greatest volatility of all, the transformation of the planet's very climate. So the idea of infrastructural power has some life left in it yet.

This is why I believe the third explanation is most convincing – that the tools Mann has forged do have insights to give on neoliberalism, but Mann himself has not been able to realize those insights.

For example, consider how Friedrich Hayek might have read Michael Mann. Hayek is discussed more often than he is read; his name has become shorthand for neoliberalism and attacks against the state. But a close analysis of his work reveals him to be not against state action in general – he writes approvingly of a whole host of regulations, including working hours legislation, environmental regulation, even state-provided health care (Hayek 1944, 38–41, 124–126) – but rather, only against state action that impedes the price signal. His argument is that direct actions to interfere with markets distort the information that price signals provide. It is an argument that greater mastery over nature – greater freedom for individuals, greater economic prosperity, and the human opportunities that it provides – requires less direct action over nature in the form of intervention against price signals. His particular worry is that because democracies are not very good at defining the collective welfare, taking seriously the desire to organize the economy in the interest of collective welfare must lead to the imposition of rule by a small minority.

Examining where this perspective fits into Mann's vision of power can help us identify where the story of neoliberalism fits into the history of power. Hayek is essentially worried about the confluence of infrastructural and despotic power – despots who, unlike despots earlier in history, can do real damage because they now have the infrastructural power to do so. In order to prevent this, he counsels abandoning the idea of planning.

Certainly, one can critique the ease with which Hayek slips from intervention against price signals to fascism, but the main point to take away is that neoliberalism fits in very well with the story that Mann has told. Hayek would have taken the crucial insight of Mann's earlier volumes that the development of infrastructural power has made history more volatile – more likely to lead to catastrophe because the organization is now present to march whole nations to suicide – to lead to the conclusion that this machinery of the state that seems to have escaped control can only be managed by binding it and keeping it less powerful. If anything, that terrifying conclusion to Volume 2, with its picture of massive armies supported by powerful infrastructure but moving blindly and out of control, is precisely what alarms neoliberals, and one can understand neoliberalism as an attempt to harness the forces that Mann has diagrammed.

French neoliberal Jacques Rueff, for example, worried about deficits because he thought they released governments from the control of the people, as had happened under Hitler. As Christopher Chivvis explains in a biography of Rueff: "the technique of government by the budget deficit had released the Nazi regime from effective civilian control, allowing it at once the leeway to carry out its public works programs, while also pursuing its military ambitions" (2010, 109) – that is, deficits allow arms buildup with impunity, a lesson that surely cannot be lost on Americans of this generation. For Rueff, budget balance was a way to force the immense infrastructural power of the state under some kind of democratic control, of trimming the dimensions of military power down and of taking that decision out of the hands of individual politicians. Rueff believed that forcing the state to live within its means was one way to control those armies that seemed to have spun out of control – an answer to the very problem that Mann brought to our attention in earlier volumes.

If one part of the Mannian vision agrees with neoliberal worries, however, there is an intellectual disagreement on a central concern. Hayek has given the most famous formulation of the theory that price signals encapsulate and aggregate information:

Assume that somewhere in the world a new opportunity for the use of some raw material, say tin, has arisen, or that one of the sources of supply of tin has been eliminated ... If only some of [the users of tin] know directly of the new demand, and switch resources over to it, and if the people who are aware of the new gap thus created in turn fill it from still other sources, the effect will rapidly spread throughout the whole economic system and influence not only all the uses of tin, but also those of its substitutes and the substitutes of these substitutes, the supply of all the things made of tin, and their substitutes, and so on; and all this without the great majority of those instrumental in bringing about these substitutions knowing anything at all about the original cause of these changes. The whole acts as one market, not because any of its members survey the whole field, but because their limited individual fields of vision sufficiently overlap so that through many intermediaries the relevant information is communicated to all. The mere fact that there is one price for any commodity – rather that local prices are connected in a manner determined by the cost of transport, etc. – brings about the solution which (it is just conceptually possible) might have been arrived at by one single mind possessing all the information which is in fact dispersed among all the people involved in the process ... It is more than a metaphor to describe the price system as a kind of machinery for registering change, or a system of telecommunications which enables individual producers to watch merely the movement of a few pointers, as an engineer might watch the hands of a few dials, in order to adjust their activities to changes of which they may never know more than is reflected in the price movement ... The marvel is that in a case like that of a scarcity of one raw material, without an order being issued, without more than perhaps a handful of people knowing the cause, tens of thousands of people whose identity could not be ascertained by months of investigation, are made to use the material or its products more sparingly; i.e., they move in the right direction. (Hayek, 1996 [1948]: 85–87)

This theory of the price signal, generally associated with the Austrian school and traced to Ludwig von Mises, is the intellectual core of the neoliberal revolution. (Although the theory actually seems to have roots in French economic thinking of the nineteenth century, see Chivvis 2010; it also appeared in the work of Max Weber, see Swedberg 1998, 78ff. It may be one of those insights that have been discovered a new multiple times.)

In Hayek's theory of price, social order is emergent, arising not from top-down hierarchies but from bottom-up, local-level coordination. Hayek critiques as a worrying aberration the rise of armies, bureaucracy and centralized control that is the crux of Mann's vision of recent history. In Mann's vision, on the other hand, social order, including economic order, is a matter of explicit coordination, and it is the inability to coordinate – as in the world war and climate change examples – that is the problem.

So we have some areas where Mann's vision resonates with the neoliberals and some areas where his vision directly challenges theirs. To be clear, the point here is not whether Hayek or other neoliberals were right or wrong to fear the state. The point is that the ideas of Michael Mann engage the ideas of the neoliberals in curious and compelling ways that Mann has not (yet?) explored. Perhaps it is asking too much for Mann himself to conduct this exploration – perhaps this is the kind of task best taken up by an author's followers rather than by the author himself. But an engagement on the heights of the question of social order could indeed fulfill the promise of comparative historical sociology of this kind by showing us new ways to think through events that we thought we had understood.

References

Chiu, Stephen W. K., K. C. Ho, and Tai-lok Lui. 2012. "Reforming Health: Contrasting Trajectories of Neoliberal Restructuring in the City-States." In *Locating Neoliberalism in East Asia: Neoliberalizing Spaces in Developmental States*, pp. 225–256. Edited by Bae-Gyoon Park, Richard Child Hill, and Asato Saito. Malden, Mass.: Wiley-Blackwell.

Chivvis, Christopher. 2010. *The Monetary Conservative: Jacques Rueff and Twentieth-Century Free Market Thought*. Dekalb: Northern Illinois University Press.

Hayek, F. A. 1944. *The Road to Serfdom*. London and New York: Routledge.
    1996 [1948]. *Individualism and Economic Order*. Chicago: University of Chicago Press.

Swedberg, Richard. 1998. *Max Weber and the Idea of Economic Sociology*. Princeton: Princeton University Press.

7   Nationalism and military power in the twentieth century and beyond

Siniša Malešević

Introduction

Whereas much of the contemporary mainstream sociology remains oblivious to the study of military power and nationalism, Michael Mann has put both of these at the forefront of his comprehensive sociological analyses of the world history. While there is no doubt that Mann has made an unmatched contribution in this area, his analyses also exhibit some weaknesses which come to light most clearly in his studies of the twentieth and early twenty-first centuries. This chapter explores some limits of Mann's IEMP power model and offers alternative explanatory remedies. More specifically I identify conceptual problems and contradictions present in Mann's diagnosis of the relationship between military power, warfare and nationalism in the context of the past 120 years. The chapter aims to demonstrate that Mann's strict separation between political and military power together with his understanding of nationalism as a direct consequence of warfare create some explanatory blind alleys that cannot be accommodated within the existing IEMP model. To deal with these pitfalls, I argue that both nationalism and military power should be analysed through the prism of the three long-term historical processes which make the link between military power, war and nationalism possible: the cumulative bureaucratisation of coercion, centrifugal ideologisation and the envelopment of micro-solidarity. I will try to show that in contrast to Mann's optimistic account[1] that emphasises the worldwide weakening of the military power and decline of warfare (but continuous persistence of nationalism), it is more likely that as the dominant social organisations transform, expand and strengthen so will coercive power, nationalism and war.

---

[1] Although Mann is quite optimistic about the continuous decline of war and military power his overall long-term outlook is more pessimistic in the context of the environmental disasters that are very likely to dramatically destabilise life on this planet (Mann 2013).

Military power

In contrast to much of contemporary sociology, Michael Mann has regularly emphasised the significance of military power in social life. From the early civilisations and modernising empires to the late eighteenth- and early nineteenth-century nation-state formation processes, organised violence has been at the heart of Mann's subtle analyses of social order. Military power has proved decisive in accounting for the key social transformations from the early Mesopotamian world, the Greek city-states, the Roman and Ottoman empires to much of European history all the way to the Napoleonic wars (Mann 1986, 1993). Although in his view the gradual expansion of infrastructural potency of the European states has partially stifled militarism in the nineteenth century, the military might have reached its pinnacle in the two world wars. In other words, despite various historical fluctuations and the continuous interdependency of all four sources of social power, it is military power that has often proved critical in instigating long-term social change.

This unusual, bold and original focus on military power has put Mann at odds with much of contemporary sociology, which either ignores the study of war and militarism or simply assumes that organised violence is just a means of economic, ideological or political power. Thus, Mann convincingly argues that the neo-Marxist, rational choice and other staunchly materialist perspectives tend wrongly to subsume violent acts and military prowess under the category of economic interests. Similarly, he equally rejects the alternative, idealist, accounts that privilege cultural interpretations of military power and simply assume, as Philip Smith (2005: 212) does, that 'war is not just about culture, it is all about culture'. However, the crux of disagreement on the relevance of military power in history has focused on the question whether military power is truly an independent force or just a segment of political power. In contrast to many traditional Weberian scholars who insist on the tripartite division of power (political, ideological and economic), Mann is tenacious in his defence of the autonomous role that military power plays in history.

Hence, taking into account this lifelong persistence in advocating the autonomy and significance of 'concentrated lethal violence' it is striking to see that Mann's recent work (2004, 2005, 2007, 2012, 2013a) tends to substantially downplay the relevance of military power in the late twentieth and early twenty-first centuries. He argues that it is now necessary to revisit and revise Tilly's (1985) well-known maxim about wars making states and states making wars to read 'wars used to make states, and states used to make wars – but no longer. Military power relations have played much lesser roles in recent advanced countries' (Mann 2013a: 36). Furthermore, he insists that 'military power has greatly declined across most of the world' and as such it is even possible to envisage a war-free world as military power is 'the only one of the four that could, in principle, be abolished' (Mann 2013a: 418, 428).

Although this particular conclusion stems from the solid evidence that the past five decades have experienced fewer wars, that warfare has become less lethal, more localised and shorter in duration, its long-term sociological reasoning is less solid. Moreover, the view that 'war and military power will decline over the coming decades' and that in the future one is likely to see 'revolutions gradually diminishing in frequency and scale' (Mann 2013a:418, 267) does not properly reflect the steadfast historical trajectory of military and political power (and also largely goes against the grain of Mann's earlier work).

In contrast to this view, I would argue that rather than witnessing a gradual decline of organised violence the world is, in fact, experiencing a continuous expansion of coercive organisational power. In this context the periodic, and temporary, decrease in interstate warfare, the reduced numbers of battlefield casualties, the greater localisation and shorter life span of wars are not in themselves the most reliable indicators to assess the ever increasing coerciveness of contemporary social organisations. For counting the percentages of human casualties and the frequency of wars are too crude a measure to adequately capture the changing patterns of coercive action in time and space. Instead of treating war, militarism and violence as a completely independent power source, it is analytically more beneficial to explore their historical dynamics through the broader prism of coercive organisational power. More specifically, as I have argued elsewhere (Malešević 2010, 2013a, 2013b), the different forms of collective violence originate and have historically spread through the cumulative bureaucratisation of coercion. This is a process that took its embryonic shape around 12,000 years ago and has dramatically intensified and expanded over the past 300 years. Although the process remains characterised by historical contingencies, periodic reversibility and geographical unevenness there is a strong cumulative component that underpins its expansion. In other words, the cumulative bureaucratisation of coercion fosters the continuous increase of organisational potency and capacity of social organisations to rely on coercive means for implementing different tasks – from states' attempts to internally pacify their domestic sphere and business corporations' efforts to weaken and topple their competitors to aspirations of the well-rounded social movements to use their organisational strength to dominate their membership. The ever increasing population numbers and the constant demand for the instant delivery of resources and services make social organisations indispensable to everyday life and in this way foster further coercive bureaucratisation of social relations. This process operates externally and internally: the social organisations deploy their coercive might to challenge, and guard themselves from, other competing organisations as well as to enforce the hierarchical relationships and rule obedience within their organisation. While there is no doubt that, as they tend to accumulate organisational power over centuries, in the modern era the nation-states are by far the most formidable social organisations, and their cumulative bureaucratisation of coercion affects just as much the non-state entities: from the business enterprises (i.e. Microsoft, Coca-Cola, BMW), religious establishments (i.e. Catholic Church, Scientology, Serbian Orthodox Church), and terrorist associations and insurgencies (i.e. al Qaeda, ISIS, Hezbollah, ETA, Continuity IRA) to various entrenched social movements (i.e. Zapatistas, Animal Liberation Front, Earth Liberation Army). In all these organisations, coercive power plays the decisive role, and it is difficult if not impossible to differentiate between the political and military aspects of these power relationships.

Thus, Mann's downplaying of military power in the contemporary world is directly linked to his conceptual apparatus that insists on the stringent separation between political and military power. By disjoining military from political power, Mann's project ends with a paradoxical conclusion that finds the end of the twentieth and beginning of the twenty-first century as a period when political power continues to increase while military power experiences dramatic decline. For example, he argues very convincingly that modern states have now 'acquired new legislative roles in areas of social life formerly considered private or taboo, like wife- or child-battering, life-style choices like smoking or junk food, consumer environmental pollution, sexual preference, and welfare rights. Thus the regulatory density of states has continued to increase' (Mann 2013a: 419). On the other hand, he maintains that 'wars like two world wars are unlikely to be repeated' and that the institution of war 'can be abolished' (Mann 2013a: 416, 35).

However, since political power ultimately relies on coercive threats, it seems highly unlikely that as state capacity expands, its dependence on force would gradually dissolve. How else could modern states implement all these new legislative roles? It is the continuous expansion of the coercive organisational power that makes certain that parents who spank their children are harshly penalised, that wife batterers end up in prisons, that smokers are heavily fined, that environment polluters are closed down and persecuted and that, in some instances, murderers are executed. There is no effective political power without the coercive prop.

The conventional Weberian critique of Mann's theory of power insists that military force is an integral segment of political power. However, the problem with this position is that it conceptualises violence solely as an instrument of political power. Rather than understanding force as a social process that often generates its own dynamics, the tendency is to reduce military power to being a mere means for, and of, politics. Nevertheless, my view is that conventional Weberianism needs to be turned on its head: rather than seeing violence as a means of political power, it is the coercive power that subsumes politics. Simply put, as social organisations emerge, operate and expand through coercive actions there is neither meaningful political power without coercive underpinning nor coercive power which would in the long term remain apolitical. In other words, coercion is nearly always political just as much as politics is nearly always coercive.

For Mann, political power equals state power. As he puts it: 'I continue to define political power as centralised, territorial regulation of social life. Only the state has this centralised-territorial spatial form' (Mann 2006: 352). In contrast, military power is defined as 'the social organisation of lethal violence' (Mann 2006: 351). In this context, military power is simultaneously much wider and narrower than political power. It is wider in a sense that it includes not only the state militaries but also any armed group or organisation willing and capable of using organised violence: paramilitaries, militias, criminal cartels, youth gangs, and the like. However, it is also substantially narrower in a sense that it disconnects military power from political processes. The main problem here is a sheer discrepancy between the two forms of power. If political power is only confined to the state, and military power involves a great variety of social organisations, does this mean that such organisations have no politics? Furthermore, if military power is reduced to the use of lethal violence, does this suggest that once populations are disarmed, and the monopoly on the legitimate use of violence is established, that political life becomes free of force? Obviously, this cannot be right.

I would argue that Mann's strict separation of the two power forms and his state-centred view of political power lead him ultimately towards an overly optimistic view of social life. More importantly, this conceptual split generates the problematic conclusion that while state power continues to increase, military might is bound to decrease. However, if one reconceptualises this model and looks at both political and military power through the prism of cumulative bureaucratisation of coercion, it is possible to avoid such a paradoxical finding.

The starting point of such an approach is the view that force cannot be reduced to the use of lethal violence. Instead it involves a large repertoire of coercive activity – organisationally enforced threats, institutionalised fear, public shame, the regulated forms of emotional blackmail, coercively induced behavioural change, self-censorship rituals, disciplinary actions, coercively imposed withdrawal of food, medical aid, shelter, and the like. If this was not the case, how would one account for actions of many social organisations that do not resort to lethal violence but are able to impose coercive pressure on their members and employees to fulfil organisational goals. For example, Amazon warehouse staff in the United Kingdom and Germany are monitored by GPS trackers during their ten-hour shifts and are not allowed to talk to their colleagues, take longer toilet breaks or call in sick. The working conditions for outsourced labour in Asia and Africa are generally much worse, including even longer working hours, a workforce exposed to unhealthy and often poisonous chemicals, the prevalence of debt bondage arrangements to secure employment, rampant sexual abuse, constant threats and humiliation, and more. This type of coercive pressure is utilised just as much by the large-scale social organisations such as states and social movements – although North Korean and Iranian governments possess vast armaments, and Hezbollah and Golden Dawn are well armed and they rarely resort to killings to implement their will. It is often enough to publically shame and privately threaten political opponents and their family members and friends. In all these cases, social organisations rely on coercive power rather than using lethal violence.

The fact that modern states control militaries and monopolise the use of lethal violence does not mean that they have become less coercive nor that other social organisations are prevented from deploying coercive might. On the contrary, as the cumulative bureaucratisation of coercion expands, states and other social organisations tend to acquire even greater capacity for coercive action. The key issue here is the purpose of coercive control. If in analytical terms the coercive acts are completely removed from political aims, the organisational reliance on lethal violence becomes less comprehensible. Why did our early twentieth-century predecessors have to wage wars and revolutions that caused millions of deaths whereas one can achieve similar goals today with a much smaller number of human casualties? This question cannot be answered properly if military power is detached from political power. To focus only on the current decline of warfare and see this as a reliable indicator of long-term trends in military power is wrong. The fact that contemporary wars have become less frequent or less deadly does not say much about the strength of military power nor the coercive ability of social organisations. If one takes a look at the military might of states and armed groups, it is quickly possible to see that this power is constantly on the increase. World military spending stands at $1.756 trillion per annum and as such is 'still higher than in any year between the end of World War II and 2010' (SIPRI 2013:

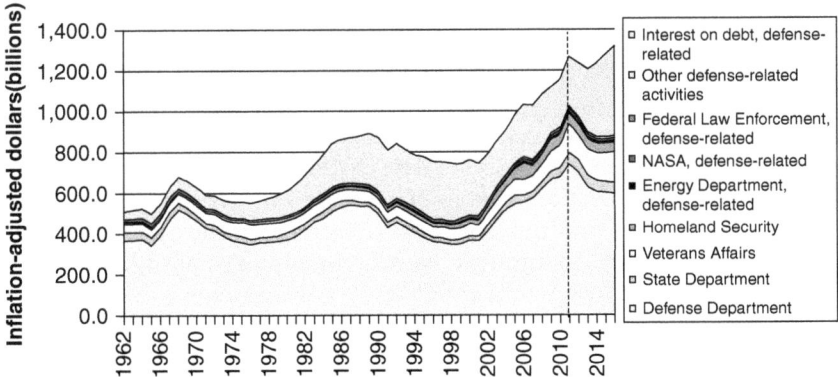

Figure 7.1 US Military budget: Per-capita military spending 1962–2014.

2). Despite some decrease at the end of the Cold War, global military spending has been on the constant increase over the past two decades. Furthermore, there is a pronounced increased concentration of military expenditure with fifteen states accounting for 81 per cent of total spending (the top five are USA 39 per cent, China 9.5 per cent, Russia 5.2, UK 3.5 per cent and Japan 3.4 per cent; SIPRI 2013: 2). The recent Global Militarisation Index (2012) shows that much of the world is in the category of high or very high levels of militarisation[2] with the Middle East as the highest militarised region in the world, but the top ten also include Singapore, Russia, South Korea and probably North Korea (for which data are not available). Over the past fifty years, the US military budget has been rising constantly: from the inflation adjusted, ca. $500 billion in 1962 to more than $1,300 trillion in 2014 (see Figure 7.1).

Furthermore, the world has experienced a substantial increase in investments for scientific research and the production of new weapons. The global arms trade has also been on the rise over the past four decades with pronounced increases in the purchase in purchase of large-scale weaponry by non-state actors such as Hezbollah, FARC, Al-Zintan Revolutionaries' Military Council in Libya, Nuer White Army militia in South Sudan, and the like. All this indicates that despite a temporary decline in warfare, military power has not declined.

[2] The Global militarisation index is calculated through the comparison of military expenditure with a country's gross domestic product (GDP), the comparison of military expenditure with a country's health expenditure; the contrast between the total number of (para) military forces with the number of physicians, and the overall population; and the ratio of the number of heavy weapons available and the overall population.

Mann's insistence on tying political power to state apparatuses only restricts one from analysing the coercive capacity of powerful non-state organisations. For example, the Russian Orthodox Church and Google have not only ideological and economic power, respectively, they are just as much, if not more so political actors, as are Paraguay and Mozambique. Google and the Russian Orthodox Church operate hierarchical social organisations that in one way or another successfully control their employees and members, make internal and external political decisions and engage in conflicts with competing social organisations. Moreover, they influence and often bully governments to achieve tax breaks and monopolistic positions and offer mutual public support in times of elections and various other financial and political deals. Although such organisations do not generally resort to the use of lethal violence, they tend to utilise all coercive powers that are at their disposal – threats, forced behavioural change, disciplinary actions, fear, emotional blackmail and the like. Thus, all social organisations possess coercive capacity which allows them to pursue specific political goals. If one reduces coercive power to warfare and the use of deadly physical force and focuses only on the human casualties one is likely to de-contextualise and ultimately misunderstand the changing nature of coercive organisational capacity. For coercive power exhibits a substantial degree of flexibility and changes over time. If we understand coercive power as the capacity to compel individuals or groups by force or authority without regard to their wishes, then this can be achieved with or without mass human casualties. In the pre-modern world, coercive might was often demonstrated and reinforced through the gruesome spectacles of public torture, witch burning and head chopping. However, despite their morbid nature, such events did not result in mass human casualties. In contrast, nineteenth- and early twentieth–century modernity was characterised by the displacement of ritualistic macabre violence with functional mass mobilisation and mass slaughter. Nevertheless, in each of these instances, the use of force was a reflection of different forms that coercive organisational power takes. The fact that we do not impale people on our public squares anymore or that we do not recruit millions of soldiers to fight trench warfare does not mean that our coercive capacity has diminished. On the contrary, it has significantly expanded as one does not need to use lethal violence to impel others to undertake tasks which, if not forced, they would not do: policing one's sexuality, family life, public interactions, political views, and the like. Moreover, with further technological and scientific advancements, it is likely that the coercive organisational power of the future will be able to wage violent conflicts without direct human casualties. As Coker (2013) and Krishnan (2009) argue, the current tendency for the US military to rely on unmanned drones is a reliable indicator of what warfare might look like in the future – violent conflict between robotic soldiers with no human death tolls but with enormous environmental destruction. In addition, sophisticated technology is likely to help gener- ate much better surveillance and policing devices that, on the one hand, would keep the borders of advanced nation-states sealed from the migrants of environmental degradation and, on the other hand, would further enhance the monitoring and regulation of one's own population (Lachman 2013). Hence by splitting military from political power one cannot properly account for the rise of coercive organisational power over the past three hundred years.

Nationalism, war and military power

Much of contemporary mainstream sociology largely remains oblivious to the study of war and military power. This is less the case with nationalism which is not ignored, but the tendency is to focus on its alleged inevitable decline in the context of intensive globalisation, cosmopolitisation and individualisation (Bauman 2000; Beck 2002). In contrast to this domi- nant perspective, Mann makes a strong case for the view that nationalism remains the most potent ideological discourse in the contemporary world. In line with the other political approaches to nationalism (i.e. Breuilly 1993; Giddens 1985; Tilly 1992; Hall 2000), Mann belongs to the modernist school which traces the rise of nationalism to development of modern state institutions. In his view, the religious conflicts of the six- teenth and seventeenth centuries gave impetus to the development of vernacular literacy, whereas the early eighteenth-century parallel growth of capitalism and state formation made sure that these forms of discursive literacy gradually spread among the top and some middle ranks of the European population. However, it is only in the late eighteenth and early nineteenth centuries that prolonged fiscal crises, geo-political instability and protracted warfare fostered the politicisation of ordinary citizens (Mann 1993, 1995). In this context, nationalism emerges slowly as a by-product of intensive state development: fiscal crisis forces rulers to co-operate with their nascent civil societies and, in exchange for war loans, higher and regular taxation, states are forced to institute greater parliamentary representation, extend citizenship rights and gradually nationalise the public sphere. This process intensified throughout the nineteenth and early twentieth centuries: with the continuous growth of infrastructural powers, most visible in communications, transport and administration, the state's ability to cage its populations firmly extends into the domain of family and civil society. With the establishment of the monopoly on education and the legitimate use of violence, state power invests heavily in the nationalisation of its inhabitants, making nationalism a principal source of one's identity in the modern era (Mann 2003, 2013a, 2012).

Nevertheless, Mann's theory of nationalism differs from other modernist accounts: unlike Breuilly (1993) or Gellner (1983) who insist that once there is a substantial degree of overlap between the state and nation, nationalist ideology becomes less relevant, Mann argues that nationalism continues to retain its ideological strength well into the late twentieth and early twenty-first centuries: 'today's Europeans barely make war anymore and yet their competitive nationalism remains vigorous' (Mann 2013b: 173). Since his approach ties the rise and expansion of nationalism to the growth of state power, as state power has continued to increase over the past centuries so has a sense of national attachment too: 'Through the nineteenth and twentieth centuries, the nation-state became more extensive over the world and more intensive for its citizens, caging their rights within its boundaries and laws. Sentiments of nationalism grew' (Mann 2012: 14). For Mann nationalism is one of the most significant forms that ideological power takes in the contemporary world: 'the ideology which lies behind the nation state is nationalism, now the world's dominant ideology' (Mann 2003: 106). Mann distinguishes between the aggressive nationalisms associated with wars and paramilitary activities and 'a latent emotional sense of national identity' that is usually banal and benign but can acquire hostile features in times of major national crises (Mann 2013b: 175). Nevertheless, for Mann, nationalism has much more to do with ideological and political power than with military might. In the modern era, not only has nationalism become a principal source of state legitimacy, but it also remains the key social glue that ties citizens and their nation-states together. Hence nationalism thrives on the expanded infrastructural powers of states: wide reaching educational systems, universal literacy, proliferation of sophisticated communication networks, extended welfare provisions, enforced citizenship rights, distributive economy and the like. Even though the origins and spread of nationalism have specific and contingent structural, geo-political and historical roots, the citizens of modern polities remain nationalist for both instrumental and value rational reasons: nation-states provide material and ideational/symbolic resources and generate shared collective meanings. The ideological power of nationalism also stems from its Enlightenment- and Romanticism-induced egalitarian principles and the view that members of any specific nation are free individuals of equal moral worth.

In this context, Mann is determined to decouple nationalism from military power and show that despite the popular views which identify nationalism as one of the key generators of wars, in fact nationalism is very rarely the cause of war. He argues that 'in Europe wars had been much more frequent in the pre-nationalism period' and that some limited link between nationalism and war 'might be found in the nineteenth and twentieth centuries when nationalism rose up and the lethality (though not the frequency) of interstate war increased, but not to the further past or to the present' (Mann 2013b: 173–174). In other words, since nationalism is a modern phenomenon it could not account for the bulk of (pre-modern) wars nor for the many contemporary cases where strong nationalism does not result in organised violence. Hence, for Mann, nationalism is more likely to be a consequence than a cause of war. Assessing the origins of the First World War, he states: 'Nationalism had not been responsible for the war; aggressive nationalism was the consequence of the war' (Mann 2013a:159). The fierce calls for national unity and solidarity could not erase strong class- or race-based divisions, and it was the technology of mass mobilisation of total war that was decisive in producing nationalism. Although the Second World War owed more to the virulent nationalisms of Nazi Germany and Japan, it too was not caused by nationalist ideology: 'with exception of Nazi Germany and militaristic Japan, the predominant causal relation was that war generated nationalism, not vice versa' (Mann 2013b:194).

Mann is absolutely right that the relationship between nationalism, war and military power is much more complex than usually assumed. As I have argued elsewhere (Malešević 2011, 2013a, 2013b), most forms of nationalism do not have a violent edge, and nationalism is rarely a principal cause of wars. The view that strong national attachments inevitably cause violent conflicts is premised on two flawed and essentialist ideas: (a) that cultural differences are given and unchangeable in a sense that shared cultural markers inexorably generate organised social action and (b) that cultural variation is in itself a source of violent discord. However, the fact that a number of individuals share the same national categorisation (i.e. Germans, Portuguese and Zimbabweans) does not in any way indicate that this category affiliation will instantly transform into a group conscious social action. Nationalism entails successful and prolonged political mobilisation, and most attempts to mobilise large-scale population end in failure. In a similar vein, the link between violence and cultural diversity is spurious: individuals do not injure or kill each other because they speak different languages or share incommensurable cultural practices but because they associate these differences with real economic, political or status disparities (Cohen 1969: Brubaker and Laitin 1998). One should not take aggressive pronouncements of nationalist ideologues at face value and assume that virulent rhetoric manifestly translates into real violence. There is nothing natural in nationalism: just as other ideological projects it, too, requires a great deal of organisational work and skill. Even in the most recognisable cases of aggressive nationalism, such as Nazi Germany, imperial Japan, late 1930s Austria and Romania, nationalism did not generate war by itself. As Mann (2004, 2012) demonstrates convincingly, it was only when nationalist ideas became mediated by geopolitical instability, weakness of the old regime, class polarisation, corporatist statism and rampant paramilitarism that the link between war and nationalism came to the fore.

Although I am in full agreement with Mann that nationalism is rarely a cause of war, I am more sceptical of his view that nationalism is a direct consequence of war. While there is no doubt that in modern conditions an overwhelming majority of wars rely on nationalist rhetoric to mobilise popular support, it takes much more than the mere outbreak of hostilities to trigger intense nationalist sentiments. Although Mann is well aware of this, his analyses of the two world wars suggest an interpretation that deduces the rise of popular nationalism directly from the war experience. For Mann (1986, 1993, 2005), just as for Tilly (1985, 1992) or Posen (1993), the strength of nationalism is more often than not dependent on the competition between states: successful interstate warfare entails the presence of nationally self-aware citizens willing to vigorously support or fight for their country. The state apparatuses encourage national solidarity by granting citizenship rights, investing in the nation-centric educational systems and providing welfare provisions that ultimately foster a greater sense of attachment to one's nation-state. Hence the onset of war is likely to galvanise intense nationalist attitudes as well as a sense of strong animosity towards the enemy nation-states. In Mann's view, the power of nationalism also rests on its ability to neutralise other social divisions, and this is particularly pronounced in times of war. For example, the Second World War was characterised by a situation in which nation often trumped class: 'the feeling was widespread that Hitler had brought a classless society, and this increased the sense of national solidarity, as it did in Britain. Nationalism was by now a much more important factor than in World War I. A sense of shared citizenship was real even in despotic regimes' (Mann 2012: 454). What is missing in this analysis is an understanding that although war can act as a potential trigger for the expression of intense nationalist feelings in the modern era, it cannot by itself produce such feelings. For if this was the case, every instance of protracted warfare would yield a strong and uncompromising popular nationalist response. However, there are many nineteenth-, twentieth- and twenty-first-century historical episodes when this simply did not happen: the list is very long, including such examples as the popular attitudes of Peruvian and Bolivian population in the War of the Pacific (1879–1884), the Mexican citizens in the Mexican-American War (1846–1848), the Bulgarian population in the Second Balkan war and the First World War to more recent and well-documented cases of changing popular views during the wars in Vietnam and Iraq (Centeno 2002; Malešević 2012). Even the textbook cases of apparently strong links between nationalism and war, such as those of the First World War and Germany require proper dissection: even though there was a substantial elite and some cross-class support in the early stages of war this did not last for long. The German experience on the eve of the Ludendorff Offensive in 1918 is a potent indicator that, despite German military victories, large sectors of the German public became less nationalist and much more focused on rising social and economic discontent. Hence, when their support was most needed to clinch the victory in the First World War, the public became disillusioned, tired of war and reluctant to provide continuous nationalist support for military actions (Howard 2002). The key point here is that although war can activate intense nationalist euphoria, this is not an inevitable form of popular response: the onset of organised violence can also produce a strong anti-nationalist outlook or sheer ignorance about nationhood and conflict.

Second, war can only trigger nationalist reactions if a nationalist *weltanschauung* is there in the first place. The experience of war cannot create a sense of national solidarity if such a phenomenon did not exist before the outbreak of hostilities. As a modernist, Mann is fully aware that pre-modern wars did not and could not generate nationalist feelings. However, it is less clear what happens to the relationship between nationalism and war in modernity. Why do some modern age wars stimulate a nationalist response and others do not provoke such effects? To better understand this relationship, it is necessary to shift one's analysis away from the actual battlefields and briefly explore the workings of coercive organisational power as well as the ideological processes that underpin the cumulative bureaucratisation of coercion.

As already argued, the cumulative bureaucratisation of coercion provides structural conditions for the continuous expansion of organisational power: it fosters internal pacification, the hierarchical division of labour and impersonal social relations, the reliance on specialised knowledge, enforced discipline and little or no toleration for disobedience. This process also operates externally with ever-growing social organisations encouraging rivalry and periodic hostility towards competing social organisations. In this context, nation-states operate similarly to other modern social organisations: they engender lasting institutions and social mechanisms that help perpetuate their existence and potential expansion.

Hence they tend to institute processes that increase state capacity: the expansion of effective civil service, wide reaching fiscal competence, advanced infrastructure and communications, the professionalised and efficient military and police forces, the centralised decision-making mechanisms and the like. All these organisational transformations create institutional conditions for the development and expansion of nationalism. More significantly, although wars foster large-scale social change, much of this organisational scaffolding develops in times of prolonged peace. In other words, the institutional setting that stimulates the perpetuation of nationalist ideas and practices emerges and develops long before any sign of looming warfare: nation-centric educational systems, full literacy in standardised vernaculars, state centralisation, constitutional order, advanced division of labour, developed communications and infrastructure, nation-centric mass media, bloated civil service, and more. For example, to properly understand the social origins of Serbian, Croatian or Slovenian nationalisms in the wake of the Yugoslav state collapse in the late 1980s and early 1990s, one has to focus on the legacies of organisational power generated by the pre-communist and communist states: none of these nationalisms was directly created by war nor were they themselves the cause of the 1991–95 wars. Instead, just as in many other cases in the modern era, nationalism was in part a by-product of cumulative bureaucratisation of coercion. Simply put, the Serbian, Slovenian and Croatian nationalist ideas and practices developed long before any sign of war, and the outbreak of hostilities has only concentrated and intensified already well-entrenched nationalist discourses (Malešević 2002, 2012, 2013a).

Nevertheless, while the development of widespread nationalist ideologies entails the presence of strong social organisations, the mere existence of institutional shells is not enough for the successful proliferation of nationalism. As I have argued in my previous work (Malešević 2010, 2013a, 2013b), the coercive edge of organisational power is regularly soothed by the ideological cushion. The success of bureaucratisation is often premised on its ability to secure society-wide normative justification. Hence, the cumulative expansion of organisational power goes hand in hand with what I call centrifugal ideologisation – a mass scale process through which specific ideological creeds became embraced by the majority of a population. More specifically, this is an organisationally generated historical process that, when successful, is capable of undercutting the existing social divisions in terms of gender, class, status or religious affiliations in the name of commonly shared ideological principles. In other words, as ideological power grows, it infuses different social strata and thus engenders a substantial degree of ideological unity within a particular social organisation. Thus, when centrifugal ideologisation is in full motion, the coercive organisational power is popularly perceived as legitimate: we tend to accept modern bureaucratic structures on the simple premise that they are more efficient and more meritocratic institutions than their pre-modern patrimonial counterparts. However, the political legitimacy of such organisations is also built on the belief that such entities justifiably represent the popular wills and aspirations of diverse individuals. Hence, although the nation-state does not possess an ultimate rationale, its functionality and its ability to project national solidarity make it legitimate in the eyes of its citizens. Mass scale ideologisation is not only a social mechanism for the popular justification of organisational power, it is also a potent mobiliser of social action. This is not to say that citizens of modern nation-states are involved in perpetual mobilisation but only that the key markers of dominant ideological discourses tend to permeate specific social organisations and as such can be invoked more strongly in times of crisis or war. Furthermore, just like the cumulative bureaucratisation of coercion, centrifugal ideologisation is not confined to the state but includes non-state actors as well: all operative social organisations require both coercive organisational and ideological powers. In contrast to Mann, for whom political power equals state power, I argue that non-state organisations including civil society groupings, social movements and kinship-based structures are just as much a locus of political power as are states. This is significant in a sense that when the state apparatuses are weak, the non-state social organisations can and often do accomplish ideological and coercive organisational work that is traditionally associated with states. For example, Hezbollah, Hamas (before they came to power in Gaza) and FARC were powerful non-state organisations involved in policing, military activities, welfare, education, jurisprudence, mass media and communications, thus contributing effectively to the ongoing ideologisation and bureaucratisation of social life in Lebanon, Palestine and Colombia, respectively.

These two processes are decisive in making sure that nationalism becomes and remains the dominant (operative) ideology of the modern era. Although Mann and I agree that nationalism is still the most potent popular ideological doctrine, we disagree over the social mechanisms that make nationalism so omnipotent. I would argue that Mann's position contains a degree of contradiction. In his understanding, the war experience by itself is a major source of strong nationalist attachments: for much of the twentieth century 'war generated nationalism' (Mann 2013b: 194). Hence, the logical corollary of this position would be that as wars decline so would nationalism too. Nevertheless, in Mann's account this is not the case: he is well aware that warfare has declined, but he also accepts that nationalism continues to expand worldwide. Although he is at pains to dissociate military power from nationalism, he does not go far enough in deconstructing this relationship. The key point here is that to understand the workings of nationalism, it is necessary to completely decouple nationalism from the battlefields and analyse its development and rise through long-term historical processes such as centrifugal ideologisation and the cumulative bureaucratisation of coercion. In this context, nationalism is not to be associated with the sudden outbursts of extremist rhetoric that often accompany wars but with the coercive organisational and ideological processes that are integral to everyday activities of key social organisations. As I argue (Malešević 2010, 2013a, 2013b), nationalism saturates most institutional and non-institutional social life in modernity and its strength is rooted in its apparent invisibility. Nationalist ideology is not most powerful when it is aggressive and red in tooth and claw but when it is normalised, taken for granted and largely unquestioned. Billig (1995) is right that habitual banality matters much more than bellicose flag waving, but he is wrong in associating such acts with present-day life in 'the established states in the West'. Since its inception in the late eighteenth century, nationalism was and remains defined by its habitual triviality as it is the habit and inertia of organisational and ideological power that maintain nationalist ideology as a dominant form of social practice for the majority of human beings.

Why do soldiers fight?

Since historical sociology's raison d'etre is the attempt to provide an analysis of long-term social change and the large-scale historical processes that bring about that change, most historical sociologists centre on the macro- at the expense of micro-level transformations. In some respects this is inevitable. If we are to properly explain significant long-term social change, the focus has to be on the macro-level. Why were the inhabitants of sixteenth-century Europe much more patriarchal than their late twentieth-century descendants? Why can twenty-first-century nation-states and powerful private corporations such as Google or Facebook store and recall an astonishing amount of information on most contemporary individuals while their thirteenth- or eighteenth-century counterparts could not even dream of being able to do this? To answer such questions, one has to look at the macro-processes involved: state formation; geopolitical transformations; the structural changes in production, distribution and consumption; the growth of science and technology; the development of social movements and more. Even the best and most comprehensive micro-sociological analyses simply would not be able to capture the significance of these long-term processes. However, despite this unavoidable focus on the macro-level, no full-fledged explanation is possible if the micro-processes are ignored. In this context, Mann's work has been criticised as lacking a strong micro-sociological dimension (Breuilly et al. 2006; Laitin 2007). Even those authors highly sympathetic to Mann's approach find his micro-sociology underdeveloped and prone to producing 'ad hoc arguments' (Kiser 2006: 57). For example, Kiser (2006: 67) argues that 'Mann does not always specify the goals of actors' and sees 'his micro-foundations as incomplete' and his arguments based on such foundations as 'difficult to evaluate'.

However, in Mann's recent work (2006, 2012, 2013a, 2013b) there is much greater engagement with both agency and the micro-level social contexts. In *Fascists* (2004) and in *The Dark Side of Democracy* (2005), he explores not only the structural conditions that gave rise to fascist social movements and genocidal groupings but also the social, and even some individual, profiles of extremist groups and the local contexts in which they emerge and operate. Similarly, in the last two volumes of the *Sources of Social Power* (2012, 2013a), there is much more analysis of the individual and small group-level decision-making processes such as Gorbachev's role and the localised rationalities in the collapse of Soviet Union, the Reagan administration's responsibility in enlarging the US state apparatus, the elite power struggle in Mao's China or the motivation of ordinary soldiers to fight in the First World War. Hence, Mann does acknowledge the significance of both individual and collective agency and the micro-level contexts in history. More specifically, in his analysis of war, military power and nationalism there is not only recognition that these phenomena are shaped by structural and non-structural forces, but, more importantly, Mann builds his key points through the synthesis of up-to-date research on both levels – the macro and micro. For example, when examining the relationship between nationalism and organised violence in the First World War, he looks at changed geo-political balances, the expanding infrastructural powers of states, and the macro-economic and ideological global transformations but also at the micro-level complexities of popular support for war: the civilian readiness to aid and labour for war and the conscripts' willingness to fight and die for others on the battlefields (Mann 2012: 145–153; 157–165).

Unlike the dominant perspectives in political science that clash over the question of whether an actor's participation in wars is motivated by 'greed' (i.e. an individual's self-interest) or 'grievances' (i.e. non-economic motives such as identity or ideology) (Collier et al. 2009), Mann offers a nuanced sociological understanding that integrates a variety of factors. To account for the willingness of millions of British, French and German soldiers to fight and die in the First World War, Mann identifies five key reasons: the dominance of a militaristic culture in pre-war Europe; youth's thirst for adventure as an attempt to escape dull working or middle class life; the popularly shared belief, reinforced by mass media and government messages, that this was a war of self-defence and 'civilisation against barbarism'; the local community pressure including the localised system of recruitment and the institution of regular pay and full employment generated by war (Mann 2012: 145–146). These factors were also present in the Second World War, although Mann argues that ideological commitment played a greater role in the Second World War when compared to the First World War. However, even in this case, ideology mattered more for some than others as he sharply distinguishes between fascist regimes and the rest. More specifically he accepts the view articulated by Bartov (1985, 1991) and others that see Wehrmacht soldiers as being more motivated by the Nazi ideology than the sense of a micro-, platoon, level comradeship associated with most other militaries (Mann 2005: 273; 2012: 147). In this view, the fascist states were characterised by a substantial degree of ideological unity between frontline soldiers and political elites. Mann illustrates this with the available research that analyses diaries and letters of Wehrmacht soldiers who adored Hitler and remained loyal until the end of the war (Bartov 1991; Fritz 1995).

However, for Mann these strong attachments to the Nazi creed were also integrated with military organisational might, so it is not easy to distinguish which comes first: 'it is difficult to separate out nationalist-rooted high morale from superiority in military organisation, both were present, reinforcing each other' (Mann 2003b: 191). This was also the case in Second World War Japan: 'a nationalist culture emphasising hierarchy and community, the growing militarisation of the Japanese state through the 1930s, and the "Imperial Way" strategy adopted by the High Command, emphasising *seishin*, spiritual mobilisation, which could supposedly overcome the enemy's numerical and technological superiority' (Mann 2013b: 1991). Hence although ideological power and nationalism in particular played an important role on both macro- and micro-levels in the Japanese and German cases, this was mediated by the strength of military organisation and other factors. For the non-fascist soldiers, ideology seems to be even of less importance as a source of personal motivation to fight. In other words, for Mann, the Second World War motivations of soldiers and other actors were complex, combining comradeship, self-interest, military pressure and hierarchy, masculinity and ideological commitment, but the balance of these factors was different as fascist soldiers were much more ideological that the rest.

Although Mann makes a very persuasive case that emphasises the complexity of individual and group motivation in deciding to support or fight in wars, there are some problems with his analysis. First, his sharp distinction between soldiers fighting in the fascist as opposed to non-fascist armies is too rigid. While there is no doubt that there were significant differences between the ideocratic militaries of fascist, Nazi and communist states, one could argue that the actual behaviour and motivation of ordinary soldiers on the battlefields exhibit more similarity than Mann envisages. To fully understand the micro-dynamics of battlefields and the complex motivations of frontline soldiers, it is necessary to briefly outline the micro-social sources of individual motivation. In my previous work (Malešević 2010, 2013a, 2013b), I have argued that success of the cumulative bureaucratisation of coercion and centrifugal ideologisation is heavily dependent on their penetration and fusion with the patterns of micro-solidarity. In other words, much of social action is rooted in mechanisms of micro-group solidarities. Human beings thrive on small scale, face-to-face interaction and a great deal of individual motivation stems from one's sense of attachment, responsibility and emotional embedment in micro-level groupings: families, friendships, neighbourhoods, peer groups and the like. Much recent micro-sociological research on intra-group behaviour shows that most human beings are substantially more motivated by chains of inter-personal interaction than by uncompromising doctrinal principles or narrow economic interests (Turner 2005, 2007; Collins 2004, 2008; White 2000). In this sense, the behaviour of soldiers on the battlefields resembles the actions of other micro-level groups such as revolutionary conspirators, terrorists, insurgents and others, all of whom tend to coalesce around the strong emotional ties generated by kinship and friendship networks. For example, Sageman's (2004, 2008) and della Porta's (2013) studies on Islamic terrorists and Italian Red Brigades, respectively, demonstrate the significance of micro-group affective bonds and the relevance of ethical fulfilment generated from inter-personal ties, friendship and family-based networks. These studies confirm previous findings on motivation of frontline soldiers, most of which indicate that the emotional bonds with one's platoon, regiment or even smaller military units tend to outweigh other motives for individual and social action (Stouffer et al. 1949; Holmes 1985, Collins 2008, King 2013). Although Mann generally accepts the significance of small-group comradeship and Stouffer et al.'s (1949) research of micro-level bonds, his account remains overly rationalist and instrumentalist. There is an underlying assumption that the intensive group bonds forged in times of war originate and operate according to the principles of self-interest. In this context, Mann (2013b:

178) emphasises 'shared living conditions', 'interdependency' and 'self-preservation': 'A man on his own was a dead man'. Furthermore, the earlier studies that identified similar processes at work among Wehrmacht soldiers, such as Shils and Janowitz (1948), are roundly dismissed. The problem with this position is twofold. For one thing, the debate is framed too narrowly: either soldiers' behaviour is motivated by the self-interest for preservation or by uncompromising ideological commitments. However, human beings are much more complex and malleable creatures. Obviously, both instrumental and normative factors play a significant part in most of our actions, and frontline soldiers are not an exception. What is distinct to situations of prolonged life-threatening hardship and extreme conditions, where the questions of life and death are present on a daily if not hourly basis, is that emotional action tends to overpower instrumental, value rational and habitual forms of social action. Both Max Weber and Georg Simmel recognised this quite well. For Weber (2004: 225), the war environment was decisive in creating intense feelings that generated communities of sacrifice: 'war ... is able to create in the modern political community pathos and feeling of community and thereby releases an unconditional community of sacrifice among the combatants ... [it] releases the work of compassion and love for the needy which breaks through all the barriers of naturally given groups'. In a similar vein, for Simmel (1917: 20) war constitutes 'an absolute situation' which contrasts with all previous human experiences and as such generates different emotional reactions. Hence, writing in the midst of the First World War, he describes this phenomenon: most of us are now living in what we might call an absolute situation. All the situations and circumstances in which we found ourselves in the past had something relative to them ... None of this poses a problem now, since we are faced with an absolute decision. We no longer have the quantitative dilemma as to whether or when we must make a sacrifice or a compromise'. Hence, the intensity of micro-group solidarity is largely based on emotional ties. In the whirlpool of armed violent conflicts, emotional energy constitutes the principal ingredient of individual and social action. As Collins (2004, 2008) argues, emotions motivate much of social life, and emotional energy is the backbone of all successful patterned social encounters, which he calls interaction ritual chains – from commuters conversing on the train to revolutionary uprisings. In this context, battlefield solidarity represents one of the most intensive forms of group attunement: a fully integrated and synchronised emotional bond. What is distinct about frontline experience is that such strong emotional attachments tend to foster non-instrumental and non-doctrinal action. As a number of studies on twentieth-century battlefield environments demonstrate, in extreme conditions, there is a

much greater willingness to die for others than to kill the adversary (Holmes 1985; Bourke 1999; Collins 2008). Thus, Mann's overly instrumentalist understanding of 'why soldiers fight' cannot fully capture the utmost dominance of emotional action on the frontline.

For another thing, despite obvious political, ideological or cultural differences between the militaries involved in wars of the past two centuries, the bonds of micro-solidarity are universal. Whereas Wehrmacht or Japanese Second World War soldiers might have been more prone to emphasise their ideological credentials, this in itself may not be the most reliable sign that their ideological commitment was stronger than their sense of micro-solidarity. Bartov's studies have often been criticised for taking the letters of frontline Wehrmacht soldiers at face value while ignoring the fact that sincere emotional expressions or criticisms of the Nazi regime could not pass the censors and could even lead to court martial. The fact that Nazis and Japanese military authorities shot 20,000 soldiers each for desertion or showing cowardice on the frontline while only 146 US soldiers were given the death penalty is in itself a powerful indicator that coercion was more significant than ideological devotion.

Much of the more recent research on both the German and Japanese cases has questioned this image of uncompromising, highly ideological, fascist soldiers. For example, Shimazu's (2009) and Hill's (2006) analyses of soldiers' diaries and interviews with surviving kamikaze pilots demonstrate that their willingness to fight originated from a variety of sources including vanity, personal sense of pride or an attempt to overcome humiliation. However, what stands out in this research is that ideological commitments played a less prominent role while the sense of loyalty and attachment towards one's family and friends dominates many personal narratives. In a similar vein, Neitzel and Welzer's (2012) recent analysis[3] of the transcripts based on the secret recordings of German prisoners of war indicates that micro-solidarity was a much more powerful source of individual motivation than any doctrinal principles. For example, the key Nazi ideas such as *Volksgemeinschaft*, 'global Jewish conspiracy', 'Bolshevik promotion of Genetic inferiority' rarely if ever appear in the conversations of PoWs (p. 237, 319). The authors demonstrate well that: 'As a rule German soldiers were not "ideological warriors." Most of them were fully apolitical' (p. 319) What really mattered is the sense of responsibility and duty towards one's comrades: 'Frontline soldiers felt an almost exclusive sense of duty to their comrades and their superiors who formed their social units'. Furthermore, the decisions to continue resisting the enemy after

---

[3] Although Neitzel and Welzer provide excellent data, much of their own analysis is quite problematic and deeply rooted in Hobbesian ontology.

obvious military defeat were often made in relation to the anticipated reactions of family and friends. For example, when a tank commander explains his reluctance to aid Allied propaganda at the end of the war, he is not invoking ideological reasons but the emotional commitment to his family: I should consider it as an utterly dirty thing to do in every way . . . There are my wife and my children. I wouldn't dream of doing it. I should be ashamed to face my wife if I did' (Neitzel and Welzer 2012: 21). Even the views of SS soldiers were characterised by their diversity and heterogeneity and, in contrast to traditional interpretations, the willingness of SS soldiers to die for Hitler or Germany was not greater than that of ordinary soldiers (p. 301). In all of these cases, the micro-group dynamic was quite similar to what researchers observed in other militaries. While micro-solidarity might operate differently in diverse social context, it remains a universal phenomenon present in all wars.

This leads us to the final point: the relationship between ideological power and micro-solidarity. Saying that the bonds of micro-solidarity often trump officially proclaimed ideological creeds does not suggest that ideology does not matter. On the contrary, in addition to coercive organisational might, ideological power is a cornerstone of much social action. The point is that a great deal of ideological power does not stem from the set of uncompromising principles and beliefs. Instead, ideological processes work best when they are in perpetual motion and when they are able to amalgamate with other forms of social action. In other words, rather than assuming that ideology is an either/or singular phenomenon directly opposed to material interests or emotional, habitual or value rational action, it is much more fruitful to focus on ideologisation as a multifaceted process that blends with different forms of social action and taps into existing social relations. Most individuals do not absorb ideological doctrines *per saltum*, as a closed and coherent set of ideas, but take in ideological principles and acts in an unsystematic, fragmentary, contradictory and disjoined fashion (Billig et al. 1988). As I have argued elsewhere (2010, 2013), centrifugal ideologisation operates most efficiently when able to deeply penetrate into the microcosm of family life, kinship networks, peer groups or friendships. Hence, ideological power is heavily dependent on the capacity to tie the diverse pockets of micro-solidarity into a shared, wider, ideological narrative. In this context, nationalism has regularly proved to be the most potent social glue that brings together patches of micro-solidarity into a society-wide common narrative in which heterogeneous individuals and groups can instantly recognise their own personal experiences. Therefore although the emotional bonds of micro-solidarity help generate and maintain much of social action, it is the long-term ideologisation, initiated and fostered by powerful social organisations, that synchronises and often successfully directs shared emotional energies so as to fulfil specific organisational demands. Obviously, this is not a simple and straightforward process but something that encounters resistance and requires periodic spurts of mobilisation. Thus, when trying to answer why soldiers fight in wars, it is necessary to explore these complex relationships between competing coercive organisations that deploy mutually exclusive ideological practices to generate diverse forms of micro-solidarity and utilise this solidarity for specific organisational purposes. This is not to say that centrifugal ideologisation and the envelopment of micro-solidarity operate in the same way all over the world. As these processes depend on infrastructural developments, substantial levels of literacy, organisational sophistication, as well as the particular cultural traditions in some organisational contexts are likely to have greater ideological penetration of the micro-world than others. Simply put, the extreme nationalist rhetoric present in the letters of Nazi soldiers or official declarations of Japanese Divine Wind pilots was not only an expression of quite particular forms of micro-solidarity associated with each individual soldier but was also a broader reflection of the organisational and ideological capacity of the state and military organisations involved in waging the Second World War. In other words, if ideology is not understood as a form of social pathology but as an integral process of organisational action, then it is not difficult to demonstrate that all militaries and soldiers are ideological to some extent.

Conclusion

There is no doubt that Michael Mann's contribution to the study of the world history of power and historical sociology is immense. His conceptual, analytical and comparative historical work is in many respects unique and unparalleled. There is no contemporary sociologist who possesses such breadth of knowledge and such subtle ability to make sociological sense of human history as Mann does. Nevertheless, Mann's complex analyses are not immune to criticisms. The principal aim of this chapter was to highlight some weaknesses in Mann's understanding of military power, war and nationalism. In contrast to Mann's more recent publications which emphasise the strong discontinuities in the development of military power and the gradual decline of organised violence, I attempted to show that there is much more continuity in the workings of coercive organisational power over the past 120 years than the past usually envisaged. In addition, I also probed and problematised the macro- and micro-relationships between nationalism and war and argued that Mann's model cannot properly account for the complexities and the long-term historical trajectories that shape war and nationalism. To fully capture the social and historical dynamics of the past, present and future, it is necessary to identify the organisational, ideological and micro-solidarity processes that underpin relationships between military power, war and nationalism.

References

Bartov, O. (1991) *Hitler's Army: Soldiers, Nazis, and War in the Third Reich.* Oxford: Oxford University Press.

Bauman, Z. (2000) *Liquid Modernity*. Cambridge: Polity Press.

Beck, U. (2002) The Cosmopolitan Society and Its Enemies. *Theory, Culture and Society*, 19 (1–2): 17–44.

Billig, M. S. Condor, D. Edwards, M. Gane, D. Middleton and A. Radley (1988) *Ideological Dilemmas: A Social Psychology of Everyday Thinking.* London: Sage.

Billig, M. (1995) *Banal Nationalism.* London: Sage.

Bourke, J. (1999) *An Intimate History of Killing.* London: Granta.

Breuilly, J.D. Ceserani, S. Malesevic, B. Neuberger and M. Mann (2006) Debate on Michael Mann's The Dark Side of Democracy: Explaining Ethnic Cleansing. *Nations and Nationalism*, 12 (3): 389–412.

(1993) *Nationalism and the State.* Manchester: Manchester University Press.

Brubaker, R. and D. Laitin (1998) Ethnic and Nationalist Violence. *Annual Review of Sociology*, 24: 423–452.

Centeno, M.A. (2002) *Blood and Debt: War and the Nation-State in Latin America.* University Park: Penn State University Press.

Cohen, A. (1969) *Custom and Politics in Urban Africa.* Berkeley: University of California Press.

Coker, C. (2013) *Warrior Geeks: How 21st Century Technology Is changing the Way We Fight and Think about War*, London: Hurst.

Collier, P., A. Hoeffler, and D. Rohner. (2009) Beyond Greed and Grievance: Feasibility and Civil War. *Oxford Economic Papers* 61(1):1–27.

Collins, R. (2004) *Interaction Ritual Chains.* Princeton: Princeton University Press.

(2008) *Violence: A Micro-Sociological Theory.* Princeton: Princeton University Press.

Della Porta, D. (2013) *Clandestine Political Violence.* Cambridge: Cambridge University Press.

Fritz, S. (1995) *Frontsoldaten: the German soldier in World War II.* Lexington, Ky.: University of Kentucky Press.

Gellner, E. (1983) *Nations and Nationalism.* Oxford: Blackwell.

Giddens, A. (1985) *The Nation-State and Violence.* Cambridge: Polity.

Global Militarisation Index (2014) - http://gmi.bicc.de/index.php?page=ranking-table

Hall, J.A. (2000) Globalisation and Nationalism. *Thesis Eleven*, 63: 63–79.

Hill, P. 2006. Kamikaze, 1943-5, in D. Gambetta (ed) *Making Sense of Suicide Missions.* Oxford: Oxford University Press.

Holmes, R. (1985) *Acts of War*. New York: Free Press.

Howard, M. (2002) *The First World War*. Oxford: Oxford University Press.

King, A. (2013) *The Combat Soldier: Infantry Tactics and Cohesion in the Twentieth and Twenty-First Centuries*. Oxford: Oxford University Press.

Kiser, E. (2006) Mann's Microfoundations: Addressing Neo-Weberian Dilemmas. In: J.A. Hall and R. Schroeder (eds.), *An Anatomy of Power: The Social Theory of Michael Mann*. Cambridge: Cambridge University Press.

Krishnan, A. (2009) *The Killer Robots*. Farnham: Ashgate.

Lachmann, R. (2013) *What Is Historical Sociology?* Cambridge: Polity.

Laitin, D. (2007) *Nations, States, and Violence*. Oxford: Oxford University Press.

Malešević, S. (2013a) *Nation-States and Nationalisms: Organisation, Ideology and Solidarity*. Cambridge: Polity.

   (2013b), Forms of Brutality: Towards a Historical Sociology of Violence. *European Journal of Social Theory*, 16 (3): 273–29

   (2012) Wars That Make States and Wars That Make Nations: Organised Violence, Nationalism and State Formation in the Balkans. *European Journal of Sociology*, 53 (1): 31–63.

   (2011) Nationalism, War and Social Cohesion. *Ethnic and Racial Studies*, 34 (1): 142–161.

   (2010) *The Sociology of War and Violence*. Cambridge: Cambridge University Press.

   (2002) *Ideology, Legitimacy and the New State: Yugoslavia, Serbia and Croatia*. London: Routledge.

Mann M. (2013a) *The Sources of Social Power IV: Globalizations, 1945–2011*. Cambridge: Cambridge University Press.

   (2013b) The Role of Nationalism in the Two World Wars. In: J.A. Hall and S. Malešević (eds.), *Nationalism and War*. Cambridge: Cambridge University Press.

   (2012) *The Sources of Social Power III: Global Empires and Revolution 1890–1945*. Cambridge: Cambridge University Press.

   (2007) Predation and Production in European Imperialism. In S. Malešević and M. Haugaard (eds.), *Ernest Gellner and Contemporary Social Thought*. Cambridge: Cambridge University Press.

   (2006) The Sources of Social Power Revisited: A Response to Criticism. In: J. A. Hall and R. Schroeder (eds.), *An Anatomy of Power: The Social Theory of Michael Mann*. Cambridge: Cambridge University Press.

   (2005) *The Dark Side of Democracy: Explaining Ethnic Cleansing*. Cambridge: Cambridge University Press.

   (2004) *Fascists*. Cambridge: Cambridge University Press.

   (2003) *Incoherent Empire*. London: Verso.

   (1995). A Political Theory of Nationalism and its Excesses. in S. Periwal (ed.), *Notions of Nationalism*, Budapest: CEU Press.

   (1993) *The Sources of Social Power II: The Rise of Classes and Nation-States, 1760–1914*. Cambridge: Cambridge University Press.

   (1988) *States, War and Capitalism: Studies in Political Sociology*. Oxford: Blackwell.

(1986) *The Sources of Social Power I: A History of Power from the Beginning to A.D. 1760*. Cambridge: Cambridge University Press.

Neitzel, S. and H. Welzer (2012) *Soldaten: On Fighting, Killing and Dying*. New York: Knopf.

Posen, B. (1993) Nationalism, the Mass Army, and Military Power. *International Security*, 18 (2):80–124.

Sageman, M. (2008) *Leaderless Jihad. Terror Networks in the Twenty-First Century*. Philadelphia: University of Pennsylvania Press.

(2004) *Understanding Terror Networks*. Philadelphia: University of Pennsylvania Press.

Shils, E. and M. Janowitz (1948) Cohesion and disintegration in the Wehrmacht in World War II. *Public Opinion Quarterly*, 12: 280–315.

Shimazu, N. (2009) *Japanese Society at War: Death, Memory and the Russo-Japanese War*. Cambridge: Cambridge University Press.

Simmel, G. (1917) *Der Krieg und die geistigen Entscheidungen*. Munich: Duncker and Humblot.

Smith, P. (2005) *Why War?: The Cultural Logic of Iraq, the Gulf War, and Suez*. Chicago: Chicago University Press.

SPIRI (2013) Stockholm International Peace Research Institute. Military Expenditure. http://www.sipri.org/research/armaments/milex

Stouffer, S. and E. Suchman (1949) *The American Soldier: Combat and Its Aftermath*. Princeton: Princeton University Press.

Tilly, C. (1992) *Coercion, Capital and European States*. Oxford: Blackwell.

Tilly, C. (1985) War Making and State making as Organized Crime. In P. Evans, D. Rueschemeyer and T. Skocpol (eds.), *Bringing the State Back In*. Cambridge: Cambridge University Press.

Turner. J. (2007) *Human Emotions: A Sociological Theory*. London: Routledge.

Turner, J. (2004) *Theory and Research on Human Emotions*. Amsterdam Boston: JAI Press

Weber, M. (2004) *The Essential Weber: A Reader*. London: Routledge.

White, R.W. (2000) Issues in the Study of Political Violence: Understanding the Motives of Participants in Small Group Political Violence, *Terrorism and Political Violence*, 12 (1): 95–108.

8   History, historical sociology and the problem of ideology: the cases of communism and neoliberalism

David Priestland

The final volumes of *Sources of Social Power* have appeared at an interesting time in the development of academic history. Over the past decade, several historians have become dissatisfied with what they see as the excesses of the 'cultural turn' which has dominated the field since the 1980s, bemoaning two effects in particular: first, the neglect of the socio-economic and, more generally, the structural; and second, the abandonment of 'macro-history' and the big picture. Indeed, both are related, as a historian who adopts an 'interpretive' approach, primarily concerned with recovering the ways in which historical actors interpreted their world, is likely to be more interested in context than in identifying the main forces that affect societies and tracing broad patterns of development over time. Historical sociologists have also been wary of the grand syntheses fashionable in the 1970s and 1980s, though professional specialization may have had more impact than the cultural turn. Even so, the British sociologist Dennis Smith has argued that works like Mann's and Wallerstein's are no longer common in historical sociology because the intellectual scene is 'awash with talk of individualism, identity, the self and social fluidity ... [which have] turned the world into one giant swimming pool' (Smith 2014: 207).

Historians have responded to these critiques of the cultural turn in various ways. One is to reject it completely; but, rather than returning to older social structural approaches (which are still unfashionable), they focus on subjects such as trading networks, migration and international institutions, as with the newly fashionable 'global history' (or a 'big history' popular outside the academy) which often, though not always, has less interest in the social (Bell 2013; Christian 2004; Morris 2010; though, for exceptions, see, among others Davis 2011; Hunt 2014). Other historians, however, have sought to combine the cultural and the socio-structural. Two of the most stimulating recent books on the state of the field in the United States and Europe by William Sewell and Geoff

Eley agree that historians have overemphasized context at the expense of structure and have therefore tended to produce highly nuanced, but excessively narrow micro-historical studies. They also accept that the achievements of cultural history have to be defended and that we cannot return to the excessively structuralist social history of the 1950s and 1960s. However, their solutions differ: Eley, always more sympathetic to structural social history, calls for a 'pluralism' in which social and cultural historians exist side by side and learn from each other (Eley 2005); Sewell proposes a combination of cultural and social history, though one with culturalist leanings, arguing that the social should be seen as a 'complex network' made up of diverse 'semiotic practices' (of many types, not just linguistic) and organized in a series of rule-bound 'language games' (Sewell 2005: 346).

In practice, neither author has had a significant impact on the field so far. Macro-history continues to be relatively unpopular in the academy (for this point, see Guldi and Armitage, 2014), as is social history and historical sociology, while the macro-historical work that is done is often materialist in approach, and the gap between culturalists and structuralists is as wide as ever. Indeed it may be widening: some of the more recent developments in cultural history have been even more hostile to structuralism than the cultural history of the 1980s and 1990s, urging a neo-phenomenological emphasis on 'experience' and 'practice' and a rejection of the Foucauldians' overly 'structuralist' conception of discourse (Spiegel 2008).

The completion of Michael Mann's *Sources* is therefore very welcome, for it is one of the few recent attempts to produce a macro-history that seriously tries to take account of both ideas and social structure, escaping from an overly materialist history and sociology, while also retaining Tilly's commitment to 'big structures, large processes, huge comparisons'.

So how successfully does Mann's methodology integrate ideology and culture with structure? One of the main themes of the last book of critical articles focused on his treatment of ideology. Mann was charged with taking an excessively instrumentalist view of ideology, concentrating on coherent 'authoritative' ideologies (like Christianity or Marxism) at the expense of the less explicit 'diffuse' ideologies identified by the interpretivists and, more generally, neglecting the ideological in preference for the political, military and economic (Hall and Schroeder 2006: chapter 6). In response, Mann argued that he is not hostile to the interpretivist agenda; he is concerned with the content of ideology and is seeking to reconcile 'ideas and practices' in all aspects of his 'IEMP' model (not just ideological, but economic, military and political too), though he admitted that the execution of this approach has not always been as successful as he would have liked. He also insisted that he does discuss the content of ideas, though he does not 'claim to discuss *all* ideas, values, norms and rituals, only those mobilized in macro-power struggles' (Hall and Schroeder 2006: 344–347); as his focus is on the 'leading edge' of power, he has to deal with the most influential and consequential ideas. His conception of ideology therefore tends to treat ideologies as relatively coherent entities, which interact with the other three power sources to push societies along certain paths of development. Adapting a Weberian metaphor, he sees ideology, like the other three sources of power, as 'track-laying vehicles', determining 'which of several tracks down which social development would proceed'. To understand the process of social development, therefore, the historical sociologist needs to study the '"moments" of tracklaying, and of converting to a new gauge' and determine the nature and balance of the various sources of power at these crucial times of change (Mann 1986: 28).

This essay will return to this debate and will argue that both Mann and his critics have a point. As Mann explains, if he is to write a macro-history which traces long-term changes in the interaction between the sources of power, he has to use a degree of abstraction when it comes to the ideology's content. On the other hand, as his critics argue, his account of specific ideologies can exaggerate coherence and neglect elements which are important for an analysis of historical dynamics; he can underestimate the role of ideas in historical change because in practice he is often more interested in ideology as an instrument of power (equivalent to military or economic power), rather than in ideologies as systems of ideas which affect the way historical actors interpret their world.

I shall suggest that the reason both Mann's and his critics' viewpoints are tenable is explained by the fact that Mann has different (though related) goals, and some conceptions of ideology are more suited to some than others. Three, I would argue, are most important: the first, and the one that most animates the project, is to show how the balance between the *sources* of social power, IEM and P, changed over time – for instance, in his argument in Volumes 1 and 2 that I was more dominant in Christendom in the Middle Ages, compared with the nineteenth century when E and P became more powerful; or in Volumes 3 and 4 his view that in the post-1945 period, E and P were more important than I and M, in contrast with the interwar period, when there was a 'surge in ideological power' (Mann 1986: Chapter 10, 1993: 1, 2012: 458, 2013: 429). The second goal is to trace the development of important *networks* of power – in particular empires, nation-states, classes, capitalism and movements inspired by religions and political ideologies. And the third, more 'micro'-level goal is to examine specific historical dynamics, exploring both sources and networks of power, while also taking account of historical contingency. Mann is particularly interested in the 'moments of tracklaying', for instance, explaining the origins of the First World War or the rise of neoliberalism.

I shall argue that Mann's approach is most successful when addressing the first set of issues and less so when dealing with the third, which requires a more interpretivist approach – hence a number of scholars have criticized his work when it deals with the specific topics they know about. This is not to question the importance of his work – indeed I shall argue that if anything the significance of Mann's use of the IEMP analysis to address the first set of issues has been underestimated and that hostility to macro-structuralist approaches has led historians in particular to neglect this insightful framework. But I shall defend another way of addressing Mann's three sets of issues while seeking to reconcile the culturalist and macro-historical sociological schools in a way that avoids an overly interpretivist 'swimming pool' view of the world. This will focus more on the networks of power than the sources of power, combining what Randall Collins calls the 'Marxian–Weberian synthesis', positing a conflictual world of competing power groups (both institutions and social classes) (Hall and Schroeder 2006: 20–21), with a more culturalist and interpretivist approach influenced by recent French sociology.

The importance of the sources of power

In the *Anatomy of Power* volume, Jack Snyder dismissed Mann's whole IEMP framework as the product of an outdated project. The typology, with its 'hoary four horsemen' 'labours under the deadweight of the history of sociological thought, especially the debate between the schools of Marx and Weber', and, since the implosion of academic Marxism, it was a non-issue (Hall and Schroeder 2006: 323). At first glance, this scepticism is understandable: is it helpful to distinguish between these forms of power and to determine which is more dominant at different times? Historians of the USSR and the communist world should be particularly suspicious of the argument that some societies or eras are more 'ideological' than others because it smacks of a Cold War liberal analysis that distinguishes between supposedly 'rational' or 'pragmatic' systems, like liberal capitalism, and supposedly 'irrational' and 'ideological' systems like fascism and communism. Surely liberal capitalist societies have their own dominant ideologies as hegemonic in their way as Marxism–Leninism in the communist world? This point was made in a different way by Philip Gorski, who argued that Mann only analyses explicit and codified 'authoritative' ideologies, like Christianity and

Marxism, rather than the more 'diffuse' ideologies and ideological networks that might be less obvious, but have become more prevalent in modern liberal societies (Hall and Schroeder 2006: 126–7).

Yet I would argue that Mann's scheme is a powerful analytical tool that should be used more widely. For different societies do indeed have different balances of power sources, and that tells us something important about the nature of their politics and also has broader social and political effects. So, for instance, ideological power was indeed greater and economic power weaker in the USSR and other communist states than in liberal democratic states. Material incentives designed to encourage people to act in order to maximize economically rational outcomes certainly existed, but they were in tension with stronger ideological imperatives. Communist parties, the power networks that were established to exercise ideological power, made sure that economic incentives remained within strict limits and did not generate 'bourgeois individualism'. But more than that, they developed techniques of economic organization that employed ideological power in order to compensate for the weakness of economic power – such as the use of agitation and propaganda to raise productivity by imbuing workers with a commitment to socialism; these techniques underlay the Stakhanovite movement and other mobilizational campaigns in the 1920s and 1930s, and indeed afterwards (Priestland 2007). The enforcement of ideological norms was therefore not simply the result of knuckle-headed dogmatism, as is often assumed, but was central to the dynamism of a political and economic system which depended not only on ideological conformity, but also on enthusiastic commitment. This explains why Gorbachev's initial analysis of the failings of the system in the mid 1980s concerned ideological weakness: the economy, he claimed, was failing because Soviet citizens were not committed to socialism, and his early reform proposals involved the renewal of the Communist Party and the ideology. The centrality of ideology also explains the development of a series of ideology-centric practices and rituals in communist societies, from the frequent party meetings to individual 'self-criticism' sessions.

Mann's efforts to trace changes in balances of IEMP over long periods of time are also invaluable in historical and political analysis. For instance, the framework forces us to think hard about the realities of modern geopolitics, in a way that less profound but more popular celebratory accounts of American ideological 'soft power' do not (Nye 2004). So the recent struggle over Ukraine suggests that not only the United States and European Union, but also Russia, with its mixture of ethnic nationalism and opposition to EU 'neoliberalism', has soft power in some regions of the world; that since the Chechen wars, the Russians have learnt new ways of using military power more effectively; and that economic power in the form of American financial sanctions, developed in the last decade, used against Iran and to a lesser extent against Russia, has become a much more important (though not necessarily always effective) source of geopolitical power (Zarate 2013).

Mann's approach also helps us to understand important differences between institutions below the level of states, including, for example, universities. For the types of power wielded in universities vary enormously. Where 'merit pay' operates – most commonly in the United States, but also increasingly in universities throughout the world – administrations use economic power to control their faculty, usually to increase academic 'productivity' in the form of publications (Amey and VanDerLinden 2002). However, in universities founded on bureaucratic statist models (still common in many parts of the world), where they have close relationships with states and academics are often seen as quasi-civil servants, administrations tend to use political power, which can be more rational-legal or more patrimonial depending on the institution. In a third form of university – the collegiate one – with its origins in pre-bureaucratic, monastic organizations and surviving in a few places such as Oxford and Cambridge, administrations have traditionally had neither much economic nor political power over faculty and rely on a much more diffuse but highly effective ideological power to keep them in line. Strong moral norms, reinforced by frequent meetings and collective meals in relatively small institutions (colleges) ensure that academics follow the informal codes of the university – codes which prize a quasi-aristocratic 'gentleman tutor' model of education, deeply rooted in the traditions of British elites (though this ideological power is being eroded by both global competition and governmental initiatives and is increasingly combined with both political and economic power).

The types of power operating in each of these systems have a significant effect on the behaviour and work experience of academics: the use of economic power loosens or periodically disrupts rigid hierarchies but encourages competitive, individualistic behaviours that tend to undermine altruistic activities, including teaching; the use of political power can promote those more altruistic behaviours, but at the cost of rigid hierarchies and the excessive power of heads of department and administrators; the extensive use of ideological power may avoid both excessive individualism and hierarchy, but gives the existing ideological system a crucial political role, which can encourage intellectual conservatism (as also occurred in Soviet-type political systems).

Alternative approaches to ideology: morphology and culture

Mann's level of abstraction therefore works very well when it comes to asking a set of questions about the changing balance of the four sources of power in power networks – and particularly in the macro-networks associated with them, such as states, religions, classes and capitalism. However, I would argue that we need to employ different conceptions of ideology if we are to understand the dynamics of societies and social groups more effectively and in a more finely grained way.

The first problem with Mann's 'track-laying vehicle' conception of ideology is its tendency to exaggerate coherence and neglect tensions within ideological systems. Joseph Bryant, for instance, has already argued that Mann assumed (in Volume 1) that Jesus's message was 'ethical, simple and rational' and ignored the apocalyptic and mystical elements which also explained its appeal (Hall and Schroeder 2006: 88–89). Similarly, Mann's treatment of ideology in the USSR can assume too much coherence (though this is shared by much of the more specialist literature). And this is not just of interest to ultra-empiricist historians but matters to anybody trying to understand the internal dynamics of Soviet politics and seeking to explain crucial events.

Mann describes Marxism–Leninism as 'a totalizing ideology involving passionate hatred of "class enemies" and a commitment to achieve utopian goals, a secular salvation' (Mann 2012: 351). But while the ideology did indeed make totalizing claims, there were fundamental tensions within it, which permitted different views on a number of issues (including attitudes to the question of the 'class enemy'). Hence diverse interpretations of the ideology emerged, which in turn justified contrasting political and economic strategies. Central was the conflict between what I have called a 'Modernist' and a 'Radical' Marxism–Leninism (Priestland 2009: introduction). The first drew on one side of the classical Marxist tradition – its commitment to technocratic, planned development; its prizing of science and expertise; and its acceptance of some market incentives within the planned system (at least during the 'lower' stage of socialism); the second was rooted in a more voluntaristic Marxism which stressed the role of consciousness over economic forces and saw a quasi-revolutionary mass mobilization as more effective in encouraging effort and commitment than stifling technocratic hierarchies – a mobilization that could be either more elitist (as in the Stalinist USSR in the later 1930s) or more populist (as in Maoist China in the Cultural Revolution era). And it is in the context of conflicts between the two, I have argued elsewhere, that we need to understand the Stalinist Terror of 1936–38.

This was a complex phenomenon, but was at least initially intrinsically connected with campaigns to replace communist 'bureaucrats' with officials who would implement a more mobilizational policy at a time of economic downturn and the threat of war (Priestland 2007: chapter 5). Mann, in contrast, provides an explanation for the Terror which neglects the role of ideology, uneasily combining a focus on Stalin's personal paranoia and drive to accumulate power common in the 'traditional' historiography (Khlevniuk 2000), with a more 'revisionist' emphasis on structural conflicts within the party-state (Getty and Naumov 1999) (though his analysis is ultimately more traditionalist than revisionist) (Mann 2012: 357–362).

An understanding of the tensions within Soviet ideology also helps to explain Gorbachev's surprisingly (and from his own perspective irrationally) disruptive reform strategy more convincingly, I would argue, than Mann's approach. In his analysis of *perestroika*, Mann describes Gorbachev as a supporter of 'reform socialist' and 'pragmatism' and argues that neither he nor his conservative opponents had an ideology – unlike the liberal reformers of the period, who did have 'an ideology, a view of an alternative society'. He then implies that this very lack of ideology contributed to his failure: he lacked a 'clear sense of economic priorities' and introduced decentralization and 'openness' for populist reasons, inadvertently helping the 'utopian', ideological liberals (Mann 2013: 4, 187). I would argue, however, that while Gorbachev's ideas were certainly confused and internally contradictory, ideology did inform his politics, which can best be understood in the context of the Marxist ideological tradition and the tensions within it; they were certainly not straightforwardly 'pragmatic' (nor, indeed, were they at root Social Democratic, as some have implied; Brown 1996: 316).

When he came to power, Gorbachev believed that the best way to raise growth in the poorly performing Soviet economy was to concentrate on the subjective element of politics and economics. For him, at the root of the USSR's problems lay with the bureaucrats and the 'authoritarian-bureaucratic system', which 'suppress the initiative of the people, alienate them in all spheres of vital activity and belittle the dignity of the individual' (Gorbachev 1989: 1). Only 'socialist democracy' – that is a non-pluralist participatory democracy in which ordinary people had some say over the details of local government and the workplace (but not the political system) – would enhance the 'feeling that they were masters' (*chuvstvo khoziaina*) and 'activate the human factor' – that is create a commitment to work and the regime. As this language suggests, Gorbachev was melding a number of ideological traditions. One was liberalism ('the dignity of the individual'), but the Radical Marxism of

Stalin and Khrushchev, which blamed 'bureaucrats' for failing to mobilize the masses, was also a strong element of his thought, as was what might be called a more participatory democratic 'Romantic' Marxism (hence references to 'alienation' and a genuine commitment to limited participation in management). And like both Romantic and Radical Marxists, Gorbachev criticized Modernist Marxism with its technocratic hierarchies. While his Marxism could be combined to some extent with market liberalism – for both were hostile to the excessive powers of state bureaucrats – and Gorbachev did indeed accept the need for some market reform (increasingly so as the economy deteriorated), as a socialist he was never a market enthusiast.

Gorbachev's early ideological preferences are clear in his first major piece of economic legislation, the Law on the State Enterprise of 1987, which combined both a Romantic-Radical Marxism and a very limited market liberalism. At its centre was an attack on 'bureaucrats' and the top-down 'bureaucratic system': power was to be radically devolved, away from state planners and down to factory managers, who were to have more control over profits, but who were also to be elected by workers and were still to operate in a fundamentally non-market system without meaningful prices (Schroeder 1987). The assault on the economic bureaucracy which this reform initiated made sense in the context of Romantic-Radical Marxism but was highly risky because the whole economic system depended on these hierarchies to hold it together; and it became disastrous when Gorbachev refused to develop a set of market and legal structures that might provide an alternative to the old structures. The result was a power vacuum which led to the mass 'self-privatization' or 'theft' of assets by officials, economic disintegration and, ultimately, the collapse of the state (Solnick 1996). Gorbachev did not intend this outcome, but it was the likely consequence of his fundamentally revolutionary politics, partly inspired by the Marxist–Leninist tradition in which he was raised (Priestland 2009: 532–541).

Marxism–Leninism was not unusual in incorporating important ideological tensions which have political consequences. Neoliberalism can usefully be analysed in the same way; and this approach helps to resolve some of the highly contentious disputes over whether 'neoliberalism' actually exists as an ideology (pro-market liberals insist that it is not 'neo' at all, but is a revival of the classical liberalism of the nineteenth century; Mirowski 2013: 37–50). Mann, like many critics of the rise of market power in the late twentieth century, uses the term and treats it a coherent ideology which sees 'markets as natural and guaranteeing individual freedom' and which champions the spread of markets and market forms of organization throughout all areas of life (Mann 2013: 130).

However, an awareness of the tensions within the ideology (Turner 2008) helps us understand its malleability and its ability to appeal to a wide range of interests and political ideas. So, for instance, while neoliberals are united on the centrality of competition, one of the central tensions lies between those (such as Hayek) who stressed the importance of markets made up of many small competing firms and those (including in the Chicago School of economists) who were satisfied with competition and market-type behaviour within oligopolistic corporations and within state organizations (Davies 2014: chapter 2). And this inconsistency helped neoliberal thinkers forge alliances between big corporate interests, who have little interest in state regulations to encourage competition, and small businesspeople, who see in neoliberalism a more populist championing of the hard-working 'little man' – an alliance that is central to contemporary Republicanism in the United States and Conservatism in Britain. It also explains why neoliberals were able to extend their agenda beyond the market sphere, and especially to state organizations, where the establishment of competitions, league tables, targets and other quasi-market mechanisms has affected the working lives of millions of professionals and non-professionals alike.

The political theorist Michael Freeden has theorized this approach to ideology most effectively. He argues that that while ideologies may seek to convert the 'inevitable variety of opinions into the monolithic certainty which is the unavoidable feature of the political decision, and which is the basis of the forging of a political identity', it is rarely successful in doing so. Even so, it sets limits, pronouncing on which conceptual combinations are available to be applied to the understanding and shaping of the political world' (Freeden 1996: 551). He therefore defends a 'morphological' approach to the study of ideologies, which examines their internal structure, distinguishing between their 'core' and more contested 'peripheral' concepts and then examining their relationships with other 'adjacent' ideologies.

Freeden's framework therefore allows us to examine the content of the ideologies in more depth than approaches which assume more coherence and to relate their constituent elements to particular institutions or groups. However, there is also a strong case for broadening our scope even further, beyond the limited number of 'conceptual combinations' allowed by Freeden's model, and adopting, in addition, another approach to ideology – a more interpretivist and culturalist one, which relates ideology to broader values and norms. For if we are to answer the question 'why did communist movements achieve power in some places and not others?' or 'what are the roots of the neoliberal ascendancy and how long is it likely to last?', we need to assess how these ideologies relate to a number of other less codified ideas and values – such as occupational, local and national cultures and everyday practices.

So, for instance, when it comes to explaining the power of different types of communist politics in various states, we need not only to disaggregate that ideology, in a Freedenite way, but also to appreciate how these ideas and the practices associated with them either succeeded or failed to root themselves in various parts of society. Thus Modernist Marxism's promises of a technocratic, developmental regime of national unity could speak to the values and experience of expanding technical intelligentsias; meanwhile Radical Marxism could mobilize more subaltern groups at times, and a neo-traditionalist pseudo-'Marxism' that legitimized a paternalistic boss politics seems to have had some purchase in rural areas. And establishing these links between official ideology and more popular values demands an interpretive approach to ideology: it requires the study of the way in which a broad range of official and non-official ideas were perceived, through the study of language, visual material, rituals and other practices.

We need similar interpretive approaches if we are to assess the power of neoliberalism. Mann's Volume 4 includes an interesting discussion of why neoliberal politics and the inequality it brings with it have been so resilient in the United States even though so few have benefited, and he discusses a number of factors, from the presence of 'lobbying and corruption' in American politics, to the electorate's 'limited knowledge of the extent of inequality' and the 'skill of Republican politicians' (Mann 2013: 335–344). However, we might also examine the continuing power of many neoliberal ideas and values at a deeper level. As Mann points out, polls show that Americans do not differ much from citizens of other wealthy countries in their views of government intervention in health, education or the provision of jobs. But they are significantly more individualistic when answering questions on more fundamental values and assumptions, such as 'is success in life determined by forces outside our control?' and 'which is more important, freedom to pursue life's goals or that nobody should be in need?', and attitudes to the first question have not changed since the financial crisis (Stokes 2013). To address these issues, political scientists like Vivien Schmidt are starting to use a discourse analysis approach to discover the relationship between neoliberalism and national identity (Schmidt 2002). But any analysis would also benefit from anthropological and ethnographic approaches, which show how various opinions fit together and how they relate to people's everyday experiences (see, for instance, Ho 2009).

Of course, the response of the macro-historian or macro-historical sociologist is obvious: all of these approaches are very valuable, but surely their interest in nuance and complexity is incompatible with grand comparisons and generalizations across time and societies? Freeden's morphological approach to ideology is easier to integrate into Mann's scheme, for while it allows for more complexity than Mann's, it treats ideology as an authoritative system of political ideas that seeks coherence and argues that any incoherence takes the form of a limited number of 'conceptual combinations'. But the culturalists' desire to treat ideology as culture is much more difficult to deal with: Mann, in seeking to find patterns in the history of power, necessarily traces a few ideas related to the 'leading edge' of power, while culturalist approaches see such a vast range of ideas, values and everyday practices as imbued with power that power can become invisible – both everywhere and nowhere. As the intellectual historian Daniel Rodgers writes of Foucault's view of power, 'if power relations are everywhere and saturated everything ... [has] not the long, complex search for power's ever more subtle faces succeeded ... in finding nothing at all?'(Rodgers 2011).

William Sewell's excellent *Logics of History* shows how incompatible some interpretivist and macro-historical approaches can be. For instance, he provides an analytical framework for a study of the effects of the Argentinian peso crisis of 2001. Ruling out reference to 'macro' concepts such as the 'systems' and 'dynamics' of capitalism, or indeed neoliberal ideology, he proposes that the historian of the crisis should study two sets of semiotic practices which have their own 'language-game'- like rules – first the 'language game of middle-class financial prudence' in Buenos Aires, involving 'complexly articulated and usually mutually reinforcing semiotic practices – discourses of thrift, practices of maintaining savings accounts, certain strategies of deferred consumption etc.'; and second the 'semiotic practices of currency traders', which is also a 'language game'- type system, even if technology gives it much greater scale and scope. The historian should then study the 'articulation' between the two semiotic systems (Sewell 2005). It would clearly be very difficult to incorporate the Argentinian crisis into a broad history of economic power using this methodology.

Towards a culturalist historical sociology

Even so, I want to argue that it is possible to reconcile macro-history with a more interpretivist approach building on the 'Marxian–Weberian' conflict school foundations that Mann uses, but we have to adopt a different analytical focus. Mann begins with the most abstract level – the four sources of power – and traces their waxing and waning through the development of macro-power structures; for instance, among the central stories he traces is the decline of churches and the intertwined rise of states and classes (Volume 2) and the 'globalizations' of capitalism, nation-states and empires (Volumes 3 and 4). In contrast, I prefer to start with the power networks, just as Sewell does, in order to permit the linkage of networks with ideology in the broad, interpretive sense of that term. The problem of course is that there are countless numbers of these networks, from Argentinian savers to international currency traders to academic historians, and the macro-historian of power has to generalize and abstract more than Sewell is prepared to do. We therefore need to find the right 'meso'-level of abstraction, one which allows us to identify broad, aggregate groups that have a significant effect on power relations across societies and history and yet are coherent enough to enable us to make generalizations about their values.

The power networks I identify are similar to those in Mann's Marxian–Weberian scheme – for instance armies, bureaucracies, churches, capitalists, working classes – each employing different combinations of the sources of power (see Priestland 2012). In communist societies, for instance, the major groups would include communist parties, economic ministries, armies, political/secret police forces, and at times (when elites ceded power to them), social groups, such as working classes, peasantries and white-collar workers. Modern post-industrial societies, meanwhile, have a larger number of significant groups, and a list of major power networks might include state organizations, financial enterprises, industrial corporations, armies (especially in the United States) and other significant social groups which influence politics through elections or lobbies – including production workers, service workers and small business owners, socio-cultural specialists ('creatives'), technical specialists, managers and self-employed professionals (I am using here a six-group model of occupational social class developed by the sociologist Daniel Oesch and others) (Oesch 2006, 2008).

All of these groups can be identified with particular interests, but they are also likely to have cultures related to the forms of power they employ. And it is here that it helps to combine Mann's conflictual historical sociology with more culturalist and interpretivist sociological approaches. Bourdieu's sociology, in positing a society differentiated by social networks, or 'fields', each of which has its own cultural character, provides one helpful way of linking power sources with the experience of actors. As Bourdieu argues, people operate in social networks, or 'fields', in which different forms of 'capital' prevail (so, for instance, they might work in commercial companies, where individuals struggle over economic capital, or in university departments, where cultural capital is more desired). And each field generates its own set of unexamined assumptions (*doxa*) and practices and dispositions (*habitus*) (though Bourdieu also argues that upbringing and education is important in the formation of *habitus*) (Bourdieu 1977, 1990). Bourdieu's framework, however, can exaggerate the role of interest-maximizing behaviour (in this case the struggle for different types of capital) and neglect the importance of other less goal-oriented forms of action (Joas and Knöbl 2009: 389–391), and Luc Boltanski's concept of 'regimes of justification' is helpful in remedying this. For Boltanski, different value systems coexist within societies, each with their own prevailing ideas of what is valuable which influence the perceptions and behaviour of social actors; for instance, some value commercial success, others technocratic efficiency (Boltanski and Thévénot 2006).

So, by uniting Bourdieu's culturalist sociology, Boltanski's more actor-oriented theory and Mann's Marxian–Weberian conflictualist scheme of competing power networks, it is possible to develop an analysis that is both macro-historical and interpretivist, establishing the connection between the major power networks I have identified and particular sets of values, or 'moral orders' as one might term them. So, in communist regimes, communist parties often used ideological power to achieve their goals, using strategies of mobilization, while economic ministries used political or economic power, adopting more technocratic or material-incentive-based approaches, and at the same time they fostered different cultures, moral orders and even *habitus*. Khrushchev and Gorbachev with their love of long-winded speeches and constant talk of 'enthusiasm' were recognisably 'party' ('*partiinyi*') types, whereas economic officials pre-ferred a more technocratic, practical and 'businesslike' ('*delovoi*') manner.

In modern wealthy capitalist societies, one of the biggest divisions is between institutions founded on market principles which value short-term transactional relationships – the purest form being financial and trading companies – and institutions based on more bureaucratic and technocratic organization (though of course there are mixtures of the two, both in increasingly marketized public sector organizations and in more bureaucratic industrial corporations). Each of these organizational prin-ciples generates its own culture, which then affects the values prevailing in those institutions. As Herbert Kitschelt and others have tried to demon-strate empirically, with some success, occupation is related to political outlook through the experience of work and work organization. So, those working in sectors of the economy more exposed to the market are likely to adopt more pro-market views and accept neoliberal values on ques-tions like competition than those who are not (for instance, in public sector organizations); meanwhile, those who have more autonomy at work, (and related to that, higher levels of education) – the educated 'creative' professionals – are more likely to favour a culturally liberal politics than production workers who, since at least the 1990s, have been more likely to support a more culturally conservative politics (Kitschelt 1994; Lachat and Oesch 2007).

The analytical unit of the socio-cultural group can therefore help us to create a synchronic picture of the balance of power within particular societies, but historians of course need to think diachronically and trace the development of the groups over time and explore the dynamics of their interaction. As Mann's Marxian–Weberian model assumes, these groups both come into conflict and forge alliances, but we also need to understand that these conflicts are often about values as well as interests. And more than that, these groups often fight for ideological and cultural hegemony, as well as political/economic/military power over others, which they justify using ideologies or 'Freedenite' 'sub-ideologies'.[1]

Thus, in the communist world, communist parties were participants in battles with the economic ministries over their respective spheres of influence, but they were also involved in struggles for ideological and cultural hegemony, which were often closely related to the ideological tensions within Marxism–Leninism discussed earlier. Communist parties sought to transform the more 'bureaucratic' (in a Weberian sense) ministries in their own more ideology-centric and mobilizational image, while on their side ministries tried to 'bureaucratize' and 'deideologize' the party. Meanwhile each tended to use a version of Marxism–Leninism in their battles: the ministries a more Modernist one and the party a more Radical one (especially in the interwar USSR and Maoist China), at times mingled with a Romantic Marxism (and particularly in the post-1960s era, whether in Dubček's Czechoslovakia or Gorbachev's USSR).

Hence, Gorbachev's reforms can best be understood in the context of both Radical-Romantic Marxist–Leninist and liberal ideas, as I have argued, but also as an attempt to promote the institutions which supposedly embodied that ideological approach. And while unusually radical and indeed reckless, his programme had several precedents in communist politics. Like Radical Marxist reformers before him – especially Khrushchev, but also Mao and Stalin (who used much more violent

---

[1] This approach owes something to Gramsci: groups struggle for ideological 'hegemony' as well as other types of power. But Gramsci's overly Marxian and insufficiently Weberian approach, which tends to see the world as a binary struggle between ruling and revolutionary classes, each with its own intellectual 'officers' undermines its utility, as does its pre-cultural turn neglect of the deeper roots of ideology in culture and experience. Therefore, we need to understand the institutional as well as class bases of competing socio-cultural forces, while appreciating the ways in which ideologies relate to culture and experience (see Bates, 1975: 360).

methods) – he sought to revitalize the system by initially reviving the party as a mobilizing force and then using it to transform an economic apparatus which he accused of 'bureaucratism'. However, like his predecessors, he soon ran into party resistance: party leaders like Yegor Ligachev, while supporting his initial plans to revitalize the system through some form of party-led ideological mobilization, resisted measures such as '*glasnost*'' (openness) and the reconsideration of the Soviet past, that might undermine the party's authority (Kotkin 2008: 81–82). Hence, Gorbachev soon found himself turning his fire on the party. What was new was Gorbachev's willingness to seek support against the party from non-party liberal intelligentsia groups and to pursue this strategy even when the party's authority began to crumble. Hence, Gorbachev's apparently irrational attacks on first the economic and then the party apparatus, and his ultimate destruction of the institutional 'spine' which kept the Soviet state together, become much more comprehensible if seen in the context of well-established conflicts over both ideas and interests between socio/institutional-cultural groups.

We can see similar power struggles, to maximize interests and ideological hegemony, in non-communist societies too (Priestland 2012: 78–88, 206–14). After the Second World War, the Bretton Woods system gave states more control over international private banks and contributed to their transformation into bureaucratic institutions: their employees were paid fixed salaries and made safe investments, and they were no longer the freewheeling, highly flexible institutions they had been in their heyday before the 1929 crash (Augar 2001). They therefore became more similar to states, and indeed to large industrial corporations, where managerial and expert bureaucracies rather than competitive networks of traders had been dominant since the 'second industrial revolution' of the late nineteenth century. However, with the economic crises of the 1970s, state control over finance crumbled and instead deregulated banks and financial markets gained the upper hand. Banks returned to their origins as highly commercial and flexible entities (Ho 2009) and then began to control and spread their market culture to the industrial sector, transforming it in their own image (Helleiner 1994). 'Corporate raiders' in the 1980s and 'private equity' in the 1990s, backed by large banks, organized hostile takeovers of American and British firms deemed to be giving too much power and resources to managers and labour and too little to the shareholders who owned the capital (O'Sullivan 2001: chapters 5–6). And partly as a result of the takeovers and the threat they posed, the organization and culture of industrial firms changed, becoming highly responsive to the short-term fluctuations of capital markets while inevitably neglecting more long-term concerns, such as investments in research and development and in the labour force. At the same time, wealth was channelled to investors and financiers, making a major contribution to the inequality that became the hallmark of the era. And the resulting changes in the experience of work has had an effect on the values of employees and helps to explain neoliberalism's resilience. Of course, financial companies were not solely responsible for these developments; they acted in alliance with other groups and institutions: academic economists, think-tank policy-makers, influential journalists and conservative political parties, each of which had different cultures and used varying combinations of economic, ideological and political power (and at times states even used military power in pursuit of neoliberal goals, most dramatically during the British miners' strike of 1984–85).

International finance did not only help to change large corporations in some countries; it also had a major transformative effect on states themselves – understandably, given that bond markets now had much more power over state financing than before and were constantly demanding cuts and market 'efficiencies'. Some parts of state activity were directly 'captured' by market institutions through privatization, but even those that remained publicly owned were increasingly 'colonized' by market cultures and organized according to quasi-market principles. The 'New Public Management' movement, influential in 'Anglo-Saxon' countries in the 1990s and 2000s, urged that state bodies replace bureaucratic hierarchies with smaller budget-holding agencies and proposed that competition be stimulated, even in the absence of actual markets, by means of league tables and targets (Connell, Fawcett and Meagher 2009). In some sectors (such as British education at all levels), this has transformed behaviour and the experience of working life.

An analysis of the struggles between these 'meso-level' socio-cultural groups therefore allows us to take account of both interests and values in explaining dynamics at the level of high politics and ideology (whether between Radical and Modernist Communism or neoliberalism and Social Democracy) while at the same time permitting us to explore their relationship with the values and experiences of non-elites within significant organizations and social groups (whether party activists and economic officials in communist societies or private and public sector employees at various levels in late capitalist societies).

This analytical framework also helps us to address the question of ideological hegemony and to ask why particular power networks with their associated value systems become dominant in particular times and places and not in others. These questions can partly be answered at the level of national societies, and we can explore the relative role of contingent events and deep institutional structures and cultural traditions in embedding the power of particular socio-cultural groups and values. A great deal of work has been done by political scientists on the institutional reasons why neoliberalism has been less powerful in many continental European countries than in North America, Britain and Australasia, in the so-called Varieties of Capitalism literature (Soskice and Hall 2001); fewer have written on cultural roots of different responses to neoliberalism, using discourse analysis to analyse variations between national political cultures (Schmidt 2002). But examining the cultures of institutions and social groups comparatively – such as the prevalent bureaucratic corporatism in nineteenth-century Prussian institutions or the gentlemanly individualism in British ones – is likely to allow us to understand different attitudes to markets in a fuller, more historically contextualized and more satisfying way (Crouch 1993: chapter 10; Price 1999).

However, we also need to examine power networks and their associated values at the international level, for they compete globally and become dominant in particular periods as they interact with each other, as well as with the changing environment. This approach allows us to identify some of the major turning points that have altered the global balance of power. It also permits us to take account of the changing balance of ideological hegemony, as well as political, economic and military power. Indeed, I have argued that we can better understand the history of the twentieth century if we identify a series of major crises, both material and ideological, which affected the major power networks and precipitated processes of 'learning' which helped to shape the orders that took their place (Priestland 2012). So, for instance, the neoliberal finance and trade-dominated global order that emerged from the end of the 1970s was in part the result of a decision by American and other elites that this system was in their economic and military interests, and in part the consequence of a broader perception among several social groups that the previous state-dominated Bretton Woods order had failed materially and morally. Meanwhile that order, founded as it was on the technocratic states and their allies, the organized working class, which had emerged from the Second World War in a dominant position, was a reaction against both a perceived failure of the free-market policies of the American hegemon in the mid 1920s and against the defeated populist militarism of interwar radical nationalist movements. And that brief 1920s order was, in turn, founded on the promise that peaceful commerce, led by international traders and financiers, could provide an alternative to the militaristic aristocratic states and armies that had allegedly caused the disastrous First World War. We can therefore see an oscillating pattern in which particular socio-cultural groups took advantage of major shifts in the balance of political, economic, military and ideological power to establish their own preferred orders founded on the promise that their strategies and values offered both a viable and moral alternative to the previous failed order.

This narrative and the approach underlying it are, of course, open to criticism. For some, they will seem overly abstract and schematic in their efforts to link interests with ideas. Sewell would probably not approve of them, for he would regard them as examples of a 'building-block' view of society that reifies social groups and neglects fluid relationships between them (Sewell 2005). For others who are more interested in how the balance of the four sources of power changes over time, Mann's framework is clearly more useful. But no attempt to find patterns in the past can fully capture the 'mess' of reality, as Mann puts it. Historians and historical sociologists alike will differ over how much simplifying abstraction they find helpful, and any abstraction will inevitably only be able to present a partial picture. But we have to use abstractions to cut through complexity, and the goal is to ensure that the models we employ approximate most closely to reality. The future therefore lies in judicious combinations of macro-historical frameworks, not the search for single, all-encompassing models, however nuanced they are.

References

Amey, M. and VanDerLinden, K. 2002. Merit Pay, Market Conditions, Equity and Faculty Compensation. *The NEA Almanac of Higher Education.*

Augar, P. 2001. *The Death of Gentlemanly Capitalism. The Rise and Fall of London's Investment Banks.* London: Penguin.

Bates, T. 1975. Gramsci and the Theory of Hegemony. *Journal of the History of Ideas* 36.

Bell, D. 2013. This is What Happens when Historians Overuse the Idea of the Network. *New Republic* 23 October 2013.

Boltanski, L. and Thévénot, L. 2006. *On Justification: Economies of Worth.* Princeton: Princeton University Press

Bourdieu, P. 1977. *Outline of a Theory of Practice.* Cambridge: Polity.
   1990. *The Logic of Practice.* Cambridge: Polity.

Brown, A. 1996. *The Gorbachev Factor.* Oxford: Oxford University Press.

Christian, D. 2004. *Maps of Time. An Introduction to Big History.* Berkeley: California University Press.

Crouch, C. 1993. *Industrial Relations and European State Traditions.* Oxford: Oxford University Press.

Davies, W. 2014. *The Limits of Neoliberalism. Sovereignty, Authority and the Logic of Competition.* London: Sage.

Davis, N. 2011. Decentering History: Local Stories and Cultural Crossings in a Globalized World. *History and Theory* 50.

Eley, G. 2005. *A Crooked Line. From Cultural History to the History of Society.* Ann Arbor: University of Michigan Press.

Freeden, M. 1996. *Ideologies and Political Theory. A Conceptual Approach*. Oxford: Oxford University Press.

Getty, J. and Naumov, O. 1999. *The Road to Terror. Stalin and the Self-Destruction of the Bolsheviks, 1932-1939*. New Haven: Yale University Press.

Guldi, J. and Armitage, D., 2014. *The History Manifesto*. Cambridge: Cambridge University Press.

Gorbachev, M. 1989. Report to CPSU Central Committee plenum, 6 January 1989. Current Digest of the Soviet Press, 45.

Hall, John A. and Ralph Schroeder (eds) 2006. *An Anatomy of Power: The Social Theory of Michael Mann*. Cambridge: Cambridge University Press.

Helleiner, E. 1994. *States and the Reemergence of Global Finance: From Bretton Woods to the 1990s*. Ithaca, NY: Cornell University Press.

Ho, K. 2009. *Liquidated. An Ethnography of Wall Street*. Durham, NC: Duke University Press.

Hunt, L. 2014. *Writing History in the Global Era*. New York: W.W. Norton.

Joas, H. and Knöbl, W. 2009. *Social Theory*. Cambridge: Cambridge University Press.

Khlevniuk, O. 2000. The Reasons for the "Great Terror." The Foreign-Political Aspect, in S. Pons and A. Romano (eds.), *Russia in the Age of Wars, 1914–1945*. Milan: Feltrinelli.

Kitschelt, H. 1994. *The Transformation of European Social Democracy*. Cambridge: Cambridge University Press.

Kotkin, S. 2008. *Armageddon Averted. The Soviet Collapse, 1970–2000*. Oxford: Oxford University Press.

Lachat, R. and Oesch, D. 2007. Beyond the Traditional Economic Divide: Class Location and Political Attitudes in 21 European Countries. www.romain-la chat.ch/papers/lachat_oesch_2007.pdf

Mann, M. 1986. *Sources of Social Power. Volume 1. A History of Power to 1760*. Cambridge: Cambridge University Press.

  1993. *Sources of Social Power. Volume 2: The Rise of Classes and Nation-States, 1760–1914*. Cambridge: Cambridge University Press.

  2012. *Sources of Social Power. Volume 3: Global Empires and Revolution, 1890–1945*. Cambridge: Cambridge University Press.

  2013. *Sources of Social Power. Volume 4. Globalizations, 1945–2011* Cambridge: Cambridge University Press.

Mirowski, P. 2013. *Don't Let a Serious Crisis Go to Waste. How Neoliberalism Survived the Financial Meltdown*. London: Verso.

Morris, I. 2010. *Why the West Rules – For Now. The Patterns of History and What They Reveal about the Future*. London: Profile.

Nye, J. 2004. *Soft Power. The Means to Success in World Politics*. New York: PublicAffairs

O'Sullivan, M. 2001. *Struggles for Corporate Control: Corporate Governance and Economic Performance in the United States and Germany*. Oxford: Oxford University Press.

Oesch, D. 2006. *Redrawing the Class Map. Institutions and Stratification in Britain, Germany, Sweden and Switzerland*. Basingstoke: Palgrave Macmillan.

2008. Remodelling Class to Make Sense of Service Employment: Evidence for Britain and Germany. www.unige.ch/ses/spo/Membres/Enseignants/Oesch-1/Publications/Background_class_Paris_Crest_20Nov08.pdf

Price, R. 1999. *British Society, 1680–1880.* Cambridge: Cambridge University Press.

Priestland, D. 2007. *Stalinism and the Politics of Mobilization. Ideas, Power and Terror in Interwar Russia.* Oxford: Oxford University Press.

2009. *The Red Flag. Communism and the Making of the Modern World* London: Allen Lane.

2012. *Merchant, Soldier, Sage. A New History of Power.* London: Allen Lane.

Rodgers, D. 2011. *The Age of Fracture.* Cambridge, MA: Harvard University Press.

Schmidt, V. 2002. *The Futures of European Capitalism.* Oxford: Oxford University Press.

Schroeder, G. 1987. Anatomy of Soviet Reform. *Soviet Economy* 3.

Smith, D. 2014. The Return of Historical Sociology. *Sociological Review* 62.

Sewell, W. 2005. *Logics of History. Social Theory and Social Transformation.* Chicago: University of Chicago Press.

Solnick, S. 1996. The Breakdown of Hierarchies in the Politics of the Soviet Union and China. *World Politics* 48.

Soskice, D. and Hall, P. 2001. *Varieties of Capitalism. The Institutional Foundations of Comparative Advantage.* Oxford: Oxford University Press.

Spiegel, G. 2008. Comment on *A Crooked Line. American Historical Review* 113.

Stokes, B. 2013. Public Attitudes toward the Next Social Contract. Pew Research Center. www.pewglobal.org/files/pdf/Stokes_Bruce_NAF_Public_Attitudes_1_2013.pdf

Turner, R. 2008. *Neo-liberal Ideology. History, Concepts and Policies.* Edinburgh: Edinburgh University Press.

Zarate, J. 2013. *Treasury's War. The Unleashing of a New Era of Financial Warfare.* New York: Public Affairs Press.

Ralph Schroeder

Introduction

Debates about globalization have waxed and waned in the social sciences. They flourished briefly after the end of the Cold War and during the economic upswing of the 1990s and early 2000s (Guillen 2001) but have subsequently receded again. Still, the debate has been left unresolved: while some continue to build social theory around the concept of globalization (Martell 2010, Walby 2009), there have also been critics (Hirst and Thompson 1996). This leaves us with the question whether social theory now embraces globalization as a master concept, or if we should revert back to earlier concepts like modernization or 'capitalism' or move beyond all of these and on to new concepts?

In Volumes 3 and 4 of the *Sources of Social Power*, Mann makes a series of arguments about globalization which I will review and assess in this chapter. I will argue that his account of the increasingly global reach of social processes can explain some aspects of social development in the twentieth century but has serious limits when it comes to explaining recent social change, especially in the post–Cold War period. Mann's theory also puts too much emphasis on the driving force of capitalism and on America's global role in sustaining it and therefore overlooks a number of tensions in contemporary globalization. To make this argument, I will focus on Mann's ideas about American empire, technoscience and the environment and consumer citizenship.

Mann proposes that there are plural 'globalizations', by which he means that the processes of globalization among the economic, political, military and ideological sources of social power are orthogonal to each other; they are not causally related in a direct way. In contrast, I have argued for 'globalizing modernity' (Schroeder 2013), whereby cultural, economic and political processes have global dimensions, but there are also causal relations between them – even if they are indirect. This difference entails that I would like to criticize Mann's theory, in a constructive way, on several counts: first, I argue that technoscientific culture is a separate source of power and autonomous vis-à-vis nature, which also means that we differ on the looming crisis of climate change. Second, I argue that markets are more disembedded than Mann allows, with the implication that the global ideological and military role of the United States is less crucial to the future of capitalism. Instead, instabilities generated by financial markets and unfettered consumerism are autonomous, with counter-forces only on a distant horizon. Finally, therefore, we differ about how different globalizing processes are separate from – or orthogonal to – each other, with different implications for how globalization should be conceptualized in contemporary social theory.

Mann's globalizations

Mann's globalizations can be analysed in three steps: first, in terms of different phases of order and disorder in the relation between states; second, from the vantage point of America's role in imposing these orders; and third, by charting these orders in detail and how the different sources of power interrelate – or fail to do so.

Mann's account of the long nineteenth century in Volume 2 of *Sources*, from the American and French Revolutions up to the outbreak of the First World War, did not make use of empire in explaining the relations between states and how this imposed an international order upon the world. However, in Volumes 3 and 4, he goes back into the nineteenth century to correct for this omission. Four phases of imperial order can be distinguished: empires were 'fractured' during the phase of their ascent and expansion up to the First World War. Then, in a second phase, European empires competed against each other for dominance during the First World War and then, in the Second World War, for global dominance. This was followed by the third phase when Europe's dominance was superseded by the ascendency of the United States dominating the global order against its Cold War rivals. The fourth phase did not begin, as in other periodizations, with the end of the Cold War, but earlier with the end of the Golden Age in the 1970s when the relative economic decline of the United States began. In this phase, which is still ongoing, the global military power of the United States has become unrivalled, leading to hubristic war-making, at the same time that American economic elites are merely part of a transnational elite spearheading a globalizing neoliberal economic order.

The United States' role in these global orders has been complex, but the main shift was that America went from being one empire among others during the first phase to being the sole informal empire upholding a global military and economic order in recent decades. Mann distinguishes between three variants of informal empire: informal 'gun-boat' empire, informal empire through proxies and economic imperialism (2012: 19). He says that economic imperialism does not qualify for the label imperialism since it lacks the use of military or coercive power. But the American empire has not just been an informal one; it has assumed various imperial forms depending on time and place: territorial rule – the defining feature of colonies (or direct and indirect, more-than-informal empire) – was rarely used by the United States, mainly early on and in certain parts of the globe. During the Cold War, apart from a number of 'hot' wars, the United States for the most part used military power to contain the communist 'alternative' and national liberation movements by means of alliances with conservative elites in the developing world – against peoples revolting or seeking reform from these elites. America's economic imperialism – or hegemony – from the 1980s onwards has consisted of foisting a neoliberal regime upon much of the world, and this order has only been partly imposed by the United States: although it has been led by America, it was also promoted by transnational finance capital.

Against this background, we can examine globalizations in terms of the overlap – or lack thereof – of the sources of social power. One initial thrust towards globalization came via markets, but global integration took place later than is often supposed (pace world-system theorists, who locate the origins of a systemic capitalism in the fifteenth/sixteenth century, or earlier). Mann cites O'Rourke and Williamson who argue that price convergence only occurred late in the nineteenth century, and even then covered only parts of the globe (2012: 41). This is one reason why there was not simply a capitalist or market logic to expanding imperial power (contra Lenin's and Hobson's theories). Even if core powers often exploited colonial peripheries for raw materials and gained economic benefits, 'most empires did not turn a profit for the mother country' (2012: 462). With the possible exception of India, the costs of empire often outweighed the benefits, and even in the British case, colonialism or imperialism were not preconditions for the rise of industrial or capitalist power. The main thrust of imperial expansion across the globe was rather via military power (see also Headrick 2010), and competition between empires was such that it was not singular but 'fractured', with the several great European powers competing for different parts of the globe. The United States was a latecomer to this competition, which unravelled during the world wars.

In any event, the First World War was fought for dominance in Europe and not driven by imperial rivalry. Likewise with the Second World War, which nevertheless escalated into a wider struggle whereby rival imperial powers competed with each other – ultimately – finished off European colonial power altogether. Only after the Second World War, after a period of fractured empires and imperial competition, did globalization become 'universal but polymorphous' in being 'driven by capitalism, nation-states and American empire'(2013: 10): a single struggle for the dominance of America's informal empire, even while ruling classes had allowed 'people' onto the national stages of political power and capitalist elites compromised on Keynesian economic policies and yielded social citizenship rights – later shifting to neoliberal policies.

The Keynesian compromise came undone during the 1970s and 1980s, when American military and economic power began to diverge: the United States could no longer afford war and shifted from informal empire through proxies to economic imperialism. Now it began to promote neoliberal economic orthodoxy under the guise of exporting freedom and democracy. After the end of the Cold War, America's military power became unrivalled, the only global empire in history. Yet neoliberalism has not been just an American project: though spearheaded by the United States, it has also been borne by other Northern powers and by a transnational financial elite or what Mann calls a 'fraction' of the capitalist class (2012:11). Thus, only the military reach of American power has been global; its economic power has been hegemonic – benefitting from the dollar as the world's currency so that the United States could run a trade deficit without penalty: 'the new economic imperialism did halt American relative economic decline for three decades'(2013: 272). Yet at the same time the United States has been constrained by the turbulence of finance capital. Thus, American hegemony will end in the future because of its relative economic decline, but Mann argues that the United States can remain the dominant military power for several decades to come (Mann 2013b).

Unlike in world-system theory, for Mann, there is thus no unitary logic to capitalism or to America's role as a hegemonic empire within the capitalist system. After the Second World War, neither the United States nor the Soviets sought empire. Hence, too, Mann agrees with Lundestad (1986) that America's was an 'empire by invitation' (2013:88), at least in Europe and then, after several wars, also in East Asia. During the first phase of the Cold War, when the United States was pushing against the Soviet alternative, several wars of containment were instigated to maintain the American global order. However, in the post–Cold War period, America's projection of military power has no longer confronted any serious global alternatives. It is not clear then whether the imposition of a particular economic regime requires coercion: for Mann, this is one place where (two – military and economic) social powers are orthogonal. For Mann, America's globalizing thrust has therefore become two-pronged, an attempt at perpetuating or extending a neoliberal economic regime, plus military adventures driven by an elite in Washington which has often gone against domestic interests, including public opinion and its economic interests.

Another aspect of globalization has been that, within neoliberalism, the financial sector has gained power over other parts of the economy, becoming more globalized – even if Mann points out that large parts of economies are contained within nation-states ('80 per cent of trade in goods and services still lies within countries', [2013: 408]). Still, the asymmetric power of finance gives an advantage to transnational capital over labour, which remains nationally caged. Within Anglophone neoliberal countries in particular, social citizenship has therefore stalled, and inequality has grown in the global North. Mann hints that this is partly to do with consumer citizenship, again, particularly in Anglophone countries, where the gains of social citizenship of capitalism's Golden Age are being displaced or becoming fragile.

Globalizations are therefore plural for Mann: as for economic power, capitalist markets have come to dominate the globe, though there are still various options for organizing economies. In terms of military power, there is now only a single unchallenged military empire with global reach. Politically, the nation-state is dominant and national sovereignty is a global norm. Ideologically, consumer culture is global though shallow. Perhaps the best way to understand Mann's conception of globalizations is therefore to highlight how it differs from other views: it is not economistic in the sense of the increasing openness advocated by the champions of capitalism, nor a system based on exploitation as for world-system theorists and Marxists. It is not a separate world of geopolitical interests of states as for international relations theorists. Instead, there is ultimately a historical shift in the leading edge of power, away from Europe, and now in a phase moving beyond America's hegemonic peak and towards a more multipolar world in which capitalism is nevertheless producing new asymmetries of economic power.

Globalizing modernity

Mann's tracking of globalization at the leading edge of power rests on the idea of the dominance of American militarism and of neoliberal capitalism. However, he also foresees that American military power is bound to decline and that various forms of capitalism will continue to thrive. Thus, he argues that a more multipolar order can be envisaged. In this respect, it is worth asking whether a different ordering of power relations more usefully explains the dynamics of advanced societies. One such ordering concerns the global reach of different powers and how they intersect or fail to do so. This reach, I argue, relates less to a leading geopolitical or geo-economic edge of dominance – and more to how different types of power have diverged in contemporary society. To make this point, it is necessary to recognize that there has been no convergence on Western norms and progressive social development, as suggested by optimistic modernization theories. Instead, social development is increasingly fraught by tensions and instabilities, and a key task is to relate these to globalization.

We can begin with the modern economic order, which is characterized by increasingly disembedded markets. Unlike Mann, I prefer 'markets' to 'capitalism', and disembeddedness means that growing economic inequalities and the instabilities of the financial sector have moved beyond the control of nation-states. There are exceptions to the disembeddedness of markets if we think, for example, of national energy infrastructures or markets that operate 'politically' or illegally, such as the arms and illegal drugs trade. However, the vast bulk of economic relations operates via formally free exchanges. Those who use the concept 'capitalism' point to systemic asymmetries of exploitation between different classes or between a core and periphery, but at least for the post-war and post-colonial era, such systemic relations are difficult to pin down.

Cheerleaders for 'capitalism' suggest that, instead of these asymmetries, there is a 'trickle-down effect' of increasingly widespread growth, but this effect has also been not been demonstrated. Instead, as Mann and Riley (2007) have shown, there are distinctive regimes of inequality in different regions across the globe, and, in terms of global economic inequalities, there are signs of greater divergence but also some indication of 'catch-up' (Milanovic 2011). Apart from this spatial unevenness, however, a more general pattern is that advanced economies everywhere have 'liberalized' (or subjected their economies to intensified disembedding) in recent decades, with the result of relinquishing control over economic distribution and over how financial markets affect economic policy.

Political power has become increasingly centralized and consolidated in the container of the nation-state, as Mann argues (see also Dandeker 1990; Giddens 1985), and state capacity, despite what has just been said, has not been undermined in a zero-sum manner by the force of economic globalization, though it may have stalled. For Mann, the dominant trajectories of modern political power are different paths of democratization, whereby states are democratized 'from below' by citizen classes. This process, however, is contained within nation-states, and Mann repeatedly argues that the locus of political power is the state. Others have argued against this, claiming that there are signs of an emerging transnational or global civil society or movements towards cosmopolitan governance which entrench democracy in institutions beyond states. Thus, Slaughter (2004, see also Hurrell 2007) argues that there are ever-denser organizational ties between bureaucrats across borders at the meso-level, making agreements which bind states (see also Ikenberry, Chapter 14 of this volume). Keck and Sikkink (1998) have similarly documented how transnational movements have put certain issues such as environmental protection and human rights onto the political agenda, though they have had less impact in translating them into policy. However, Collins (2010) points out, in a more 'realist' vein, that to implement human rights and other binding laws or reforms at the transnational or global level depends on a geopolitical coalition of strong and highly bureaucratized powers. Mann similarly notes that social movements, transnational or otherwise, always still need to take aim mainly at the state in order to achieve their achieve goals of transnational reform. In other words, the state's organizational strength is needed for rules to be implemented within states in order to be binding across them.

In terms of ideology – or culture – Mann thinks there are only two forceful ideologies in today's world: religious fundamentalism and neoliberalism (2013: 405–5). As for fundamentalism, Cook (2014) has argued that Islamism is unique among modern world religions in its relations with political change. Does this go against the secularization thesis and the decline of religious ideology in the developed world? That depends partly on whether countries with strengthening Islamism are counted as part of the developing world. Further, as Norris and Inglehart (2004) point out, even if the number of adherents to religion is growing worldwide, this is because of population increases in the developing world, not in the secularizing developed world.

Of greater relevance to advanced societies is neoliberalism which, as we have seen, Mann thinks is partly responsible for extending a particular type of economic and political regime. In my view, in contrast, there has been a continuous disembedding or liberalization of markets, a process that was interrupted mainly by the two world wars, so that it is not necessary to identify a new and separate phase of 'neoliberalism'. It is true that the recent relative decline in economic growth throughout the global North has meant an end to the push for the extension of social rights, but I would argue that this is due to an exhaustion of forces pushing for this extension from below, combined with fiscal pressures, rather than to a new political ideology. To support this point, it can be noted that the disembedding of markets is not limited to neoliberal Anglophone countries but rather a dominant trend worldwide: Mann, as we have seen, thinks that there is a variety of forms of capitalist economies outside the Anglophones, but the direction of travel for even the most statist of these, China, is towards a more disembedded economy and greater consumerism (Gerth 2010).

Thus, on my view, there has been no fundamental break in the ongoing disembedding of markets as between a period of Keynesian and neoliberal capitalism. Mann argues that neoliberalism depends crucially on ideological power: 'Only in the Anglophone countries', he says, has neoliberalism 'possessed overwhelming power, and then *only in alliance with a conservative revival*' (2013a; p. 130, emphasis added). Yet financialization, which has played a powerful role in the recent intensification of disembedding of markets (or of Mann's neoliberalism), has also taken place beyond the Anglophone world, though it has been stronger there. Moreover, American militarism after the end of the Cold War has also largely become divorced from the promotion of a particular type of economic regime. The social bases of recent economic changes must therefore go beyond the dominance of a particular type of ideology or geopolitical push.

One place to look for this basis is in the deepening and spread of consumer culture, driven by technoscientific innovation (Schroeder 2007). There is an internal logic of this process whereby culture is increasingly mediated by new technologies, creating an ever greater role for consumption in everyday life in turn. This internal logic depends on conceptualizing technoscience as a separate source of power, which Mann wants to avoid. Yet technoscience cannot be subsumed under ideology since, as Mann admits, it is 'cold' and does not generate meaning (2012: 8, 2013: 363). Further, it is not, pace Mann, subservient to his other three powers: true, technoscience has in certain respects been driven by military needs. However, technoscience has also been harnessed to peaceful ends and promoted by the whole range of modern economic and political regimes. Put differently, the logic of technoscience is the transformation of the physical and human environment before it is put to social or ideological purposes. One consequence of this aimlessness is that scientific knowledge and technological innovation cannot but amplify market growth and enhance technocratic governance without being subject to these powers.

There is another implication of a separate source of technoscientific power that can be related specifically to one of Mann's global crises, climate change. Here, Mann looks towards a political and economic solution, even though he also mentions the possibilities of technological means of mitigation. Yet the alternative, if technoscience is a separate source of power, is to foreground the role of technology and science per se. Technoscience may separately produce new systems to transform the environment differently or to mitigate the effects of climate change, though these could also introduce new instabilities into the relationship between the physical and human environments. It can also be noted that any change to existing large technological systems – say, transport or energy – would require major technoscientific and social resources to reshape their workings.

In any event, the point is to highlight that scientific expertise provides an autonomous and exclusively legitimate means of assessing the severity of the climate problem and of the adequacy of different options: in this way, economic and political power can be held to account by experts with an autonomous power base. Mann says that new ideologies arise to meet new societal problems or crises, and perhaps environmental or 'green' ideology will rise to the challenge. But technoscience cannot become part of such ideologies because it is 'cold' or impersonal, but that does not prevent it from providing a separate basis to change thinking about climate change based on its own, non-political or ideological legitimacy. This, again, 'cold' appeal, may be weak, though its strength lies in an objectivity which serves only to increase further knowledge rather than provide support for any particular social grouping.

Technoscience is global and institutionalized on a supra-national level in scientific communication and collaborative organizations. It is mirrored on this global level by the threat from climate change, also with a global scope and brought about by the technoscientific transformation of nature. Climate change potentially affects everyday life 'from below' at a global scale, and so, apart from solutions that change the transformation of nature, only everyday patterns of consumption at a global scale can make a difference. Yet the threat of catastrophic climate change also lies on an indeterminate horizon in the future, and there is as yet little by way of response to it. While technoscience and the threat produced by it is driven by a consumer culture, it has become nearly global. This is also a rather diffuse culture, propelled by political power only insofar as politicians are forced to promise economic growth (as Mann notes, 2013: 396).

But Mann also makes a separate argument related to consumerism, which is that, recently, a new type of citizenship has emerged: consumer citizenship. Here, we must recall that Mann follows T.H. Marshall that citizen rights have progressed through three types – civil, political and social – even if he argues that these rights do not progress in a linear fashion or in stages. Whatever the sequence of these three citizenship rights, Mann argues that after the entrenchment of social citizenship rights in the postwar period in the global North, there is now also 'consumer citizenship'(2013: 408). The origins of this right are discernible in the American era of mass production in the 1920s, but, unlike the other three rights, Mann does not spell out its lineage in detail except to associate it most strongly with the Anglophones and with neoliberalism. But despite its American origins (de Grazia 2005), consumer citizenship is not particularly neoliberal or particularly American or Anglophone: in today's world, it is deeply entrenched in everyday life throughout advanced societies and beyond (Stearns 2001). Another problem of Mann's view is that consumer citizenship, even if it may have become part of belonging to a society (T. H. Marshall's criterion for citizenship rights), it is not really a 'right' at all and goes beyond being part of any particular national community.

Instead, I argue that consumerism is driven by the disembeddedness of markets, making transactions 'open-ended', and by a culture in which technology provides ever more means to extend consumerism. This makes consumer citizenship different in kind from social citizenship: it is true that social citizenship rights can be commodified (and de-commodified) such that it is not mutually exclusive with consumer citizenship and instead they may compete with each other (as when health, education and social protection are privatized). Yet civil, political and social citizenships are binary: they are either provided or ensured or not and inclusive or exclusive on this basis (potentially on a universal basis within the nation), whereas consumer citizenship rights are a matter of degree and divisible, like markets.

Thus on the global level discussed here, cultural change is either on a distant horizon (the rebounding of the transformation of the nature, which is largely a future prospect), regional (Islamism in its heartland stretching from Morocco to Indonesia) or diffuse or mixed such that little cohesion or otherwise can be expected from this (consumerism). Of course, there are many diverse routine cultural practices, important in everyday life. Yet, in relation to culture (or ideology, as Mann prefers to label it), it is worth bearing in mind Mann's theoretical stance; viz. that ideas do not effect social change unless they have some organizational instantiation and force (2012: 7–9). This constraint should also apply to culture and ideology on a global or transnational level: it must be identifiable in patterns on the ground rather than floating freely without being embedded in organizations or institutions, as is often the case with norms in 'international relations' theory (though some international relations scholars avoid this: for example, Westad's analysis of China's role in the world, see 2012: 14).

In the context of examining globalization, it is worth noting that there have been several challenges to understanding global processes primarily from the perspective of the developed countries of the North. Hobson (2012), for example, thinks that Western centrism has informed and biased the study of international relations. He argues that all the major schools of thought in international relations theory – liberal, realist, hegemonic stability theory and Marxist or world-system theory (see also Hobson 2000) – are based on a hierarchy whereby the West is assumed to have 'agency' which is denied to developing societies. This is an interesting argument to consider here, if only to reject it: the decline of American and Western military and economic power is foreseeable, so that while a residue of these hierarchies may linger, they are bound to be replaced in due course, shifting to parts of the world such as Asia that were previously denied agency. In any event, 'agency' can only be related to macro-structural patterns by locating it in institutions which affect these patterns, and it is difficult to discern such institutions in what has been said so far (though Mann's conception of American global military power would be an exception and is clearly at the apex of a hierarchy of 'agency').

Similarly, there has been a challenge from post-colonial scholars and others who questioned the Western-centric association between the West and modernity. But again, whatever associations with the West or modernity existed in the past (industrialization, the scientific revolution, democratization, imperial control), the allegedly misguided implications of making such a direct connection in a globalized world are avoided in Mann's account, as they are in mine: first, because once the several sources of social power are separated and do not overlap (or they do not provide functional perquisites for each other or for social development), there is also no single model of development. Second, there are benefits but also costs associated with the development of the sources of power: Mann mentions some of the most evident benefits of economic growth in the twentieth century, such as better nutrition and longer lives (2013: 409–410). Yet he balances these with, for example, looming environmental catastrophe, financial instability and growing inequality in parts of the globe. Misleading implications about a necessary connection between modernity and positive social development must be put into this context.

Mann's focus on the leading edge of power suggests that Western dominance – first European and then American – cannot be divorced from imperialism. But the global hierarchy associated with imperialism and, with it, Western centrism rested largely on technologically based military superiority (Headrick 2010). With hindsight, the escalation of military and of technoscientific capabilities also led to unprecedented destructiveness during the two wars and subsequently the threat of nuclear war (as well as to a destabilized natural environment (McNeill 2000)). For Mann, the enormous military power of the United States has conferred advantages on its economy in the past. Nowadays, however, as

Mann admits, American military power is a drain on its resources and its wars have generated backlash. The military shield or umbrella for America's informal empire, including economic imperialism, may have been useful in the past for the American empire (and British empire before it), opening and extending markets. Yet arguably it no longer plays this role: Mann's ideas overlap here with Ikenberry's, except that Mann thinks that American empire has been on balance negative while Ikenberry thinks it has been mainly positive. Both ideas are, in my view, trumped by the perspective that Mann himself articulates when he says that capital cares about profits rather than about war (2012: 464), which also sets him apart from those who argue that American imperialism is driven by economic aims.

Again, during the Cold War, Mann argues that American military power played a malevolent role and Ikenberry disagrees because of the non-military benefits on that side of the ledger. But it is possible to question Mann's association between imperialism and a Western – now American – leading edge of power. Mann himself seems unsure of the connection: he explains America's recent wars by reference to imperial hubris and how foreign policy has become divorced from peoples' wishes and tied instead to 'interests' in the Middle East and to exporting liberal democracy for ideological reasons. At the same time, he says of the four sources of social power that 'military power is ... the only one of the four that could, in principle, be abolished' (2013: 428). It is possible to go further to say that it no longer shapes social relations in the global North and that American military power, as all are agreed, will decline eventually. This leaves nuclear weapons which are, according Mann, among the truly global forces nowadays, though as these are rather difficult to theorize, they can be, rather optimistically perhaps, be left out here as a macro-social or global force.

Hence, it is not clear if there are any systemic properties or independent logics on the transnational or global level. Before pursuing this question further, it is worth summarizing the spatial – globalizing – dimensions of power. The global reach of the fourth source, American military power, has just been mentioned, but its most far-reaching devastating force, nuclear weapons, will hopefully not rebound on the globe. Apart from military power, the other three sources of social power have different spatial reaches: nation-states have become the global norm, but they are spatially bounded power containers. Markets (or capitalism on Mann's view) and their consumer culture have become global or near global. Technoscience finally (on my view) and how it has transformed the natural and human-made world is not just global in spatial terms but bounded by the planet and how resource exploitation may come to rebound on us. In this respect, Mann's idea of ideological power is different, with only indications of a neoliberal and fundamentalist revival.

In view of these different spatial dimensions, the three (or four) powers also have different constraints: for exploiting resources via technoscience, the constraint is the natural world, with scientists beginning to measure a 'safe operating space for humanity' (Rockstroem et al. 2009). It has been argued that there is a connection between geopolitics and the environment via the idea of 'resource wars'; yet currently this applies mainly to a single resource in a single region – oil – in relation to the North, though both this resource and the region are also part of a larger picture (other resource conflicts over water and the like can be found in the South). Apart from this exception, environmental issues are global vis-à-vis nature and so require cooperation that may depend on geopolitics, but to avoid rebounding ultimately rests on changes in the transformation of the natural world. Fortunately, geo-economic advantage is no longer directly coupled to geopolitical expansion, and this 'orthogonality' of power has benefits (avoiding wars) but also costs (the inability to enforce a transnational regime of conserving resources).

With American decline, and if by transnational or global 'order' we mean leading geopolitical powers, then the world is moving either to a tripolar one which includes a North American, a European and an East Asian pole, or a bipolar competition between two major powers, the United States and China. On current evidence, China does not promote an alternative economic order; in fact, the aim is to promote the extension of its capitalist economy (Westad 2012: 465), so it does not directly threaten the model of American capitalism. Second, China's military prowess lies mainly in its large armies, and thus mainly relates to neighbours rather than to more global ambitions. Finally, as Westad (2012: 462), points out, 'when China becomes the world's largest economy sometime in the 2030s, the United States will still be the world's leading military power, and it is set to remain so for another decade or more after that' – so this will be a highly asymmetric bipolar order. No matter where the United States winds up in a global (bi- or multipolar) hierarchy of powers, the economic order it promotes will not necessarily be challenged, but nor will the United States be able to impose a distinctive economic regime elsewhere.

Mann's sociology in his first volume contained an alternation between 'empires of domination' and 'multi-power-actor civilizations' (1986: 533–538). In his account of the twentieth century, however, he has abandoned this dialectic and in his outlook on the twenty-first century sees an unrivalled American military amidst a shift in economic power to the East. Elsewhere, in international relations theory, there is a 'stratification' of greater and lesser powers (as we saw earlier), while in sociology, the closest to 'stratification' is either cultural 'hegemony' or a systemic economic exploitation by a capitalist core of the periphery. Where Mann differs from these two views is in highlighting America's unrivalled military power. Yet unless military power shapes the other sources in the global North, and if there is no direction in the imbalance or asymmetry of core/periphery economic relations, then we are left with a non-systemic international order. The systemic and asymmetric relations which might be extracted for the purpose of a global analysis are the military gap between the North and South, which Mann occasionally touches upon but which fall outside the scope of an essay about the leading edge of power and developed societies, and the inequalities in economic power between the nations on the two sides which continue to favour the North (ditto). Global hierarchies used to be more easily recognizable during the heyday of imperialism and colonialism with centres ruling formally or informally over peripheries and during the lopsided Cold War; nowadays such relations are no longer so clear since the asymmetry between North and South has fuzzy boundaries.

Global power in the North now rests on capitalism as a 'hegemonic order' which is 'not just of the United States', Mann says; it is a 'kind of dual hegemony – of both a class fraction and an American-led geopolitical alliance'(2011: 16). Mann identified the reciprocal influences between the two, or between the transnational level and internal social development in the United States, up to the end of the Cold War. In this period, the suppression of progressive forces was internally legitimated by the need externally to champion economic 'freedom' against communism. Yet, in the post–Cold War era, and with capitalist or market relations dominant globally, it has become more difficult to see this connection. Of course, it is true that the United States may be aiming to use its overwhelming military advantage to promote its economic interests. But with military power divorced from its popular domestic base and decidedly mixed success in foreign and military strategy, it has become ever more difficult to identify tangible gains here.

The United States no longer represents a unique model of social development, and no export of such models via military or economic power – at least in the North – is on the horizon. Mann argues that the power of capitalist elites ('capital') is able to shift economic resources across national borders and thus outflanks the power of workers ('working classes') that are nationally 'caged' (to use his terminology). Yet, as Crouch (2004) points out, the 'parabola' of class politics in the West has been on a long-term descent since the 1970s. Mann similarly recognizes that the era of class politics is past – or stalled – at least in the North. In this respect, it is notable that although Mann analyses the Great Depression as a global crisis with ramifications for class relations (the New Deal, for example) and argues that in this respect there are similarities with the recession of 2008 (2013), there are – perhaps regrettably – few signs that the Great Recession has led to political upheaval or realignments, even if there has been a major impact on economic hardship and inequality.

The conclusion that Mann's theoretical apparatus therefore leaves us with is that the different sources of social power are 'orthogonal' to one another (2012: 5); that is, they are non-determinative of one another. For Mann, this orthogonality or the separation between the four sources is nowadays positive since, for example, economic and political conflicts do not reinforce each other directly. On my view, there are both positive aspects (for example, the de-coupling of economic instability from political conflict) but also negative ones (such as the lack of capacity to govern or set curbs to markets in relation to environmental transformation). The problem is that two of the social orders (markets and technoscience) simply expand without the state or other forces setting limits to them (though market instabilities and the physical constraints of nature do so), and in this sense instead of orthogonality, there is a de-coupling of markets and of technoscientific transformation from the political order (even if they impact on each other over a different timescale). Mann's outlook is that a major problem is that America's military descent may cause disorder in the world and that the promotion of a particular version of capitalism will be detrimental to economic well-being. My theory, which also hinges on powers or orders being separated from each other, foresees that the continuing differentiation between social orders leads to greater economic and environmental instability, without counter-forces.

To sum up: in terms of globalization, we agree that markets (or capitalism) are becoming global. We also agree (indeed, I borrow the idea from him) that different types of power are becoming separated and that it is positive for social development that this is so – for example, inasmuch economic conflicts do not systemically exacerbate political ones and vice versa. However, in Mann's schema, political power could potentially overcome the fallout from the financial crisis and from American neoliberalism, reining these in. In my view, only political longer termism (avoiding legitimation by promising growth), constraint on consumption, and technoscientific change could do so, all involving tensions. Much of this Mann could agree with, but our emphases are different. Finally, I have focused here on the implications of our respective theories which stem from different analyses of modernization and globalization. These are very large-scale and therefore abstract topics, and I agree with Mann when he says that 'the most one can do is to give alternative scenarios and what might happen given different conditions, and in some cases to arrange them in order of probability'(2013: 432). It can also be agreed that hope should not replace analysis (Hall 2006: 33). But, finally, there is also no reason to shirk these abstract issues: unless social science continues to pin down patterns of macro-relationships, there will be voids in which unexamined economic or cultural reductionisms or determinisms (to take just two examples) can continue to prevail. Hence, these differences can be summarized in an even more condensed and abstract way as: differentiation without de-differentiation of a globalizing modernity (Schroeder) versus dominant globalizing forces (Mann). Or, for Mann, globalizations entail domination, by neoliberalism and empire. In my view, domination takes place within each of the three orders, with tensions within and between all three. Put in a nutshell, pluralizing the processes within modernity, rather than the global, as Mann wants to do, in my view provides a more penetrating account of the limits of globalization.

Conclusion

In contrast with Mann, this chapter has argued that there is no longer a shaping of the transnational/global level by the dynamic of dominant powers (nowadays, American empire or hegemony). Thus, while agreeing with Mann that the interplay between domestic and more global patterns has played an enormous role – indeed, perhaps the most important contribution of Volumes 3 and 4 is to show how this is so – this interplay has come to an end in the global North since the Cold War. For Mann, one global force is American military empire (and again, the possibility of nuclear war is one potential global threat). Yet the transnational/global level has another systemic pattern, though it is on an uncertain future horizon, which is that environmental crises may force states and techno-scientific expert (or 'epistemic') communities and resource-intensive technological infrastructures to address the catastrophic effects of the transformation of nature. Apart from this, a shift among economic powers from West to East and from North to parts of the South can be foreseen (Maddison 2007), but this is a slow and diffuse shift. A range of political options, though within a range, persist in the North, all facing increasing fiscal burdens (Tanzi and Schuhknecht 2000) that are constrained by diminished growth rates and unstable financial markets.

What is new after the end of the Cold War is not the 'end of history' (Fukuyama 1992), but a transnational/global condition in which nature and economic resources provide (respectively) a looming hard and an ongoing softer constraint on political and social development – without dominance by great powers shaping these. Nation-states within and beyond the North face similar pressures to maintain or improve upon existing levels of consumption and social rights. Yet, pace functionalists (such as Meyer, Boli, Thomas and Ramirez 1997), and as Mann argues, there is no sign that a world society of nation-states is emerging which would entail convergence towards a single model of how to govern nation-states and the relations between them. In sum, the dynamics of the cultural/technoscientific (environmental transformation and rebound), economic financial instability in global markets and democratizing politics bounded within states – follow different logics, without any super-ordinate logic at the transnational or global level.

Whether great powers will return to shaping this otherwise drifting transnational/global level or order remains to be seen. The notion of 'globalizing modernity' is useful in providing a yardstick for how the three processes that characterize modernity face constraints and possibilities and whether we can generalize about them or where there are departures from them (such as with theocratic states or single-party states, or pockets of the economy that are resistant to disembedding, like vast agricultural or energy subsidies). 'Globalizing' is useful because these three processes are still expanding spatially and they are deepening, even if limits of this process in developed societies are discernible. Further, this yardstick can gauge the extent to which these constraints and possibilities impact on the scope for enhancing human capabilities, deepening them or universalizing them or curtailing them – though this is a separate normative question. Apart from this, the absence of a systemic or structural hierarchy of economic or geopolitical powers should not be taken to indicate greater transnational/global order or disorder: instead, the possibility of an externally unfettered improvement of social development in the nation-states of the North can open up spaces for social theorists to think anew about major concepts rather than being straitjacketed by older ones such as hegemony and capitalism, even as it forces them to address new global patterns such as environmental rebounding and market instabilities.

References

Collins, Randall. 2010. 'Geopolitical Conditions of Internationalism, Human Rights, and World Law', *Journal of Globalization Studies*, 1 (1): 29–45.
Cook, Michael. 2014. *Ancient Religions, Modern Politics: The Islamic Case in Comparative Perspective*. Princeton: Princeton University Press.
Crouch, Colin. 2004. *Post-Democracy*. Cambridge: Polity Press.

Dandeker, Christopher. 1990. *Surveillance, Power and Modernity*. Cambridge: Polity Press.

De Grazia, Victoria. 2005. *Irresistible Empire: America's Advance through 20th-century Europe*. Cambridge MA: Harvard University Press.

Fukuyama, Francis. 1992. *The End of History and the Last Man*. London: Hamish Hamilton.

Gerth, Karl. 2010. *As China Goes, So Goes the World*. New York: Hill and Wang.

Giddens, Anthony. 1985. *The Nation-State and Violence*. Cambridge: Polity Press.

Guillen, Mauro. 2001. 'Is Globalization Civilizing, Destructive or Feeble? A Critique of Five Key Debates in the Social Science Literature', *Annual Review of Sociology*, 21: 235–60.

Hall, John A. 2006. 'Political Questions', in John A. Hall and Ralph Schroeder (eds), *An Anatomy of Power: The Social Theory of Michael Mann*. Cambridge: Cambridge University Press, pp.33–55.

Headrick, Daniel. 2010. *Power over Peoples: Technology, Environments, and Western Imperialism, 1400 to the Present*. Princeton: Princeton University Press.

Hirst, Paul and Thompson, Grahame. 1996. *Globalization in Question*. Cambridge: Polity Press.

Hobson, John. 2000. *The State and International Relations*. Cambridge: Cambridge University Press.

2012. *The Eurocentric Conception of World Politics: Western International Theory, 1760–2010*. Cambridge: Cambridge University Press.

Hurrell, Andrew. 2007. *On Global Order: Power, Values, and the Constitution of International Society*. Oxford: Oxford University Press.

Keck, Margaret and Sikkink, Kathryn. 1998. *Activists Beyond Borders: Advocacy Networks in International Politics*. Ithaca: Cornell University Press.

Lundestad, Geir. 1986. 'Empire by Invitation? The United States and Western Europe, 1945–1952', *Source: Journal of Peace Research*, 23 (3): 263–77.

Maddison, Angus. 2007. *Contours of the World Economy, 1–2030 AD*. Oxford: Oxford University Press.

Mann, Michael. 1986. *The Sources of Social Power, Volume I: A History of Power from the Beginning to 1760 AD*. Cambridge: Cambridge University Press.

2011. *Power in the 21st Century: Conversations with John A. Hall*. Cambridge: Polity Press.

2012. *The Sources of Social Power, vol.3: Global Empires and Revolution, 1890–1945*. Cambridge: Cambridge University Press.

2013a. *The Sources of Social Power, vol.4: Globalizations, 1945–2011*. Cambridge: Cambridge University Press.

2013b. 'The End may be Nigh, but for Whom?', in Immanuel Wallerstein, Randall Collins, Georgi Derluguian and Craig Calhoun (eds), *Does Capitalism have a Future?*', Oxford: Oxford University Press, 71–97.

Mann, Michael and Riley, Dylan. 2007. 'Explaining macro-regional trends in global income inequalities', *Socio-Economic Review*, 5, 81–115.

Martell, Luke. 2010. *The Sociology of Globalization*. Cambridge: Polity Press.

McNeill, John R. 2000. *Something New under the Sun: An Environmental History of the Twentieth-Century World*. New York: W. W. Norton.

Meyer, John; Boli, John; Thomas, George; Ramirez, Francisco. 1997. 'World Society and the Nation-State', *American Journal of Sociology*, 103 (1): 144–81.

Milanovic, Branko. 2011. *The Haves and the Have-Nots: A Brief and Idiosyncratic Guide to Global Inequality*. New York: Basic Books.

Norris, Pippa and Inglehart, Ronald. 2004. *Sacred and Secular: Religion and Politics Worldwide*. Cambridge: Cambridge University Press.

    2009. *Cosmopolitan Communication: Cultural Diversity in a Globalized World*. Cambridge: Cambridge University Press.

Rockstroem, Johan. et al. 2009. 'A Safe Operating Space for Humanity', *Nature*, 461: 472–75.

Schroeder, Ralph. 2007. *Rethinking Science, Technology and Social Change*. Stanford: Stanford University Press.

    2013. *An Age of Limits: Social Theory for the 21st Century*. Basingstoke: Palgrave Macmillan.

Slaughter, Ann-Marie. 2004. *A New World Order*. Princeton: Princeton University Press.

Stearns, P. 2001. *Consumerism in World History: The Global Transformation of Desire*. London: Routledge.

Tanzi, Vito and Schuhknecht, Ludger. 2000. *Public Spending in the Twentieth Century: A Global Perspective*. Cambridge: Cambridge University Press.

Walby, Sylvia. 2009. *Globalization and Inequalities: Complexity and Contested Modernities*. London: Sage.

Westad, Odd Arne. 2012. *Restless Empire: China and the World since 1750*. London: The Bodley Head.

Part III

American exceptionalism

10 Ethnicity, class and the social sources of US exceptionalism

Liliana Riga

An analysis of the character and consequences of US political development is centrally threaded across Michael Mann's magisterial account of the twentieth century. In fact one of the most compelling arguments of the last two volumes of *The Sources of Social Power* is that enduring exceptionalism cannot consistently explain US political development. Mann shows that through most of the nineteenth century, and especially in the era of intense industrialism between 1872 and 1902, US labour organization was not much behind that of Britain. But then the United States began to lag compared to other capitalist democracies of the Progressive Era in terms of labour welfare and other social protections, with comparatively weak socialist or trade union organizations, an absence of labour parties and exceptional levels of violent labour repression. It was, Mann aptly argues, a labour movement without a working class. By the New Deal years, however, social welfare provisions and a lib-lab welfare regime had generally caught up to make it again unexceptional, and union membership in the 1940s was roughly comparable to that of other industrialized states – before falling behind once again in the post-Second World War conservative drift (Mann 2012 Vol. 3: ch. 3, 8; 2013 Vol. 4: ch. 3).

This account is powerful and persuasive. Mann (2013 Vol. 3: 70–74; 1993: 642–644) shows that labour's Progressive or industrial era weakness involved a number of possible factors, concluding that while a certain class organization was indeed present in the 1890s and 1900s, broad class identities eventually 're-tracked' into a combination of localism, sectionalism and factionalism. Region and sector generally outmaneuvered class and prevented lib-lab politics, while in the South race was determinative. So these distinctive racial and regime crystallizations, including an exceptional level of domestic militarism, meant that underlying sectoral, regional, ethnic/racial diversities and localized politics undermined class solidarity, making it hard to mobilize on a class basis (Mann 2013 Vol. 3: 70–74, 172; Vol. 4: ch.3).

185

Taken together, these findings imply a central tension around US exceptionalism. In its formative industrial decades, the United States was also characterized by a complex and paradoxical combination of repression and liberalism. On the one hand, it was in comparative terms a democratic and inclusive male democracy with full political citizenship; but on the other, it also had high levels of coercive repression of labour, with workers regularly and often violently outflanked by capitalists supported by the state (Mann 2013 Vol. 3: ch.3, 172–173, and *passim*).

This paradox notwithstanding, the United States is usually sociologically placed at the liberal end of a wider comparative historical typology organized around the character of the state. This typology holds that the character and actions of the state – inclusive and liberal, or exclusive and repressive – are central to theorizations or explanations of the comparative character of working classes (e.g. Katznelson and Zolberg 1986; Mann 1993: ch. 18–20). So arrayed along a liberal-repressive continuum, the United States and Britain are at the liberal end with the weakest organized working classes, followed by France and Germany, and finally Tsarist Russia – the only truly fully excluded, and therefore fully radicalized, working class. That the character of the state's policies had a determinative impact on the shape of its working class formations is now settled political corrective to those rather more structural accounts (e.g. Lipset 1997) deriving from Sombart's (1906) famous early explanation in *Why Is There No Socialism in the United States?*.

But the United States' complex combination of liberal democratic inclusion and brutal repression of worker organization arguably sits uneasily on this continuum. Therefore, my aims here are two. The first is to begin to think about how to substantively address a somewhat neglected social process in Mann's account of US political development: nation-building. And, in light of this, a second aim is to offer some additional – albeit preliminary – data on the character of the American industrial labour force. I hope that together these enable further reflection on the United States' placement on this continuum and therefore add to Mann's assessment of what was, and what was not, 'exceptional'.

Beyond race exceptionalism, which Mann rightly and consistently acknowledges as unique, I find that Progressive America's industrial labour was also distinctive among western democracies in its *ethnically* differentiated access to full political citizenship. To be clear, this is not an argument about the collective action problems occasioned by working class ethnic or racial fragmentation – although this might be worthy of reconsideration given an under-theorized causal relationship, which is that industrial labour's considerable cultural diversity itself contributed to political elite unity in these unsettled decades. In fact, the striking consensual nature of the era's nation-building or Americanization's content and practices offers compelling evidence that this might indeed have been an important sociological dynamic.

Rather, my argument rests on drawing a different set of implications from labour's cultural diversity, beginning with two empirical claims. First, these years of formative industrialism and first imperial expansion were also ones of nation-building or, to put it more precisely, of the disciplining of new and powerful cultural diversity. US nation-building – in the form of the Americanization Movement – critically shaped the character of industrial labour, something to which Mann's more class-focused account is perhaps too little attentive. Mann (2013 Vol. 3: 204–207) concludes that class conflict was suppressed and nationalism was quite weak. But I find that here the United States was actually rather unexceptional: it, too, engaged in homogenizing nation-building comparable to other industrializing states (with or without culturally saturated class conflicts). So early imperial extension, industrialism and nation-building were empirically related in the United States in these formative decades in ways slightly neglected in the last two volumes of *The Sources of Social Power*.

I explore capitalism's cultural embedding in a particularly intensive nation-building moment by turning more careful attention to how labour's character, organization and repression might also have been shaped by nation-building policies – extensive and often intrusive policies that impinged upon 'alien labour's' political, work and community lives. I anchor this around a second and related empirical reconsideration, which is the extent to which industrial era America was a fully politically inclusive male democracy given, as I show later, that most of its critical industrial labour force was non-citizen and politically excluded from the nation as much as it was excluded or repressed as labour. And indeed it was perhaps the former that enabled the latter. So a better grasp of the cultural disciplining of 'alien labour' might bring into view another dimension of the United States' militant repression of its labour force.

More specifically, I hope to extend Mann's account by offering some empirical adjustments to his data on the composition and nature of industrial labour in the decades between the 1880s and the late 1920s. My provisional data are not directed at labour's relationship to capital per se, or to intra-labour factionalism, or to state support of capitalists and industrialists, although it does imply something about each of these. But it does demonstrate, I think, some of the ways in which non-citizen, 'alien labour' sat intersectionally between the industrial era's class conflicts and its cultural, nation-building tensions.

Adding nation-building, or the cultural disciplining of 'alien industrial labour', to Mann's rather more class-weighted analysis suggests that the strength of organized labour may have been less a predictor of social citizenship, as *Sources* argues, than it was its indirect consequence. It suggests, too, that to better understand its militarist repression of labour, we might need a clearer political sociological account of the United States' comparative placement in the inclusion–exclusion typology. And it suggests that socialism's appeal as an alternative class-organizing ideology might not simply have been related to the liberal-autocratic character of the state, or indeed to its moral disciplinary qualities, but also very integrally to nation-building processes and cultural diversity. Put simply, a better understanding of the social sources of American (non)exceptionalism involves greater attention to the political mediation of class conflict with nation-building. And finally, all of this hints at a more general reflection on Mann's masterly Volumes 3 and 4 of *The Sources of Social Power*: their relative Weberian silence on the cultural shaping of the contours of twentieth century capitalism.

Americanization: foreign-born labour and the nation

I begin by contextualizing industrial labour within Americanization's nation-building efforts, before offering data on the character of industrial labour. Between 1880 and 1924, more than 30 million Catholic, Jewish and Orthodox immigrants arrived in the United States from Southern and Eastern Europe, comprising 15 to 20 per cent of the population and 80 per cent of residents in the urbanizing Northeast and Midwest. They constituted the largest proportion of labour in those industries most central to the United States' industrial takeoff.

This rapid and significant increase in ethnic diversity generated worries among Progressive reformers about social cohesion and assimilation; it challenged settled conceptions of 'Americanness', which had barely adjusted to the integration of earlier immigrants from northern and western Europe; it threw open legislative and Census debates around how a multiracial democracy might be defined and grasped; it prompted shifts in racialized boundaries of whiteness; and it caused 'the nation' to question whether it now did, in fact, have 'classes'. This latter anxiety was especially pronounced and focused on the urban immigrant working classes because emergent social inequalities were virtually indistinguishable from visible and socially prominent cultural distinctions, beyond those historically settled ones between whites and free blacks.

This dimension of Progressivism gets some attention in Volume 3, but Mann's (2013 Vol. 3: 65–68) focus is on two strands of the era's social

reform: its modernizing control of capital and industry and its redistributive policies. He argues that labour issues were marginal to Progressive
programs and that ultimately Progressives failed to redistribute power,
something that in turn allowed the cause of labour to lag as capitalists
were largely unfettered by the state (Mann: 2013 Vol. 3: 69). Despite
moves towards egalitarian and progressive taxation (such as the 'confis-
catory tax' on excessive incomes to curtail wealth's economic and political
power [Piketty 2014: 505–508]), the state's characteristic reliance on
corporate benevolence and 'private welfare capitalism', and its failure to
enact a range of social provisions, shaped industrial America into a non–
risk-sharing society.

And yet Progressive reformers were middle-class urbanites and agrar-
ians in a moment marked by comparatively less rancorous labour relations and more prosperity than the Mugwumpery and Populism that had
preceded it and the post-war reactionary nativism and labour repression
that followed (cf. Hofstadter 1955: ch. 4; Link 1959; McGerr 2003).
Ideological rhetoric aside, Progressives were as much culturalists as they
were 'redistributionists'. Indeed, Progressivism collapsed in the 1920s
because intellectuals defected from the cultural project; their central aim
had been to de-radicalize the increasingly diverse social forces from below
by disciplining them culturally, by re-shaping them in their own class
image (cf. Crocker 1992; King 2000; Gerstle 2001; McGerr 2003). So,
between the 1890s and the late 1920s, they homogenized. They imposed
a nation-building, cultural discipline on an ethnically diverse labour
force.

This involved one of the largest (and most under-theorized) social and
political mobilizations in US history: the Americanization Movement of
the early nineteenth century, which marked the effective cultural transformation of its industrial working class from 'alien' and racialized non-
citizen labour into 'white ethnic' citizens. The Americanization
Movement was a large-scale grass roots social mobilization for assimilation, a political project involving more than 80,000 federal, state, local
and private agencies, including a fully mobilized civil society across more
than 30 states, 2,300 cities, 1,200 Chambers of Commerce, more than
800 industrial or trade organizations, 50 national religious organizations,
and countless patriotic groupings, churches, shop floors, schools, neighbourhoods, libraries, YMCAs and even funeral parlours.[1] 'The scale of

---

[1] I draw here variously on materials from the National Archives and Records
Administration (NARA), College Park, MD, and Washington, DC Records of the
Immigration and Naturalization Service; Records of the Committee on Public
Information; Records of the Council of National Defense/Records of the Educational
Propaganda Department; General Records of the Department of Labor; Records of the

the movement is difficult to exaggerate', McClymer (1978: 23) wrote, and as the *Chicago Tribune* dryly noted on 14 April 1919: 'only the most agile and determined immigrant, possessed of overmastering devotion to the land of his birth can hope to escape Americanization by at least one of the many processes now being prepared for his special benefit' (quoted in McClymer 1978: 23).

Only one dimension of this complex and sprawling effort is relevant here: political elite anxieties around the assimilation and 'naturalization of alien labour'. Indeed, an important dimension of Americanization was almost entirely coextensive with federal and state governments' relationships to 'alien labour'. Americanizers in the Bureaus of Education, Labor, Immigration, the Census and that of Naturalization worked to Americanize 'alien labour' through the Justice Department and agencies and organizations at every level of state and municipal government, and through all manner of civic association. State-level bureaus developed the most extensive Americanization efforts, and Americanization filled the interstices of Progressive politics' reach across more than 16,000 cities, counties and localities (cf. Gould 2001; Zeidel 2004; Flanagan 2006). In order to reach 'alien labour', they systematically targeted national and local Chambers of Commerce and associations of manufacturers and industries as well as labour unions. These included, for example, the United Brotherhood of Carpenters and Joiners, the National Committee for Organizing Iron and Steel Workers, Bethlehem Steel's workers, the Pennsylvania Railroad, the American Federation of Labor (AFL) and the United Mine Workers. In other words, Americanization targeted *both* capital *and* labour.

In this effort, the Bureau of Naturalization crucially operated as an *institutional section of the Bureau of Labor*. Because citizenship fell under the control of the Department of Labor, in practice, this bureaucratically rendered the Americanization problem and the labour problem largely indistinguishable. So the Bureau of Labor Statistics' new 'labour statistics movement', the Congressional Immigration Commission's forty-two-volume report on 'Immigrants in Industries', countless legislative hearings and extensive efforts by the Naturalization and Census Bureaus all demonstrated the critical importance given to grasping or making socially legible 'alien labour' (see especially, Carter et al. 1991; Cohen 1999; Ngai 1999, 2004; Perlmann 2001; O'Connor 2001: ch. 1; Zeidel 2004). Between 1874 and the First World War, more than 130 published reports

Office of Education; Records of the US Commission on Industrial Relations; the University of Chicago Archives and Library Robert Ezra Park, William I. Thomas, Sophonisba P. Breckinridge and Americanization Collections.

were undertaken by twenty-nine state labour bureaus and local authorities to gather detailed data on industrial and foreign-born labour, union organizing, citizenship applications and strike rates, working conditions, living standards, family demography, household economies, wages and earnings and so on (cf. Carter et al. 1991). In fact, it was not at the federal level, but at the state level that Progressivism's labour regulations and legislation were most extensive: there were more than 135 distinct state-level labour laws enacted before the 1930s and the New Deal (Fishback et al. 2008).

So, with the exception of the federally regulated railroads and health and unemployment insurance, state legislatures actually had great regulatory and legislative control over labour markets because key industries were highly localized. The coal and copper mining industries, for example, were limited to a few states, so despite some variation, both labour regulation and ethnic discrimination were state and industry specific (see, for instance, Hannon 1982; Ziegler-McPherson 2010). This is important for understanding geographic and industry variations in labour repression, union density and organization and anti-strike violence, and, because of their sectoral distribution, for understanding the ways in which foreign-born (non-citizen) labour and black labour were converging around similar levels of political power at the municipal and state levels.

Therefore, the concerns of state-level agencies, capitalist and industrial elites on the one hand, and those of Progressive Americanizers on the other, were equally focused on foreign-born 'alien labour'. Industrial elites viewed their economic interests as aligning with those of the nation-builders: Americanization reduced accidents and made factory floors run smoothly in a single language, it reduced tensions among workers of different nationalities in a factory and it eroded internal *padrone* systems of ethnic policing. Similarly, social and industrial relief policies like adult education, labour conditions regulation, environmental protections and conflict resolution were used as key instruments in the cultural assimilation of foreign-born labour, and they were therefore central to Americanization efforts (cf. Flanagan 2006; Ziegler-McPherson 2010).[2] All of this was intended to create a 'more homogenous body of labour'.[3]

As a result, key industrial sectors became sites of both compassionate and coercive assimilatory nation-building. And Americanization became

---

[2] 'Washington America First Campaign to Increase School Attendance of non-English Speaking Immigrants: How Chambers of Commerce Can Cooperate', Circular 9, n.d., Department of Interior, Bureau of Education, Division of Immigrant Education, NARA.
[3] Ibid.

part of working-class life in neighbourhoods, communities, shop floors and factories. For example, the Ford Motor Company's famous 'Sociological Department' built classrooms for the Americanization of more than 1,700 workers (Barrett 1992); the cloth and cotton producing Sicher Company worked with the New York Board of Education in 1913 to allow employees – mostly women because the 'alien man is best reached through the alien woman' – to attend English and civics classes on company time and with a promise of increased wages on successful course completion (McClymer 1978: 40); the Pennsylvania Railroad's 33,000 foreign-born workers were offered preferments in employment and promotion in 1919 for taking out naturalization papers; a Detroit nut and bolt company did not lay off any foreign-born worker who attended civics night school in pursuit of naturalization papers; twenty-two small industries in Cleveland offered Americanization and naturalization courses on company time; Westinghouse Electric Company organized its own committees of foreign-born labour into citizenship classes; and the Akron Goodrich Tire and Rubber Company employed twenty-seven teachers in their own Americanization school, on the realization that 'the very best place to carry our Americanization work is in the factory' (Hill 1919: 622–638; cf. also Ziegler-McPherson 2010).[4]

In its most coercive dimensions, of course, this cultural disciplining moved slightly away from the nativist-inspired argument that aligned Catholicism with radicalism, towards one in which Jewish, Italian, Polish and Russian workers were (often wrongly) associated with anarchism, socialism and Bolshevism. So Americanization's homogenizing policies urgently targeted male 'alien labour' illiteracy as a national security problem: 18 per cent of the army in 1917 was foreign born, 3 million un-naturalized foreign-born males in the wartime labour force were of military age, and 500,000 non-citizen draft-age males could not speak enough English to understand military orders (Hill 1919: 612). The Justice Department similarly defined assimilation negatively and politically, as a way of preventing espionage and sabotage, which were perceived to derive from foreign labour's 'hyphenated loyalties'.

Critically, then, the deportation of 'alien radicals' required the cooperation of the Department of Labor. 'Alien labour' was deported if workers lost their jobs or became a 'public charge'; and federal intervention in the labour movement was invoked in cases of 'criminality', 'anarchism', political dissidence or so-called wartime misconduct. And labour deportations or forced removals of striking workers by vigilantes, employers and

---

[4] 'Americanization' (newsletter), No. 3, Vol. 2, Washington DC, 1 November 1919, pp. 13, 15, Department of Interior, Bureau of Education, Americanization Division.

local governments affected hundreds of non-citizen workers (see extensive discussion in Kanstroom 2007: ch. 4). Indeed, as John Higham (1955: 220) wrote, 'in deportations the nation grasped its absolute weapon against the foreign born radical'.

In this 'deportations delirium' of the era, citizenship petitions were also regularly denied at naturalization proceedings on evidence that the petitioner-as-worker had participated in strikes (McClymer 1978: 28–29, 35–36). This important practice needs much more detailed research than I can offer here, particularly in terms of whether individuals who were refused papers were then deported, and certainly the actual number of deportations was lower in the pre-1924 period than after passage of the Quota Laws when the term 'illegal aliens' formally entered immigration practices (Ngai 2004: 58–60, 274).[5] But striking workers' citizenship applications were indeed at risk, as Americanization bureaucratically entwined with the need to exclude radicalized labour. This made workers cautious of joining unions, and it made a number of unions equally wary of organizing foreign labour. As importantly, the Department of Labor's Naturalization Service responded with a record number of denials of petitions for naturalization and citizenship, as I show herein. Anarchism and socialism, naturalization petitions and industrial challenges were conflated, with the result that political inclusion or citizenship was in complex ways contingent on labour (in)activism. Indeed, it was in this context that the term 'social control' first emerged (Kanstroom 2007: 131).

This political and legal re-inscription of the perceived association of (socialist or class-based) Leftism with cultural difference – that is, the withholding of political inclusion or citizenship because of labour activism – was followed by more permanent legislation: a culturally disciplining social closure, legislatively achieved in the Quota Acts of the 1920s. Adding to the 1917 literacy test criteria, the Quota Board used national origins to restrict immigration from Southern and Eastern Europe based on assessments of the assimilability of foreign-born white labour. The Congressional Dillingham Commission had recommended the restriction of unskilled labour because of worries of the 'racial displacement' of natives by foreign-born labour, but in practice the equivalence of cultural difference with socialism made citizenship eligibility central to this effort.

---

[5] Between 1901–1910, 119,769 'alien radicals' were deported; the figure rose to 206,021 between 1911–1920, and 281,464 in the subsequent decade. Figures in Ngai 2004: 274.

Liberalism and repression, citizenship and 'alien labour'

The state's relationship to foreign-born 'alien labour' was at the core of the ways in which nation-building intersected with working class formation. In light of this, I hope to anchor this Americanization data with some additional, though provisional, data to illustrate how we might reconsider an important theme in Mann's Volume 3: an account of the United States as a male democracy (exclusive of African Americans and women), characterized by political citizenship and full political inclusion, and yet also distinguished by exceptionally high levels of coercive repression of labour.

The depth of labour exclusion is in itself rather important. So we might elaborate its character a bit further than Mann does in Volume 3, reaching back in fact to his fantastic Chapter 18 in Volume 2, on the comparative analysis of working class movements between 1880 and 1914. I begin by noting that the decades after 1877 in the United States were the most violent anti-labour among all western democracies, with at least 1,129 strike-related deaths between the 100 killed in 1877 and the 1947 Taft-Hartley Act (Lipold and Isaac 2009: 189). Here, Mann's (1993: 635) figure of c.500–800 for workers killed in labour disputes between 1872 and 1914 is at the rather low end, but, nevertheless, between 1899 and 1905 there were at least 1,000 strikes per year with more than 375,000 strikers and 500 deaths between 1894 and 1924.

These figures are not too far off the roughly 150 Lena goldfield workers killed in 1912 Tsarist Russia – usually placed at the other end of the liberal-autocratic spectrum. US strike fatalities were double those of France, and only one British worker was killed after 1911, but more than 5,000 were killed in Russia in these years. So this takes us directly to this repression–liberalism paradox that characterized the US working class. Mann (1993: 644) rightly observes that 'what is strikingly exceptional or extreme about the United States in this period was its level of industrial violence and paramilitary repression'. And yet the brutality of labour repression is seen as 'exceptional', in part because it occurred in what is otherwise characterized as a politically inclusive party democracy:

[i]t seems that employers and regime responded to industrial action in fundamentally different ways. But their level of domestic militarism did not correlate with their position on the representative state crystallization: Russia was the most authoritarian monarchy, but the United States was the most advanced party democracy. (Mann 1993: 635)

Now this may be accurate, and there may be no need to alter settled political sociology. But the underlying data is undeniably stark: US repression of organized labour actually lay between that of post-Bismarck

Germany and Tsarist Russia – indeed far closer to that of the latter and nowhere near that of liberal Britain. A sociological account of this level of violent domestic militarism – and all manner of associated legislative, police, paramilitary and judicial repression – requires, I think, a substantive social explanation that treats the United States' coercive labour exclusion as *fundamentally integral* to its working class formation, not as exceptional to it.

So I would like to try to re-contextualize some of this data in a way that brings a slightly different narrative framework into view. Variations in the institutionalization of class struggles were significantly shaped by variations in state crystallizations, as Mann's work brilliantly demonstrates. But the vast majority of labour in key US industrial sectors (mining, metalworking and transport) was actually increasingly being excluded from even minimal male democracy. The most meaningful daily citizenship privileges had been historically dependent on local state-level inclusions from the beginning of the Republic to the Progressive Era: individual states had had relatively wide latitude in terms of granting the franchise to resident 'aliens', for instance (Smith 1988: 237–238; Raskin 1993). State-level governments had used citizenship privileges like the franchise as a way to attract immigrant settlement (even in the South in the immediate post–Civil War period), so there were few citizenship requirements for the franchise for white males over age 21 in 22 states through most of the nineteenth century.

But between the 1890s and 1927 – or through the course of the Progressive Era – state-level recognition of 'alien' or non-citizen suffrage was removed from resident aliens in every state, leaving them without political representation, and, as struggling workers, effectively without what Judith Shklar (1991) famously termed 'citizenship as standing'.[6] Exclusions were first made contingent on Americanization and naturalization, that is, 'declarant aliens' could vote locally on proof of intention to 'naturalize' or take out first papers; political inclusion shifted from 'inhabitants' and 'residents' to 'would be citizens'. But with growing immigration that brought greater 'foreignness' from Southern and Eastern Europe, these local- and state-level electoral practices were everywhere in retreat. The Progressive Era's Americanization's nation-building had fully undone any limited 'alien labour' suffrage.[7]

---

[6] Shklar's (1991) 'citizenship as standing' broadly includes not only voting but also the opportunity to earn (the good life, union organizing, etc.) and a public recognition of respect and social belonging, all as distinctively American marks of US citizenship.

[7] There remained a certain bifurcated citizenship, then: 'alien labour' was taxed and drafted as citizens, but had no effective voice in the political process.

This nation-building context, I think, crucially contributed to shaping the social valorization of labour vis-à-vis capital. And while the data I can offer here are by no means comprehensive, it might nevertheless build on Mann's work and begin to open a way to a more inclusive social explanation of US labour repression. If the decades of greatest industrial unrest and violent labour repression were also the decades of greatest nation-building and cultural anxiety, then, for purposes of illustration, we might consider some 'demand side' data to complement Mann's more 'supply side' data and allow an otherwise obscured dimension of this liberal-repressive contradiction to come into view. Drawing on data from mid-level federal bureaucracies such as that of Naturalization and Immigration services within the Bureau of Labor, Congressional studies on state and regional industrial labour conditions and local studies contained in state-level labour bureau surveys, where most anti-labour violence was sanctioned, I offer the following cumulative data points, roughly approximating the formative decades of the industrial labour movement.

First, while native-born labour was largely rural, foreign-born (and second-generation) labour comprised nearly 85 per cent of the urban working classes in the Northeast and Midwest – particularly consequential industrial regions and the intellectual homes of Progressivism. Of the total first-generation foreign-born population in the United States, 61.3 per cent worked in four key sectors of the new industrial economy (manufacturing, mining, construction and transportation/railroads) as compared to 39.9 per cent of the native-born working population (Carter et al., 2006: 621–622, Table As874–937). This was not simply immigrant or ethnic labour; it was *foreign-born* labour, and its dominance in key industries gave it a disproportionate relevance in the triadic state-capital-labour relationship. It also placed the cultural disciplining of the foreign born at the centre of the social control of the heavy war industries – and this made the United States rather exceptional vis-à-vis other states, where labour in comparable key industries was actually more ethnically homogenous, even in multiethnic Tsarist Russia depending on region.

Beyond the ethnic diversity of US industrialism in these formative decades, a second and more layered data point is offered in Table 10.1. If we also add Census statistics on the working classes' *naturalization rates* and *citizenship status*, which are often oddly neglected in accounts of labour and immigration in this period, in 1890, one-third of all foreign-born males over age 21 were *'un-naturalized'*, *non-citizens* (defined as having no papers or only first papers),[8] and no citizenship status was

---

[8] First papers refer to the 'declaration of intention' to become a citizen. Usually taken up two years after arrival, they could be held for years.

Table 10.1 *Foreign-born males and citizenship*

	Foreign-born males over 21	Naturalized citizens	Non-citizens (no papers or only first papers)	Citizenship status unknown
1890	4,348,459	59% (2,545,753)	33% (1,425,513)	9% (377,193)
1900	5,010,286	57% (2,848,807)	28% (1,426,490)	15% (734,989)
1910	6,780,214	49% (3,038,303)	44% (2,961,947)	12% (779,964)
1920	7,063,594	44% (3,320,226)	48% (3,379,292)	5% (364,076)
1930	7,218,977	59% (4,247,704)	38% (2,740,170)	3% (231,103)

Source: Data extracted from Carter et al., *Historical Statistics of the United States* Vol.1, Part A Population, Table Ad280–318, p. 1–598.

known for a further 9 per cent. This increased to 48 per cent in 1920: nearly one-half of the white US male labour force over age 21 was 'alien', citizenship-less labour, with a further 5 per cent of unknown status (Carter et al., 2006: 598, table Ad280–318). At the crucial state level, where most direct labour repression was sanctioned and practiced, and where the franchise and citizenship privileges were everywhere contracting even for 'declarant resident aliens' and depending on the state, between one-fourth and one-half of all eligible labour was non-citizen. This challenges something of the idea that this was a working class characterized by liberal political inclusion or full male democracy or even by 'citizenship as standing'.

Interestingly, *trends* on naturalization data or citizenship rates show a steady increase from 1907 (when data were first systematically collected) to a peak in 1919, followed by a brief period of stabilization and then slow decline from the end of the War through the 1924 Immigration Act. Then the numbers rise again during the New Deal and Second World War years. The peak years of successful naturalization were 1918 and 1919, when, respectively, 42 per cent and 59 per cent of 'naturalized aliens' were made citizens under military provisions (all figures, Carter et al., 2006: 641, table Ad1030–1037). The majority of petitions for naturalization in 1919 – only available to free white persons – came largely from Illinois, Massachusetts, New Jersey, Michigan, Ohio and Pennsylvania. Not surprisingly, these were also some of the states with the most intensive and coercive Americanization efforts because of the ways in which industrialism and assimilation efforts so closely entwined.

Equally suggestive is the trend in the proportion of petitions for citizenship *denied*: in 1910, 20 per cent of 'alien' naturalization petitions were denied; this decreased to 14 per cent in 1916, but during a crucial moment of military mobilization in 1918–1919, and in line with military naturalizations, only 0.05 to 0.08 per cent of petitions for citizenship were rejected. Non-citizens were eligible for military service, of course, something that helped their subsequent petitions for citizenship.

This important military carve-out in a context of exclusion from other democratic processes suggests, of course, that wartime exigencies outran other concerns. So, as the war ended, and following the large coal, steel and railway strikes, in 1922–1923, rejection rates returned to pre-war levels (17 per cent). By then, however, the practice of denying papers to striking 'aliens' had been generally institutionalized and routine – and understood as such by political elites, industrialists, unions and workers alike. Once foreign-labour migration was closed to new immigrants with the Quota Acts, and as the cultural coercion of the Americanization movement took hold and steadied nation-building anxieties, rejection rates again returned to their 0.05 per cent historic lows between 1927 and 1930 (all figures, Carter et al., 2006: 641, table Ad1030–1037).

I make only two brief observations. First, in addition to concerns about low rates of naturalization petitions among the eligible male (working) population, a very worrisome category for officials between 1900 and 1910 was that of 'no known citizenship status', because this meant that 12 to 15 per cent of the foreign-born population remained 'illegible' or 'unknowable' and therefore potentially threatening. And second, legislators and mid-level federal bureaucrats also worried about trends: while the proportion of new-immigrant foreign-labour increased until its closure in 1924, the proportion of those seeking citizenship or taking out first papers steadily decreased relative to numbers. Indeed, as both premise and conclusion, the Dillingham Commission's report asserted with alarm and urgency that among the crucial iron and steel manufacturing industries in 1911, 'the tendency toward acquiring citizenship among the foreign-born male employees ... was very small, only 32 per cent being naturalized and 11.4 per cent having taken out first papers' (Dillingham et al. 1911: part 23, vol. 2 p. 18).

Table 10.2 disaggregates the data further, focusing more precisely on those sectors most crucial to the industrial moment. These are where the most violent labour repression occurred. Most immediately, foreign-born labour was disproportionately sectorally and geographically concentrated in industrial manufacturing. This affected wages and inequalities (Restifo et al., 2013), but it also suggests how we might begin to re-contextualize anti-labour hostility and repressive labour practices. Industrialism

Table 10.2 *Non-citizen labour in key industries*[a]

	Percentage of foreign born in sampling of industry (second generation)	Percentage of non-citizens or only first papers of eligible males older than twenty-one at the time of immigration and in the United States more than five years in sampling of industry	Percentage of foreign born who were affiliated with trade union based on sampling of industry (% of native born)
Iron and steel	57.7% (13.4%)	56.6%	1.5% (3.6%)
Clothing/textile manufacturing	59% (25%)	69.9%	n.a. n.a.
Wool/worsted manufacture	61.9% (24.4%)	63.9%	4.1% (21.9%)
Silk goods (textile)	34.3% (44.9%)	38.7%	3.1% (18.2%)
Cotton goods	68.7% (21.8%)	70.2%	n.a. (11.3%)
Clothing manufacturers	72.2% (22.4%)	70.1%	18.4% (3.6%)
Boots/shoes	27.3% (25.6%)	66.9%	37.1% (35.3%)
Extractive/ mining:[b]			
Bituminious (soft) coal	61.9% (9.5%)	73.3%	31.8% (55.8%)
Anthracite (hard) coal	59.4% (38.7%)	71.6%	77.5% (25.8%)
Oil refining	67.7% (21.5%)	63.7%	1.2% (5.8%)
Copper mining/smelting	57% (12%)	59.5%	0% 0%
Iron ore mining	52.6% (4.3%)	62.1%	1.2% (6.9%)
Construction/ railroads[c]	50% (21%)	n.a.	n.a.
Diversified industries: representative communities[d]			
Community A	63% (14%)	64.4%	8.3% (13.7%)
Community B	59% (19%)	50.5%	23.2% (29.3%)
Community C	85% (4%)	68.2%	2.8% (3.1%)

Table 10.2 (*cont.*)

	Percentage of for-eign born in sam-pling of industry (second generation)	Percentage of non-citi-zens or only first papers of eligible males older than twenty-one at the time of immigration and in the United States more than five years in sampling of industry	Percentage of foreign born who were affiliated with trade union based on sam-pling of industry (% of native born)
Community D	86% (7%)	79.9%	7% (14.1%)
Community E	73% (10%)	57%	27.1% (15.7%)
Community F	88% (5%)	62.1%	3.8% (13.3%)

[a] Each column is based on slightly different industry populations, so baseline numbers for percentages vary.
[b] Excludes agriculture and fishing.
[c] Includes tool manufacture; electric railway transport, supplies and manufacture; locomotive building; steam railway transport; zinc smelting/manufacture; foundry and machine shop products manufacture; other related industries.
[d] Case studies of households in representative industrial communities.Source: Data extracted Dillingham, et al. *United States Immigration Commission (1907–1910)* (1911) (Washington, DC: GPO), Vol. 24 'Immigrants in Industries', Part 23: Summary Report on Immigrants in Manufacturing and Mining; Vol.18 "Immigrants in Industries": Part 21, pp. 95, 117, 156, 198, 260, 292, 331, 360, 395, 420, 480, Diversified Industries; Vol. 16 'Immigrants in Industries', Part 17, pp. 11, 41–42, 70 (Copper mining/smelting), Part 18, pp. 205, 209, 248, 277, 279 (Iron Ore Mining), Part 19, pp. 587, 620, 639, 641, 699 (Anthracite coal mining), Part 20, pp. 745, 766, 835, 853, 863 (Oil refining); Vol. 9, Immigrants in Industries, Part 2 Iron and steel manufacturing; Vol. 6 'Immigrants in Industries', Part 1 (bituminious coal mining).

generally and the war industries in particular were highly dependent on first-generation immigrant or foreign-born labour, comprising nearly 62 per cent of workers over age 21 in coal mining; 50 per cent of those over age 21 in railroad and construction industries; between 52 per cent and nearly 68 per cent in hard coal, oil refining, iron ore and copper mining; and nearly 58 per cent of those over age 21 in iron and steel.

In key industrial sectors, even higher proportions were *non-citizen 'alien labour'*: nearly 57 per cent of the iron and steel industry; 60 to 73 per cent of the extractive sector (soft and hard coal, oil, copper iron ore); and, depending on region and location, on average 64 per cent of transport and railroad labour was non-citizen. Drawn from Dillingham et al. (1911), these figures correspond roughly to the 1907–11 years, but both foreign-born and non-citizen labour proportions increased from these levels in the 1914–19 period – something that requires more systematic data than I can offer here.

State- and federal-level labour repression had remarkably similar patterns of geographical or sectoral concentration. We know that 46.5 per cent of US strike fatalities occurred in the extractive sector (with coal mining accounting for one-third of these) and in the transport and rail-road sector. Indeed, more than 80 per cent of strike fatalities were in these two industrial sectors, while only 1.4 per cent of strike deaths occurred in construction or the building trades (Lipold and Isaac 2009: 189, 196–199). Because of its sectoral distribution, industrial violence also had geographical patterns: it was worse in the mining and industrial states (e.g. Pennsylvania, Colorado, West Virginia, Illinois, Ohio, New York) and in the south, where 'southern exceptionalism' is sometimes noted given the historically distinctive ways in which southern political elites aligned with capitalists, but also, and as importantly, given the lesser valorization of black labour (Lipold and Isaac 2009: 201).

Of course, labour unrest in the extractive and transport sectors posed a greater threat given these sectors' centrality to industrialism and its war efforts, making its repression rather more predictable, and mining usually tends to generate unions and more cohesive working class communities, as well as greater repression. And I stress this needs much more granular empirical data at the intersection of 'alien suffrage' and ('alien') labour repression. But it is the case that those industries that had the highest proportion of foreign-born labour also had among the highest levels of local and state-level repression. And at moments and locations of peak labour repression, a numerically substantial and politically consequential proportion of the US working class was increasingly restricted in its access to political citizenship.

Moreover, and again based on non-exhaustive data (Table 10.2), citizenship status across industries also had an intimate and complex, though non-linear, relationship to trade union density. Sectoral, regional and ethnic compositional variations mattered of course; and historically the most organized were native-born workers. The attractiveness and openness of trade unions for foreign-born 'alien labour' was variable and affected by local conditions of employment, the relative proportions of ethnicities employed in different localities, and workers' disruptive capacities, including the availability of (usually foreign-born) replacement workers. In the Midwest, Southwest and West, organized labour controlled the labour supply and unionization among foreign born were generally higher, but

Pennsylvania had the largest proportion of new foreign labour (Italian, Lithuanian, Russian) in unionized localities, and in the 1900–02 coal strikes, its localized, extractive-industry concentration raised worker replacement costs and therefore boosted union density (Dillingham et al. 1911: vol. 6: 100–104; Kimeldorf 2013).

An additional dynamic was also in play. Trade union membership of non-citizen labour tended to increase initially with greater length of residency across industries, but then it stabilized: in the coal industry of Pennsylvania, for instance, trade union membership was 20.6 per cent for those in the United States less than five years and 38.3 per cent for those resident between five and nine years, but it then remained steady at 38.7 per cent for those resident more than ten years (Dillingham et al. 1911: vol. 6: 104). Similarly, assimilation, if measured strictly by rates, was higher in the Southwest, where their numbers were smaller and union-ization rates were high: 68.1 per cent of foreign-born labour in the Southwest had papers, in the Midwest as a whole it was 39.6 per cent, but only 12.3 per cent in Pennsylvania and 10.8 per cent for the minority of foreign-born in the South. In the form of full citizenship, then, Americanization did not necessarily lead to greater unionization, though the relationship between 'alien labour' and unionization rates is worthy of greater consideration.

Moreover, the strength or presence of national unions did not seem to make a difference in terms of the extensiveness of liberal protective labour legislation: between roughly 1899 and 1919, the ten states with the great-est amount of labour regulation and state labour spending per worker were largely in the West (North Dakota, Idaho, South Dakota, Nevada, Montana, New Mexico, Arizona, West Virginia, Minnesota, Colorado), while the bottom ten were in the South and parts of the Mid-Atlantic (South Carolina, Mississippi, Florida, Georgia, Alabama, Louisiana, Virginia, North Carolina, Texas, New York) (Fishback et al. 2008). These patterns are suggestive not only of the important role of larger manufacturing employers and their ability to influence state legislatures, but also of the possible role played by the relative size and homogeneity or heterogeneity of labour's composition. Taken with the data above, there was greater protective legislation where labour was more rural and homo-genous with political citizenship and less where it was largely black or foreign-born, urban non-citizen. My suggestion is simply that these cul-tural contexts contributed to both the social (de)valorization of labour and to the shaping of capital-labour-state relationships.

This is not evidence of ethnic diversity fractionalizing or sectionalizing what would otherwise be a more fully articulated working class, a process that was, as Mann rightly notes, only part of the story. But this kind of data is significant in terms of what it implies about the tension between democracy and repression – and to where we might comparatively place the United States. If between one-half and two-thirds of its labour force in key industries at a moment of peak labour repression were non-naturalized 'aliens' whose earlier state-level citizenship rights were being curtailed, then this was not really a labour force characterized by full male democracy or liberalism in the most meaningful sense. Foreign-born, non-citizen labour – much like black labour – found itself at the intersection of the class conflicts generated by industrialization and the cultural conflicts generated by nation-building processes. And this meant that *political exclusion* materially and consequentially characterized a critical segment of the US working class.

What's exceptional and what's not?

I offer a few tentative reflections to complement Mann's analysis. Most generally, my preliminary findings suggest that the underlying cultural de-valorization of labour in this nation-building moment may need a more prominent role in our accounts of both labour formation and of its violent repression in the decades of greatest industrialism. These provisional data also carry more specific implications. First, it is perhaps *easier to repress* 'alien' non-citizen labour than citizen workers, or those democratically included workers armed with the vote and political voice. This is most especially true at state and local levels given 'alien labours' even more limited ability to compete with the legislative power of industrialists and organized capitalism in state legislatures and local politics. But it was precisely in these political locations where (i) anti-labour violence, (ii) protective labour laws and (iii) contractions of historical citizenship practices originated. These relationships clearly need more granular empirical research.

Their combined effect reinforced 'alien labour' exclusion, and it arguably had a conservative role on labour organizing, not least because workers knew that they risked citizenship. Indeed, the lessons workers generally draw from capital's alignment with political, police and judicial power and from intimidation and violence can hinder willingness to organize (Goldstein 2010: 276). Of course this fear may have been mitigated in certain contexts: in the Southwest, where all labour was in collective bargaining arrangements, or in some of the extractive industries (agriculture, fishing, mining), where geographic isolation raised worker replacement costs, or where non-citizen labour was locally a dominant majority with hard-to-replace skills (cf. Kimeldorf 2013). But the climate of serious repression and fear of permanent political exclusion no doubt had its effects. So we cannot substantively explain US working class formation in these decades and the capital-state-labour relationship without taking a fuller measure of its cultural shaping and of the ways in which an enormous segment of its labour force experienced nation-building practices.

In this regard, sometimes Mann (2013 Vol. 3: 278–279, 282) notes that 'the strengthening of nation eases class conflict, part of the dialectic between class and nation'. But I think that nation-building might perhaps need to be more causally central to a historical sociological account of the formation of the US industrial working class in the decades *before* the New Deal. In the American case, Mann argues that class struggle enabled the extension of nation, that nation was rendered more cohesive because of class struggle. And yet some of the data offered here on 'alien labour' suggests that actually the causal relationship in this period may have run the other way: the prior expansion of nation is what subsequently allowed labour in.

The Progressive era's nation-building and cultural disciplining of 'alien labour' culminated in a legislative social closure around foreign-born labour with the Quota Acts and the 1924 Immigration Act. Immigration legislation was quintessential nation-building (Ngai 1999; Zolberg 2006). But it was also critical labour policy: by removing urban manufacturing competition from 'native labour' for forty years, in effect by decreasing unskilled foreign labour from a high of 13 per cent to 15 per cent in 1920 to 5 per cent by 1965, the Quota Acts decisively shaped the skills composition of the labour force and the contours of organized labour for decades. This social closure around white foreign labour created a temporary repose in cultural and nation-building anxieties – perhaps a permissive condition for both subsequent New Deal inclusion *and* for allowing attention to class inequalities. Indeed, Mann (2013 Vol. 3: 257–259) notes that by the mid 1930s, striking workers had national sympathies, as nation and class solidified and ethnicity weakened with more workers born in the United States.

So if the Progressive Era created the white ethnic out of 'alien labour' for inclusion in nationhood, the New Deal embedded them as recipients of its welfare and housing policies, with race not an exception to social inclusion and citizenship but its permissive condition. Fox (2012) nicely shows how white immigrants, African Americans and Mexicans constituted three different 'faces of dependency' in the early New Deal. Setting aside the conspicuous omission of Asian immigrants (dealt with in Ngai 2004), for white immigrant labour this was actually a re-inscribing of the earlier broad set of relief policies aimed at cultural disciplining in Progressive era industrialism.

To put this differently, prior attention to homogeneity can allow attention to both social inequalities and to the inclusion of the working class. Nation-building was as causally important to the expansion of social citizenship as was the strength of labour organization. As Edwin Amenta's work has convincingly shown, greater democracy or political voice along certain political process dimensions better enables redistributive social policies. But, in this moment at least, this was itself premised on a prior or contextual cultural inclusion in the nation: redistributive policies are easier when there is a cultural consensus with few identity fractures, so a real or imagined sense of nation-building homogeneity may have enabled *both* labour's subsequent (if brief) inclusion *and* supply-side redistributive attention to inequalities. In those historical moments when the United States looked more like Europe in terms of social citizenship (i.e. became more risk-sharing), it also viewed itself as more culturally cohesive.

Understood in this way, we can better grasp a persistent and 'exceptional' feature of US labour development, which runs through much of the twentieth century: the social equivalence of Leftism with cultural difference. Industrial capitalism was dependent on an 'alien labour' that was politically excluded from meaningful democratic processes and 'citizenship as standing' but remained the target of an intensive cultural disciplining. It also opens the way to a better sociological theorization of the extensiveness of labour's violent and brutal repression in these industrializing decades, beyond caveating this to domestic militarist exceptionalism. Instead, we might begin to better situate US anti-labour violence and the ways in which the composition and character of industrial labour was socially valorized, challenging the extent to which we continue to characterize the United States as a fully inclusive male democracy in terms of its early working class formation and the social sources of its exceptionalism.

As arguably the most critical segment of the United States' second industrial takeoff, 'alien labour' sat intersectionally amid an intense industrialism and a culturally disciplining nationalism. In this respect, actually, it was rather unexceptional. As a nation-building or culturally disciplining project, Americanization was more liberal and less state led than those that made 'peasants into Frenchmen', or that Magyarized, or Polonized or Russified their populations. Indeed, comparatively situating Americanization in this way needs more research. But, as a general reflection, these were the same industries at the centre of the revolutionary Central Black Earth region of the Russian working classes in roughly the same years, and in Russia they were similarly among the most viciously repressed between the 1880s and 1917, although they were ethnically also more homogenous. Moreover, the US pattern of political inclusion or exclusion of migrant segments of the working classes was more similar to Germany's trade union exclusion of Polish labour than it was to France's inclusion of Italian migrants.

Besides nationalism, of course, given my tentative account here, Mann's (1993) wonderful political sociology, which holds that socialism occurs when production also fuses with political exploitations, would imply a stronger socialism for the United States, not a weaker one. But this typological construction might itself be a little too narrow. Socialism as an elite political ideology for organizing labour often tends to be more appealing in contexts where nation-building processes are more fractured or less developed, in the way that nationalism and socialism-as-universalism can compete intensely in contexts of deep cultural diversity. So there may perhaps be room for a more textured analysis of the ways in which the strength or weakness of socialism – both at the level of organized working classes but also as an appealing elite ideology – is related not only to the liberal or autocratic character of the state per se, as Mann's sociology tells us, but also to underlying cultural exclusions or inclusions and nation-building processes. In other words, we might comparatively reflect a little more on the ways in which capitalism and socialism might both be in some measure shaped by the politics of underlying cultural diversities, and the United States should not be exceptional to this theorizing.

References

Barrett, James. 1992. 'Americanization from the Bottom Up: Immigration and the Remaking of the Working Class in the United States, 1880–1930' *Journal of American History*, Dec.: 996–1020.

Carter, Susan et al. (eds.). 2006. *Historical Statistics of the United States, Earliest Times to the Present* Vol. I. New York: Cambridge University Press.

Carter, Susan, Roger Ransom, and Richard Sutch. 1991. 'The Historical Labor Statistics Project at the University of California' *Historical Methods*, 24 (2): 52–65.

Cohen, Patricia. 1999. *A Calculating People: the Spread of Numeracy in Early America*, 2nd edn. London: Routledge.

Crocker, Ruth. 1992. *Social Work and Social Order: The Settlement Movement in Two Industrial Cities, 1889–1930*. Chicago: University of Illinois Press.

Dillingham, W.P. et al. *United States Immigration Commission (1907–1910)*. 1911, multivolume. Washington, DC: GPO.

Fishback, Price, Rebecca Holmes, and Samuel Allen. 2008. 'Lifting the Curse of Dimensionality: Measures of the Labor Legislative Climate in the States During the Progressive Era' *National Bureau of Economic Research*, Working Paper 14167.

Flanagan, Maureen. 2006. *America Reformed: Progressives and Progressivism, 1890s–1920s*. New York: Oxford University Press.

Fox, Cybelle. 2012. *Three Worlds of Relief: Race, Immigration, and the American Welfare State from the Progressive Era to the New Deal*. Princeton, NJ: Princeton University Press.

Gerstle, Gary. 2001. *American Crucible: Race and Nation in the Twentieth Century*. Princeton, NJ: Princeton University Press.

Goldstein, Robert. 2010. 'Labor History Symposium: Political Repression of the American Labor Movement during its Formative Years – A Comparative Perspective' *Labor History*, 51 (2): 271–293.

Gould, Lewis. 2001. *America in the Progressive Era, 1890–1914*. New York: Pearson Education Limited.

Hannon, Joan. 1982. 'Ethnic Discrimination in a 19th-Century Mining District: Michigan Copper Mines, 1888' *Explorations in Economic History*, 19 (1): 28–50.

Higham, John. 2002 [1955]. *Strangers in the Land: Patterns of American Nativism, 1860–1925*. New Brunswick, NJ: Rutgers University Press.

Hill, Howard. 1919. 'The Americanization Movement' *American Journal of Sociology*, 24 (6): 609–642.

Hofstadter, Richard. 1955. *The Age of Reform*. New York: Vintage Press.

Kanstroom, Daniel. 2007. *Deportation Nation: Outsiders in American History*. Cambridge, MA: Harvard University Press.

Katznelson, Ira and Aristide Zolberg. (eds.). 1986. *Working-class Formation: Nineteenth-century Patterns in Western Europe and the United States*. Princeton, NJ: Princeton University Press.

Kimeldorf, Howard. 2013. 'Worker Replacement Costs and Unionization: Origins of the U.S. Labor Movement' *American Sociological Review*, 78 (6): 1033–1062.

King, Desmond. 2000. *Making Americans: Immigration, Race, and the Origins of Diverse Democracy*. Cambridge, MA: Harvard University Press.

Link, Arthur. 1959. 'What Happened to the Progressive Movement in the 1920s?' *American Historical Review*, 64: 833–851.

Lipold, Paul and Larry Isaac. 2009. 'Striking Deaths: Lethal Contestation and the "Exceptional" Character of the American Labor Movement, 1870–1970' *Internationaal Instituut voor Geschiedenis*, 54: 167–205.

Lipset, Seymour Martin. 1997. *American Exceptionalism: A Double-Edged Sword*. New York: W.W. Norton and Company.

Mann, Michael. 2013. *The Sources of Social Power: Vol. 4 Globalizations, 1945–2011*. Cambridge: Cambridge University Press.

   2012. *The Sources of Social Power: Vol.3 Global Empires and Revolution, 1890–1945*. Cambridge: Cambridge University Press.

   1993. *The Sources of Social Power: Vol.2 The Rise of Classes and Nation-States*. Cambridge: Cambridge University Press.

McClymer, John. 1978. 'The Federal Government and the Americanization Movement, 1915–1924' *Prologue: Journal of the National Archives*, 10 (Spring): 23–41.

McGerr, Michael. 2003. *A Fierce Discontent: The Rise and Fall of the Progressive Movement in America*. Oxford: Oxford University Press.

Ngai, Mae. 2004. *Impossible Subjects: Illegal Aliens and the Making of Modern America*. Princeton, NJ: Princeton University Press.

1999. 'The Architecture of Race in American Immigration Law: A Reexamination of the Immigration Act of 1924' *Journal of American History*, 86 (1): 67–92.

O'Connor, Alice. 2001. *Poverty Knowledge: Social Science, Social Policy, and the Poor in Twentieth Century U.S. History*. Princeton, NJ: Princeton University Press.

Perlmann, Joel. 2001. 'Race or People: Federal Race Classifications for Europeans in America, 1898–1913' Jerome Levy Economics Institute Working Paper No. 320.

Piketty, Thomas. 2014. *Capital in the Twenty-First Century*. Cambridge, MA: Belknap, Harvard University Press.

Raskin, J. B. 1993. 'Legal Aliens, Local Citizens: the Historical, Constitutional and Theoretical Meanings of Alien Suffrage' *University of Pennsylvania Law Review*, 141 (4): 1391–1470.

Restifo, Salvatore, Vincent Roscigno, and Zhenchao Qian. 2013. 'Segmented Assimilation, Split Labor Markets, and Racial/Ethnic Inequality: the Case of Early Twentieth Century New York' *American Sociological Review*, 78 (5): 897–924.

Shklar, Judith. 1991. *American Citizenship: the Quest for Inclusion*. Cambridge, MA: Harvard University Press.

Smith, Rogers. 1988. 'The 'American Creed' and American Identity: The Limits of Liberal Citizenship in the United States' *Western Political Quarterly*, 41 (2): 225–251.

Sombart, Werner. 1976 [1906]. *Why Is There No Socialism in the United States?*. New York: Sharpe.

Zeidel, Robert. 2004. *Immigrants, Progressives, and Exclusion Politics: The Dillingham Commission, 1900–1927*. DeKalb, IL: Northern Illinois University Press.

Ziegler-McPherson, Christina. 2010. *Americanization in the States: Immigrant Social Welfare Policy, Citizenship, and National Identity in the United States, 1908–1929*. Gainesville, FL: University of Florida Press.

Zolberg, Aristide. 2006. *A Nation by Design: Immigration Policy in the Fashioning of America*. Princeton, NJ: Princeton University Press.

11 Mann's big picture of US social citizenship: "Road to World Empire" with Bob Hope

Edwin Amenta

Most scholars argue that US social policy has been late to develop and smaller in size and influence than that of other rich democracies. This underdevelopment of direct social policy has produced higher poverty rates than those of rich democracies. To explain the distinctiveness of US social policy, some argue that US labor has been comparatively weak, without its own political party, or that US capitalists have been comparatively powerful, dampening the forces for social policy advancement, or that pro-social policy coalitions of labor and farmers never emerged on the US political scene. Others argue that the unusual construction of US political institutions hamstrung potential change. Their extensive fragmentation made it easy for opponents to block social policy measures, and a state that was slow to bureaucratize and democratize also thwarted social policy advocates (see review in Amenta 2003).

Where does Michael Mann stand on these debates about the characteristics of US social policy and what accounts for them? How well do his characterizations of and arguments about the development of social policy in the twentieth century, especially regarding US social policy, work? Mann's volumes do not focus on social policy, but he does write extensively about it and the US case. And his take is of special interest. No expert on social policy has anything like his worldwide comparative and historical perspective, not to mention one that centers on major social changes and power conflicts that range far beyond domestic policy. To answer the first question, Mann largely follows the consensus characterization in the specialty literature, arguing that US social citizenship lagged. Mann argues that US social policy caught up with that of English-speaking and Nordic countries during the 1930s (mainly in Chapters 8 and 9 of Volume 3, as well as in Chapter 3 of Volume 4) and sees social citizenship advancing across the democratic North between the wars and immediately afterward. The United States did not gain as much from the Second World War and postwar periods, however, and fell behind again. From his vantage point, he sees the United States as truly exceptional, however, not in its social policy, but in its race relations.

To explain the advance of social citizenship and its unusual US career, Mann draws in part on demand-side arguments, such as those of Huber and Stephens (2001) and Korpi (1983); political institutional arguments, such as those by Skocpol (1992) among others; and those that combine both, such as my own (Amenta 1998). Unlike these others, however, Mann sees the central determinants of US social policy not as predominantly internal. His argument works mainly from the outside in, based on the contingencies of depression, war and geopolitics. He relies on various historical conjunctural analyses, employing mainly Weberian ideas, with some Marx, Gumplowitz and others sprinkled in. For Mann, the Great Depression explains much about how the United States built social policy. Then war and geopolitics combine to explain why it fell behind. The war came late to the United States, and having its citizenry shielded from direct attacks provided no impulse to promote social citizenship. Yet the war thrust world leadership upon the United States, creating a militarized state that came at the expense of the domestic one.

Mann's big picture perspective is bracing, and his overall account of the main developments in social citizenship and many of his individual arguments are compelling, though I have some significant disagreements with him. One way to indicate these differences is this: if I were to work Mann's account of US social citizenship in comparative and historical perspective into a full-length book and then convert that book into a film, it would be a war comedy titled "Road to World Empire," featuring Bob Hope. In the mid-twentieth century Hope starred in a series of "Road to . . . " films, in which he usually played a shiftless and cowardly though-good-underneath everyman, with a pal played by Bing Crosby. They seek fortune and romance in exotic-sounding places (Rio, Morocco, Zanzibar, etc.), where they inevitably find trouble, while vying for the affection of the female lead, usually Dorothy Lamour. What the heroes are trying to accomplish takes fourth place to events, gags and the agency of others. Through little effort of his own, the Hope character lands on his feet, though he never gets the girl.

In Mann's big picture, the hero (Hope, as the US welfare state) and his sidekick (Crosby, European welfare states) are buffeted by severe depressions, catastrophic wars and imperial incursions. Our feckless protagonists advance, not in spite of all the trouble swirling around them, but because of it. Hope (US social policy) improbably gains from the Depression and Crosby (European social policy) from the Second World War. Hope joins the war late and reluctantly, whereas Crosby is in, if involuntarily, from the start. Sympathetically injured in war and then swearing it off, Crosby wins the love of Lamour (a more complete welfare state). Meanwhile, scaredy cat Hope emerges unscathed from the war, but somehow gets promoted to general and sent on a long-term mission, putting romance (and further social policy gains) on hold. Everyone lives happily, for the moment at least, though Crosby is happier.

As with the "Road to ... " movies and their agency-poor protagonists, Mann's account of social policy development is a secondary plotline running counter to larger and often disastrous developments. Mann's account also has a comic and happy ending for its social citizenship subplot. In the North, social citizenship advances, though not quite as well in the United States as in Europe, abetted by a world of trouble. Mann's perspective is unique and valuable, as I detail below. The disadvantage of this treatment, however, is that social policy does not fully come into focus. The characteristics of the leads seem to matter little, and the key determinants of their fates are played as mainly accidental. I would put the characters and the internal features that drove their different levels of success more at the center of the story. To explain their relative status in social citizenship, I would focus on the character of democracy in their respective political systems, with that perhaps being analogous to how good underneath the characters were. I would portray the Hope character, and US social policy, as being flawed because of democratic deficits, not from his failure to suffer sufficiently during the war or his promotion to a position of military leadership after it. But first, let's go to the review. (Warning: many spoilers ahead.)

Reviewing Mann's "The Road to World Empire"

From his global and deeply historical point of view, Mann provides a plausible big picture of the development of what he refers to as "citizenship rights" in the United State. In the 1930s, he argues that it joined other institutional democracies in forming a "lib-lab welfare regime," borrowing from the work of Alexander Hicks (1999) among others. In his account, Mann focuses on the major reforms connected to the Social Security Act, as well as labor regulations and changes in tax policy. He notes as well that the United States was an early leader in compulsory mass education, well before Roosevelt's New Deal of the Depression era, but a laggard in public health policy, which did not advance very far in the first half of the century and mainly for the elderly in the second half of the century. By citizenship rights, Mann means something beyond standard understandings of social policy, which usually center on specific social insurance and welfare programs to reduce insecurity and inequality. Instead he provides a model based on T. H. Marshall's (1950) concept, developing four criteria that include standard welfare-state transfers, but three other considerations: a low level of inequality in market incomes, including state interventions in labor markets; a progressive tax system; and a universal education and health system. Mann argues that each of these four aspects is functionally equivalent and works at the level of the nation state.

Mann deftly situates the US trajectory in citizenship rights in comparative and historical perspective. He sees the democratic North developing lib-lab citizenship rights throughout the interwar period and the United States as largely catching up with its democratic counterparts during the Depression era. In most of the North not much was happening in social citizenship during that period; most of the other countries had seen gains in social protections after the First World War. As a result, Mann argues that the English-speaking and the Nordic countries were largely similar in their lib-lab policies by the time of the Second World War. Mann explicitly and more tellingly, I believe, uses the regional terminology of Francis Castles (Castles and Mitchell 1993) rather than the "welfare state regime" types of Gosta Esping-Andersen (1990), as the social policy of the European continent was very much unsettled during this period. As for the English-speaking countries, he sees mainly similarities, but some differences. The US policy leaned toward progressive taxation and welfare state policies (along with Britain and Canada), whereas Australia and New Zealand provided social citizenship rights more centrally by way of labor arbitration, again following Castles (1985).

Mann focuses on the steep upward trajectory in US social citizenship rights during the so-called New Deal: the rise to power of President Franklin Roosevelt, which began in 1933 during the trough of the Depression and is usually thought to have continued until the United States entered the Second World War at the end of 1941. This period notably brought the 1935 Social Security Act, National Labor Relations Act and the Works Progress Administration (WPA). The first is viewed as the cornerstone of the US welfare state; the second as the main guarantor of the rights of organized labor, which grew dramatically in the next few decades; and the third was the central US approach to social policy in the Depression, rocketing US social policy to the forefront of welfare state spending efforts among democracies (Amenta 1998). The period also saw legislation specifying minimum wages and maximum hours and instituting overtime pay. Mann argues that during the war, social policy was placed on the back burner. Less well addressed are the 1939 amendments to the Social Security Act, which turned the focus of US policy to old age for the long run, and some key fiscal changes that happened during the war (more later), but on the whole the presentation is coherent and plausible.

In explaining this sharp upswing in social citizenship, Mann features two main causes, the first being centered on the Great Depression itself. He zeros in not on the generic or direct influence of depressions on social policy, but on the contingent discrediting effects of the Depression; its influence depended on the nature of regimes in power when it happened. And happened is the operative word. Although that worldwide catastrophe cannot be attributed plausibly to individual governments in power, each one bore the brunt of public dissatisfaction. As the United States had in power a severely right-wing regime throughout the 1920s, the Depression discredited its entire ungenerous approach to social citizenship and state-economic relations. Mann also makes the case that US deficits in social policy were brought into bold relief, as it were, by the Depression, creating a kind of functional need for action that was more pressing in the US case. In short, this disaster proved salubrious for US social citizenship.

Mann also sees political causes for these developments. Here, he enters a terrain fought over by many historians and social scientists wielding arsenals of different arguments. These include "pluralism," "state autonomy theory," encompassing "state elites" and "state institutions," "path dependency," "power resources" theories, including "class struggle" and "class fractions," the latter focusing on the influence of corporate liberals. The pluralist perspective is associated with Alexander Hicks (1999) among others, state elites with Theda Skocpol's earlier work (e.g. Skocpol and Ikenberry 1983), path dependency with Paul Pierson (2000), state institutions with both of them and several others, class struggle theory with Evelyne Huber and John Stephens (2001) and Walter Korpi (1983), among others, and the corporate liberal argument with William Domhoff (e.g. 1996).

Mann downplays most of these conflicts, identifying many similarities in their arguments that help to explain these developments. He also notes that pluralist, political institutional and class struggle perspectives all focus on the role of elections, and each sees a strong role for the South in slowing social citizenship. Democracy is important in Mann's treatment. He sees bottom-up forces for change working mainly by way of elections rather than the direct action of protesters ranging from farmers and workers to veterans and the elderly. He also indicates that, institutionally speaking, US democracy was laggard and that the underdevelopment of US democracy meant that the popular voice was not more directly transformed into political power. However, Mann takes aim at Skocpol and Pierson and their respective state-elite and the path-dependent vantage points. Mann argues that there were many elites of different sorts arguing for and against different social policy proposals and that state elites mattered far more in fascist countries than in the United States. He also argues that path dependency did not matter much, as US social policy was mainly being formed at the time (more later).

The main villain in the piece is war, though for our tertiary social citizenship heroes, war is mainly a self-sabotaging comedy villain. For all its devastation and evil intent, war inadvertently aids social citizenship. Many European social policy advances happened after and, in his view, partly because of the First World War. Similarly, following Richard Titmuss (1969) and Arthur Marwick (1974), whose argument makes an uncredited cameo appearance, Mann sees the Second World War as spurring social policy, notably in Britain. As with the Depression, he argues that the influence of the war was contingent. This time its influence on social citizenship depended on who suffered most from it. The entire British people were buffeted by Nazi Germany's extensive bombings, leading in Mann's view to tremendous pressure for enhanced social citizenship. However, for the United States, the process had a different result. US citizens were only mildly affected by war, and only the US group that sacrificed the most, veterans, got advances in social citizenship, its own private welfare state through the 1945 GI Bill of Rights. Key items, like health insurance, designed for the entire citizenry and remaining on the New Deal social policy agenda were cast aside. As with the Hope franchise, the initially war-shy one (Hope) survives but does not get the full benefits of social citizenship gained by European democracies (Crosby).

Indeed, the results of the Second World War further and uniquely disadvantaged the prospects of social citizenship in the United States by elevating its geopolitical status to hegemonic power. In Mann's account, the war and the ensuing Cold War fractured the New Deal, and this overwhelming triumph brought social policy defeat in two important ways. With the new geopolitical status came the rise of an extensive military industrial complex, which crowded out social policy in the standard fiscal competition between guns and butter. This is an argument made notably by Harold Wilensky (1975), who applied it not just to the United States, but also to other countries that failed to demobilize fully after the war. This military turn also had a general conservative effect on US politics, possibly partly as a result of its new geopolitical opponent being the Soviet Union. A somewhat similar, if more narrow argument and analysis is made by Hooks and McQueen (2010), who focus on the conservative influence of extensive military procurement. For all these reasons, the United States fell behind other Northern countries in social policy, including the other English-speaking ones. Mann notes another minor bid to improve the lib-lab citizenship regime in the mid 1960s through improvements in the health care system but also indicates the great limitations to them, as well as the much-talk-little-action "War on Poverty."

This social policy expert found Mann's account thrilling. His big picture is so much bigger than most scholars that work in this area that it is as if he were shooting in CinemaScope while others had been pointing at the issue with their iPhones. It is not just that these developments are situated across the entire world. It is not just that he considers them for more than a century. It is that they are also situated with respect to depression, war, empire and revolution, all of which are conspicuously, if not surprisingly, missing in the accounts that zero in on social policy in the richer countries or just in the United States. For that reason alone, this is worth the price of admission, as Mann provides an original, vital and useful point of view on policy development. From his angle, he makes us see that social policy changes were typically extensive in countries that retained democratic institutions, in comparison to developments where such regimes fell. He also provides the first real historical comparative appraisal of the Esping-Andersen (1990) thesis about the rise of different types of welfare state regimes and finds it lacking. If such regimes developed and began to diverge from one another, they were largely a post–Second World War phenomenon, as Mann plausibly argues.

Despite his reliance on the wide angle, Mann's close ups are also very fine. As I note above, Mann can entertain several different arguments about what is driving social policy and the evidence advanced for them. Here, he works from the secondary literature and uses broad comparisons, logic and the evidence advanced by others to make his judgments. In the main, I do not see much wrong with his assessments and his conjunctural arguments, in which systematic and contingent forces converge to produce major social policy developments. For instance, he sees popular movements as pushing citizenship rights forward in ways that were partly class based and partly not. He also finds that state institutions strongly influenced the ways that struggles played out.

All in all, Mann's very wide angle provides something that experts in the area never see – an entirely new look at old issue. All the same, he can focus on the details regarding the way specific policies turned out the way they did. His account of the development of US social policy in the first half of the twentieth century gets most things right. I was consistently impressed by how much work Mann has considered and the judiciousness of his treatments. Mann's heuristic ideological, economic, military and political power model and historical approach provide him considerable freedom, focusing the contingent influences of economic crises and war and never being constrained to support or apply some more general argument. Unlike most social science scholars, whose readers are battered with sustained arguments about systematic causes of policy, Mann's account rarely seems as though it is attempting to hammer home a message. In comparison, most expert studies seem like afterschool specials, promoting their arguments in the way that specials warn of the dangers of drug use or bullying. So this reviewer of Mann's "Road to World Empire," a nonexistent movie based on a nonexistent book about social policy, starring the late Bob Hope, gives it four stars (out of four).

Deeper into Mann's account of social citizenship

Moving from movie review to film criticism, I want to dig deeper into some of the empirical, methodological and meta-theoretical issues Mann's discussion raises. (Warning: social science jargon to follow.) The difficulties are often the flip side of the highlights. In some debates over nitty-gritty policy issues, he gets lost in the details and in others he seems less than impartial (discussions that stand out because they are rare). The reliance on other scholars that makes possible his bracing wide-angle approach is not without its problems. Mann is sometimes failed by the secondary literature, a standard hazard of comparative historical analyses without primary evidence and a central reason that we see so few studies like Mann's. His historical approach to argumentation makes for a freewheeling and exciting discussion, but contingency seems to matter so much that major outcomes seem overly accidental. Also, although there is much discussion of the big picture and excellent depictions of details, there is little in the mid-range theoretical ground where most social policy studies reside. I think that both of these issues are linked to how Mann views social citizenship. For him, in addressing power on a world scale, he sees social policy as something isolated to national states and as a tertiary concern, and so his treatment of it is more unanchored than that of revolutions and empires.

Let me start with the smaller stuff. Despite being largely trustworthy Mann sometimes runs off course in rehashing old battles. His sequences treating 1980s-era battles between Skocpol and Domhoff make them seem as if they still are at the center of the debate. In his chapter on the influence of the war, sometimes he is partying like it's 1989. Notably, he criticizes a piece by me and Skocpol (1988) for minimizing the influence of war on the British citizenry, with only a brief citation to a passage from my 1998 book that supersedes and corrects it. This gives some discussions an unfortunately dated, rather than timeless, feel to them. Also, in attempting to demonstrate the influence of corporate liberals and arguing that state experts do not independently matter, the account misses the important role that political appointees, such as Harry Hopkins and the

(WPA), the Children's Bureau and aid to dependent children, and other policy officials, made to the construction of US social policy. In these moments, the account degenerates into the sort of marginally compelling message treatment of which Mann's volumes are usually blissfully free.

As for methodology, most scholars in comparative and historical sociology have abandoned the Barrington Moore (1966) model of relying on secondary literature to make claims across many disparate countries, issues and centuries – and for several good reasons. One set of them has to do with the problems of bias initially identified by Ian Lustick (1996). Even a comprehensive knowledge of the secondary sources on a given subject may be insufficient to address some questions, as secondary sources are far from comprehensive. Historical social scientists addressing their own questions typically have to go beyond careful reading of the related historiography and social science and engage in some independent inspection and interpretation of the historical materials. For one thing, arguments in historical social science often concern the thinking of key actors behind their actions, and historiography may give only a partial or biased account of this thinking. For another, scholars often conceptualize what they seek to explain differently from secondary treatments. These strictures tend to channel historical social scientists into studies of more self-contained phenomena in fewer countries or places within a country over briefer periods of time.

These gaps and biases vary across areas of study, and some of the problems are mitigated by the fact social policy has been so extensively researched by social scientists that Mann has a lot to work with, almost enough to get by on. All the same, by relying so much on the scholarship of others, he leaves himself open to errors of fact, providing little support for the superstructure of explanation. For example, in the discussion of US social policy, Mann zeros in on the Second New Deal of 1935 and the Social Security Act. Its creation and passage are central to his description of the advancement of US social citizenship, and, based on it, he appraises a series of arguments about why the legislation passed in the form that it did. Yet Social Security changed in a major way in 1939. It was transformed not only into a pay-as-you-go program, but also into a pension program for the first generation of beneficiaries (Amenta 2006). Mann misses this change, mainly because he is failed by the social science literature, which also focuses on the initial legislation.

Mann's divergences from what the literature typically seeks to explain also hamper his account. He conceptualizes citizenship rights more broadly than most other studies. These studies in turn, unsurprisingly, do not engage the issues specifically as Mann sees them. He has four dimensions of citizenship that are treated as functionally equivalent and to provide a kind of historical scorecard of these developments, he would need country or issue experts to detail each aspect over a long stretch of history. Since no one does that, Mann is forced to do a lot of reading between the lines, which he admittedly does very well. But without any additional research that explicitly addresses these outcomes, his claims about them are sometimes difficult to assess.

My biggest objection to Mann's account involves contingent explanation, on which I believe he is overly reliant. Mann's argument can be categorized as historicist in the valuable sense of the term as deployed by Arthur Stinchcombe (1968). That is to say that Mann is constantly examining and entertaining conjunctural causes in critical periods and arguing that contextual and political factors combined to produce a specific institutional outcome, one with lasting influence well beyond the critical period. Although he addresses both structural and contingent influences, perhaps because he is not much constrained by any over-arching argumentation, he usually errs on the side of contingency.

One example of this is his claim that the Depression forced the United States to deal with its inadequacies in social policy. The United States had no unemployment insurance or benefits for old age when unemployment overtook more than one-fourth of the population by 1933. However, there was no reason that a presidential administration might not have addressed these problems in simply a short-term way, providing emergency relief until the crisis lifted. This is largely what Roosevelt's Republican opponents and southern Democratic allies sought and, to some extent, what Roosevelt did just after assuming office that year. But two years later, he turned the New Deal toward permanent reform. (This point and the following two are lifted from my 1998 book.)

Moreover, although Mann's point is well taken that the United States avoided the destruction of war and missed the potential benefits of that for social citizenship, quite a lot happened during the war to shape US social policy, though not necessarily because of it. In the early 1940s, the income tax made a great leap forward, becoming more progressive and a mass tax. In part that was because of the revenue needs of the war, but also because the revenue requirements allowed the Democratic regime in power to advance this part of its agenda because progress on social spending policy was stalled. This was a way that the left Democratic regime exploited the crisis to make a long-lasting change in citizenship rights – a right regime would have handled it differently. The 1942 elections, however, returned an extremely conservative Congress. It used the administration's preoccupation with war and short-term high employment to dismantle the WPA. It is easy to say that the war caused the end of the employment programs, and therefore contingency happened to harm US social policy. But it is also plausible and possibly more consistent to say the war simply provided an opportunity for a very conservative Congress to stop a program it had fought from the beginning. In short, the war was attended by both permanent positive and negative outcomes for social citizenship and influenced their character but was not the direct cause of them.

Some social policy decisions and bets of the New Deal simply did not pay off. But they failed because of mismatches between the character of the policy and economic realities, not external reasons. Notably, having made great strides in social policy during the Depression, US policy architects more or less assumed that unemployment would be severe for the long run and that their public employment approach would remain necessary. The Roosevelt administration set the WPA on a permanent footing in 1939 and rechristened it the Work Projects Agency. A lot of political capital was invested in the public employment program, but it resulted in no long-term gain in social citizenship. One can imagine an analogous situation if President Barack Obama had placed all his bets and spent all his capital in his first two years in office on a stimulus package rather than the Affordable Care Act. Economic growth would have come sooner, but permanent social citizenship would not have been as greatly advanced.

More generally, Mann's historical argumentation makes it often difficult to assess or place his claims. Even sociologists shedding the general linear reality of standard quantitative methods, as Abbott (1992) has called it, usually seek to develop or appraise theoretical arguments that are in some ways or in some parts transportable to other situations, however defined. Comparative and historical scholars like Mann are more concerned with causes of important effects or outcomes than the effects of specific causes (Mahoney and Goertz 2006). But a key part of the social science project is to isolate theoretical argumentation of some form or another that would be expected in well-defined circumstances or contexts to produce similar phenomena (George and Bennett 2005). Although Mann's overall approach expresses doubt on the validity and usefulness of extensive theorizing, in line with some other scholars (Collier and Mazzuca 2006), he does work to some extent along these lines for the development of states, capitalism and empires.

Mann's overall argument about the development of social citizenship is a path-dependent one of the sort associated with Pierson (2000), but with a difference. In Stinchcombe's (1968) account of historicist causation, accidental factors provoke impervious institutional change, such as when societies choose religions. In that style of argument, some causes in a configurational sequence may be accidental (Sewell 2006), but these developments are argued to happen in a critical period that yields major institutional change. As Pierson points out, these institutions have self-reinforcing mechanisms. In social policy research, the standard positive feedback loop is that policies greatly encourage new political constituencies, who mobilize around them and fight reductions in them. In such an argument, a set of conditions provokes institutional change, but afterward the reappearance of these conditions would not have the same effect. For instance, control of the US government by a right-wing regime in the late 1930s would have been sufficient to abolish Social Security, but a Republican regime holding all branches of government after 2004 could not do so given how far the program had developed and the large constituency backing it.

Unlike Pierson, however, Mann sees US policy freezing in place not because of self-reinforcing mechanisms in the policy itself but from ones that work from the outside. That is, hegemonic geopolitical status for the United States prevented further progress in social policy of the sort seen in the 1930s. It was locked into its fairly well developed, but somewhat substandard social citizenship. Presumably, a rise to geopolitical eminence in a world of competing empire hopefuls would have been problematic for any state, providing the guns/butter trade-off and overall conservative tinge, but it applied to the United States alone, or possibly to the United States and the Soviet Union, and to a lesser extent to some other allies.

Still, I would choose a different main line of explanation, one centered on democratic political institutions. Mann sees the process of social citizenship as being internal to national states but does not entertain explanations sufficiently at this level. In standard political institutional explanations, macro-level aspects of the polity, such as electoral procedures, party systems, and state bureaucracies, are argued to mediate the impact of both internal political forces, such as bids by workers or social movements for change, and external forces, such as economic changes, such as crises or modernization. To the extent that Mann addresses arguments at this level, they have to do with the degree of democratization and the character of democratic institutions. Mann's main insight along these lines was that countries that were able to maintain their democratic structures in the turbulent interwar period were able to advance social citizenship rights. He also makes the key point that US democratic institutions were less well developed than those of other democracies and dampened the influence of popular forces in the 1930s at the key moment when social policy had its greatest chances for advancement. I am convinced of its plausibility because I initially made it (Amenta 1998). This would also explain the comparative historical trajectories of social citizenship as he portrays them, with the United States lagging behind other democracies despite various efforts to catch up.

This somewhat different movie would unspool with a greater focus on comparative democratic political institutions. Though an early democracy, the United States suffered from extensive democratic hindrances as well as other political institutional circumstances that make it difficult for political advocates of social policy. The main hindrance was a region, the South, that was only barely democratized and depended on a labor-repressive economic system; in states of the former Confederacy and ones that previously allowed slavery, a series of restrictions ranging from legal ruses to physical intimidation prevented African Americans and poorer whites from voting. Another deficit was based in a patronage-oriented party system that fought social programs with guaranteed benefits and which dominated much of the Northeast and Midwest (Mayhew 1986). In addition to these obstacles to democracy, which were mainly worn down by the last quarter of the twentieth century, the US political system was born fragmented, with numerous so-called veto points, providing opponents of far-reaching policy reform with many opportunities to stop it (Immergut 2010). In addition, the majority electoral requirements of the system discourage labor or socialist parties and promote right-slanted party systems (Iverson and Soskice 2005).

From this point of view, the US pattern of being slow to start in social policy and subject to quick bursts of reform and then extensive bids at retrenchment is not so much the result of contingent influences like war and depression as of democratic deficits. The United States simply had fewer chances to have in power the sort of political regime that would advance social policy. It is true, as Mann argues, that the Depression discredited the conservative political formation that held power, but the odds are that something would have done so some time in the first half of the twentieth century and would have led to a chance for a different political formation. The odds were also that this formation would not last long. And so the opportunities to develop social citizenship rights were simply going to be far less frequent and shorter in duration in the US setting. When they did happen, they were constantly being undermined by a business-oriented Republican party and Southern Democrats who liked social spending directed at its region but were desperate to ensure that money would be under local control and that no generous or liberal national standards would appear in any program. This line of argument is also in fitting with Mann's view of American exceptionalism regarding its internal race issue that other proto-empires lacked. That situation was thoroughly bound up with US backwardness in democracy.

Although Mann is convincing that war and geopolitical status had an overall dampening effect on US social citizenship, the political institutional argument helps to explain developments since the 1940s. There was a burst of legislation in the mid 1960s, when northern Democrats and a reform president dominated Congress. President Lyndon Johnson was able to pass much of his Great Society legislation, which notably helped fill the gap in health insurance, though only for the elderly and the poor, through Medicare and Medicaid. Also, the first two years of the Obama administration, when the Democrats had the supermajority needed in the Senate to overcome Republican obstruction, led to the 2010 Affordable Care Act. That legislation in turn upgraded Medicaid and is insuring a high percent of those neither poor, elderly, nor with health insurance through their employment. The reform was partial, immediately attacked and almost nullified by the Supreme Court, and the Democrats suffered stinging defeats in the 2010 election, drying up further possibilities for reform.

Conclusion

Overall, Michael Mann's account of the development of social citizenship is compelling, both in his overall characterizations of social policy developments and in his various explanations for them. There is considerable value added in his account, beyond what one might gain from reading the secondary literature on its own, and it derives from his good judgment, his above-the-fray outlook and, most of all, his encompassing comparative and historical perspective. Mann is a keen judge of secondary materials, digs into the details of empirical debates over policy changes, works through all the main arguments and the evidence advanced for them and referees them with considerable, largely impartial skill. From his long historical and wide comparative perspective, he provides compelling critiques of important arguments in the literature, notably those by Esping-Andersen about the origins of different types of welfare regimes.

As I note above, my main issue with the account is that it relies too much on contingency. And I think the problem stems in part from Mann's wider outlook on power relations. Most of the people writing on social policy see its historical expansion as central to changes in power relations despite their confinement to specific groups of citizens in individual countries typically ruled by powerful national states. For Mann, in contrast, social policy advances are not unimportant, but are far removed from the developments in empire and revolutions in which he is mainly interested. From his point of view, the forward march of social policy and citizenship rights in the English-speaking and Nordic countries do not matter as much as developments in fascism, communism, revolutions and wars surrounding European empires. Social policy is a subplot in a story mainly about other things. And so it is not surprising that Mann treats social citizenship developments mainly as resulting from external and contingent forces such as depressions and wars.

I would focus more than Mann does on the internal conditions of national states, notably those connected to political and democratic institutions. A more sustained treatment at this level would help to explain the social citizenship trajectories of democratic countries in the interwar years versus others, as well as the social citizenship of the United States versus other democracies. These countries differed in important structural considerations, mainly the construction of their political institutions. They differed in the nature of their social policy frameworks and thus the possibilities for further reform. And they differed as well in important ways regarding their party systems and the organizations pressing for and against social policy. Focusing on these political institutional circumstances that varied across democracies is consistent with Mann's arguments, which occasionally move in this direction. Attention to political institutions would also provide the missing link between his geopolitical and contingency arguments and the more detailed analyses of which groups and their collective action advanced social citizenship when they were able to do so.

References

Abbott, Andrew. 1992. "From Causes to Events: Notes on Narrative Positivism." *Sociological Methods & Research* 20: 428–455.

Amenta, Edwin. 1998. *Bold Relief: Institutional Politics and the Origins of Modern American Social Policy.* Princeton: Princeton University Press.

2003. "What We Know about the Development of Social Policy: Comparative and Historical Research in Comparative and Historical Perspective." Pp. 91–130 in *Comparative Historical Analysis in the Social Sciences*, eds. D. Rueschemeyer and J. Mahoney. New York: Cambridge University Press.

2006. *When Movements Matter: The Townsend Plan and the Rise of Social Security.* Princeton, NJ: Princeton University Press.

Amenta, Edwin and Theda Skocpol. 1988. "Redefining the New Deal: World War II and Public Social Provision in the United States." Chapter 2 in *The Politics of Social Policy in the United States*, eds. Margaret Weir, Ann Shola Orloff, and Theda Skocpol. Princeton, NJ: Princeton University Press.

Amenta, Edwin and Amber Celina Tierney. 2014. "Political Institutions and U.S. Social Policy." Chapter 8 in *The Oxford Handbook of U.S. Social Policy*, eds.

Daniel Beland, Christopher Howard, and Kimberly J. Morgan. New York: Oxford.

Castles, Francis G. 1985. *The Working Class and Welfare: Reflections on the Political Development of the Welfare State in Australia and New Zealand.* Sydney, London: Allen & Unwin.

Castles, Francis G. and Deborah Mitchell. 1993. "Worlds of Welfare and Families of Nations." Chapter 3 in *Families of Nations: Patterns of Public Policy in Western Democracies*, ed. Francis G. Castles. Aldershot: Dartmouth.

Collier, Ruth Berins and Sebastian Mazzuca. 2006. "Does History Repeat?" Chapter 25 in *The Oxford Handbook of Contextual Political Analysis*, eds. Robert E. Goodin and Charles Tilly. New York: Oxford University Press.

Domhoff, G. William. 1996. *State Autonomy or Class Dominance? Case Studies in Policy Making in America.* New York: Aldine de Gruyter.

Esping-Andersen, Gosta. 1990. *The Three Worlds of Welfare Capitalism.* Cambridge: Polity Press.

George, Alexander L. and Andrew Bennett. 2005. *Case Studies and Theory Development in the Social Sciences.* Cambridge, MA: MIT Press.

Hicks, Alexander. 1999. *Social Democracy and Welfare Capitalism: A Century of Income Security Politics.* Ithaca, NY: Cornell University Press.

Hooks, Gregory and Brian McQueen. 2010. American Exceptionalism Revisited: the Military-Industrial Complex, Racial Tension, and the Underdeveloped Welfare state. *American Sociological Review*, 75 (2): 185–204.

Huber, Evelyne and John D. Stephens. 2001. *Development and Crisis of the Welfare State: Parties and Policies in Global Markets.* Chicago: University of Chicago Press.

Immergut, Ellen M. 2010. "Political Institutions." Chapter 15 in *The Oxford Handbook of the Welfare State*, eds. F. G. Castles, S. Leibfried, J. Lewis, H. Obinger, and C. Pierson. Oxford: Oxford University Press.

Iversen, T. and D. Soskice. 2005. Electoral Institutions, Parties, and the Politics of Class: Why Some Democracies Redistribute More Than Others. *American Political Science Review*, 100 (2): 165–182.

Korpi, Walter. 1983. *The Democratic Class Struggle.* London: Routledge and Kegan Paul.

Lustick, Ian. 1996. "History, Historiography, and Political Science: Historical Records and Selection Bias." *American Political Science Review* 90:605–618.

Mahoney, James and Gary Goertz. 2006. "A Tale of Two Cultures: Contrasting Quantitative and Qualitative Research." *Political Analysis* 14: 227–249.

Marshall, T. H. 1950. "Citizenship and Social Class." *Citizenship and Social Class and Other Essays.* Cambridge: Cambridge University Press.

Marwick, Arthur. 1974. *War and Social Change in the Twentieth Century: A Comparative Study of Britain, France, Germany, Russia, and The United States.* New York: St. Martin's Press.

Mayhew, David R. 1986. *Placing Parties in American Politics: Organizations, Electoral Settings, and Government Activity in the Twentieth Century.* Princeton, NJ: Princeton University Press.

Moore, Barrington Jr. 1966. *The Social Origins of Dictatorship and Democracy.* Boston: Beacon Press.

Pierson, Paul. 2000. "Path Dependence, Increasing Returns, and the Study of Politics." *American Political Science Review* 94: 251–267.

Sewell, William Jr. 2006. *Logics of History*. Chicago: University of Chicago Press.

Skocpol, Theda. 1992. *Protecting Soldiers and Mothers: The Political Origins of Social Policy in the United States*. Cambridge, MA: Belknap Press.

Skocpol, Theda and G. John Ikenberry. 1983. "The Political Formation of the American Welfare State in Historical and Comparative Perspective." *Comparative Social Research* 6:87–147.

Stinchcombe, Arthur L. 1968. *Constructing Social Theories. New York: Harcourt. Brace, and World.*

Titmuss, Richard. 1969. *Essays on the Welfare State.* Boston: Beacon Press.

Wilensky, Harold L. 1975. *The Welfare State and Equality: Structural and Ideological Roots of Public Expenditures*. Berkeley: University of California Press.

Part IV

Empire

12   Mann and the problem of empire

John Darwin

The resurgence of interest in 'empire' and empires has been one of the more striking academic developments of recent years. Inevitably, it has been driven in part by polemic and political debate. But something more interesting has also been happening. Not long ago it was usual to assume that empires – certainly modern empires – represented a great aberration from the High Road of history on which all the sign posts clearly pointed 'This Way to the Nation State'. Empires delayed, distorted and even destroyed the (supposedly) universal impulse towards the formation of national communities. They were also invariably predatory, despotic, militaristic and, since they often seemed under the sway of a powerful individual – the 'emperor' – they could also be seen in varying degrees as psychopathic phenomena in their drive for what Schumpeter called 'objectless expansion' (Schumpeter, 1951). Except to their benighted champions, they were obviously a 'bad thing'. Indeed some historians felt obliged to assert their hatred for empire in case writing about them was mistaken for admiration. That empires possessed all these defects, and worse still were bound to fail, was amply proved to most commentators' satisfaction by their post-1945 collapse. Alas, we are no longer so sure.

If contemplating the contemporary scene has discouraged the belief that empires belong to the irrelevant past, another powerful influence has been the revival of *longue durée* global history. To an extent that would have struck many observers in the 1970s and 1980s as remarkable (and shocking) it is now almost a commonplace to say that empires have been the default form of political organisation above the pettiest scale for most of the world and most of world history. Two implications might follow, one perhaps easier to swallow than the other. (1) It becomes more difficult to treat empires as a metahistorical blockage to human progress. That is not to say that they become a 'good thing'. But they become an object of study without overriding moral preconceptions, even if we might conclude that some were better than others by certain criteria of human happiness. (2) If we are ready to grant some indulgence to empires where the constituency of the aggrieved is no longer very vociferous (like the

Iceni or Dumnonii), then it might be possible to view more recent types of imperialism in a less pejorative light as the products of world-historical conjuncture rather than flawed moral choice – not to approve of them, but to approach them more as historians and social scientists than as white knights on high horses. Part of that exercise might involve recognising the remarkable extent to which they rested on consent.

One final introductory point may be in order before we turn to Michael Mann's contribution. It is usual when discussing empire to assume a threshold of scale. Empires are 'extensive'. They are 'large-scale' political units – although no one has fixed what that scale should be. It's not clear why this presumption has become so ingrained. The *core* definition of empire is a system of rule or influence exerted by the leaders of one ethno-cultural group over others and embodying, in more or less systematic fashion, the allocation of functions among them to subserve the (imagined) interests of the imperial centre. This form of polity can exist on almost any scale (indeed many past empires might strike us as puny) and with widely varying degrees of sophistication and 'intensity' (to invoke one of Mann's terms). We might even be tempted to say that many if not most of today's 'nation-states' are really petty empires or display marked imperial tendencies in their internal organisation. This is not an argument for rebranding the world but for acknowledging that empires are not a radically distinct species of polity but merely part of the spectrum of state forms; that imperial characteristics are exhibited by many superficially 'national' states; and that globalisation is as likely to strengthen that tendency as to weaken it.

In the remainder of this chapter, I would like to discuss five aspects of Michael Mann's treatment of empire, drawing upon the first three volumes of *The Sources of Social Power* where Mann's views on empire are set out.

We begin with *origins*, on which Mann's account is exceptionally original and stimulating. It opens conventionally enough by suggesting that the impulse to territorial expansion by the early city states of the Mesopotamian plain arose from the need to extend their control over trade. But it is in exploring the *logistics* of conquest that it presents a compelling insight that should be of interest to any historian of empires. Drawing on a specialist military literature, Mann argues that the practical limits of a city state's military reach were approximately three days' march. Three days' ration was as much as an army could carry with it, unless it was able to exploit waterborne transport. The implication was drastic. Unless it was able to seize the food arsenals of its enemies at once, it would need to buy or levy supplies from the local population. The alternative – to disperse its strength in search of nourishment – might be fatal to its military aims. Hence the logistics of conquest forced the would-be imperialists into a search for clients almost as soon as their empire-building began – and clients of course expected a bargain. Even after the conquest was accomplished – supposing it was – the same logic applied. If the new ruler was to avoid fragmenting his force into a mass of small garrisons, with all the attendant risks were he threatened by an invasion or uprising, his authority would have to depend to a greater or lesser degree upon the cooperation of local clients or allies.

The suggestion that imperial rulers need local allies is not new. The value of Mann's account lies in its insistence that the actual process of conquest enforced a *simultaneous* search for clients as the price of military success. Of course in different periods and places, the time scale might be different, but not drastically so. When the British marched to Kumasi in 1873–74, to coerce the Ashanti, their first task was to recruit local labour not so much to supply their rations as to carry them (Brackenbury, 1874). They were also oppressed by the need to reach their target and then withdraw as quickly as possible. In their conquest of India after c.1750, the British relied very largely upon hiring local soldiery, the ubiquitous sepoy, and also upon advances from Indian bankers (perhaps here *they* were the clients) (Kolff, 1990; Subrahamian, 1987). Even after they had imposed their rule upon much of the subcontinent (by c.1820), they were desperately anxious not to disperse their limited military manpower but to husband it in large garrisons or cantonments. Indeed, fear of invasion from Afghanistan (a recurrent fear as late as the 1920s) required much of their military strength to be concentrated in the northwest, in modern Punjab and the North West Frontier Province. That reinforced the case for finding allies among the Indian elite to reduce the need for armed coercion of the subject population. Indeed, there is a powerful case for arguing – as Mann's account would suggest – that the pattern of clientage was laid down at the very moment of conquest or annexation precisely because they could not be achieved without it. Here, Mann's description of the methods of Alexander the Great, the world's grandest conqueror, is also suggestive. Alexander relied not so much on the laborious besieging of cities as upon the fear that his military reputation inspired. It was usually enough for a detachment of his troops to appear to persuade local rulers that it would be wiser to come to terms quickly than risk an encounter with the main force over the horizon. Colonial generals, like Alexander, preferred to rely upon this 'moral effect' whenever they could (Callwell, 1896).

What might we add to Mann's treatment of origins? First, we might want to stress that empires are often a consequence of the 'connectedness' that arose from the human instinct to 'truck, barter and exchange' on which Adam Smith famously insisted. Connectedness between different communities was always liable to create stresses that weakened some while strengthening others. The agents and influence of the stronger community would begin to subvert the cohesion of the weaker. Sooner or later, fear of domination on one side, or fear for the safety of now-profitable interests on the other, would bring on a crisis. Thus, empires – as the forcible expansion of territory or predominant influence – can be seen as a response to the need to control the *mobility* of people, goods and ideas, sometimes by encouraging it, sometimes by limiting it and almost always by the surveillance of it. For empires should be imagined not as mere slabs of landmass but rather as a series of nodes, and as skeins of routes (over land or sea), giving mastery over the flow of information, instruction, revenue, trade and personnel. Beyond these corridors of control, authority on the ground might wax and wane according to circumstance. But if *they* were lost, and with them command of mobility, the empire could not survive. Second, we might want to qualify the assumption that imperial expansion invariably arose from the will of the ruler. If connectedness is often the predisposing cause, then it is likely that the impulse to expand was felt by a *range* of interests, some perhaps already established in the target region, who exert their political influence to persuade the ruler to act on their behalf. The poverty of sources may make this conjecture hard to test on the earliest empires. But it is a common enough occurrence in more recent times to make it plausible (Darwin, 2009: ch. 2).

But how was an empire once conquered to be preserved? What were the causes of its *persistence*? Here again Mann offers a perceptive analysis. The essence of imperial rule, he says, is 'compulsory cooperation'. The local allies whose role was so vital in the achievement of conquest have (or believe they have) little option but to acquiesce in their over-rule. Of course, this is very similar to the famous assertion by Gallagher and Robinson that the British (and other imperialists) depended upon what they called 'collaboration' (Gallagher and Robinson, 1953). Lacking the means or the will to extend their power and influence worldwide by force, the British fell back on a series of bargains with 'collaborating elites': Indian, African or South American (in their 'informal empire' in Argentina and elsewhere). Gallagher and Robinson were at pains to stress that the bargains made varied according to the strength of the local ruling class and the demands of the imperial power (which might be commercial or strategic). Mann's use of 'compulsory' is, nevertheless, a useful reminder that to extract collaboration from recalcitrant locals required an initial 'investment' by the imperialists, usually of military or naval force. This might be modest. The imperialists' real advantage lay not in numbers or even in technology (contrary to the old adage about the maxim gun). It typically derived from having the means to maintain a disciplined standing force (often of local mercenaries) in the field against local armies of cultivators or pastoralists that lacked cohesion and staying power. Where they faced well-trained and well-led opponents, as in the Indian wars of the 1780s and 1790s, it was a close-run thing (Cooper, 2003). For the success of an imperial 'intervention', much depended on how successfully the initial investment was able to leverage local resources. If it did, then empire became a going concern: if not, it might be confined to the narrowest of bridgeheads. In most cases, however, limited military force obtained massive additional advantage from the lack of political or ethnic solidarity among 'colonial' populations and the relative ease with which the invaders could recruit supporters from those who hoped to profit from the overthrow of the *ancien regime* (Darwin, 1997).

Cooperation, however, was not once and for all: it had to be maintained. It had to be in the interests of both sides if it was not to break down. Writing at a time when much of the literature on colonialism stressed the propensity to resist and revolt in pursuit of nationalist freedom, Mann struck a much more realistic note. Most 'provincials', he remarked, preferred to 'reconsolidate' the empires they lived under, not to destroy them. The reason for this lay in the material benefits that empire conferred: the opportunity to accumulate wealth, to privatise assets once collectively owned and to use reliable systems of value on which they soon came to depend. Empire could also inject new material resources, often by redistributing the tribute or taxes it raised from the conquered. In the Roman Empire, the presence of the legions and the military roads they constructed acted as a form of 'military Keynesianism', a military multiplier galvanising local economies. In modern empires, the equivalent was railways – funded in British India by borrowings from London secured on Indian revenues. 'Reconsolidation' meant a refashioning of the empire's ruling system to admit the provincials to its citizenship or concede them more local autonomy. It reflected the cultural as well as the material attractions of imperial over-rule.

Much of the modern history of empire bears out the shrewdness of this analysis. The preference for 'reconsolidation' is vividly seen in a multitude of colonial (and European) settings. The politicians of the Indian National Congress (founded 1885) made much of their loyalty to 'British connection'. Their most vociferous leaders, including Motilal Nehru (father of the more famous Jawaharlal), argued not for 'independence' but for self-government *within* the Empire. Perhaps more surprisingly, they thought the British gene of 'manliness' was essential if

Indians were to govern themselves successfully (this was why Jawaharlal was sent to Harrow and Cambridge) (Kumar and Panigrahi, 1982: 256). Overseas Chinese in Singapore and Malaya, and Christianised Africans in British West Africa shared much of this outlook. They aspired not to a national independence but to political authority over their hinterlands in partnership with British rulers whom they hoped to persuade to devolve much of their power. But perhaps we should add three further ingredients that helped to make 'reconsolidation' the only practical option. In most cases if not all, revolt seemed out of the question. Indian politicians had only to look back to the Great Rebellion of 1857 and the savage indiscriminate reprisals meted out by the British (in which perhaps 100,000 Indians were killed) to see the objections. Second, the British (like other imperialists) made much of their liberal instincts and constantly promised (not entirely insincerely) to widen the scope of political representation. Third, colonial rule was remarkably successful at internalising in the minds of its subjects much of the imperialist ideology, not least the impossibility of independence in a predatory imperial world. It took the genius of Gandhi to see that freedom was impossible until Indians threw off their mental and moral (as opposed to their physical) subjection. The message of his famous manifesto *Hind Swaraj* ('Indian self-rule'), published in 1909 and promptly banned by the British, was that the British ruled because the Indians allowed them to. We shall discuss in a moment why the appeal of 'reconsolidation' eventually failed and how 'provincials' discovered an alternative order that made 'imperial downfall' preferable.

The third theme for discussion is Mann's notion of 'fractured imperialism'. This is his term for the way in which the rival European imperial powers divided the globe in the later nineteenth century. Twelve empires brought about a 'fractured globalisation'. For Mann, the driving force behind the explosion of European imperialism in the nineteenth century was a combination of 'intensive militarism' and industrial capitalism. Both require some scrutiny and raise further questions. It is now a commonplace of European historiography to detect the rise of a 'military fiscal state' perhaps as early as the late fifteenth century, certainly widely in place by the mid-seventeenth century (Glete, 2002; Yun-Casalilla and O'Brien, 2012). The main result was to endow the majority of the larger European states with the resources to maintain a standing army in peacetime and to finance its expansion in war. In the late seventeenth century, the army of Louis XIV, an imperialist *par excellence* but with his ambitions fixed on Europe, reached the astonishing size of 400,000 men. Britain, France, the Netherlands and Spain also maintained substantial navies whose field of operations extended to the Mediterranean and to the Caribbean, the cockpit of rival mercantilisms since the late sixteenth century. Yet for the most part this dramatic scaling up of military power was applied not to conquest beyond Europe but to internecine struggles within it, culminating in the 'Great War' of 1793–1815. In fact, European armies fared badly outside Europe, especially in the tropics where malaria, yellow fever and dysentery destroyed their manpower with remarkable efficiency (McNeill, 2010). A partial exception might be made for the European conquest of India after 1750. The techniques of the fiscal military state had been exported to India and taken up enthusiastically by some Indian rulers, who also hired European expertise in artillery and infantry warfare. Here, the ultimate success of the British East India Company lay in being a marginally more efficient fiscal militarist than its Indian competitors, especially the 'modernising' rulers of Mysore, Hyder Ali and Tipu Sultan.

After 1815, the European continent remained the primary focus of European militarism. But Mann is right to claim that Europe's militarist culture – embodied in what might be called the 'court-aristocratic-military complex' – created an appetite for adventurism and (sometimes) a vociferous constituency for military conquest. The French occupation of Algiers in 1830, originating in an obscure diplomatic incident, rapidly widened into a military struggle for what is now Algeria in which the generals displayed a notorious indifference to instructions from Paris. 'If I don't like the orders from Paris', remarked one, 'I tear them up' (Fremeaux, 2010). It was a tradition carefully upheld in the subsequent French conquests in North and West Africa (Kanya Forstner, 1969). The Russian advance into the Caucasus – scene of a bloody guerrilla war that lasted into the 1860s – and Trans-Caspian Central Asia might also be seen as reflecting the virtual autonomy of the army so long as it enjoyed the Tsar's approval. The British were different, but not all that much. In their case, the navy was the vanguard of military ambition. By the 1830s, its reach was worldwide. In 1842, its advance up the Yangtse forced the Qing emperor into the first of China's 'unequal treaties'. Maritime policing sucked it into the Indonesian archipelago, the Persian Gulf and up China's rivers. Suppressing the slave trade (not very effectively) gave it a (malarious) toehold on the West African coast. Of course, a naval presence fell short of territorial conquest and Britain's own army was small compared with those of its main European rivals. But the British had a second army in India, mainly of Indians and paid for by Indians. Its Anglo–Indian militarist culture lay behind the progressive subjection of the Indian subcontinent – a process that continued up to 1857 – and extended into Burma and even (in 1904) to Tibet.

Some qualifications are needed, nevertheless. First, European armies typically made very slow progress against non-European opponents and their 'victories' often existed only in the official imagination (and military communiqués) (Belich, 1986). The 'logistics factor' was usually against them: their wars were as much 'against nature' as their human foe (Callwell, 1986). Setbacks and even disasters were not so uncommon: Kabul and Maiwand in Afghanistan, Isandhlwana and Adowa in Africa were signal defeats. No European power showed any appetite for the military conquest of China. In Africa, as in India, conquest was achieved mainly by the recruitment of local mercenaries and by a careful adaptation of local methods of warfare. France's West African mercenaries were reputedly paid in captured slaves, Britain's Maasai allies in East Africa in captured cattle (Klein, 1998; Waller 1976). The all-powerful machine gun used up ammunition so fast that it had to be used very sparingly if at all (Marjomaa, 1998). As we saw earlier, the impact of Europe's 'intensive militarism' was massively amplified not so much by its superior technology as by its deployment as part of a Machiavellian diplomacy of clientelism, the real foundation of European imperialism across most of the world. For all that, we should acknowledge that it was the fear inspired by Europeans' capacity to deploy (sometimes very small) military force with unprecedented rapidity (aided by the steamship, railways and telegraph) that made the overthrow of their colonial regimes hardly more than a pipe dream before the mid-twentieth century.

As Mann suggests, 'intensive militarism' is best understood in alliance with 'industrial capitalism'. It can hardly be disputed that the combination of industrial technology – above all the advances in steam propulsion, mechanised textile production and metallurgy – with the commercial and financial techniques that they stimulated – above all the large-scale mobilisation of capital – endowed Europeans with a technical superiority over non-European cultures that they had lacked before c.1800. Together, they drastically cheapened the cost of empire and simultaneously created a new appetite for it. This was not just a matter of finding new markets or new raw materials. Industrial societies 'at home' became more internally mobile and demographically dynamic. One by one, beginning in the British Isles, they produced a huge stream of migration – some 20 millions alone from the United Kingdom up to 1914. The most durable (and often the cruellest) face of European empire was settler colonialism, including that of the largest of 'white men's countries' the United States, Old Europe's semi-detached wing. Yet even if we acknowledge the power-shift that Europe obtained from militarism and industrialism, many puzzles remain. Perhaps the greatest is the extraordinary, irregular and apparently arbitrary pattern of territorial conquest. It had little to do – on the face of it – with the pursuit of markets or economic advantage. If it had, then Latin America, coastal China and the 'unoccupied' territories that fell into American hands – Texas, California and Oregon – would have been obvious targets for European imperialists. The African interior, so often regarded as the proxy for Europe's voracious expansionism, would have been left alone, especially after the general outlawing of the slave trade and slavery. The 'strange career' of British imperialism (the British were, by a huge margin, the largest traders and investors outside Europe up to 1914) nicely captures this paradox. Much of the greatest share of their trade outside Europe flowed across the Atlantic, to and from the independent United States, the independent republics of Latin America and their colonies in British North America, self-governing since the 1840s. By 1914, two-thirds of their overseas capital was concentrated there. The significance of industrial capitalism needs to be identified with some care if its true role is to be appreciated.

So far, the most persuasive explanation for the 'arbitrary' pattern of imperial conquest has been that advanced some sixty years ago by Gallagher and Robinson. In a long-famous article on 'The Imperialism of Free Trade', they argued that the British adopted a parsimonious and highly selective approach to territorial expansion. Wherever they obtained their economic *desiderata* – an open economy and a minimal tariff barrier to their manufactured exports – by negotiation with the local elites (those 'collaborators' again), they were disinclined to use force or contemplate annexation. Against a less 'cooperative' regime – like Qing China – they applied limited force to impose economic openness. By contrast, their territorial acquisitions were chiefly motivated by the geo-strategic imperative to guard the sea lanes that connected their empire and their extra-European markets: thus Malta, the Cape of Good Hope, Aden, Ceylon (Sri Lanka), Singapore, Hong Kong, the Falkland Islands and (later) the 'veiled protectorate' of Egypt and Egypt's colony, the Sudan. But we might want to add a second powerful constraint to this self-denying doctrine of minimum effort and maximum gain. Those parts of the world where the British abstained from an annexationist imperial-ism were also the places where trying to impose it would have been exceptionally difficult. This was partly because local resistance would have been fierce as it would have been in China as well as in the Americas. But it was also because (as in China or the Near East) they would have been met by Great Power opposition to any unilateral land grab. In all these cases, discretion proved the better part of imperial valour, and pragmatism ruled the pursuit of riches. It was Africa's mis-fortune in the late nineteenth century that its fragmented polities were dangerously susceptible to the subversive tactics of European interlopers and their rag-tag following of adventurers, ne'er-do-wells and unemployed soldiers. Political weakness not enviable wealth was Africa's downfall.

The colonial invasion of Africa brings us to the key question posed by Mann's 'fractured imperialism'. How can we explain the crazy quilt of Europe's overseas empires – the partitions that shared out Africa, the Pacific and South East Asia in a frenzy of line-drawing between 1885 and 1914? As Mann rightly points out, the bottom line was the inability of Britain to uphold what had briefly promised to be a global supremacy. The British lacked the strength (and the will) to knock their competitors out of the ring. The military power available to Russia and France – their most dangerous rivals up to 1904 – was intimidatingly large. The British had to give ground or, as an alternative, insist on defending the 'sick men' of Europe and Asia (the contemporary view of the Ottoman Empire and China) against vivisection by the European Powers. A more difficult question is why the partitions were carried through without the spilling of blood *between* Europeans. For this is the era when, in so many conventional accounts, European imperialism was 'red in tooth and claw' and European rivalry in the 'outer world' a rehearsal for the blood-letting of 1914. It is a striking fact that no two European states went to war over a colonial question between 1870 and 1914 despite the best efforts of lobbyists, publicists and patriots. They settled instead for a form of 'competitive coexistence' in the imperial sphere. The best explanation is also the simplest. For all the European Powers, the arena that mattered was Europe itself. Three of the five great powers were also the rulers of multinational empires at home, where the tide of ethnic nationalism was rising. A European conflict might be the locomotive of nationalist politics. What the European chancelleries dreaded was an 'accidental' war that deranged the continental balance of power. That is why, despite their resentment of Britain's overweening claims, they refused to coalesce against her. That is why partition diplomacy was designed not so much to maximise territorial gains as to prevent the hyperactive 'men-on-the-spot' from dragging Paris, London, Berlin or St Petersburg into unwanted wars for acres of desert and scrub. Where they could not agree on a bloodless partition, they left matters alone – sometimes to simmer at a dangerous heat. The breakdown of this 'huff and puff' diplomacy in July 1914 occurred because the patched-up solution to the collapse of Ottoman power in the Balkans suddenly threatened a catastrophic upheaval in the European balance of power.

Two other facets of 'fractured imperialism' deserve some attention. When the European Powers drew a line on the map, declaring one side to be British and the other to be French, the administrative zones they created were mere bundles of districts ruled on a shoestring where governed at all. The colonialists' compact not to attack each other meant that there was neither need nor incentive to endow the colony with more than the barest trappings of statehood. Indeed, for most of the period up to 1945, colonial rulers found it convenient to treat these possessions as a random collection of ethnic fragments unified only by common subjection to a tiny cadre of aliens. These were the 'shallow states' that they bequeathed to the 'nationalists' at the end of empire. In Mann's terminology, they were 'fragile interaction networks' with an emphasis on the 'fragile'. The second point arises from Mann's (surely correct) observation that in the inter-war years Hitler showed little interest in forging a global empire and was willing to acquiesce in the 'fractured imperialism' with its huge British component. But the contrast with the handling of imperial ambition by the 'old diplomacy' of before 1914 is certainly stark. The three main aggressors of the world crisis of 1937–45 all displayed a ruthless indifference to the existing balance of power, partly because they saw themselves as its victims, partly because the economic depression seemed to demand the creation of vast autarkic empires. The anomalies and absurdities of 'fractured imperialism', congenial to Conservative Europe before 1914, made little sense in this 'beggar-thy-neighbour' world. The 'shallow states' that it had fostered went down like ninepins under the strains of war and its gruelling aftermath. This can be seen in the ease with which Japan carried through the conquest of French Indo-China, the Netherlands East Indies, and British Malaya and Burma (Bayly and Harper, 2004). It remains to turn to the last of our themes, Mann's analysis of the end of empire.

Perhaps it needs to be said first of all that Mann does not think that the age of empires and imperialisms is over – a view with which the present writer agrees. So it less a question of why empire has ceased to be a viable form of polity than of why particular versions of empire have failed to survive. One way of framing the problem is to ask why collaboration or 'compulsory cooperation' breaks down, or why, in Mann's terms, the 'provincials' begin to prefer the break-up of the imperial system to its 'reconsolidation' in a more acceptable form. Mann's instinct is to see the breakdown of an empire as a consequence of its failure to be inclusive, to satisfy the aspirations of its subject peoples. Thus, in reflecting on the fall of the Roman Empire, he rejects the commonplace explanation (at least since Gibbon) of 'overstretch' or, in Gibbon's language, of 'immoderate size'. On the contrary, it was the 'boundedness' of the Roman system that brought on its downfall. This was because, by imposing closed frontiers and *limes*, guarded by its legions, it deliberately excluded 'barbarian' peoples who longed to enjoy the fruits of *Romanitas*. Like angry *sans-culottes* shooed away from the gates of the rich and respectable, their response was to smash their way in and take what they could. Under huge sustained pressure, the Roman defences gave way, and the imperial system collapsed. Interestingly, this thesis has once again become fashionable among ancient historians (Heather, 2005). For modern empires, Mann proposes a variation on the theme of exclusion. Here, however, the active ingredient is the racism of the Europeans: their refusal to admit the civilisational equality of their subject peoples or – in many cases – their *potential* for civilisation. Denied any prospect of a reasonable share in the government of their own societies, colonial elites saw no alternative except to work for the overthrow of the empire, having despaired of its reform.

There is much in the record of anti-colonial nationalism that lends plausibility to this argument. We might note in passing that a sense of victimhood, exclusion and disparagement by arrogant master-races has fuelled nationalist movements within Europe as well as outside it. The language of empire in every part of the world (and perhaps in every era) proclaimed the superior moral virtue of the rulers and, quite often, their superior physique. If the 'lazy native' flourished in colonial Africa, *Polnische Wirtschaft* justified German rule over lazy Slavs. But the function of racism in colonial societies was not quite as straightforward as these examples suggest. The British are sometimes considered the most unambiguously racist of the European imperialists. Yet they imposed a colour-blind franchise (as in Cape Colony in the 1870s), rejected the claims to self-government of tiny white minorities, acknowledged the claims of Indian elites to a share in provincial government (in the reforms of 1892 and 1909) and eventually accepted (in August 1917) the principle of India's eventual self-rule. Moreover, as we have seen already, the contrast they drew between their moral and physical 'manliness' and the timidity or 'effeminacy' of Indians was endorsed by some of the early leaders of the Indian National Congress. Much as we now deplore its expression, racism was not entirely dysfunctional in the management of empires. Indeed, it might be argued that a carefully cultivated ethno-cultural solidarity has been a vital part of the tool-kit of imperial rulers in every place and time. The Manchu elite in Qing China practised segregation and exclusion (of the Han majority) with as much enthusiasm as the British in India. Racial solidarity among the British wherever they formed a tiny ruling cadre was well understood as the key to their survival (and safety) in the face of a suspicious and resentful subject peoples. It was deliberately reinforced by commemorative practice (as in the remembrance of the Cawnpore massacre in 1857) and local literary production (especially where there was a local press) as well as by vulgar prejudice. In the British empire, race served a further vital function. A sense of shared racial origins and destiny bound the 'British peoples' in Canada, Australia, New Zealand and South Africa (where they made up 40 per cent of whites) to the 'mother country' in Britain. Long after they attained almost complete self-government, they self-identified as 'British' ('English' in South Africa) and claimed to embody an invigorated version of the racial virtues of the British 'at home'. It was this 'British' identity, as much as any notion of shared *interests*, that prompted the astonishing manifestations of loyalty in the two world wars of the twentieth century: some 1 million volunteers from the 'white dominions' served in British armies in Europe and the Middle East between 1914 and 1918. The 'blood sacrifice' of the white dominions equalled or exceeded that of the British at home.

Whether resentment at racial exclusion and the political mobilisation it stimulated was enough in any modern case to pull down an empire is, however, a moot point. For some of the reasons we have discussed already, a direct assault by subject peoples on their rulers (however modest in number) was rarely practicable. Most colonial regimes were guarded by (small) local armies carefully recruited from communities that were unlikely to sympathise with the local elite: often from hill peoples or other minorities who saw themselves as oppressed by *local* rather than imperial 'master-races'. The Indian Army, with its British officer corps, was disproportionately Muslim: the Indian National Congress was predominantly Hindu. Most colonial regimes enjoyed or obtained a range of emergency powers to jail or 'extern' troublesome local politicians. Moreover, local elites were rarely united enough to present a common front and withdraw 'collaboration' on a large enough scale to make imperial rule unworkable. Worse still, they were extremely wary of employing the tactic that could have broken the back of most colonial regimes: the fomenting of *mass* opposition. The reason is obvious enough. Living in deeply unequal societies where public order was largely dependent on the social authority of local 'big men', mass unrest could easily get out of hand. Indeed, it might as easily be turned on the most immediate sources of grievance – landowners, rent collectors, money lenders, shopkeepers, oppressive chiefs – as upon the remote, rarely seen agents of empire. Thus the most dynamic anti-colonial movement of the first half of the twentieth century, Gandhi's 'non-cooperation' movement of 1920–22, collapsed when its supporters turned on the police, burning a number to death at Chauri Chaura in the United Provinces (today's Uttar Pradesh) in March 1922. Gandhi's main allies drew back in horror. Nor, of course, did imperial rulers simply sit on their hands as the political scene shifted. They could dole out concessions – safeguards to some constituencies, benefits to others – as a potent reminder that any change of regime would bring upheaval and loss as well as the promise of freedom.

Indeed, there was little sign anywhere before 1939 that nationalist movements were capable of the forceful overthrow of colonial rulers: even in India the Congress leaders had resigned themselves to an indefinite 'war of manoeuvre' with the British. The critical factor there (indeed, we might think this was true of most empires in history) was geopolitical – the external environment in which the empire existed. Almost universally, the *sine qua non* of imperial rule, of the effective exercise of 'compulsory collaboration', was the exclusion of disruptive influences from outside, certainly in its physical form and preferably in its ideological as well. Nothing gave more hope to even the weakest of oppositional movements than the promise of outside help to distract or intimidate their rulers. And if the rulers were embroiled in a war and were forced to conscript 'provincial' resources in the struggle, they were likely to breach the informal covenants that bound their local allies to them. It was at this point, to return to an earlier discussion, that 'provincials' might decide that 'reconsolidation' had finally lost its appeal and a new regime was essential to preserve their interests. In the classical era of decolonisation between 1945 and 1975, these internal and external pressures converged in a 'perfect storm'. In the Second World War and its aftermath, the colonial powers exploited their empires as never before in their struggle for survival. At the same time, the outcome of the war discredited much of the ideological underpinning of 'fractured imperialism' and drastically demoted the colonial powers in the face of the new (and ideologically 'anti-imperialist') superpowers. One consequence was to raise the costs of maintaining imperial rule to the metropolitan societies – in some cases dramatically. In a new world order in which the sovereignty of all 'nations' – a term defined very liberally – became the basic law, the weakened collective of European colonial powers abandoned their empires with almost indecent haste. Two qualifications are needed. First, it was of crucial importance that a global Cold War formed the geopolitical setting for this imperial exit shaping both its course and chronology. Second, two great empires remained in being: the Soviet and the Chinese. Both were exempt (in the Soviet case until the later 1980s) from the geopolitical forces that acted upon the old colonial powers. Both remained free to coerce their subject peoples physically and ideologically in ways that were no longer open to their old Western rivals.

A final point might be made. As Mann reminds us, empire could come in several forms, including what is often termed (in the language of

Gallagher and Robinson) 'informal empire'. It was this version, he suggests, that the United States adopted after 1945. Not everyone would agree with this characterisation of the global power that the United States has exercised since the 1940s, if not before (as can be seen elsewhere in this volume). Indeed, carelessly used, 'American imperialism' becomes merely a term of abuse. Nevertheless, the arguments for assimilating America's global expansion to the history of empires is hard to deny so long as we recognise that the *form* empire takes is bound to reflect the geopolitical and cultural setting in which imperial aims are pursued. It would be hard to deny that American leaders and 'informed opinion' were eager to exploit the great geopolitical opportunity that opened up in 1945. They were anxious to break out of the economic prison of the 1930s when America's economic recovery appeared to be constrained by the autarkic regimes of Germany and Japan and (even more) by the British sterling bloc. They wanted to shore up their geostrategic security after the traumatic discovery that their 'fireproof house' was alarmingly fire-prone. And they were naturally keen to promote friendly, ideologically sympathetic regimes among their neighbouring states, a category that was now bound to include Western Europe. The British in 1815 were similarly determined to reap the economic and geopolitical benefits of victory. They encouraged the break-up of the Spanish–American empire, primarily for commercial reasons, and set out to force open markets wherever they could. They urged the merits not of democracy but of 'representative government', believing that it would make for friendly, peace-loving neighbours. Of course, unlike the British, the United States had no Indian Empire: it was too late for that. Nor did it have settlement colonies, although Alaska and Hawai'i bore a close resemblance. But it rapidly acquired a vast string of globe-spanning bases, the latter-day equivalents of Gibraltar, Malta, Aden, Singapore and Hong Kong, and invested enormous resources in a globe-commanding navy. It already possessed an inner ring of quasi-protectorates in Central America and soon began to acquire an outer ring of client states scattered broadcast across the globe.

The most distinctive feature of America's global expansion was the close defensive alliance with the West European states and Japan, an alliance on the face of it between sovereign states. Yet even here there was a certain likeness to the relations between Britain and its self-governing and (after 1931) formally sovereign 'white dominions'. They too long depended upon the development capital and strategic protection supplied by their patron, occupying a position of 'dignified dependence'. The British at home were careful to avoid the language of subordination when dealing with the notoriously prickly dominion leaders, just as they pretended that Egypt after 1922 was an independent state despite the restrictions they imposed upon it. Indeed, much British opinion in the 'heyday' of empire was curiously indifferent to an explicitly 'imperial' ideology of the 'white man's burden' variety and preferred to think of Britain's world mission as the spread of free trade and a Christian humanitarianism. Certainly, the United States has eschewed the language of empire (in its formal sense) and renounced the confiscation of sovereignty as a weapon of statecraft: it was forced to pursue its geopolitical interests in an emerging bi-polar world order in which both sides employed (however disingenuously) the rhetoric of democracy and national liberation and in a world in which formal empire had become morally disreputable. But if we attend to *function* rather than *form* (and remember how much British world power depended upon cooperation rather than rule), we might want to conclude that the parallels between the American trajectory and that of the only real world-system between 1830 and 1940 (uncontroversially described as the British 'empire') are surprisingly close.

But even informal empire is not a cheap option, as London discovered in the 1950s and 1960s, and Moscow in the 1980s. Nor is it a stable category. It is arguably even more susceptible to the vagaries of economic and geopolitical change than its territorially defined counterpart. But while vast discrepancies in the power of states persist – as they will do indefinitely – the potential for empire-building in one form or another will also remain. No fixed definition of empire will be helpful to grasp this phenomenon since the geopolitical, economic and ideological conditions for empire-building are in constant flux. If we keep that caution in mind and acknowledge that empire is a sempiternal element of world history, then the conceptual framework laid out in *The Sources of Social Power* will serve as a uniquely insightful guide to the dynamics of empire-making and breaking.

References

Bayly, C and Harper, T 2004 *Forgotten Armies: Britain's Asian Empire and the War with Japan*. London.
Belich, J 1986 *The New Zealand Wars*. Auckland.
Brackenbury H, 1874 *The Ashanti War: a Narrative Prepared from the Official Documents*, 2 vols. London.
Callwell, CE 1986 *Small Wars: Their Principles and Practice*. London.
Cooper, RGS 2003 *The Anglo-Maratha Campaign and the Contest for India*. Cambridge.
Darwin, J 2009 *The Empire Project: the Rise and Fall of the British World-System*. Cambridge.

1997 'Imperialism and the Victorians: the Dynamics of Territorial Expansion' *English Historical Review* cxii, 447.

Fremeaux, Jacques 2010 *De Quoi Fut Fait l'Empire: les guerres coloniales au xix siècle*. Paris.

Gallagher, J and Robinson, R 1953 'The Imperialism of Free Trade' *Economic History Review* vi.

Glete, J 2002 *War and the State in Early Modern Europe: Spain, the Dutch Republic and Sweden as fiscal-military states 1500–1660*. London.

Heather, P 2005 *The Fall of the Roman Empire*. London.

Kanya-Forstner, AS 1969 *The Conquest of the Western Sudan*. Cambridge.

Klein, M 1998 *Slavery and Colonial Rule in West Africa*. Cambridge.

Kolff, D 1990 *Naukar, Rajput and Sepoy*. Cambridge.

Kumar, R and Panigrahi D (eds.) 1982 *Selected Works of Motilal Nehru*, Vol 1. Delhi.

Marjomaa, R 1998 *War on the Savannah: the Military Collapse of the Sokoto Caliphate*. Helsinki.

McNeill, JR 2010 *Mosquito Empires: Ecology and War in the Greater Caribbean 1620–1914*. Cambridge.

Schumpeter, JA 1951 'Imperialism' in *Imperialism and Social Classes*. English Translation. New York.

Subrahmanian, L 1987 'Banias and the British: The Role of Indigenous Credit . . . in Imperial Expansion in Western India' *Modern Asian Studies* xxi, 473–510.

Waller, R 1976 'The Maasai and the British: The Origins of an Alliance, 1895–1905' *Journal of African History* 17, 4, 529–53.

Yun-Casalilla B and O'Brien PK (eds.) 2012 *The Rise of Fiscal States: A Global History 1500–1914*. Cambridge.

13 Hegemonic power during the Cold War and beyond

Odd Arne Westad

Michael Mann's work has stood at the centre of debates among historical sociologists and historians ever since the first volume of his magnificent *Sources of Social Power* appeared in 1986. Although I have far too often failed to make explicit reference to it, Mann's writing has deeply influenced my own work, both in terms of orientation and explanations.[1] With the publication of Volumes 3 and 4 in 2012, Mann has completed the best synthesis yet of concepts of power and their uses through history. It is a superb achievement, because Volume 4, which I will discuss in this chapter, caps a series of books that are stimulating, thorough and exceptionally useful for both social scientists and historians.

I am particularly impressed by how Mann's approaches develop throughout the four volumes and, I suppose, the almost thirty years of work that they encompass. Although the basic preoccupations remain the same, as do the primary definitions of social power, the focus expands massively in the final two volumes. They move away – sometimes quite dramatically – from the Eurocentrism that Mann was accused of holding in the two first volumes. And they become deeper and more positioned in an empirical sense: While the two first volumes took the discussion through two millennia, the final two deal with what could be called the (very) long twentieth century, from the 1870s to 2010, or thereabouts.

As a historian of contemporary international affairs, I appreciate the increased depth that comes with Mann's twentieth-century focus. I also very much agree with him that it makes sense to speak of a long twentieth century, one that starts with the great recession of the 1870s and ends with the great recession of the 2010s, rather than the short twentieth century from the outbreak of the First World War to the end of the Cold War, which the great historian Eric Hobsbawm among others present.[2] This is

---

[1] This is especially true for *The Global Cold War* and *Restless Empire*, but also the project I am working on now, provisionally entitled *Worlds Apart: The Cold War in the Twentieth Century.*

[2] Hobsbawm (1994).

not economic determinism but a serious attempt at getting to grips with the impact that increasingly rapid economic change has had on people's lives and therefore on their concepts of what constitutes social power.

As Mann's account becomes broader and deeper, it also becomes less theoretically parsimonious. This is, as can be imagined, both a strength and a weakness. More theoretical generosity means an ability to explain phenomena that were left aside in the first two volumes. But it also opens up for explanations that are too broad or contradictory. One such example, to me, is Mann's summing up of the reasons why the United States did not acquire formal colonies around the turn of the century, which ranges from having been burnt by their experiences in Cuba and the Philippines, via lacking pre-existing imperial institutions, to the rise of corporate capitalism.[3] All of these are probably correct, to some extent or other. But there may be a need for more authorial guidance on what matters most to Mann, especially as the US non-expansion in territorial terms becomes a key element in defining the bases of US power in the century that follows.

Cold War origins

The international conflict that dominated much of the twentieth century – the Cold War between the United States and the Soviet Union – stands at the core of Mann's fourth volume. The Cold War was, as Mann recognizes, always a complex phenomenon. In many ways it fits very well into Mann's four dimensions of power. In terms of economic power, it is about the expansion of capitalism in a global sense. In terms of political power, it is about the development of highly centralized states. In terms of military power, it is about the preoccupation with weapons of mass destruction. And in terms of ideological power, it is about the conflict between American liberal capitalism and communism, with the former emerging victorious.

As Mann presents the conflict in Volume 4, the outcome is almost over-determined. The United States was more powerful than its main enemy, the Soviet Union, at least on the first three of these dimensions of power. There is no doubt that Mann is right on this; it is not difficult to see the Cold War primarily as a relentless expansion of US power on a global scale. The Soviet alternative could score minor successes as long as it could isolate itself from globalizing capitalism, centralize science and production, and have easy access to plentiful domestic raw materials.

---

[3] Mann (2012a).

But in the end, the United States out-produced, out-managed and out-gunned the Soviets.

The only aspect of power in which the Soviet Union could compete with the United States was in terms of ideology. The appeal that communism as 'scientific socialism' had in most corners of the world (except the Anglo-American core) at different times during the Cold War was remarkable. The promise of an alternative way of organizing human affairs – emphasizing social justice and a planned and purposeful use of the powers of production – gave rise to new states from China to Cuba and produced results that are very notice-able today. I wonder if Mann sometimes passes over the ideological dimension a bit too easily in Volume 4 (also compared to what he does in the first two volumes): the transformative power of ideology is to me one of the key elements to understanding the twentieth century (and especially the Cold War).

Where I would disagree with Mann is in terms of the deeper origins of the Cold War as a Soviet–American conflict. There is a recent tendency among historians to attempt to avoid over-determining the Cold War by making its origins dependent on the outcome of the Second World War. The story-line goes, roughly, that there were many challengers to American power at the beginning of the twentieth century – Britain, Russia, France, Germany and Japan all at different times and by different means attempted to frustrate the growth of US hegemony. They all failed, but they failed *slowly*, and it was therefore only by 1945 that the United States ruled supreme, with the exception of the Soviets and their allies who had to be overcome through a Cold War.

The advantage of this interpretation, which reconfirms the orthodox view that the Cold War started in the late 1940s, is that it is neatly packaged in an almost teleological fashion while verbally stressing the diversity and complexity of the international history of the early twentieth century. It also hints that post-1945 history could have turned out differ-ently if the Second World War alliance between Soviets and Americans had been allowed to develop further.

Mann does not share the emphasis on mutual misunderstandings and strategic folly in the immediate post-war period that some analysts of the Cold War prefer. But he does seem to think that the United States and Soviet leaders of the 1940s and 1950s were caught in their own rhetoric and that they believed that they were acting defensively while in reality building up military capabilities that the other side could only view as aggressive. He also stresses that both the United States and the Soviet Union came to see other conflicts as inherently connected to the Cold War conflict between them; Stalin, for instance, was obsessed by fear of a

German resurgence and worried that the United States would assist in such a venture.

My own view is somewhat different from this. Increasingly, I see much deeper causes not only of Soviet–American antagonism, but of the emergence of the Cold War as a global system. Already from the 1870s (if not before), the United States and Russia were emerging as new kinds of great powers. Their transcontinental expansion had given them control over amounts of territory that the British and French empires could only mobilize non-contiguously and that had an almost unlimited resource base for production. Both saw rapid increases in population. And, at least from 1917 on, elites in the two countries had ideologies that were sharply different in content but which shared a universalist approach to world affairs. Avoiding any determinism, it seems overwhelmingly likely that these two states would come into conflict with one another. And it seems more likely than not that they – not Britain, France, Germany or Japan – would become the ultimate challengers for global hegemony in the twentieth century. Stalin, in the late 1940s, worried not about German revanchism, but about the harnessing of German industrial capacities to the purposes of American power.

This is not a realist argument in the sense that conflict was preordained; as I show in my own work, political leaders made decisions that produced the Cold War. Nor is it an argument for analysing political developments at the state level only: there were disagreements among both Soviet and US leaders on how to approach the Cold War conflict (though both states were more ideologically cohesive than the lesser powers in international affairs). But it is realist in the sense that it emphasizes material potential as a precondition for a state's global reach. The form of production that both the United States and the USSR engaged in depended on easy access to raw materials and a centralization of productive capacity. During most of the twentieth century, this gave advantages to large countries with large and growing populations (different from, say, the seventeenth century).

Unlike much of the existing literature, I do not argue for the kind of Cold War parallelism that the era of the conflict itself was so full of. The United States during the length of this period became a much more powerful state than the Soviet Union *on all scores*, except perhaps nuclear weapons (although I strongly doubt whether the kind of parity that Cold War nuclear theologians spoke about ever truly materialized). My point is rather that in terms of power potential these two were in a league of their own. That is why they emerged as the main victors of the Second World war, and why they became the two poles in the Cold War system.

The Cold War is therefore both part of the history of the growth in US predominance in the twentieth century and linked to histories that were going on on a global scale. That the Soviet experiment ultimately failed is not an argument against giving it its place in history. In its heyday it was the only other state that could have challenged the United States for supremacy within all the dimensions of power that Mann rightly is pre-occupied with, and especially with regard to ideology. The attention that others paid it – its American or European and East Asian enemies, or its adherents and admirers there and elsewhere (especially in the Global South) – was therefore not misplaced; it was a reflection of what was going on at the time.

The global expansion of the Cold War system was also connected to the existence of the Soviet Union as an alternative to capitalism. Obviously, the United States expanded its control globally in order to draw material benefit from that expansion, especially in economic and resource terms. But it also intervened in order to stop radical movements that were inspired by communism and the Soviet example. Only a few US Cold War interventions took place against agrarian reformers and liberal progressives – most of them were against communists (as in Korea and Vietnam) or other socialists energized by Soviet-style forms of development (Cuba, Laos, Angola, Ethiopia, Nicaragua). These people and their projects were real and not just invented by American anti-communists in order to justify their country's global expansion. The existence of the Soviet Union, both during the Comintern period and after the Second World War, meant at least the opportunity for anti-capitalist groups and movements to get material support for their aspirations from outside their own borders.

This, to me, is the only meaningful way to talk about Cold War 'bi-polarity': A number of political experiments which otherwise would probably have been scuppered at the outset survived at least in part because of Soviet support. The People's Republic of China is of course the biggest example (and the most relevant one for us today). But there were numerous others scattered around the globe. In some cases, their political programs set off civil wars which often continued for a very long time because of US support for their enemies. The same, of course, can be said the other way around: the Soviets (and their allies) supported rebel movements that were out to overthrow regimes held up by the United States. The result in both cases tended to be the same: long, out-drawn conflicts with terrible human costs because neither side was capable of gaining an overall victory.

Cold War endings

Mann's observation that US power is very diverse in different parts of the world is very well taken and one I fully agree with. It is not particularly important here, I feel, to engage in a discussion about whether the United States is an empire – in some cases it obviously behaves like one, in other cases not. It clearly engages in imperial behaviour on a large scale: in Japan in the post-war era, or in Iraq today, or in a lot of other places in between. But the main point, at least to me, is to show how US policies and strategies are historically linked to an epoch of what could be termed European 'high imperialism' that began in the late nineteenth century and continued through the Cold War (and to some extent up to today).

I therefore agree with Mann's observation that 'US dominance became more hegemony than empire'.[4] It also became profoundly ideological in a universalist kind of sense: only by replicating key aspects of the US experience, most Americans believed, could other countries become efficient, prosperous and free. This was in many ways as true for the post-war US presence in Western Europe as it was when the United States organized, funded or staffed interventions against various Third World projects in the 1960s, 1970s or 1980s. But it was in the latter countries that the gap was widest between what the United States and its local allies attempted to achieve and what conditions allowed for. The US 'high imperialism' therefore had a very destructive aspect to it: it caused massive dislocation at the local level, especially among the peasantry, such as in Central America, in Indochina or in southern Africa.

The Cold War warfare and other forms of coercive operations that the United States engaged in link in a somewhat ironic form to the development of US hegemony in the final phase of the Cold War, from the late 1970s onwards. Yes, interventions and overall preponderance of power were costly and contributed to the US deficits of the late 1960s and early 1970s, which – in turn – provoked Richard Nixon to destroy the Bretton Woods system in order to allow a de facto devaluation of the dollar. But American power also helped convince first allies, in the 1970s, and then former enemies, in the 1980s, that the United States should have its way in terms of financial regulations and access to markets elsewhere. Combined with the massive expansion of finance capital on a global scale, which was – to some extent – an unintended consequence of the collapse of Bretton Woods – this gave the United States the chance to buy into and to some extent control a massive expansion of the world capitalist system.[5]

Seignorage mattered in this, as did the increasing – and to some extent self-inflicted – weakness of the opposition, meaning the Soviet Union and its allies. Soviet-style wastefulness and lack of productivity, excessive military expenditure and accompanying political oppression

---

[4] Mann (2012b).   [5] See, on this, Arrighi (1994, 2010).

delegitimized not only the Communist Party of the Soviet Union (CPSU), but also hurt attempts at creating states inspired by the USSR in Africa, Asia and Latin America. Still, this is the minor part of the story. By the mid-1980s most countries that diverged from free market capitalism, ranging from the USSR's communism to the import-substitution economies of Latin America, were hit by what seems a perfect storm: as global financial markets expanded and the US economy internationalized, autonomy increasingly meant marginalization. With prices of raw materials under pressure and the international financial institutions, the International Monetary Fund and the World Bank under US control, most socialist countries had nowhere to turn. The US model seemed, increasingly, the only game in town.

The timing of this global transformation is essential. It came as the Soviet Union (as Mann correctly observes) experienced historically low internal growth rates. It also coincided with China emerging from the worst years of the Maoist nightmare. And China is, in many different ways, perhaps the best illustration of how the end of the Cold War determined what the world looks like today.

China and the future

While I agree with Mann that the Maoist regime in a way prepared China for its current economic expansion, I would argue that it mainly did so involuntarily and accidentally. As for Eastern Europe, some historians argue that the centralized use of resources, the emphasis on education and health and the priority given to industrial growth prepared the way for other forms of growth. But for China this can only be said about the first decade of communist rule, when the country – more or less – followed the Soviet planning model.

And even then growth was limited, especially if one takes into consideration the very low starting point for China in 1949. China had been going through hell ever since the collapse of the Qing in the early part of the twentieth century (or some would say since the mid-nineteenth century). Wars had been followed by civil wars, which had been followed by even more disastrous wars. A key reason for the high growth rates during the first five-year plans was simply catching up on a backlog of unrealized potential (a bit similar to the high Soviet growth rates from the late 1940s to the late 1950s, or in the inter-war years).[6]

---

[6] Dikötter (2014) is a good overview, though a new economic history of China in the 1950s still needs to be written. For the Soviet Union, see Mark Harrison (2011).

After 1958, political excesses in Chinese communism increasingly got in the way of any rational planning regime, with disastrous results. Not only did Chinese industries atrophy and its science and technology get cut off from the rest of the world, but large-scale starvation led to the worst decimation of the population ever known in peacetime, with an estimated 45 million excess deaths between 1958 and 1961. Maoism may have prepared China for what came later, but primarily through destroying what remained of 'old' China in social and psychological terms.

After the military-led coup against the Maoists in 1976, the new regime found very little from Maoism worth rescuing. Deng Xiaoping's adherents had to pay lip-service to China's past (Mao had been 70 per cent right and 30 per cent wrong, Deng said – curiously the same percentage score that Khrushchev had given to Stalin twenty years before). But in reality, the search for a new model started almost immediately and reached its high point as Deng's regime solidified in the early 1980s.

This is where the timing of China's 'reforms' come into play. Deng had to feel his way towards a new model of economic development for China just at the time when global finance and global markets were expanding rapidly. These matters obviously influenced his decisions, to the extent that some Chinese historians have argued that if it had not been for Deng's observations of the international scene, his political instincts may well have driven him back to some form of state planning as was the vogue in the 1950s and the Soviet Union. Instead, Deng concluded that only the United States was in a position to further China's economic growth substantially, and only the US form of markets would help to get China quickly out of its economic quagmire. Leaving for his first visit to the United States in 1979, Deng is supposed to have told his audience that a key lesson of twentieth-century history is: whoever works with the Americans will gain, while those who try to oppose them will fail.[7]

China benefitted immensely from its security alliance with the United States. Mao had set it up to prevent a Soviet attack. But Deng made use of it for economic and commercial reasons as well. In turn, the commercialization of daily life in China expanded rapidly. By the 1990s, it is clear that any meaningful Chinese claim to be a socialist state was gone. The state may think that it governs the economy through ownership of the 'commanding heights' of the economy, such as banks and energy companies. But in reality, these companies have to live within the market system, domestically as well as internationally, and their main purpose is to make a profit. Social services are worse in China than in any capitalist

---

[7] Information from Ambassador Wu Jianmin in conversation with author, London, October 2013.

254 Odd Arne Westad

country in Europe or North America; social inequality even more so. China is now one of the most unequal countries in the world in terms of its Gini score. And more Chinese believe that the market will find solutions to their main problems than is the case in the United States (74–68 per cent; in Spain the score is 47 and in Mexico 34).[8]

I therefore disagree with Mann (225) that China today carries with it a non-capitalist mode of development. The more interesting discussion, which Mann also touches on, is whether China (and other countries such as Russia, Vietnam, Angola, Algeria, etc.) are developing kinds of stable politicized capitalisms similar in nature but different in form from the United States, Germany or Japan.[9] Although I agree with Mann that there has always been significant differences in how capitalism is practised within individual states, my main point is that I do not believe that China's capitalism will have much of an influence on how markets are organized internationally. Nor will it serve as an example for other states, except in a purely negative way, as for instance when more than a few African politicians see nothing wrong in cronyism and corruption because that is the way matters are handled in China.

My sense is that the future pattern of development is likely to be the other way around, with Western and perhaps especially Japanese forms of capitalism influencing what is happening in China. Just as Xi Jinping's new government is intent on strengthening the political dictatorship, they seem preoccupied with expanding the role of the market in the Chinese economy. The program of deregulation and financial liberalization now announced would change Chinese capitalism even more towards models existing in other countries with a longer history of capitalist development. Mann is of course entirely right when he points out that there is, through the history of the past two hundred years, a propensity for making private confiscations and expropriations of common property permanent through property, stocks and corporations. Having witnessed how this has already happened in China over the past thirty years, I can testify that it is not a pretty sight. But neither was the introduction of capitalism in Britain and the United States, of course.

What China does have, however, is an opportunity to reform its polity in manners that will be different from the political systems in the West. Time will show whether those who do away with the current dictatorship will choose such a course. Is there a chance that China will use the existing capacity of the state, which at present is concentrated on avoiding popular

---

[8] Pew Global Attitudes Project: www.pewglobal.org/2012/07/12/pervasive-gloom-about-the-world-economy/
[9] Mann to author, August 2014.

unrest, and thereby facilitate the exploitation of ordinary people by robber barons to improve public welfare, access to education and social justice? My answer to this is that it can happen, but only if China's democratization helps empower those very groups that the People's Republic has excluded so far – first and foremost the working class, young people and those who want to learn from grassroots democratic experiments elsewhere.

References

Arrighi Giovanni. "The World Economy and the Cold War," in *The Cambridge History of the Cold War*, ed. Melvyn P. Leffler and Odd Arne Westad, vol. 3 (Cambridge: Cambridge University Press, 2010).

Arrighi Giovanni. *The Long Twentieth Century: Money, Power, and the Origins of Our Times* (London: Verso, 1994)

Dikötter Frank. *The Tragedy of Liberation: A History of the Chinese Revolution, 1945–57* (London: Bloomsbury, 2014)

Harrison Mark. "The Soviet Union after 1945: Economic Recovery and Political Repression," *Past & Present* 210 (January 2011): 103–20.

Hobsbawm E. J. *Age of Extremes: The Short Twentieth Century, 1914–1991* (London: Michael Joseph, 1994).

Mann Michael. *The Sources of Social Power. Volume Three: Global Empires and Revolution, 1890–1945* (Cambridge: Cambridge University Press, 2012a).

Mann Michael. *The Sources of Social Power. Volume Four: Globalizations, 1945–2011* (Cambridge: Cambridge University Press, 2012b).

14 The last empire? American power, liberalism, and world order

G. John Ikenberry

"How is the Empire?" King George V asked as he lay dying. "All's well, sir, with the Empire," replied his secretary.

Introduction

Michael Mann's fourth volume surveys the rise of the post-1945 global order. In these decades, American power holds center stage. In Mann's account, the world wars of the first half of the twentieth century bring the European era to an end. The great European empires and the "segmented" global system built around them are swept away. Out of the rubble emerges the United States. Unrivaled in power, it seizes the opportunity to reorganize the world. America's interest in an open world economy and the threat of rising Soviet power trigger an ambitious world order-building project. What emerges is a new type of empire – built not around colonies but client states and a global system of alliances. This American-style imperial system thrives, backed by the sword and the bible – that is, backed by military power with global reach and a sense of mission. It is, as Mann argues, "the only global empire there has ever been." Despite its novelty, the American empire is nonetheless an empire, a global order built and maintained by American power and self-regard. With the collapse of the Soviet bloc and the end of the Cold War, the United States now stands alone as a global power – the last empire.

This American-style empire plays a leading role in Mann's world-historical narrative. It is one of three pillars of the global system, together with transnational capitalism and the nation-state. It is a protean force as Mann tells the story. Under American auspices, the world economy entered a "golden age," non-Western states gained independence and stable geopolitical relations were "cemented" among most of the advanced countries of the world. But despite these wider advances in the global order, Mann insists that America runs an informal empire. Mann notes that most Americans "deny they ever had an empire," but with this volume he intends to "prove them wrong." By insisting on this label, Mann is emphasizing that the postwar global order is built on an organized system of American domination. The implication is that it is – like the empires of the past – an imposed system of hierarchical rule. Like past empires, American military force stands ready to enforce the terms of order. Indeed, the history of the last half century is one of repeated and unsanctioned US military intervention. Americans might think that they are "leading" the world and championing anti-imperial forms of order, but, as Mann insists, the United States is really playing the same old game of empire. Indeed, precisely because the American postwar order is an empire, Mann can confidently expect it to eventually unravel and disappear – the fate of all past empires.

But does Mann really prove his empire thesis? Is "empire" the best way to capture the character and logic of the American-led global order? Certainly, the United States built an international order – and it had lots of features and forms, including crude imperial ones. But does placing this American-led order in the company of other empires illuminate its deep logic or obscure it? These questions bear on the more substantive questions. What motivated the United States to build and lead the postwar international order? What gave it its distinctive character? How do we assess its accomplishments and the damages it inflicted on the world? And, finally, what is its future?

In engaging Mann on the origins, character, and future of this American system, I argue that the notion of "empire" misses the more distinctive and novel forms of order that it manifests. Unlike traditional empires, the American order has been both built upon and circumscribed by two great order-building projects of the last century – the Westphalian project and the liberal internationalist project. The spread of the nation-state and the rise of new forms of institutionalized cooperation have fundamentally reshaped the terms of American global domination – doing so to such an extent that the term "empire" itself misses the larger logic, character and trajectory of international order.

The United States might be best seen not as the "last empire" but as the first post-imperial global power. To be sure, the United States has dominated the global system in the twentieth century, imposing itself and its ideas on the world. It has intervened to prop up and overturn regimes in South America, the Middle East, and Asia. But the overall effect of America's efforts to establish its dominance has been to undermine imperial forms of order. The United States used its rising power to defeat the great mid-twentieth-century empires – Japan, Germany, and the USSR. It also used its power – finance and trade – to undermine the British empire. Indeed, because of its ideas, interests, geopolitical setting and historical timing, the United States tended to build international order around anti-imperial logics and movements. It is an order that has established institutions and norms of legitimacy that serve to restrain old-style imperial despotism and the exercise of indiscriminate and arbitrary power. It is an order that has not prevented the United States from intervening in weak states in the periphery, but it has imposed costs on doing so – as the Bush administration discovered with its war in Iraq. It is a hierarchical order, but one that enshrines democracy, human rights and the rule of law. It is an international order where sovereignty, liberalism and multilateral cooperation coexist with power, inequality, and domination.

Varieties of empire and international order

Empire is an evocative term. It has been wielded by scholars to describe an extraordinarily diverse array of ancient and modern systems and realms of order. Mann does not explicitly define what empires are in the fourth volume. It is used as a descriptive term – referring to powerful states that dominate others. It is an organized hierarchical system; a structural configuration of power and control.[1] Within this overall category, leading states exhibit the logic of empire in widely differing ways across eras and regions. In the second volume, empires are introduced by tracing the development of Japanese, British, and the early decades of the American empire. The imperial state dominates secondary and peripheral societies, usurping their sovereignty and imposing hierarchical rule on their polity and economy.[2]

Indeed it is the variety of imperial forms that come through in Mann's work. There is formal empire and informal empire. There are spheres of influence. There are military protectorates. In one categorization, Mann offers a spectrum of types of domination by cores over peripheries, the first four of which are empire – direct empire, indirect empire, informal empire, economic imperialism, and hegemony.[3] Mann argues that the Soviets started out with an informal empire but, after the Second World War, turned it into a "semi-direct empire." When Mann turns to the United States, he also finds an extraordinary variety of styles and forms of leadership and domination. The United States is an informal empire, manifest through military intervention and military proxies; and in

[1] For discussions of empire as an organizational form, see Doyle (1986); Motyl (2001); Lieven (2001); Darwin (2008); and Burbank and Cooper (2011).
[2] The best discussion of empire in Mann's work is in Volume 3, pp. 17–28. There is also a discussion of the differences between multistate civilization and hegemonic empire as the two forms of geopolitical diplomacy in Volume 1, p. 27.
[3] Mann (2013).

relations with other advanced countries, American domination takes the form of hegemony.

Mann gets at the richness of these types of domination. What is less clear is what explains these variations – and how grand shifts across the modern era, particularly in the twentieth century – have altered the deep structures of domination. Mann chronicles the other deep sources of power and order in the past two centuries – nationalism, democracy, liberalism, capitalism, and so forth. But Mann does not fully connect how these world-historical shifts in modern society have implications for the character and logic of empire. Mann argues that the United States is the first "global empire," but is the American-led postwar global order an empire as such, or is it an international order that has "imperial characteristics" as well as other types of characteristics?

This question – whether "empire" is a description of the American global order or a facet of it – is important. And Mann forces us to ask this question. His description of the American-led order does emphasize variety – or, as Mann puts it, "the sheer variety of forms of domination the United States has deployed."[4] Particularly noteworthy are hegemonic relations, which are in Mann's terms a non-imperial form of domination. Hegemony refers to more consensual forms of association, where the United States establishes order through the building of rules, institutions and markets. States are not coerced, strictly speaking, to join the order. They join the order seeking benefits. Mann sees this dynamic primarily in the economic arena. Over Europe, Mann argues, American domination has primarily been hegemonic, leading to various sorts of dependency on the United States for markets and security. American postwar relations with East Asia were originally a mix of informal and indirect empire, marked by wars to defend client states. But over time, Mann observes, domination in East Asia has become more benign and hegemonic.

So, in Mann's rendering, America's relations with the two major regions of the world – the home of the most advanced industrial societies – are not imperial at all. The terms of the relationships are more reciprocal and consensual. Mann provides the example of the American dollar to illustrate this hegemonic dynamic. The international role of the dollar provides benefits to other states – creating a stable financial and monetary order. But it also gives the United States benefits. The United States can export the costs of macroeconomic adjustment onto other states and it can run balance of payment deficits without triggering a run on its currency. This is not empire. It is a hierarchical order in which states play different roles, pay different costs and experience different benefits.

---

[4] Mann, Vol. 4, p. 24.

States might like to live in a different type of order, but given the alternatives, this one is better than the available alternatives. In the financial and monetary order, hegemony is manifest as an open system organized around various sorts of rules and institutions. The United States plays a disproportionate role – a hegemonic role – in setting the terms of order, but it also operates more or less within the rules and institutions. Hegemonic order is less despotic than empire, and where rules and institutions do in fact hold sway, the order takes on liberal characteristics.[5]

Mann does not want to pursue this logic of hegemony too far. He has promised to show that America does run an empire. But not doing so risks giving an incomplete picture of the logic and character of the wider global order, which is decidedly not imperial. Indeed, it might be useful to describe the American-led order as hierarchical – but one with different types of hierarchy. In some places and times, it is "hierarchy with imperial characteristics." In other places and times, it is "hierarchy with liberal characteristics." No one disputes that the United States has pursued crude imperial policies of military intervention in Latin American and the Middle East. It has client states and exercises various forms of informal and indirect rule or influence over them. But it also has established more open and rule-based forms of order across the world. These might be hegemonic realms of order or they might simply be liberal internationalist in character.[6]

The problem with Mann's framing of the American-led order is his initial move – depicting the United States as the "first global empire." What is important to observe is that the United States built an international order. Other major states built empires. To build an empire is to establish zones of more or less exclusive control. It is a transnational political formation; it is a hierarchical structure of politics and economics; it is a geopolitical hub and spoke system. When European great powers were building empires, they were not building international order. They were building geopolitical and economic zones of control. To build international order is to establish the wider framework for relations among great powers and other states and societies around the world. To focus on the search for empire in the American-led postwar system is to miss this larger order-building project.

The shift from building empire – as zones of exclusive control – to building open and rule-based international order emerged in the

---

[5] For discussions of the distinction between empire and hegemony, see Doyle, *Empires*; Munkler (2007); and Nexon and Wright (2007). See also Go (2011).
[6] This formulation is offered in Ikenberry (2011).

nineteenth century with Great Britain. It did run a formal empire. But it also used its power – naval, commercial, financial, geopolitical – to promulgate rules and institutions of order. These were essentially liberal-oriented rules and institutions – open trade, freedom of navigation, and so forth. It simultaneously presided over an authoritarian empire. The United States stepped forward after 1945 and offered a much more ambitious vision of an open and loosely rule-based international order. And, as Mann notes, the United States pursued informal and indirect types of imperial policies as well.

My point is that Mann's volume does not pull back to look at the wide structures of international order. This wider order is not simply a globalized order built on Mann's three pillars – the nation-state, transnational capitalism, and American empire. To speak of it as an international order is to open up an inquiry into is logic and character, placing it alongside other manifestations of international orders in other times and places. International orders might be seen as the settled array arrangements that define and guide relations among states and societies. As such, international orders can differ in terms of their geographic scope – they can be regional or global. They can differ in terms of their functional scope – they can be organized around security arrangements – such as the balance of power or a set of alliance relations – or they can have more elaborate rules and institutions to deal with economics, politics and so forth. International orders can be highly institutionalized or based on informal rules and institutions. They can be more or less hierarchical – relations between states can be highly vertical with a dominant or despotic lead state or they might be less hierarchical, where states operate according to more equal and horizontally organized rights and authority. Finally, international orders can be organized to benefit the leading state or the gains of operating in the order may be more widely and evenly distributed.[7]

The imperial features of America's global order coexist with a wider international order. As I suggest below, this wider order is quite unique in world-historical terms. It has more liberal hegemonic and liberal internationalist features, most of them supported by the United States. Mann provides hints of some of these features when he notes the way that postwar developing states in East Asia and elsewhere were able to generate remarkable economic growth through outward-looking development strategies. Meanwhile, during the same decades, the United

---

[7] For discussions of these and other dimensions of order, see Ikenberry (2001, 2011); Hurrell (2007); Lake (2009); Clark (1987); Katzenstein (2005); Hall (1996); Gilpin (1981); and Bull (1977).

States and Europe were able to expand their social welfare systems while pursuing trade liberalization and opening the world economy. During the Cold War, the United States did turn itself into the leading military power and it intervened militarily or covertly in most regions of the world. At the same time, it became the world's leading exporter of security. In each successive decade since the 1950s, the United States has taken on more military partnerships or alliance commitments. Mann argues that this global security system is an important – perhaps even the defining – feature of the American-led global order. But for Mann, it is fundamentally a tool of domination, or as he suggests, quoting Chalmers Johnson, it has created an American "empire of bases."[8] But as Mann also notes, in at least Western Europe, this American security system is best seen, this time quoting Geir Lundestad, as an "empire by invitation."[9] Other authors have also sought to capture this more muted and restrained character to American power, using terms such as "consensual empire," "empire by consent," and "empire of trust."[10]

The shift in focus from "empire" to "international order" allows us to better capture these diverse manifestations of American power – imperial, hegemonic, and liberal. It allows us to appreciate the complex ways in which the United States has been greeted by other states and peoples. The United States has been a purveyor of violence to some peoples in some dark moments of the Cold War and in recent Middle East wars. It has also been a purveyor of security to states in most regions of the world. Japan and Germany have been able to rebuild and reintegrate themselves into the global system under the auspices of these America-led alliances. Even after the Cold War, most countries with security ties to the United States moved to reaffirm these ties. These patterns of alliance security and political solidarity are not comprehensible if we only look at them through a lens of empire.

Origins of the American empire

Mann offers an extraordinarily rich portrait of the American postwar order. It is an order, as he stresses, that is marked by its variety of relations and structures. Democracy, nationalism, capitalism, and extensive forms of international cooperation coexist within it. As Mann notes, the advanced industrial West experimented with various sorts of social democratic and neoliberal visions of capitalist democracy. Non-Western states rose up within this order, pursuing their own models of development. The Cold

---

[8] Johnson (2005).   [9] Lundestad (1998).
[10] See Maier (1991); Gaddis (1997); and Madden (2009).

War also played a role in generating a sort of "Cold War liberalism," backed by a military industrial complex. After the Cold War, the United States entered a new era of unipolar military domination and interventionism. These domestic and international, economic and security spheres interacted in complex ways, shaping and reshaping international order.

But why did the United States undertake this grand exercise in building global order? Mann says that the United States "might have turned inward upon itself," but he notes that "this was never very likely since enough politicians and corporations saw American prosperity as tied to the fortunes of the global economy, one that also needed military defense against communism."[11] This seems about right. The United States was overflowing with power – economic, financial, military, and technological. Indeed, the war itself had made the United States a global power – almost overnight. Its troops and arms were spread across Europe and East Asia. In this sense, American global domination was "acquired suddenly," as Mann notes, through a war that the United States did not seek to enter and with armed forces it did not wish to mobilize. The United States did not seek to build an empire. The United States was "inward-looking" until it was attacked by the Japanese. But, Mann argues, "as with many empires," their suddenly mobilized military forces could be deployed after the war to fill power vacuums and establish new realms of domination.[12]

Mann nicely captures what might be seen as the core impulse behind America's postwar push for domination. The United States saw its economic fate tied to a stable and open world economy. Openness and stability were both important. Openness was a question pressed on the United States by the economic upheavals of the 1930s. The world economy had broken down into blocs, empires, and spheres of influence. In the late 1930s, American strategists debated whether the United States could exist as a great power within a world divided into blocs and spheres. This would entail limiting its trade and resources to perhaps only the Western hemisphere. So the question was: how large did the "grand area" need to be? That is, how large a geopolitical space would the United States need to have access to in order to prosper as a great power? By the time the United States was in the war, the answer to American leaders was clear. The "grand area" would need to be global. The United States would need to have access – for trade and resources – to all regions of the globe.[13] This judgment seemed to settle the matter. The United

---

[11] Mann, Vol. 4, p. 24.   [12] Mann, Vol. 4, p. 25.

[13] Mann briefly mentions the notion of the "grand area." The Council on Foreign Relations, which conducted intensive postwar planning exercises, focused on this question of the "grand area." It was also taken up by scholars – most importantly, in

States would need to seek to open up and gain access to a full-blown world economy.[14]

But the world economy would need to be stable as well as open. This was another lesson that the United States drew from the 1930s. It was the fear of economic contagion, where unwise economic policies pursued in one country threatened the stability of others. President Franklin Roosevelt stressed this point at the opening of the Bretton Woods conference in July 1944: "the economic health of every country is a proper matter of concern to all its neighbors, near and far."[15] There would need to be new international mechanisms to manage and stabilize the postwar open world economy. This was a bit of an intellectual sea change in thinking about global economic relations. Jacob Viner, a leading American international economist, captured this new thinking in 1942: "There is wide agreement today that major depressions, mass unemployment, as social evils, and that it is the obligation of governments ... to prevent them." Moreover, there was "wide agreement also that it is extraordinarily difficult, if not outright impossible, for any country to cope alone with the problems of cyclical booms and depressions ... while there is good prospect that with international cooperation ... the problem of the business cycle and mass unemployment can be largely solved."[16] The point was that the United States would need to work with other states to build frameworks for cooperation that would give governments the ability to reconcile movements of trade and capital with policies that promoted stable and full-employment economies.

The United States had an overriding interest in a postwar international system that was open and stable. Widely recognized by American elites, this interest was not embedded in an ideology or vision of American domination, at least not until after the Cold War took off. It was simply a straightforward belief about how the international environment in which the United States operated would need to be arranged. Moreover, it was an interest that was decidedly anti-imperial in its substantive implications. In an open and cooperatively managed system, imperial zones and regional spheres would need to be destroyed. As the "grand area" thinkers concluded, summarized by Santoro, "the only area sufficiently large was the one equivalent to the world economy as a whole

Spykman's (1942). For a detailed discussion, see Santoro (1992). I discuss the American policy debate on the "grand area" in Ikenberry, *After Victory*, pp. 179–80.

[14] The American interest in an open world economy followed directly from its economic growth and trade. Between 1860 and 1940, raw materials rose from one-tenth to one-third of total imports. Meanwhile, between 1914 and 1939, Europe ceased to be the main source of imports. During this period, Europe's share was almost halved and Asia's share was doubled.

[15] Quoted in Ikenberry, *After Victory*, p. 190.   [16] Viner (1942).

and driven by the United States."[17] The imperial great powers of the 1930s sought to build blocs and spheres of control – that is, to gain exclusive control over regions and geopolitical zones. The United States saw its interests tied to breaking down these blocs and spheres to construct an open global system.

This impulse toward creating an open and managed world economy was reinforced by the distinctive geographical and world-historical setting in which the United States found itself. Specifically, the United States is unique in that it is the only great power that is not neighbored by other great powers – and it emerged in these remote geographical circumstances as a "late developing" great power. This has had several implications. First, geographical insularity made the rise of American power during the twentieth century less threatening. Remarkably, the United States became the world's leading power without triggering war or balancing. Indeed, even after the Cold War, when the United States was truly unipolar, other great powers – who were oceans away – did not balance against it.[18] None of the other major states – including Great Britain, France, Germany, Japan and China – has this geographical advantage. Each lives in a crowded geopolitical neighborhood where shifts in power are routinely met by counter-balancing. China is discovering this today as its growing power is greeted by hedging and balancing reactions, manifest as surrounding states engage in military modernization and the reinforcement of alliances.

Second, America's geographical remoteness reinforced its incentives to champion universal principles that allowed it access to the various regions of the world. This is an observation about geography and historical timing. The United States emerged as a great power relatively late – only in the first half of the twentieth century. By the 1930s, the United States confronted a situation where most of the regions of the world were closed, divided into empires, blocs and spheres of influence. As noted earlier, the underlying judgment that the United States acted on was that the size of the "grand area" necessary for viability as a major state needed to be global. The United States needed to open up and gain access to these regions. So the United States championed global rules and institutions rather than old-style imperial organizing ideas. It championed the open door, self-determination and anti-colonialism, not for idealist reasons but because of the practical need to get Europe, Asia, and other regions open for trade, investment, and diplomacy. In this sense, geography and its late arrival as a great powers are what launched the United States on its project to organize a global order. It was globally oriented

[17] Santoro, (1992).   [18] For elaborations, see Ikenberry (2002).

G. John Ikenberry

because it needed to open up and link itself to the major regions of the world. This, in turn, gave it incentives to articulate anti-imperial principles and rules, such as openness, non-discrimination, and self-determination. If the United States built the first "global empire," it did so by elevating universal principles and multilateral rules and institutions. It had to turn the old organizational logic of empire on its head.

Third, America's off-shore geographical position also turned on its head the way many states in Europe and East Asia thought about American power. They worried more about abandonment than domination. States in postwar Europe and East Asia sought to draw the United States into playing economic and security roles within their regions. They looked for ways for American military commitments to help solve regional security problems. For example, France and Great Britain wanted an ongoing American security commitment as part of a wider regional system that would help restrain and integrate West Germany into Europe. Japan was also able to use the alliance with the United States to solve its security problems and find a pathway back to growth and modernization. As Mann argues, these are characteristics of hegemonic – rather than empire – relations of power. But it was America's distance from these regions that made it less threatening. The challenge was – and still is – to find ways to make America's security commitments credible. Given America's remote geographical setting, the upside of getting the United States to provide security is greater than the downside of lost autonomy and risk of domination that is associated with being a junior partner or client state. It is not that American domination goes away. It is that the cost-benefit calculations are different from they would be under other circumstances.

Fourth, America's geopolitical setting also reinforced its incentives to support various sorts of national movements toward statehood and self-rule. Again, this is an anti-imperial order-building impulse. It has a realist-style logic. If a great power cannot directly dominate a weaker state, its second best option is to support that state's sovereignty and independence, precisely so that it will not be dominated by a rival great power. Ian Chong, for example, argues that the United States championed sovereignty and self-determination in East Asia as a way to avoid being excluded. Chong argues that great powers do prefer outright domination if they can get away with it. But within East Asia – and for most of the world, except the Western Hemisphere – this was not a realistic option. So in postwar states such as China, Indonesia, and Thailand, the United States eventually put its weight behind movements toward national self-determination.[19] In Chong's view, the United States is not

[19] Chong (2012).

unique in pursuing this "second best" strategy. Great Britain and other European powers have promoted state building – that is, self-determination and sovereign independence – in various parts of the developing world to undercut bids by rival great powers for regional domination.[20] But geography and historical timing made this a dominant American postwar strategy of order building.

The way the United States rose up and shaped twentieth-century international order was unique. It grew powerful in relative isolation from other major powers. It became a world power during the high tide of great-power empires. It did not become a great power through conquest. It stepped into vacuums and postwar moments to shape the geopolitical settlements. In one sense, it was like Great Britain in an earlier era. It tried to shape events as an "off-shore" power. It did not seek to become a continental power. Its comparative advantage was in offering other countries security protection, undercutting bids for dominance by land powers in Asia and Europe. Unlike Great Britain, the United States did this through a system of alliances and client states. In seeking to build a global order it advanced universal principles and multilateral rules and institutions. These tools of domination made the order more hegemonic and less imperial.

Liberal hegemony and global order

In Mann's portrait, the postwar global order is built on three pillars – American empire, transnational capitalism and the nation-state. These are important facets of the existing global system. But there is more to it as well. Today's international order can be seen as a complex and multi-layered political formation. It is an order that bears the marks of empire, hegemony and liberal internationalism. It is not just a crystallization of the distribution of power – it is constituted with authority relations, shared expectations, and settled practices through which states do business. Order is indeed built on the structured asymmetry of power. The most powerful states dominate – or try to – and seek to impose their ideas and interests. But, at least in the postwar era, international order has become a sort of de facto and loosely organized system of politics and governance. It is marked not by empire but by politics and institutions. There is give and take. It is a political order with a hegemonic leader, differential roles, rules and norms, and complex moving parts.

There are several features to this order that underscore its post-imperial or liberal hegemonic character. One is simply its integrative tendencies.

[20] See Jackson (1990).

States of various sizes and types have found pathways into this loosely organized order. Germany and Japan were the first major states to reconstitute themselves and integrate into postwar security and economic institutions. Some states joined the order in ways that Mann describes – as client states or front line allies during the Cold War. After the Cold War, many of the post-Soviet states and some of the former Soviet republics joined the European Union and NATO. Many countries integrated into the order by making political and economic transitions. One can see this as the steady expansion of the Organization for Economic Cooperation and Development – a club of the developed market economies – which has grown from twenty countries at its founding in 1960 to thirty-four countries today. The point is that a wide range of states outside the West have sought to get into this order, to rise up and seek gains within it. The institutions and ideology of this order – hegemonic and liberal internationalist – seem to facilitate this integration.

A second characteristic is shared leadership. Hierarchical orders can differ in terms of the presence or absence of coalitions of states and stakeholders. That is, order can be more or less dominated by a single state. A leading state can organize and dominate the international order, standing above other states. Alternatively, the order might be made up of a wider coalition of major states that cooperate together – and lead the order – in various ways. In this regard, the existing international order is not really an order in which one state "rules." It is an order organized around an array of great powers, junior partners, client states and other stakeholders. In the economic realm, authority and decision making is shared. This is true for the formal multilateral institutions – the IMF, World Bank, and WTO. It is also true for the informal leadership groups such as the G-7 and the G-20. These are still hierarchical institutions, but they are inhabited by a coalition of leading states. The United States and Western Europe remain overrepresented in many of these organizations, but they are not based on fixed membership or voting rights.[21] Doors are open and bargains are on the table. The movement of activity from the G-7 to the G-20 also suggests ways that leadership mechanisms are evolving as power shifts away from the old West great powers.

A third characteristic is the way economic gains are spread across the international order. Orders can differ in the way that economic and other material rewards are distributed across states. The economic gains from the order can accrue disproportionately to the leading state, or those gains can be shared more widely. In traditional imperial orders, the profits and

---

[21] On the difficulties of accommodating rising non-Western states in global institutions, see Wade (2013).

gains have flowed overwhelmingly to the imperial core. In colonial and informal empires, economic gains have flowed disproportionately to the wealthy and powerful states, classes, and societal groupings that organize and run the order. In the existing order, with its system of open trade and investment, the profits and economic gains seem to be more widely shared.[22] In the case of the American-led postwar order, trade and investment across the system allowed states near and far to grow and advance, often outpacing the United States or its Western partners. States in all regions of the world over the past half century have made systematic efforts to integrate into this American-led order in pursuit of trade and growth.

A fourth characteristic of order is the degree to which it accommodates diversity of models of capitalism and strategies of development. In this regard, the postwar global order has been – in practice if not in ideology – remarkably broad-minded. There have been three general types of capitalist models. One is the Anglo-American neoliberal or fundamentalist model. This takes center stage beginning in the 1980s and dominates thinking in Western capitals into and past the 2008 global financial crisis. A second is the older postwar model of "embedded liberalism" which is more social democratic in its emphasis on the social welfare state and "managed" openness. A third is the statist development model that has been pursued throughout East Asia and the developing world.[23] What is interesting is that these different models have tended to coexist. As Mann notes, "The United States might not like such policies but it lumped them." The United States set the "global rules" but they were implemented "with some autonomy by a world of nation-states."[24]

These aspects of the American-led order reflect its hegemonic and liberal internationalist character. Integrative tendencies, shared leadership, distribution of economic gains and tolerance of diversity are features or dimensions of international order. The argument is not that the existing global order conforms to some ideal type of liberal hegemonic system. Rather, it is that orders can be compared along these dimensions – and the current order seems to have more integrative tendencies, shared leadership, distribution of economic gains and tolerance for diversity than past international orders – and certainly more than one would expect from a

---

[22] There is a literature that explores "who benefitted" from empire. But there is less systematic work that explores the distribution of economic gains across the wider global and regional orders in different historical eras. D.K. Fieldhouse has done some of the best work on the economics of empire. See Fieldhouse (1973, 1999). On the American case, see Woodruff (1975).

[23] See Amsden (2001). For a discussion of the struggles between the United States and developing countries over development and economic policies, see Amsden (2007).

[24] Mann, Vol. 4, p. 28.

global empire. The sharp edges and steep hierarchies of empire seem to be missing in today's global order.

In the background, two great long-term order-building "projects" have helped shape today's post-imperial global order. These are the Westphalian project and the liberal internationalist project. The Westphalian project is associated with the creation and expansion of the modern state system. This is the project that has seen the promulgation of rules and principles associated with state sovereignty and norms of great power conduct. The other is the liberal order-building project led by Great Britain and the United States over the past two centuries. This project has been pushed forward by the "liberal ascendency" – that is, the rise of liberal democratic states to global dominance in the twentieth century. Both these order-building projects have unfolded in waves, phases and historical turning points, marked most importantly at postwar moments of peacemaking and reconstruction.

The Westphalian project has involved the development of rules and institutions that enshrine the system of sovereign states. At the heart of this order is the notion of state sovereignty and great power relations. The founding moment of this project was, of course, the Westphalian peace of 1648, but the rules and norms of state relations have continued to evolve. The founding location of this project was, of course, Western Europe. Great powers, empires and universal religious authority competed for dominance on the continent. Through wars and peace settlements, rules and norms of the Westphalian order took shape and evolved. The result has been the rise and evolution of the so-called Westphalian system of states. The great powers compete, cooperate, and balance each other within a wider framework of rules and norms. In the background, Westphalian norms of sovereignty enshrine states as formally equal and independent, possessing the ultimate authority over their own people and territory.

Over the centuries, the Westphalian system has evolved as a set of principles and practices and expanded outward from its European origins to encompass the entire globe. Despite this unfolding, however, states have retained their claims of political and legal authority. The founding principles of the Westphalian system – sovereignty, territorial integrity and non-intervention – reflected an emerging consensus that states were the rightful political units for the establishment of legitimate rule. Norms and principles that subsequently evolved within the Westphalian system – such as self-determination and non-discrimination – served to further reinforce the primacy of states and state authority. These norms and principles have served as the organizing logic for Westphalian order and provided the ideational source of political authority within it. Under the banner of sovereignty and self-determination, political movements for decolonization and independence were set in motion in the non-Western developing world. Westphalian norms have been violated and ignored but they have, nonetheless, been the most salient and agreed upon rules and principles of international order in the modern era.

The succession of postwar settlements – 1815, 1919, 1945, 1989 – also provided moments for the great powers to develop principles and practices that have shaped and updated the functioning of great power relations. Along this historical pathway – through war and settlement, learning and adaptation – it is possible to see an evolution in how the great powers have operated within a multipolar balance of power system. The source of order remained rooted in a decentralized states system in which major states compete and balance each other. But the practices and principles of competition and balance have evolved to incorporate strategic notions of restraint and accommodation, providing the great powers – Western and non-Western, rising and falling – with an accumulation of mutual understandings and experiences with which to manage their relations.

The liberal order-building project followed from and built upon this evolving system of Westphalian relations. In the nineteenth century, liberal internationalism was manifest in Britain's championing of free trade and freedom of the seas, but it was limited and coexisted with imperialism and colonialism. In the twentieth century, liberal order building was pushed forward by the United States in several phases. After the First World War, Woodrow Wilson and other liberals pushed for an international order organized around a global collective security body in which sovereign states would act together to uphold a system of territorial peace. Open trade, national self-determination and a belief in progressive global change also undergirded the Wilsonian world view – a "one-world" vision of nation-states that trade and interact in a multilateral system of laws creating an orderly international community. But this experiment in liberal order collapsed into an inter-war period of closed economic systems and imperial blocs.

After the First World War, the Roosevelt administration again engaged in liberal order building, embracing a vision of an open trading system and a world organization in which the great powers would cooperate to keep the peace. American architects of postwar order – drawing lessons from the Wilsonian failure and incorporating ideas from the New Deal period – also advanced more ambitious ideas about economic and political cooperation embodied in the Bretton Woods institutions. This vision was originally global in scope and spirit, but it evolved into a more American-led and Western-centered system as a result of the weakness of postwar Europe and rising tensions with the Soviet Union. As the Cold War unfolded, the United States took command of organizing and running the system, taking on new commitments and functional roles in both security and economics. Its own economic and political system became, in effect, the central component of the larger liberal hegemonic order.

A development of liberal internationalism was also quietly launched after the Second World War, even if it took root more slowly and in tension with aspects of the Westphalian system. This was the elaboration of universal rights of man, enshrined in the United Nations and the Universal Declaration of Human Rights. This human rights revolution is deeply embedded in the postwar liberal international project. A steady stream of conventions and treaties followed that together constitute an extraordinary vision of rights, individuals, sovereignty, and global order. In the decades since the end of the Cold War, notions of "responsibility to protect" have given the international community legal rights and obligations to intervene into the affairs of sovereign states – one more ingredient in the layer cake of ideas, norms, rules, and institutions that has resulted from two centuries of the Westphalian and liberal international projects.

Seen in this light, the modern international order is not really American or Western – even if, for historical reasons, it initially appeared that way. It is both wider and deeper. In the post–Second World War decades, the United States did step forward as the hegemonic leader, taking on the privileges and responsibilities of organizing and running the system. It presided over a far flung international order organized around multilateral institutions, alliances, special relationships, and client states – a hierarchical order with liberal characteristics. These implications of America's geopolitical position and the historical timing of its rise – together with the grand unfolding projects of the Westphalian state-system and liberal internationalism – have transformed the terms of global domination during the era of American dominance.

Militarism and interventionism

There is a sort of paradox of American power in the postwar era – the United States dominated the global system during the decades when there was an almost universal unraveling of empire and colonialism, but during these same decades the United States also engaged in manifold military interventions and covert actions across this transforming developing world. How do we square these contradictory impulses at the heart of the American century? How does the "dark side" of American power relate to the more "enlightened" aspects of the American order-building experience?

The unraveling of empire and colonialism – formal and informal – is well documented in Mann's volume. From the 1950s to the early 1960s, the previous century's era of imperial expansion underwent a radical reversal. As Robin Winks notes: "One after another, the colonized territories tried to establish their independence from European control. From Guinea to Somalia, from Morocco to India, the flags of France, Britain, Italy, Holland, Belgium, Spain, and Portugal came down. In their places were hoisted newly designed flags of the newly sovereign states. By the mid-1980s, no substantial area was under colonial rule, although the racially discriminatory regime prevailed in the Republic of South Africa."[25] America's rise as a global power took shape during this great shift from empires to nation-state – and, indeed, the building of an American-led order was premised on the breakdown of rival empires and illiberal projects.

But the other side of the American experience is also well known – the wars, the covert inventions, the coups and the illiberal client states. Mann nicely helps out here by noting the very different American impulses and policies that were manifest in the different regions as empires melted away and independence movements – nationalist, communist and otherwise – took hold. Much of the imperial behavior that Mann describes takes place in the chaotic Cold War decades when the United States found itself drawn into these regions in various ways. In East and Southeast Asia, the United States fought costly wars. The United States saw itself fighting international communism, as Mann notes, not anticolonial nationalism. In Latin America, the United States engaged in a more recognizable form of gunboat diplomacy, covert operations, and proxy foreign policy. In the more strategically located Middle East, the United States imposed order and secured access to oil through client states. As Mann argues, the American motives for intervention ranged from anti-communism to the profit motive. On occasion, more "progressive" impulses found their way into American relations with the developing world – immediately after the Second World War, with JFK's Alliance for Progress, and during the Carter years. Ultimately, as Mann concludes, "US imperialism was neither very beneficent nor very rational, except where communism did loom large."[26]

Mann's observation is astute. America's experience with the "dark arts" of empire was not particularly successful or integral to its larger order-building efforts. At least this is what we can conclude in retrospect. Yet, at the time, American officials did seem to think that interventions to shape political outcomes in the developing world were critical to fighting

[25] Winks (1993).   [26] Mann, Vol. 4, p. 127.

the Cold War. This is where the logics of imperialism and liberal order intersect. The United States waged a Cold War struggle in which openness and access to the world's regions – indeed capitalism, liberalism, and democracy – were on the line. The interventionism of these decades was justified and legitimated on the basis of this larger struggle. In postwar Europe and East Asia, the states were developed and capable, and the United States needed their cooperation. So the United States built liberal hegemonic relations. Where the United States encountered weaker and less important states, it was less liberal or restrained.

When the United States did engage in imperial-style wars or interventions, these episodes were mostly unsuccessful and damaging to American global interests. The Vietnam War was terribly costly and brutalized not just Southeast Asia but also America itself. The Iraq War of 2003 met a similar fate. Indeed, this war damaged American leadership and its reputation for power – and it undermined the willingness of other countries to work with it on shared interests. The full costs of the Iraq War will not be known for years or even decades, but the price tag will certainly exceed $1 trillion. The war also reduced the willingness of the American people to support future military adventures. This is important because it reveals not just where empire and liberal world order intersect – but also where they diverge and contradict. These self-styled imperial pursuits have tended to diminish and undermine America's global power position. It is precisely because the United States does have a non-imperial vision of itself that these costs are felt and generate a backlash.

Going a step further, the liberal international order – America's great project – provides at least a weak brake on American imperial pursuits. A large part of the international resistance to the Bush administration's war in Iraq was based on standards of conduct that the United States has championed. In particular, Western Europeans attacked Bush's war as a violation of Western notions of sovereignty, multilateralism, and international law. Two scholars have called this "liberal anti-Americanism."[27] The charge is that the United States is hypocritical – that it is not living up to its professed principles and values, standards of foreign policy which they also embrace. The United States has unrivaled military power, so it has capacities to intervene in weak states around the world, and it can offer enlightened rationales for these actions based on ideas about "responsibility to protect" and anti-terrorism. But it still finds itself constrained by global rules and institutions that it pushed on the world in the postwar era.

[27] Katzenstein and Keohane (2007).

Conclusion

Mann provides a rich and illuminating portrait of the United States and postwar global order. But the narrative of empire is forced and limiting. Ultimately, it obscures as much as it illuminates. The United States led in the creation of a global political formation that is not best seen as empire – informal, indirect or otherwise. Indeed, the proliferation of qualifiers to the term empire shows how inadequate it is as a concept to capture the character of American power and global domination in the current era. To be sure, the United States has had more opportunity than any other state in world history to shape the terms of world order. It has had power and historical openings. In the past century, it has engaged in an extraordinary amount of global activity – building, engaging, opening, intervening, spending, manipulating, announcing, and so forth. Along the way, the United States has shown the world many faces – isolationist, militarist, hegemonic, nationalist, realist, neo-conservative, and liberal internationalist. The political formation built under American auspices is complex and distinctive, and seen in world-historical terms, it is not best described as an empire.

Mann hints at why this is true when he notes that the United States is the first "global empire." But a global empire, simply by aspiring to span the world, is a fundamentally different sort of formation or project than the classic empires of the past. Classical empires are based on efforts to carve out exclusive zones or blocs. In contrast, a globe-spanning political order is by necessity premised on breaking down and abolishing exclusive zones and blocs. To organize and manage a global system requires a different set of rules and institutions than imperial orders. It requires frameworks for cooperation. It requires universal rules and institutions. The task of building global order takes states down a different road than the imperial projects of the past. Two additional considerations reinforce this anti-imperial logic. First, the United States also embraced capitalist and liberal democratic ideas about order that are deeply anti-imperial, at least in implication. Second, behind the scenes, two longer-term projects have been unfolding over the centuries – the Westphalian project and the liberal international project. These are not projects that the United States put in motion, but they are projects that the United States harnessed as it built postwar order. They are projects that shaped the logic and character of the American-led order, undercutting empire as a dominant political form.

Finally, Mann is quite skeptical and critical of America's role in the postwar world. He sees an American empire that will end soon – and it is an ending that he seems to welcome. His commitment to an "empire narrative" makes this view easier for him to hold. After all, who is not against empire? But Mann is too harsh. There is so much more that has gone on within this American-led order since 1945, beyond lamentable American military actions and imperial pursuits. Mann notes some of these accomplishments mostly in passing. The global economy was opened up. Germany and France composed their differences and launched the European project. Japan and Germany were integrated into the postwar order and acquired wealth, power, and authority within it. States across Asia, Latin America, Africa, and Eastern and Southern Europe have made political and economic transitions. There have been no major wars among the great powers during this era – the longest period in the modern era that leading states have not fought each other. Liberal democracies are struggling with problems of inequality, fiscal deficits, and political stability – but liberal democracies have spread worldwide and they articulate the norms and principles of world order that command the most legitimacy. These are accomplishments, and they have been realized precisely because we live in a post-imperial era.

References

Amsden Alice H. *Escape from Empire: The Developing World's Journey Through Heaven and Hell* (Cambridge: MIT Press, 2007).

Amsden Alice H. *The Rise of "The Rest:" Challenges to the West from Late-Industrializing Economies* (Oxford: Oxford University Press, 2001).

Bull Hedley. *The Anarchical Society: A Study of Order in World Politics* (London: Macmillan Press, 1977).

Burbank Jane and Fredrick Cooper, *Empires in World History: Power and the Politics of Difference* (Princeton: Princeton University Press, 2011).

Chong Ian. *External Intervention and the Politics of State Formation: China, Indonesia, and Thailand, 1893–1952* (Cambridge: Cambridge University Press, 2012).

Clark Ian. *The Hierarchy of States: Reform and Resistance in the International Order* (Cambridge: Cambridge University Press, 1987).

Darwin John. *After Tamerlane: The Rise and Fall of Global Empires, 1400–2000* (London: Bloomsbury, 2008).

Doyle Michael. *Empires* (Ithaca: Cornell University Press, 1986).

Fieldhouse D.K. *Economics and Empire, 1830–1914* (London: Weidenfield and Nicolson, 1973).

Fieldhouse D.K. *The West and the Third World: Trade, Colonialism, Dependence and Development* (Oxford: Blackwell 1999).

Gaddis John Lewis. *We Now Know: Rethinking Cold War History* (New York: Oxford University Press, 1997).

Gilpin Robert. *War and Change in World Politics* (Cambridge: Cambridge University Press, 1981).

Go Julian. *Patterns of Empire: The British and American Empires, 1688 to the Present* (Cambridge: Cambridge University Press, 2011).

Hall John A. *International Orders* (Cambridge: Polity Press, 1996).

Hurrell Andrew. *On Global Order: Power, Values, and the Construction of Internationnal Society* (Oxford: Oxford University Press, 2007).

Ikenberry G. John. *After Victory: Institutions, Strategic Restraint, and the Rebuilding of Order after Major Wars* (Princeton: Princeton University Press, 2001).

Ikenberry G. John, ed., *American Unrivaled: The Future of the Balance of Power* (Ithaca: Cornell University Press, 2002).

Ikenberry G. John. *Liberal Leviathan: The Origins, Crisis, and Transformation of the American World Order* (Princeton: Princeton University Press, 2011).

Jackson Robert H. *Quasi-States: Sovereignty, International Relations, and the Third World* (New York: Cambridge University Press, 1990).

Johnson Chalmers. *The Sorrows of Empire: Militarism, Secrecy, and the End of the Republic* (New York: Henry Holt, 2005).

Katzenstein Peter. *A World of Regions: Asia and Europe in the American Imperium* (Ithaca: Cornell University Press, 2005).

Katzenstein Peter and Robert Keohane, eds., *Anti-Americanism in World Politics* (Ithaca: Cornell University Press, 2007).

Lake David. *Hierarchy in International Relations* (Ithaca: Cornell University Press, 2009).

Lieven Dominic. *Empire: The Russian Empire and Its Rivals* (New Haven, CT: Yale University Press, 2001).

Lundestad Geir. *"Empire" by Invitation: The United States and European Integration, 1945–1997* (New York: Oxford University Press, 1998).

Madden Thomas F. *Empires of Trust: How Rome Built – and America in Building – a New World* (London: Plume, 2009).

Maier Charles S. "Alliance and Autonomy: European Identity and U.S. Foreign Policy Objectives in the Truman Years," in Michael Lacey, ed., *The Truman Presidency* (Cambridge: Cambridge University Press, 1991).

Mann Michael. "The Recent Intensification of American Economic and Military Imperialism: Are They Connected?" in George Steinmetz, ed., *Sociology and Empire: The Imperial Entanglements of a Discipline* (Durham: Duke University Press, 2013), pp. 213–44.

Motyl Alexander. *Imperial End: The Decay, Collapse, and Revival of Empires* (New York: Columbia University Press, 2001).

Munkler Herfried. *The Logic of World Domination from Ancient Rome to the United States* (London: Polity, 2007).

Nexon Daniel and Thomas Wright, "What's at Stake in the American Empire Debate?" *American Political Science Review*, Vol. 101, No. 2 (July 2007), pp. 256–61.

Santoro Carlo Maria. *Diffidence and Ambition: The Intellectual Sources of U.S. Foreign Policy* (Boulder, CO: Westview, 1992).

Spykman's Nicholas John. *America's Strategy in World Politics: The United States and the Balance of Power* (New York: Harcourt, Brace, 1942).

Viner Jacob. "Objectives of Post-War International Economic Reconstruction," in William McKee and Louis J. Wiesen, eds., *American Economic Objectives* (New Wilmington, PA: Economic and Business Foundation, 1942).

Wade Robert. "Protecting Power: Western States in Global Organization," in David Held and Charles Roger, eds., *Global Governance at Risk* (Cambridge: Polity Press, 2013), pp. 77–110.

Winks Robin W. *World Civilization: A Brief History* (San Diego: Collegiate Press, 1993).

Woodruff William. *America's Impact on the World: A Study of the Role of the United States in the World Economy, 1750–1970* (London: Macmillan, 1975).

Part V

Response

15   Response to the critics

Michael Mann

I want to thank all the contributors to this book for having taken the time and trouble to critique my recent work. It is an honor that I have experienced before, and I love it.

The third and fourth volumes of *The Sources of Social Power* bring to an end my history of power relations in human societies. Volume 3 begins for the most advanced countries in 1918. Yet since my second volume on the long nineteenth century largely ignored the empires of that time, in Volume 3, I actually start my discussion of empires much further back. Volume 3 then takes the narrative forward to the end of the Second World War, and then Volume 4 takes over up to (almost) the present day. The amount of empirical material I read for these volumes is large but very far from exhaustive, since an enormous amount has been written about the modern period. It would be very surprising if I did not make mistakes or depended on unreliable historians or took one viewpoint in highly controversial debates.

But my narrative is not merely empirical. It is informed by sociological theory. As before, I structure my narrative in terms of the interplay of four power sources, each one of which generates its own networks of interaction. The four are ideological, economic, military and political power. Although all four are often entwined with each other, each has its own distinct logic of development, and so their relations with each other are ultimately "orthogonal," independent and irreducible one to another. Thus, while in these periods I persistently stress the importance to social development of capitalism, I am also persistently critical of economic determinism, whether this comes from Marxism or neo-classical economics. Similarly, while recognizing the importance of ideologies in these periods, I reject the idealism which pervades much of the so-called cultural turn in sociology. For military power I try to correct the opposite tendency, the neglect until very recently of the importance of war and armed forces in social development. I would like to believe that the recent revival of interest in military power owes something to my influence. I will say something later in this essay about the continuing political importance of the nation-state.

I show in these two volumes that all four of the power networks have been important and sometimes dominant in the modern period. However, I also stress that major social institutions are composed of blends of power sources. I claim that, armed with this model, I can understand better the development of major power institutions in human societies. This is not a "hard" theory in the sense of generating a simple, universal explanation, but this is because human societies are not simple. They are extremely messy. But I do aspire to what are generally called "theories of the middle range." To fully appreciate this, you would have to read large slices of my four volumes. Here I will reply to my critics while trying to reveal pay-offs from my model. I also seek to relate these debates to more general theoretical issues.

General theory

Monica Prasad strikes hard at the core of my theory. She says it is useful in rejecting single-factor theories like economic or cultural determinism but says that I go to the opposite extreme since my four power sources end up in a multi-causality in which anything can determine anything. There is some truth in this. When I first presented my model in a diagrammatic form in Chapter 1 of Volume 1 of *Sources*, I recognized that there were many causal sequences too complex to theorize and which lay outside of my model. Societies are varied and messy. We cannot have a theory of everything.

Nonetheless, her point is overstated. My model is less multi-causal than "quadrilateral," which is to say that the fundamental structures of societies are determined by relations between four, and only four, sources of social power. These are the four alternative ways in which both collective and distributive power can be exercised; that is, they provide the ability to compel others to do things that they would not have otherwise done. Such power is the key to social structure as a whole. All four sources possess this capability, which means that each one can in certain situations be ultimately primary (in Engels' sense) in determining human action. In the period covered by Volume 4, examples would be socialist versus capitalist ideology, the role of capitalism in bringing prosperity to more and more of the world, the tremendous impact of the Second World War and the continuing role of the nation-state. It would be nice if we could specify in determinist terms invariant relations between the four, but alas that cannot be done. Each of the power sources may have its own logic of development, but as I explain later the conjunctions between them are much more contingent. There is no "ultimate primacy" in Engel's sense across the whole human experience. All we can do is specify the relations between them in particular times and places, as I have persistently tried to do. My volumes are full of "theories of the middle range," which combine different elements of the four sources.

My model offers a general injunction to social scientists: you have not explained human development unless you have considered ideological, economic, military and political powers held by concrete groups and institutions. In some contexts, we can strip this down in some cases where one or even two sources may be largely irrelevant to outcomes. Thus, in my chapter on the New Deal, which is Prasad's main focus, military power played very little role after the shock waves of the First World War had played out, and though there were ideologies constraining and permitting action, the main actors involved behaved more in pragmatic than ideological ways (always excepting "liquidationists," communists and Southern racists). This is why I conclude the chapter by offering an essentially bi-causal explanation of the New Deal era in terms of economic and political power relations.

I have also emerged from my broad-ranging research project with some generalizations concerning the nature of each source of power. Ideological power, I say, is intermittent; most of the time it is institutionalized and rather conservative. It mostly reflects the other power sources, and it is unable to mobilize deep sentiments from the people. But in occasional crises, when those ideologies seem not to offer plausible explanations of or solutions to the crisis, new ideologies emerge interstitially from the cracks of existing structural relations, and then some of them become game-changers, like the emergence of salvation religions, or of socialism, fascism, and current Islamism in recent times. Military power has some of the same properties, normally quite subdued but erratically erupting into wars which may restructure human societies. In contrast, economic power is much steadier, consistently penetrating the everyday lives of the people, inducing social change gradually but most persistently. Political power involves the institutionalization of the dynamism provided by other sources over a demarcated set of territories. All four have "emergent" properties. Although they may owe their origins to other power sources, once in place they have their own logic of development.

Derluguian, Timothy Earle and Will Reno bring their combined expertise to bear on the evolutionary history of the human race from prehistoric to neoliberal times – in twenty pages. Their general model is broadly similar to my own, though they regard human history through a social evolutionary lens, which I regard skeptically. I see the rise and fall of empires interspersed with more primitive feudal periods as more of a cyclical than an evolutionary process. But they argue that enough successive feudal periods borrow from the techniques of preceding empires, adding innovations of their own, for this to count as evolution. This is a debate to which I am contributing elsewhere – as Dennis Smith notes. They also believe that "chiefs" have dominated most of human history, equipped with the ability to establish "chokepoints" in the circulation of resources so that they can grab possession of some of them. This makes them the main drivers of distributive power (the power of some over others). The three authors use the term chief much more broadly than I do, extending it beyond what is normally seen as its role in the origins of the state to embrace religious leaders, mafias, corrupt politicians and capitalists – who they say are the main species of chief still flourishing today in an era of institutionalized, regulated societies. Capitalists are able to take advantage of neoliberalism to establish their own chokepoint of economic resources. I doubt whether the term "chief" should be applied here but the chokepoint metaphor is quite insightful.

A sustained critique of my writings is made by Ralph Schroeder. He questions my conception of economic power, my notion of "plural globalizations," preferring "globalizing modernity," my conception of "consumer citizenship," and my unwillingness to categorize science as a fifth source of power. I will attempt to discuss all four critiques.

I start with economic power relations. I use the master concept of capitalism, whereas he prefers markets. This is an old controversy. I agree with him that market competition is probably the most efficient form of economy, certainly in a complex society with extensive division of labor. Economic competition also encourages political democracy, for both are pluralistic. Yet contemporary markets are also defined by corporate and capitalistic elements establishing "chokepoints," which tend toward monopoly and oligarchy, serve the interests of some over others, often corrupting political democracy. The role of bankers today is a good example. I think that his elevation of markets tends to neglect the capitalist social relations which set the basic terms under which markets operate – the profit motive, class dominance and the presence of authoritative economic organizations like corporations, professions, and governments. Capitalist markets cannot operate without being "embedded" in other power relations – a point made by many contemporary sociologists. I specifically show the importance of classes, states, and ideologies like Keynesianism and neoliberalism – other sources of power – in helping constitute markets. Moreover, markets never quite function in the ways described by neo-classical economists. The natural tendency of capitalist markets in established industries is toward oligopoly and monopoly, with capitalists often preferring stability to pure profit.

Schroeder's stress on markets leads to his argument that the "disembedding" or liberation of markets from social institutions has been a continuous process during modernity, interrupted only by the world wars. I disagree. As is evident in my Volume 3, I follow Karl Polanyi in seeing capitalism as oscillating between periods of relative market dominance and relative collective controls – what Polanyi called a "double movement." In the United States, the drive for more control of market processes began well before the First World War with the rise of populism, the anti-trust movement, the emergence of labor unions, and the establishment of the Federal Reserve Bank. This drive for more collective control intensified through the various New Deal programs regulating industry, farming, banks and housing, as well as giving labor unions more rights. President Roosevelt even introduced massive price controls, though these soon collapsed.

The Second World War intensified controls, as Schroeder acknowledges. This time price controls worked and endured. Then, after the war, markets were restored but they were regulated by what has been called "business Keynesianism." Internationally, this was in the form of the Bretton Woods agreement and in the rejection, above all by the US Congress, of the "free trade" agenda which was to be implemented by an International Trade Organization. Instead, the United States worked to found the much weaker General Agreement on Trade and Tariffs (GATT) institutions which achieved little liberalization of trade until the rise of neoliberalism in the 1970s. Domestically within the United States "business Keynesianism" was biased less toward the market than to the giant corporations which formed the core of the military–industrial complex. American politicians trumpeted free market rhetoric, but the practice was different. The history of different countries and groups of countries differ from each other, but there was almost everywhere in the advanced world a surge in collective regulation of capitalism lasting past the mid-century mark, usually boosted by military power relations.

So I stick by my argument that it took neoliberalism to significantly "free" markets from the 1970s onward. As he says, the process of marketization still continues, reaching more and more areas of social life. But although this is a very diffuse process, at its base it serves particular group interests, especially corporations and finance capitalists. This has not been a spontaneous process. It has involved considerable coordination and regulation, both by individual nation-states and by international bodies like the World Bank, the IMF, and various macro-regional banks. Their highest administrations are staffed by the representatives of states. Capitalists still need states, just as states need capitalists. As for the future, Schroeder sees "disembedding" continuing indefinitely, whereas I see regulation as likely to make a comeback, especially to combat climate change and if there is a populist reaction against the rising inequality and exploitation that neoliberalism brings. If climate change is effectively combatted, the regulation of capitalism and consumerism would be considerable. If it is not, the ensuing last-minute regulation of market forces amid disastrous times would be much more punitive domestically and probably often vicious geopolitically. Capitalism cannot exist without political regulation, but the degree of regulation varies – and I argue that it very roughly approximates to Polanyi's "double movement" involving cycles of market and regulative activity.

Schroeder's stress on markets also leads to his conception of "globalizing modernity." Whereas I argue that globalization today is a plural process involving several distinct sets of power networks – principally capitalism, American empire and the nation-state system – he sees no shaping of the world by such distinct networks. Instead, he says, markets diffuse through everything, increasingly in neoliberal forms. He specifically rejects the notion that the United States is dominant – it is subordinate to markets, he says. Though there is some truth in this, we also find the reverse process of America shaping markets – for example, in having the dollar as the reserve currency, and in leading the international institutions I have just named. If American economic power weakens, then a more multilateral regulatory process will be needed. I also argue that the power of neoliberalism is often exaggerated, being variable in its influence across the world. To come to power, neoliberals had also to make alliances with conservatives who have quite different views on many things. The result is that neoliberals themselves are rather disappointed and perceive that free markets do *not* rule the world. But I leave it to the reader to decide whether globalizing modernity or plural globalizations is the better model.

Schroeder does not like my term "consumer citizenship" since he says consumption confers no rights and is not attached to national citizenship, since it is a transnational process. His argument is essentially correct. I should have only written that people feel they have a right to an equitable level of personal consumption, and if they do not obtain it they will express their discontent against the nation-state. This has some similarity to T. H. Marshall's observation that social citizenship means the right to participate in the economic and social life of the community. Traditionally, this was conferred through the welfare state; now it is also popularly viewed through the lens of consumption, though as Schroeder says, consumption is a substantially transnational process.

Finally, Schroeder wants to make science and technology into a separate, fifth power source, analogous to the others. We have argued about this before, and I have come to agree with a part of what he says. But I do not quite view it as a fifth source of power. I now see modern science as "half" an ideology, a marginal part of ideological power, though it is a very distinctive ideology, since unlike others it does not claim to know the "meaning of life" or of the "good society." It does not fill in the "gaps" between known facts with a leap of faith. It is "cold," failing to provide the fanatics and persecutions involved in other ideologies. But it does have three main ideological elements: it applies a universal stance of agnosticism in relation to the unknown, it has a distinctive and systematic methodology, and it tends to have an unwarranted belief that scientific and technological improvements will solve all problems. For example, in medical science technological interventionism often greatly outstrips its benefits. To take one example, women are persuaded by physicians and national governments to have routine mammograms. These most often reveal tiny cysts which would never be life-threatening. Yet the doctors cut their breasts off. Technological activism outstrips need because it becomes a believed end in itself. So science is half an ideology, tepid rather than cold.

Schroeder's argument also concerns only modern science. Europe's "scientific revolution" beginning after about 1600 CE has been identified by Collins (1994) and Schroeder himself (2007) as the origin of what they call "high consensus, rapid discovery science" now dominant. As Schroeder notes, this was technologically led. The ability to produce endless refinements and recombinations of techniques to solve practical problems of the world led to confidence that the process could go on indefinitely. However, there is nothing comparable to this role in prior history. There would be no payoff from adding it as another source of power throughout history, unlike my four power sources. Of course, that does not invalidate his argument. All it does is to reduce its historical scope.

I accept Schroeder's argument expressed here and in previous work that modern science and technology have enabled human beings to effect major objective changes in nature itself, as well as in society. They have indeed become a source of great collective power, exercised through mastery over nature. Yet changes effected through science are different to those effected through the four power sources. First, the actual changes to nature and society may be substantial but they are not implemented by scientists but by other power holders. Most lines of scientific enquiry are costly, and they are financed by other power actors – economic, military, and political. Scientists can be considered a caste, for they have a corporate identity, they have their own institutional complex of universities and laboratories, and they speak an esoteric language which no one else can understand. But while most have good salaries and the few who can patent their innovations can become very rich, they do not possess much distributive power over others. They retain a fair degree of status and institutional autonomy and jealously guard their laboratory independence, yet in many respects they are the servants of the three great power holders in modern society, the state, the military, and capitalists – modified by democratic pressures where they exist. Modern science is a major mechanism of the power of others.

For example, I agreed in Volume 3 that rapid discovery science led in the late nineteenth century to the Second Industrial Revolution which caused massive changes in society. But the scientists and technologists pioneering new techniques (the supreme one was electricity) either became employees of capitalists or they took out patents and became capitalists themselves in partnership with entrepreneurs. Across World War II militaries then dominated science. Physics was turned into nuclear weapons. After the war states and big corporations joined in, both sought advantage in international competition between countries and enterprises. Science has not conveyed either distributive or collective power to scientists, and that is unlike those persons wielding ideological, economic, military, or political power. It would be wonderful if in the future environmental scientists can persuade these power holders that climate change must be combatted by radically new policies to avoid the looming catastrophe, or alternatively that scientists and technologists discover a new form of emission-free energy. However, I do not expect this to happen without a combination of assistance from states and from capitalists seeing profit in it.

My conclusion, therefore, is that science/technology is different – almost an ideology, but only in recent history, and conveying no significant distributive power to its practitioners. Indeed, it mostly serves other power holders. That leads to a conclusion which is not quite Schroeder's, but which is uncomfortable for my own model. Modern science and technology lie partly outside my model of the sources of social power. I have tried to explain their origins in terms of interactions between my four power sources in my discussion of the "European Miracle" in Volume 2, revised in later essays. But then science developed "emergent" properties within scientific institutions themselves to pioneer invention after invention. This emergence is hard to theorize in terms of my model. Nonetheless, inventions continued to be put into social practice by others, just as they had been since the seventeenth century.

The third general critic is Risto Heiskala. His summary of my four volumes is admirable, but he also seeks to replace my IEMP model with his own NACEMP model. This is certainly a better arrangement of letters than IEMP since it yields a pronounceable word. He changes my "Ideology" to "Culture" and he adds two more sources, "Artefactual" and "Natural." As I have argued elsewhere, I think "culture" is too broad a term since it is usually employed to refer to the entire ideational side of human activity. This leads toward the dualism of ideas versus material activities which has long bedeviled social theory. Nor can I accept his statement that "cultural categorizations have also . . . . some autonomous power independent of any human intermediaries." Cultural categorizations are always carried by intermediaries. Even with messages carried via technologies like the Internet, there are always human actors with interests, ideals, and power capacities who are diffusing them across the world.

His concept of "artefactual power" is closer to Schroeder's fifth power source than I think he realizes, for Schroeder always writes of "science and technology" and he tends to stress the impact of technology more than science. So I have already given my response to the suggestion that science and technology should be added as a fifth source. Heiskala adds to his artefactual category "all infrastructures" which I think is too broad, since some of them are not technological but social, as will become clearer later. The examples he gives of artefactual power seem reducible to the other power sources. The social exclusion of people because they lack automobiles and the Internet basically flows from their lack of economic power resources, while the Berlin and Mexican border walls are expressions of political power sometimes backed up by military power. So I do not find artefactual power very convincing.

The power of Nature in the two senses of Mother Nature and human nature is another matter. My model is explicitly one of *social* power and so it is not surprising that I exclude both natures from it. But I agree with Heiskala's criticism of Durkheim's statement that social facts must always be explained by other social facts. As he notes, in my volumes I have enumerated many instances of Mother Nature constraining or enabling social activity, but I have not tried to be systematic about these interactions. It is easier to see the environmental constraints in earlier societies. In Volume 1, I showed how civilizations only first emerged in valleys whose rivers could be harnessed, and how the armies of ancient empires if self-supplied could only survive for three days and cover thirty kilometers a day. I also emphasize that we are beginning to confront the devastating environmental consequences of the human exploitation of nature. But all of this is under-theorized. Maybe I will try to remedy this in the future, but I do not want to add an N to my model, since it is a model of social power. Though "Mother Nature" may often help or hinder collective and distributive power, "she" is not an actor but a passive enabler/hinderer.

Though we can see the looming environmental crisis as Nature "fighting back" against many centuries of human exploitation, this is really an anthropomorphic expression. It is human action which is producing a threat to the planet, and it will be human action that will succeed or fail to rescue the planet.

Human nature is a little different. I am not generally impressed by either evolutionary psychology or attempts to directly transpose Darwinian categories onto human societies. Human biology has not changed since early hunter-gatherers and farmers and we remain the same species, limited by our biological nature. There are genetic differences among us, but they do not seem to yield different macro-social relations, except for the process of aging and relations between the sexes. These do introduce major natural differences into society, as do qualities like strength and beauty, even though all are also partly social. Heiskala is too kind when he says that I discuss extensively gender relations in Volumes 3 and 4, since I write only of gender discrimination, and I avoid questions of sexuality. As he says, the relevance of sexual biology to gender relations has changed, but I have contributed nothing to the understanding of this. Of course, many aspects of social life lie outside my model – the family, gender, sexuality, aging, and indeed micro-phenomena in general. No theory can do everything. But if others suggest that these involve further sources of social power, my response would be that changes in them – for example, in gender relations – are probably the product of some combination of ideological, economic, military, and political power. However, that must remain a hypothesis since I have not done the research necessary to demonstrate it.

Finally, Dennis Smith says some very nice things about my work but points out two things which I neglect. He notes that though I do from time to time assert the importance of human emotions in social life, I nowhere attempt to theorize them. He is correct. He then goes on to point out the many places in my narrative where the fear of humiliation played an important role in power relations. He is again right. My apparent unwillingness to dig deeper here flows partly from my ignorance of psychology and partly from my neglect of social status (in the sense of prestige) and its loss, a concept with which I have always been uncomfortable. The second neglect is of China and India. As he observes, if I spend much time on medieval Europe in Volume 1 on the grounds that Europe later came to dominate the world, why do I not spend more time analyzing the rise of China and India, which many believe will come to dominate the world in a few decades time. I should respond first by saying that I do not share this belief since I think that American hegemony will give way to a multipolar world with no one or two power dominant. Nonetheless, his general point about my neglect of Asia still stands. Though in both Volumes 3 and 4 I discuss China at some length (though much less than the United States), I only discuss India under the British Raj. I can only reply in terms of practicability. If I gave more attention to China and equal time to India, I would still be writing Volume 4.

For me, the most interesting part of his essay is the sustained comparison between Immanuel Wallerstein, Gary Runciman, and myself. I know that he gets me right, and I think he gets my colleagues right too. I like the role of "examining magistrate" in historical sociology which he assigns me, for it gives me an aura of dignified authority. But it is curious that in the past we have rarely referred to each other's work. If we were French intellectuals in Paris we certainly would have engaged each other directly in what the French like to think is the capital of global intellectual life. But in the more dispersed and more international Anglo-Saxon world, we can all graze among our separate and supportive networks of like-minded intellectuals. It is an Anglo-Saxon weakness.

Empire

John Darwin has written a brilliant short essay on empires, focusing especially on the British Empire. This is a wonderful overview of the subject, and not only because he is generous in his praise of my own arguments! I agree with his notion that empires were weaker than is generally thought. In his words, they have been less "slabs of territory" than strategic "nodes" and thin "skeins" of control, and they have always needed collaborating clients (which I have argued the United States forgot in Iraq). I am reminded of the book by Karen Barkey (2008). Seeking to explain how some empires managed to successfully rule for centuries, she emphasizes, alongside coercion, the flexible deals and informal contracts that the ruler makes with the diverse powerful social groups of his/her realms. In the Ottoman Empire, her main case, this meant local notables, peasants, nomads, bandits, and minority communities. Like me she emphasizes the "hubs and spokes" model of empire whereby the ruler seeks to communicate and compromise with each region and ethnic or religious group but seeks to prevent their communicating with each other. Darwin also tells me things I did not know –for example, that the machine gun needed too much ammunition to be used routinely, if at all, by the empire-builders.

Only on definitions do I disagree with him. He defines empire as a system of rule or influence wielded by one group over another, to the advantage of the former – with no mention of violent coercion. I think this is too broad to be helpful or to be able to distinguish different types of empire. In my definition, violent coercion is essential, but it is present in degrees which help us identify four or five different types of domination. Violence diminishes as we move from direct empire, to indirect empire, and to informal empire, with purely economic imperialism being a marginal type of imperialism, since there is almost no physical coercion. Finally, hegemony is definitely non-imperial, since its leadership is recognized as either legitimate or natural. These contain different degrees of military power. But in general, empires rule by killing people. The American Empire has been recently killing a lot of people. The killing is the main reason I don't like empires, including this one.

Geopolitics and American empire

I have a great deal of respect for John Ikenberry and for his books *After Victory* (2001) and *Liberal Leviathan* (2011). But I cannot quite accept the main thrust of his argument expressed there and in his essay in this volume. He argues that the United States is not an empire but a hegemon, its leadership legitimated by consent. He says the United States has sponsored the creation of a new international order based on rules, openness, democracy, and capitalist expansion, resulting in peace, prosperity, and human rights. It has sponsored international institutions which restrain the arbitrary actions of individual states, including the United States itself, in a "constitutional order" whose design helps weak and strong states alike. Thus he says in response to my chapters on American Empire that America is not an empire but a legitimate hegemon. This liberal order-building project is not yet fully accomplished, he says, but is ongoing. He does qualify this, saying that during the Cold War, American policy had two faces, one in relation to the communist bloc which relied on traditional political, military, and economic power realism, and the other in relation to the West in which conflict was "captured and domesticated in an iron cage of multilateral rules, standards, safeguards, and dispute resolution procedures." Since then, the latter has expanded across the world. He repeats again and again the word "liberal" as the key to American rule.

There is obviously some truth in these arguments. American power, allied to war weariness, did bring a period of peace and prosperity to large parts (though not all) of the world. The creation of many international organizations in which the signatory powers accept rules and restraints on their actions is indeed a feature of the post–World War II international order. Ikenberry agrees with me that the character of American dominance has varied between different regions. But there are still differences between us, notably whether American dominance has been as beneficial as he says, and whether the cage of international institutions has been quite so American led as he says.

I have already referred to my typology of empires according to how much coercion they involved. The most coercive was direct empire (with colonies), then indirect (mostly protectorates), then informal (involving no colonies or protectorates but instead variant forms of ""gunboat diplomacy," intermittent application of military force), economic imperialism (a borderline case involving only economic and not military coercion), and finally hegemony (domination regarded by the dominated as either legitimate or normal), which I said was not imperialism at all. The United States had acquired colonies and protectorates at the very beginning of the twentieth century and had not much liked the experience. So, as I noted in Volume 4, the United States has been neither a direct nor an indirect empire (excepting short-term military occupations after the world wars) and it is on this basis that most Americans reject the idea that they have an Empire. Ikenberry agrees with them. He says that the United States must not be seen as the last empire standing, as I say, but as the first post-imperial great power. He says that the United States has opposed empires – I say that it has only opposed rival empires. He says that during the Cold War, US policy built an "iron cage" of international institutions, though I note that this was based on a hard-nosed view of American interests and a desire to constrain countries to its Cold War goals.

The development of the European Union was by the Europeans themselves. The United States supported it but the main international institution sponsored by the United States in this region was NATO, built to counter the perceived Soviet threat. Then the Soviet Empire collapsed, partly as a consequence of American pressure, though mainly because of domestic discontent and division. Now there were no imperial rivals, and so we might think that the United States might relax into more liberal internationalism. But no, after 1991 came a period of both aggressive NATO expansion to the borders of Russia plus American unilateral military actions. The consequences of these are still ongoing today, most notably in the shape of the Ukrainian civil war, the emergence of IS, and over a 100 drone strikes a year.

Let me address the question of American beneficence. I first list all incidents since 1949 in which US military force, including US- or CIA-financed foreign forces, have significantly helped a coup d'état, or helped repress a rebellion, or bombed or invaded foreign countries. I have excluded the twenty or so cases where US forces entered foreign countries merely to protect US embassy staff or other Americans. Of course, it is difficult to assess what "significant help" is, and some might reduce this list a little, others might increase it. For example I have not included recent US military aid to the Colombian government, though this has dual aims: to suppress drug cultivation, of course, but also to repress peasants in a class-based civil war. I begin my list in 1949 so as to exclude the military occupations and skirmishes which were the consequences of World War II. Here it is:

Greece 1949 the last year of its civil war, Ukraine 1949–53, Syria 1949, Korean War 1950–53, Iran 1953, Guatemala 1954, Tibet 1955–70s, Lebanon 1958, Indonesia 1958, Cuba Bay of Pigs invasion 1961, Vietnam War 1959–75, Congo 1960–65, Iraq 1960–63, Dominican Republic invasion 1961, Thailand 1962, Laos 1972–75, Brazil 1964, Ghana 1966, Cambodia 1970, Chile 1970–73, Argentina 1976, Afghanistan 1979–89, Turkey 1980, Nicaragua 1981–89, Angola 1980s, Grenada invasion 1983, Panama invasion 1988–89, first Iraq War 1991, Somalia 1992, Bosnia 1994–95, Serbia 1999, Afghanistan 2001, Venezuela 2002, second Iraq War 2003–11, Haiti 2004, Pakistan drone attacks 2004 to the present and extended to at least six countries, Gaza Strip 2006–, Somalia 2006–07, Iran 2005, Libya 2011, Syria 2012–present.

Most of these interventions were violations of state sovereignty and of the international "constitutionality," which Ikenberry says the United States represents. In many cases the United States was invited in, sometimes by a legitimate democratic government but more often by elites facing popular opposition and refusing reforms. A minority of cases improved the local situation, but the majority made things worse or had no impact – as in all the twenty-first century cases I noted. But the most striking feature of the list is its length. There have been at least thirty-five separate uses of American military power since 1949, and if we counted each year of intervention as a separate case, the total would be between eighty and hundred. A few could be considered benevolent, but most were in the interests of locally dominant classes and/ or of the United States. This list does not fit well with liberal internationalism or legitimate hegemony, but it does with informal imperialism laced with gunboat diplomacy. We might wish to set against this list more positive interventions like American aid programs, of which the largest have been Marshall aid to Europe, post-war aid to Japan and South Korea, and more recent aid to Israel. We can see the hard-nosed geopolitical motives for these programs, of course, and apart from these cases US aid programs are useful but smaller in per capita terms than those of all other advanced countries.

Notice the uneven geography of the activism – which Ikenberry accepts. There were no cases in Europe west of the Ukraine and the

Balkans, but considerable activism including two major wars in Asia until about 1975 (if we exclude Afghanistan). This is exactly what I discerned in Volume 4. I argued that the United States has not been imperial in Western Europe since 1950. Its military umbrella over Europe, welcomed by the Europeans, made this legitimate hegemony. Yet I would not go as far as Ikenberry does in crediting Europe's multilateral institutions to US hegemony, since the Europeans themselves developed the European Union and they have been far more active than the United States as participants in institutions of international justice, human rights, and climate control.

Second in East and Southeast Asia the United States began as an aggressive indirect or informal military empire, sometimes through devastating "scorched earth" tactics. Yet from the 1980s came a milder hegemony. This is not unusual among empires. The Roman, Chinese, and British empires became milder once institutionalized. However, I would not credit the development of Asian democratic institutions to the United States, for it supported authoritarian regimes until local popular movements forced through democratic reforms. And of course the biggest democracy in the world, India, owed nothing to American influence.

In Africa, there have been few American interventions and little interest. The United States had little role in developing international institutions in the continent. It played no role in the formation of the Organization of African Unity (now the African Union), which first enshrined the principle of state sovereignty and so which sought to restrain foreign interventions and which has more recently become more interventionist itself.

The bulk of continuing US interventions have been in Latin America and a swathe of Muslim countries from Libya through the Middle East as far as Iran, Pakistan, and Afghanistan. The trends here have been opposite ones, milder in Latin America since the 1990s, more severe in Muslim countries. The two trends may be connected since the "war on terror" focused on Muslim countries has diverted US attention and resources away from Latin America. This amounts to informal empire laced with a very tough form of gunboat diplomacy, including major wars over almost half the world in which the United States has an interest. This is empire, not hegemony, but hegemony now characterizes most of the other half, Europe and East and Southeast Asia. Ikenberry correctly notes that the latter comprises most of the economically advanced countries of the world, but the rest of the world counts too, and in any case it is not clear that the democracy prevalent across this zone is due to US hegemony rather than to indigenous democratizing tendencies. So one should not use single terms like "liberal internationalism" or "imperialism," across the whole realm of American foreign policy. Note the extraordinary size of the zone which has been subjected to what Ikenberry calls traditional hard-nosed geopolitics, for American anticommunism was deployed in across three quarters of the world, then reducing to one half.

Another of Ikenberry's key terms is democracy. I will not repeat the arguments and evidence I used in Volume 4 to show that the United States has consistently favored capitalism over democracy and has persistently intervened to overthrow center-left movements wrongly labeled "communist" or "socialist." It has believed that what are in fact normal levels of class conflict around the world will lead to "chaos" and thence to "communism" and so it is happy to support repression – as in many of the interventions I listed above. The United States usually stood behind reactionary forms of capitalism and landlordism. Had it sponsored land reform over this whole zone, as it did in the case of South Korea (after it had first suppressed rural radicals), it would have been more liberal and also served its own interests better. In fact, repression by local elites with US support drove many opponents leftward to become socialists or communists. I described this policy as irrational, although I will qualify this term later in my essay.

So here I disagree also with Westad's statement that only a few US interventions were directed against agrarian reformers and liberal progressives. Elsewhere he admits that what he calls American high imperialism "caused massive dislocation at the local level, especially among the peasantry, such as in Central America, in Indochina, or in southern Africa." In Indochina, those who wanted agrarian reform were pushed by American hostility in the direction of communism, whereas in Latin America there was never much of a communist threat. The Chilean movement led by Allende was not communist, while the United States pushed the Sandinistas into seeking help from the Soviet Union. The Soviets were pessimistic about their chances of attracting clients in the hemisphere and they were caught by surprise by Fidel Castro's embrace. So though Westad is right in emphasizing the "bi-polarity" of the world during the Cold War, the United States and the Soviets played a large role in determining this outcome. Without their pressures, the countries of the Third World would have developed in all kinds of hues rather than being forced to choose between red and red-white-and-blue. Freed from the Cold War countries of what we now call the "South" of the world are in fact currently developing in all kinds of ways.

It might be thought that our disagreement is caused by concern with different periods and places. I am concerned with the whole of the period of US dominance and with the whole world, whereas Ikenberry focuses on more recent periods and on the advanced countries. So he stresses hegemony more than I do. But his view has difficulty dealing with the recent revival of American militarism toward Muslim countries. American paranoid anti-Islamism strikingly resembles its prior paranoid anticommunism. The past is not past. Distrusting market mechanisms for acquiring oil, allied to reactionary Arab monarchies, committed to supporting Israeli governments almost whatever they do, the United States has once again perpetrated military interventions which undermine local moderates and create more extreme enemies – as I predicted would be the case in Iraq in my book *Incoherent Empire* (2003) and which I showed came true in Volume 4. Islamic terrorism has several causes, but one of them is foreign military intervention. We have unfortunately arrived at an impasse. Only US military power could in principle destroy the truly barbaric extreme Islamists who have now surfaced in the Middle East, yet this would not now be popular among Americans and it would likely create more terrorists. In this region, American imperialism, for good or ill, and for all its military prowess, is now helpless. It can bomb but not stop the terrorist virus. Economic aid or even covert funneling of military goods to the moderates may achieve something, but not a lot.

Of course, the United States is not merely a military power. It also uses its economic power to achieve both its own dominance and a measure of collective benefit. The dollar acts as the world's reserve currency and this benefits the United States, but all countries benefit from having a stable currency system, so this system is seen by them as a combination of legitimacy and inevitability. It was set in motion by the Bretton Woods international conference, dominated by the United States, but it was arbitrarily terminated by the Nixon administration in 1971, with no advance consultation with other countries. The United States has coped with its deficits by printing money, as no other country can safely do. This triggers inflation in other countries across the world which knew that they were paying for American debts. They were discontented but knew they were powerless. This was not really "liberal internationalism" since it contained a strong streak of economic imperialism. But in financial institutions like the IMF and the World Bank global dominance is shared with Europe and Japan.

On matters of trade, we must rid ourselves of the notion that the United States favors an "open" world economy or free trade. This is true where its geopolitical interests favor it, as in relations with Japan and Korea. But for the most part, like most countries, it wants foreigners to open up but not itself; unlike most countries it has had the ability to enforce this inequality. In 1948–50, the US Congress repeatedly blocked the proposed International Trade Organization on the grounds that it would mean foreign interference in the American economy. Instead it agreed to the much weaker GATT that slowly inched its way forward in reducing tariffs, but the pace was too slow for most Third World countries. In the 1960s, they pressed for the establishment of a new UN agency, UNCTAD, which would sponsor free trade, export-oriented production, market expansion, and banking and financial flow expansion.

At the founding UNCTAD conference in 1964, one Third World delegate urged: "This conference must also establish in plain terms the right of all peoples to unrestricted free trade and the obligation of all states signatories of the agreement emanating from this conference to refrain from restraining trade in any manner, direct or indirect." These apparently neoliberal words were spoken by the Cuban delegate, Che Guevara!. Third World countries favored free trade which they believed would enable them to penetrate rich countries' markets. But the rich countries did not want this and they succeeded in starving UNCTAD of funds and blocking most of its initiatives (Bockman, 2014). This was part of its offensive against what it saw as a Third World–friendly UN. This culminated in 1996 when the United States used its Security Council veto to block the re-appointment of UN Secretary General Boutros Boutros-Ghali after his first term in office. He was the only Secretary General not to be reappointed to a second term. Instead the United States successfully pushed for the more compliant Kofi Annan.

The 1990s and 2000s saw a determined attempt by the poorer countries to change the policies of the WTO. They particularly wanted to end the rich countries' tariffs against their agricultural products. But the United States opposed this, as did Europe and Japan, and consequently the WTO has been stalled since 2002, since the poorer countries will not accept further tariff reductions without the inclusion of agriculture. This episode reveals failed multilateralism. Since then the United States has turned toward bilateral trade treaties with individual countries, agreeing to carefully demarcated spheres of reduced tariffs. The United States has from time to time sponsored free trade, as for example in its relations with Japan, but that came less from principled free market concerns than from its need to secure Japanese support during the Cold War. Most often, the United States has supported tariff reductions when they have suited America – which, of course, is normal reasoning by countries.

The United States has signed up to relatively few international treaties. Here is another list of treaties that at least half the world's countries have signed on to, but not the US. Congress has usually been a greater stumbling-block than has the President, but the consent of both is constitutionally required to sign foreign treaties.

• Convention on the Elimination of All Forms of Discrimination against Women

- Convention on the Rights of the Child (including child soldiers)
- The International Criminal Court and the International Court of Justice
- Convention for the Protection of all Persons from Enforced Disappearance
- Convention on the Rights of Persons with Disabilities (CRPD)
- Optional Protocol to the Convention against Torture
- Various other human rights treaties like banning religious intolerance and endorsing civil and political rights, economic, social, and cultural rights
- Mine Ban Treaty
- Convention on Cluster Munitions
- International arms-trade treaty
- The Moon treaty
- The Law of the Sea
- Ten international environment agreements, including the Kyoto agreement, the Basel convention on waste, the treaty on genetic resources, the Antarctic Liability Annex, the biodiversity convention, the UN convention on the law of the sea
- The United States is not complying with the Chemical Weapons Commission or the Nuclear Nonproliferation Treaty

Of course, US citizens already enjoy full protection at home against some of these abuses – for example, the humans rights violations – whereas the citizens of many countries do not, whatever their government has signed on to. But foreigners often do not have rights against the US government since the American courts are increasingly restricting their rights of redress if the President and Congress have not explicitly signed onto the relevant international treaty. The trend is toward according foreigners fewer rights than citizens. Once again this is incongruent with Ikenberry's notion of international constitutionality. And the length of this list is once again evidence that the United States is not leading the way toward this.

I am baffled by Ikenberry's repeated use of the word "liberal" for the internationalism he detects. He is using the word in a positive sense, and has liberal values himself, as I do. But which of the many American practices I have discussed could be described as liberal? So we disagree over the nature of American domination, though we do agree that it varied.

I also draw a second conclusion. I like his notion that the post-war period has seen a great increase in international institutions which act like an iron cage, restraining state sovereignty. I have hitherto used the cage metaphor only to describe the nation-state strengthening its hold on us, but he has found another use for the cage metaphor. Yet I see the United

States as being less central to this expansion than he does. The core of American power has been its military and the dollar. Neither restrain its own sovereignty, quite the reverse. The UN and its agencies largely escaped US control after about 1980, hence the frequency of the American veto, which has accounted for about 80 percent of the total number of vetoes in the Security Council since then. The iron cage of European integration has been an indigenous European affair, now producing indigenous blowback. As we have seen, the United States has been marginal to many of the initiatives of constitutional institutionalism, though its power is such that its opposition can often stymie them. But if the United States does not join in this trend, it will be increasingly on the sidelines, since Ikenberry is probably correct in predicting more international constitutionalism in the future.

My conclusion is that the United States is *both* the last empire and the last global hegemon. Neither will last much longer. The dollar may last another decade as the single reserve currency, but probably not much longer. The US military interventions have also become less successful, reflecting the growth of nationalism and other forms of ideological resistance to imperialism like Islamism. Drone warfare saves American lives but increases the number of terrorists. Many of the states of the world are alarmed by the arbitrary and ineffective militarism of the United States, by its "extreme rendition" and torture programs and by its massive espionage program directed against them – though there is much hypocrisy in the last two denunciations. I agree with Ikenberry that constitutional institutionalism should dominate the world, but unfortunately it does not yet do so. The United States has only erratically helped it along and has recently been on a downward slide away from it. But it will have a better chance in the multipower-actor geopolitical era which will succeed the American Empire.

Odd Arne Westad, in an argument reminiscent of Mackinder's classic article "The Geographical Pivot of History" (1904), sees the emergence of the two post-war land-based superpowers as a very long run and almost inevitable process. Mackinder believed that the era of the naval powers was drawing to a close, to be replaced by nations occupying vast land spaces which could now be integrated by railroads. Thus Russia and America would generate in the future far more industrial and military power than the colonial powers. During 1942–45, Mackinder (and Westad) was proved right, though I think that Germany might have been the third Superpower but for its suicidal jumps into two world wars. Though I insert less rationality into geopolitics than Westad, as I do he adds ideological power into the Superpower conflict. It supports his notion of a long-term conflict between Russia and America that the

United States was obsessed with the danger of "Bolshevism" ever since the Bolsheviks seized power in Russia. Indeed, as I show in Volume 3, even before World War I State Department documents reveal a profound fear that leftist forces might open the way to socialism and chaos.

I must defer to Westad's superior knowledge of China, though he appears to be more negative about the country than I am. Whether the Great Leap Forward killed 30 million Chinese, as I say, or 45 million, as he says, we agree that the death toll was horrendous. Yet economic growth rates before and after the disastrous Great Leap Forward were substantial. Westad focuses on that atrocious period and only briefly on other less disastrous periods. But Chinese growth rose steadily before the marketization period, if the statistics given by Naughton (2006) are to be believed. Of course, marketization increased that rate of growth quite substantially. Vietnam has also followed this sequence, while the Soviet Union in the inter-war period had a growth rate inferior only to Japan. State socialism was not without its economic achievements, even though it contained contradictions which could not be maintained in the long run. In fact, most of the successful recent developers have seen a shift from milder forms of state-led development to greater marketization – like South Korea or India. The sequence seems to be the way to success. As for Gini coefficients, I agree with Westad, and I said so in Volume 4, that China has a very high level of inequality, but it is lower than in other successfully developing countries like Brazil, half of Latin America, South Africa, and Nigeria. It is slightly higher than in Russia and the other half of Latin America (and in the United States), and if Indian figures are to be believed, it is much higher than in India. So China compares quite well in terms of inequality with comparable countries. But in the Chinese case, high inequality has been somewhat offset by the very great fall in mortality rates and the substantial rise in literacy rates ever since the 1950s. Again, state socialism has not been without its achievements, though at enormous social cost, as I underscore in these volumes as well as in my book *The Dark Side of Democracy* (2005).

We also disagree about how to label the Chinese economy. Unlike Westad and many others, I prefer not to call it simply capitalist since the degree of inter-penetration (often informal and corrupt) of state officials and capitalists is unlike the political economy of the West. I called it a capitalist party-state, indicating the entwining of political and economic power. Nee and Opper (2007) have suggested politicized capitalism, which I think suggests that capitalists have the upper hand over the state. State capitalism would have been a simpler alternative, but Trotsky and his followers had already appropriated it for quite different purposes. I noted in Volume 4 that the most common form of political economy across the world is a family of politicized capitalisms in which access to the state confers ownership of economic resources. This was egregious in cases like Mubarak's Egypt, where the political and military elites were simply given major economic enterprises, hitherto nationalized. It is more discrete in countries like Rwanda, where those connected to the ruling party have much better chances for acquiring government and foreign aid contracts. China is a distinctive and extreme member of this family. Of course, cronyism is not unknown in the West, but it is far less than in any of the other countries I have just mentioned.

The degree to which economic and political power are entwined gives us varieties of capitalism much more significant than, say, the difference between the United States and Germany, which is the core comparison involved in current notions of the varieties of capitalism. Just as I have argued that we need distinctions between different degrees of coercion in empires, so we need distinctions between different degrees and forms of politicization within capitalism too. In Volume 4, I ordered a few types in terms of the balance of power between the state and capitalism, with China being the most statist contemporary case. But this is fairly rudimentary and it might be made more systematic, as Heiskala points out. Maybe I will attempt this in the future. However, I do accept Westad's judgment that China will move in a more capitalist direction. That is what the top leadership since Deng have wanted, and he is right to stress their admiration for the American economy.

Yet in post-Soviet countries, politicized capitalism has tended to settle down into straight capitalism, including fully private corporations. Just as tax farmers in earlier historical periods gradually acquired permanent and heritable rights over what were originally temporary grants of benefits, so today we find that many economic enterprises initially acquired through political corruption or force tend to settle down after some years into normal corporations quoted on stock markets and with absolute and heritable property rights. The oligarchs of contemporary Russia and its neighbors are the supreme examples today. The entwining of economic and political power varies through both time and place.

Ideological power

It is a relief not to be accused of neglecting ideological power in these volumes. Indeed, I provide extensive discussion of racism, socialism, fascism, neoliberalism, and Islamism. David Priestland has written an excellent book *Merchant, Soldier, Sage* (2012) whose title reveals its affinity with my sources of social power (adding the word "Politician" to the title would have increased the affinity). He rejects standard criticisms of my treatment of ideologies but notes correctly that I focus on world-changing ideologies, like the ones listed above, while neglecting less dramatic ones. In the introduction to Volume 3, I do add to my two world-changing types of ideology (which I call transcendent and immanent) institutionalized ideologies, important in maintaining everyday life and tending to reinforce existing power structures. Since my focus is on change, I do not discuss them much except when they fail. Then people feel that such ideologies have lost their ability to explain and solve major social crises. At that point they are challenged by rising transcendent or immanent ideologies and they may lose the ensuing struggle. My most sustained example is the failure of institutionalized, liberal, and social democratic ideologies to explain or solve crises arising between the end of World War I and the Great Depression in the countries defeated in that war. Thus, for example, Germany saw a rise in both extreme leftist and rightist ideologies, with the fascists eventually triumphing. So it is true that I neglect ideologies in "normal times."

But Priestland also makes the point that by focusing on the world-changing capacities of ideologies, I tend to exaggerate their cohesion and fail to analyze tensions and even contradictions within them. As a corollary to this, he adds that I do not quite appreciate the incoherencies and tensions existing within the minds of actors, even those who are committed to a world-changing ideology. His Soviet examples are convincing. I stand corrected, since I only referred to these obliquely. I did observe the struggle within National Socialism between nationalists and socialists, and the intermittent ideological struggles in the United States between the State Department and the Department of Defense, but if you know with hindsight what happened next, and who won, there is a tendency to exaggerate the cohesion of the winners.

I have never believed that ordinary people possess clear-cut ideologies or even consistent values, despite what Malesevic says in his critique. In my first published works (Mann, 1970; Blackburn & Mann, 1975), I analyzed the values and norms of American and British people as revealed in social surveys and came to the conclusion that people had confused, often contradictory values and norms. In fact, they did not live at the ideological level but at a level of pragmatic acceptance of existing social structures because this was the only reality they knew, with all its imperfections and contradictions. They would flourish different and often contradictory values according to different aspects of their lives. The exception to that *bricolage* occurs in crises when institutionalized ideologies seem not to work, and when masses of people may be attracted to simplified versions of ideologies, endorsing slogans like "land, bread, and peace" rather than Marxism, and "knocking their heads together" (the heads of capitalists and unions) rather than fascism. But in both these cases, militants and leaders, with more developed ideologies, were the prime movers, especially in defining the kind of society they wanted to move toward. Of course, they often disagreed quite strongly among themselves about the route.

John Hall examines the ideological implications of my work amid a more general elucidation of what he considers to be a "decent society." Thus he is more concerned with the normative aspects of ideologies. But he makes a parallel point to Priestland's arguing that I overdo the totality of ideologies. Only some are totalizing, he says, while others are really single-issue beliefs, like environmentalism. This is a good point in general, but not in this particular case, for many environmentalists do have an ideological world view. They deify nature and argue that human society as a whole must live in tune with nature, not exploit it. Of course, there are also many who are pragmatists, just as there were pragmatic socialists and fascists. But this is different from the moral fervor of the "tree huggers" or of those who invoke the Gaia principle that self-regulating interaction between organic and inorganic entities is necessary to maintain life on the planet. The degree to which ideologies "totalize" obviously varies considerably within and between social movements.

But the core of his contribution is his identification of three and only three meta-theoretical ideologies. The first is liberalism understood in "generic Enlightenment terms," respecting reason and science, with a strain toward individualism and its passions, while containing a tension between relativistic doubt and universal agreement on minimal liberal values like tolerance. The second is the tradition of belonging to communities, exemplified by Durkheim. It rejects individualism since individuals require social support and communal values and they are defined by spiritual values more than interests. Hall notes that a shared sense of belonging is incompatible with the division of labor which dominates modern society. This is exactly what Durkheim spent his life trying to resolve. The third tradition, exemplified by Nietzsche and Freud, stresses the instinctual desire for domination. Hall then elegantly traces out the various interactions between the three that actually constitute real human life while at the same time plumping for the liberal tradition, which he argues carries more "decency" than the others.

I think this is an original and suggestive model. My own normative preference is for a combination of the first and second traditions. I accept the virtues of liberalism which Hall has identified, but I would combine them with the virtues of community solidarity. This is why I am a social democrat. I believe strongly in the virtues of market competition. Hall (echoing Adam Smith) notes that it encourages political decency. I agree but add that markets must be regulated for the public good. Either tradition in extremis can be dangerous. Rampant individualism and unregulated markets are harmful, but so are state socialism, aggressive nationalism, and racism. As for the third tradition, domination, it figures large in my empirical analysis but I do not theorize the desire for domination as an end in itself. On reflection I think this is a weakness. My discussions of distributive power tend to center on rational interests, as in empire-building, for example, where I stress the importance of economic and military interests, that is the search for profit and for security. Yet imperialists also become arrogant, overbearing, and contemptuous of those they rule over. When faced with revolt or resistance, especially one that kills a few of its own citizens, the response is sheer fury generating repression which is out of all proportion to the actual threat. I gave the British response to the Indian Mutiny as a modern instance of this, but the utter destruction of Carthage by the Romans was an ancient example, and the sentiment is alive and well in imperial Washington today.

Of course, domination is not my normative preference (not many would admit that). As I remarked earlier, I like the market more than capitalism, which involves domination by property owners over the property-less. Societies vary considerably in the extent of internal and external domination, and there is no reason why current societies might be more egalitarian and peaceful than they actually are. But I am not as sanguine as he is about the decline of militarism. Not that I am pessimistic either. I do agree that it is likely that China will play by the rules of the game. But it seems to me to be unknowable whether the United States or any other country will continue obliterating its enemies from the skies, to the applause of its citizens in what I have called "spectator-sport militarism," where the citizens watch but do not have to actually fight. It seems unknowable whether somebody, state or terrorist, will set off a nuclear weapon, or whether in some dire climate change scenario there might be conflagration between states or mass extermination of surplus population. War in this last case would be a preferred economic goal. But I do hope not.

Military power

Nobody has done more in recent years to remedy the neglect of military power in human societies than Sinisa Malesevic. Here he is in critical mood. He says that in focusing on the coercion involved in military power, I neglect the role of other forms of coercion, exercised through bureaucracies, corporations, churches, and the like. He says in rather

Orwellian or Foucaultian fashion that these coercions have been intensi-fying in modern society.

I agree that such institutions have their coercive side. But what I wanted to do was to distinguish the kind of coercion which kills from milder non-life-threatening forms of coercion. Military power I define as the social organization of lethal violence – the threat or actuality of killing. I believe this form of power is quite distinct from other forms. Not only does it kill, but its threat terrifies people. People living under American bombing or in proximity to IS beheadings have quite different emotional states to those subjected to a corporate, bureaucratic, or church hierarchy. Moreover, the discipline and comradeship necessary for soldiers to kill while facing the risk of being killed is much more intense than bureaucrats, workers, or corporate executives experience. So it is useful to distinguish between lethal and nonlethal coercion, between military power and the other three forms of power. Remember, of course, that my four forms of power are ideal types. Real-world institutions use varying mixtures of them all. Nonmilitary institutions occasionally kill people but this is not the main basis of their power. However, regimes like Stalin's and Hitler's clearly do blur the distinction between political and military power.

I am puzzled by the accusation that I neglect nonlethal forms of power, for they are explicitly central to my entire model. One of my basic distinctions is between collective power which comes through coopera-tion with others and distributive power exercised over others. The latter is normally nonlethally coercive, whether coercion is economic, ideological, or political. My books are full of examples of states, corporations, banks, and ideological movements exercising nonlethal coercion. So the charge that I neglect coercion is baseless.

Nor do I share Malesevic's vision of constantly growing coercion. The nonlethal coercion emphasized by him is normally double edged. Modern technology and social organization do potentially permit greater surveil-lance and control over subordinate populations, and this is exercised in the name of national security. But it also allows the people to exercise more counter-power. Modern corporations have less control over their employees than in former times when unions and strikes were illegal, the law gave capitalists absolute private ownership of their businesses to do as they liked with their workers, and protective legislation was absent. Catholic congregations now have more control over priests than in the past – witness the exposure of clerical sexual abuse. Pope Francis offi-ciated in Rome on September 16, 2014 at a marriage ceremony for twenty couples in which several couples were already living together, one woman was a divorcee and another was a never-married single mother. Previously, neither of the last two women could have had a Catholic

Church wedding. Even the Catholic Church is listening more to its congregation. And why does Malesevic believe that the punishment of marital abuse brings more coercion into society, rather than less? Moreover, democratic states give the people – especially women – more political power than they possessed in the past.

In my book *The Dark Side of Democracy* (2005), I argued that a wave of civil wars, about half of which have an ethnic or religious base, is still passing through the world. The issue in would-be democratizing states, seeking rule by the people, is who is to count as the people. This is problematic where there are two or three ethnic or religious groups each with a plausible claim to have its own state. Did Rwanda really belong to the majority Hutu and not the Tutsi, does Iraq really belong to the largest community, the Shi'a, and is the Kurdish people entitled to claim its own state in the north of the country? Does the Eastern Ukraine belong to its majority Russian speakers or to the Ukrainian speakers who form a majority elsewhere in the country? I argued that the West went through the same difficult process, which culminated in most countries becoming dominated by a single ethnic or religious group. I speculated that the present wave will eventually end, either with single ethnicity/religion countries, "cleansed" by mainly nonlethal coercion, or with countries with many ethnicities, none of which can plausibly claim to own the state. Either outcome would be less violent. I also thanked the Second World War for finally convincing Europeans – who had previously domi- nated the world's wars – that war was a bad thing. And I thanked the Cold War for providing a balance of nuclear terror restraining warlike confron- tation between the two usperpowers. Of course, their wars through proxies involved in small-scale fighting have not been restrained, as I emphasized in Volume 4. The balance of terror has so far restrained other emerging nuclear powers. But I added that nuclear proliferation might weaken these restraints and that we cannot count on the rationality of human beings avoiding nuclear war, witness the two world wars.

I also warned that if humanity does not take radical steps to combat climate change, then "fortress states" erected around countries, which are relatively privileged in terms of climate might emerge and be involved in wars of extermination. If you drastically reduce the population, you reduce harmful emissions. And I conclude my discussion of war in Volume 4 with a passage from which Malesevic selectively quotes. This is my full statement: "The global balance of probabilities is that war and military power will decline over the coming decades, though future cli- mate crises might well terminate this relatively pacific era. But so far in the period covered by this volume, military power has greatly declined across the world" (2013: 418). The "global balance of probabilities" indicates a rather cautious "prediction" and the last paragraph of the book adds "All good cheer might be overwhelmed by the two great looming threats to contemporary society: nuclear war and climate change." (p 432). The charge that I see peace as inevitably spreading across the world is false. I do say that war could in principle be abolished – but reality differs. Humans are too aggressive, emotional, ideologically charged, and irrational to guarantee a peaceful future.

Malesevic not only believes that nonlethal coercion has inexorably increased in modern times but that lethal violence has also intensified. He cannot claim this in terms of the incidence of warfare so he turns to military expenditures which he believes indicate that military power "is constantly on the increase." The first is a "Global Militarisation Index" created by the Bonn International Center for Conversion. This combines several variables into a single index which the Center believes represents the degree of militarization in each country. Military expenditure looms quite large in this Index. The Index data are said to indicate a high or very high level of militarization for most countries in 2010. But Malesevic gives no trend data, and in fact the Center's Index number has declined since 1962 for most countries. Malesevic does present a trend graph of American military spending in inflation-adjustment dollars and this reveals rising expenditure over the period 1962–2010, followed by slight decline afterward. But the United States is now almost the only country which regularly makes war and the United States is responsible for over 40 percent of the world's total military expenditures. This obviously dominates global trends. Data from the Stockholm International Institute of Peace Research (SIPRI) available from 1988 to 2013 show that global military spending in inflation-proof dollars neither increased nor decreased over the period. A substantial decline in spending by advanced countries was canceled out by increases in most other regions of the world.

However, if we control for economic growth and ask whether military expenditures are increasing as a proportion of total GDP we find a substantial decrease, since this has been a period of sustained economic growth for most of the less developed countries. In fact, there is a positive correlation between economic growth and military spending and also one with the extent that revenue comes from minerals. In most countries the state either owns or takes a cut from these, so states flush with funds from oil or growth like to use some of it to buy military toys. There is also a positive correlation between military spending and the extent of conflict in a state's neighborhood. Consequentially, the Middle East is the area with greatest growth in military spending.

These data indicate that global military spending is declining a little, but in some regions – above all, the Middle East and China – there are increases. States still like to flourish their weapons. But using military expenditures as an index of militarism has a drawback. Since war has become far more capital intensive, it is more costly. By and large, rising expenditures in the Middle East, Africa, and China are the consequence of the growing cost of weapons, not of soldiers. Since militaries are now much less labor intensive, the abolition of forcible conscription is spreading, and this removes weapons and war from the everyday experience of most young men. That surely reduces the militarization of society. And apart from a handful of states led by the United States and Israel, they flourish but do not use their toys. We can be thankful for that.

Malesevic also discusses my treatment of twentieth-century wars. Here he has some interesting things to say. However, he persistently turns my arguments about specific phenomena into universal generalizations. I have never said that nationalism is always a consequence of war, or that all wars generate nationalism. I noted in the case of both world wars that the declaration of war produced short-term nationalist fervor and that mobilization then tended to increase national self-identification. But not all wars involve mass mobilization and the course of the war often changes things.

I noted that experience of the front during the the First World War was not conducive to jingoism – or any ideology. Soldiers kept their heads down and grimly hoped for survival. Victory or defeat also made a big difference. Russia, Austria–Hungary and Germany took more defeats and I noted a growing perception of class or national (in the case of Austria–Hungary) exploitation among them. I argued that the Russian Revolution was a consequence of a war which produced among both worker and peasant soldiers a sense of exploitation as "cannon fodder" – and the war put weapons in their hands. I argued that these two factors were decisive for revolutionary success rather than defeat as happened in other cases of attempted revolution in the aftermath of the First World War. It was also the case in China in the Second World War. But the Second World War produced a very different outcome in countries like Britain and in India, where bargains had been struck: we the people will fight but for the promise of a better society at the end of the war. This reinforced a reformist sense of national identity, which war alone could not do. There are virtually no generalizations which will apply to all wars. It depends on the nature of the war experience.

Malesevic's claim that "in the wars of the last two centuries the bonds of micro-solidarity are universal" is also over-argued, since he downplays the role of both ideology and the officer hierarchy. I stressed the role of ideological power in World War II among German and Japanese soldiers. He questions whether many soldiers subscribed to the abstract precepts of fascism. But that misses the point. German fascism and Japanese quasi-fascism both elevated the notion that disciplined comradeship was the basis of the good society and the good soldier. Obedience to authority and a comradeship based on a sense of being a martial and often racist elite were heavily instilled, while the harshness of discipline was also a part of fascist ideology in practice. Ideology was not abstract but grounded in the everyday practice of the army. And what we must explain about these armies is why they continued fighting to the bitter end, long after defeat was inevitable, with comparatively few desertions. This is very unusual among armies, which usually break when defeat looms. Malesevic's micro-group solidarity theory would have to argue that micro-solidarity was greater in these two armies than in others. But no one has suggested this.

Of course, micro-solidarity is important in war but it can lead to an overly "democratic" theory of warfare in armies that are essentially hier-archical and authoritarian. Thus the efficiency of the chain of command is more important. Russian soldiers in World War I revolted because the chain of command could not deliver them supplies yet pressed them to advance without adequate arms and ammunition. The Italian army at Caparetto in World War I fled because of the tactical incompetence of their officers, whereas the Austrian foe had been stiffened by an influx of German officers and NCOs. I noted that German armies were the most effective for two main reasons: a higher proportion of the army were fighting troops rather than support staff, and the chain of command was more decentralized, with lower level officers encouraged to make their own decisions on the battlefield. Micro-solidarity was important but the main stimulus to fighting well was their confidence in their officers. This is much less important among guerillas and terrorists, but I was not discussing them. So in the case of military power, I have dismissed almost all of the charges leveled against me.

Capitalism, states, and neoliberalism

Monica Prasad is uneasy that in Volume 4 I seem to move back to a nation-statist model after having earlier argued that societies are com-posed of intersecting networks of interaction with only a degree of bound-edness at their edges. But it is an empirical matter as to how bounded particular societies or power networks are, and they have differed con-siderably over time and space. In Volume 1, I identified a cycle of move-ment across ancient civilizations between multipower-actor networks, relatively unbounded, and empires of domination, more caged. Much later, I emphasized the open-endedness of medieval European networks in which villages, feudal estates, monastic estates, artisanal and merchant brotherhoods, states, and churches were all to some extent conflicting sources of boundedness. Then I narrated the simultaneous expansion and hardening of states and transnational capitalism. States crystallized further into nation-states alongside the expansion of empires, Christianity, and capitalism, all generating secular ideologies transcending the boundaries of states, like socialism and fascism. I also argued that modern revolutions have come in macro-regional waves assailing states in a single region – Eastern Europe, then East Asia, then Latin America. The balance between states and transnational forces has continually shifted.

Since 1945, nation-states in the North of the world have become more obdurate. Their passports constrain our movements and our rights to work, they have penetrative political economies and welfare policies, they have massive surveillance powers, and any social movement wanting to change the law must go to the nation-state to effect reform. As Prasad notes, nation-states also collect the statistics of the world. Anyone analyzing political economy, welfare states, education, and health indicators – in fact just about any social activity which can be quantified – must willy-nilly rely on national-level statistics, as Prasad says. These are all reasons why today's nation-states approximate to what I have called "cages," especially in the North of the world. In the South populations are much less caged since their supposed nation-states often do not actually control their territories or peoples and are subjected to both transnational forces and the power of stronger states.

In my post-1945 chapters, I identified three primary pillars of global order: the nation-state, capitalism, and the American empire. A fourth pillar enters empirically into many of my analyses – macro-regional cultures, as for example among the Nordic countries or the Anglophones – but I did not develop this concept theoretically. These four overlap, intersect, and undercut one another in complex ways. I emphasize nation-state boundaries more than do enthusiasts for transnational globalization, like Bauman and Beck. Yet I see nation-states and a capitalism which has very strong transnational networks in continuous tension in the contemporary world. The degree of caging by states varies considerably across the world today, as it has in the past.

Prasad then focuses on my treatment of neoliberalism and the Great Recession of 2008. She doesn't say that I am wrong, only that other scholars have said the same thing. That is often true, of course. At one level, my volumes strive for a synthesis of present wisdom but spattered I hope with doses of originality. I differ from most sociologists in arguing that the reach of neoliberalism across the world has been quite limited. Her own excellent book (2006) is the fullest treatment of the political roots of neoliberalism, but I hope I have added more. I note that post-war "business Keynesian" consensus in the United States was purely a pragmatic one, and all the main actors continued to declaim free market rhetoric, unlike their European counterparts. They could pretend that markets not states ruled. So when the neo-liberals emerged, they had an ideological head-start in America, as they did not in continental Europe. I show that in American politics two rival blame-games emerge as responses to the Great Recession – blaming it either on Wall Street or Washington, capitalism or big government. She does acknowledge the originality of my analysis of the links and tensions between neoliberalism and traditional conser-vatism – tensions which are at present ripping apart the Republican Party. My main originality is to attempt to consider systematically the interactions between economic, political, and ideological power sources – the military having little impact in this area.

As she says, I might have discussed further the circuits of high finance across the world, which is a part of her criticism that I focus too much on the nation-state. But economic policies are mainly decided at the national level, as her own book clearly shows. I spend most time on the United States, since it has led the way in imposing neoliberal policies on weaker countries, and since it exported its financial crisis through global capitalist institutions to much of the world. However, I also note that the liberal Anglo-Saxon countries were more receptive to neoliberalism than were other macro-regions of the world, and that many of the poorer parts of the world were not so affected by the crisis. The concept of the macro-region also plays a part here as it does in my two chapters on the development of welfare states. Notions of best practice diffuse most to neighbors or culturally similar countries, like the Anglophones or the Nordics.

I left the United Kingdom in 1987 when the LSE turned down my proposal to teach a course on the Sociology of Globalization, something I have now taught at UCLA for many years. But when others caught onto globalization in sociology, many of its practitioners reified it just as they had earlier reified the nation-state. They now claimed that globalization was killing the nation-state, and that a global culture and even a global polity were emerging. These are gross exaggerations: the nation-state is not dying but changing, while there are only cultural and political glim-merings at the global level. The nation-state is neither totally dominant nor falling before the sword of globalization, for both globalization and nation-states are intensifying. Indeed, an important aspect of globaliza-tion is the globalization of the nation-state form and ideal. Now almost all states claim that they rule bounded sovereign territories in the name of the people, though they often fail to live up to the claim.

Infrastructural power

Prasad is correct in implying that my treatment of infrastructural power in Volume 4 is quite weak. In my work, I have distinguished two dimensions of state power: despotic power, whereby rulers can arbitrarily make important decisions without routine consultation with civil society groups and infrastructural power, which is the capacity to actually get decisions routinely implemented throughout the realm. I termed states low on both forms of power "feudal," those with high despotic but low infrastructural power "imperial," those high on both dimensions I now call "authoritarian" (earlier I termed them "bureaucratic"), and those which are low on despotic power but high on infrastructural power I termed "democratic." This model loomed large in Volumes 1 and 2, and still figured in Volume 3, but I mention it least in Volume 4 – though since the term infrastructural power is not in the index the reader might think it was totally absent. I made the obvious points that the infrastructural powers of modern states increased through the twentieth and early twenty-first centuries and that authoritarian powers increased with the advent of fascism and state socialism and then declined as these collapsed. The increase in the number of democratic regimes continues, slowly. But there is much more to be said than that.

In Volume 3, I identified the "party-state" as the core of Nazi and Soviet power. The invention of the mass ruling party gave a great boost to infrastructural power for it provided the party leaders with a loyal mass following which would then implement their directives throughout the realm. The party was a social infrastructure of power. However, I noted some limitations on their power. Totalitarianism might have been the ambition of rulers, but it was impossible to actually reach. The rulers themselves were despotic in the sense that they could arbitrarily decree almost anything, but they themselves believed their orders were being constantly subverted from below. Supposedly monolithic parties were actually quite factionalized. The rulers reacted with purges or by setting up surveillance agencies like the SS and the NKVD to keep the party and the state bureaucracy in line. But purges resulted in the survivors desire above all to protect their own backs, while surveillance led to the emergence of three rival hierarchies, the state bureaucracy, the ruling party, and the surveillance apparatus. Their rivalry weakened the regime's infrastructural power. I argued that most democracies have more infrastructural power than authoritarian regimes since their institutions confer legitimacy on laws and directives, which have received the stamp of parliamentary approval and so which can be implemented throughout the realm. On the contrary, authoritarian rulers can take decisions and make laws, while the plural power actors of democracies may cancel each other out, making decisions difficult and law-making almost impossible – as in the United States today.

I have subsequently written about the limitations of authoritarian power in the contemporary Middle East and North Africa (MENA) (Mann, 2014). As usual, I define infrastructural powers as those that enable regimes to penetrate their territories. But I stress that these powers are not confined to what Prasad calls "literal infrastructures" like roads and telecommunications. These are the technological side of infrastructural power, which Schroeder and Heiskala would both fit within their categories of, respectively, scientific/technological and artefactual power. But I want to add social infrastructures, like the ruling party, security police, clans, and tribes related to the ruling families, supportive religious sects, plus in some cases the provision of social benefits, i.e. social citizenship, financed by oil revenues. All these are used to try to undercut opposition.

Almost all are double edged, however. Oil revenues are the exception for they enable authoritarian regimes to distribute broader material benefits to the people without having to tax them – as long as the flow and price of oil remain satisfactory. Some technologies (like the Internet) can be used by both the regime and opposition forces. The distribution of benefits to privileged and supposedly loyal in-groups (clans, sects, etc.) has the downside of creating alienated out-groups excluded from the spoils of office. The ruling party, the "party-state," is potentially the most penetrative infrastructure, as it was in Nazi Germany, Communist China, and the Soviet Union. In the Middle Eastern countries, the Ba'athist parties have been much paler versions of the party-state.

But the reliance of most rulers on particular families, tribes, regions, or sects who actually implement the ruler's instructions through the realm, while taking their cut of the spoils, is reminiscent of the weaker infrastructures of premodern imperial states. They also set up Roman-style praetorian guards (usually security police) as a counterweight to the army. These practices alienate powerful elites and the army who are left out of the spoils, and induces elite factionalism, which weakens rulers' infrastructural power and makes them more vulnerable to coups and civil wars. If the regime responds by relying more on groups it defines as being particularly loyal, and uses them to help repress the rest, this will further narrow their base of support. Walking the fine line between rewarding the particularly loyal and providing benefits more broadly to powerful elites requires considerable skill from authoritarian rulers. We saw the consequences of some regime failures in the Arab risings of 2011. Mubarak in Egypt and Ben Ali in Tunisia had narrowed too far their distribution of privilege and they had alienated their armies by relying more on the security police. They fell to opposition forces denouncing their corruption, while the army stood aside.

In democracies, infrastructures are also double edged, though in a different way. Democratic infrastructures are a two-way street, for civil society can use them to control the rulers. If popular opposition reaches a certain level of dissent, the government will be thrown out and the opposition will succeed it through highly institutionalized elections which preserve the democratic system. Of course, the electorate only exercises indirect control. The opposition parties must also be responsive to the needs of those who finance them, usually business groups but also labor unions and large voluntary associations like the National Rifle Association. I emphasized that full democracy remains a goal to be struggled toward.

Two major imperfections can be observed. First, foreign policy is rarely democratic. It evokes little public interest except from particular interest groups like the pro-Israel lobby in the United States or businesses trading with a particular country. Even most politicians do not develop much expertise in foreign policy. Thus presidents and prime ministers have considerable autonomy. They can dominate the flow of information concerning countries and movements abroad, sometimes fabricating or amplifying threats and crises in far-off countries, as in the invented second Tonkin Bay incident in Vietnam or the "weapons of mass destruction" supposedly held by Saddam Hussein. Because of their enormous infrastructures of military power (rightly emphasized by Prasad), they can plunge the country into war, with or without parliamentary approval. Two of my examples of this concerned the run-up to World War I and the 2003 invasion of Iraq.

Information control spills over into domestic politics by leaders brandishing and amplifying the threat of alien terrorism. This has led to a dramatic increase in state surveillance infrastructures. The actual level of threat is often exaggerated by politicians who believe both that maintaining a climate of fear will boost their electoral chances while fearing that any outrage committed on their watch will lead to electoral defeat. Thus military and political power relations are now entwining to generate the "deep state" long known to Middle Eastern peoples – murky, secretive, practicing torture, giving great powers to security agencies. The war on terror has no obvious end, since the actions of the states themselves repeatedly generate more terrorists. This is especially true of the United

States. The exercise of power is not always rational, as I stress in these volumes.

The second structural defect of existing democracies is that elected governments are pushed around by those wielding economic power. The prime movers are capitalists who finance most parties, and today this primarily means finance capitalists. They wield economic power sufficient to dictate state economic policies. They may persuade them that the program on which they were elected is at odds with economic reality, that there is "no alternative" to doing what business wants. This advice is backed by sanctions like capital flight. In my volumes, I noted this happening in the 1920s, the 1980s, and the 2000s, so it is not new. But as I noted in Volume 4 (and Prasad and Derlugian et al agree), these constraints have become stronger in recent years as capital has become more transnational, better able to outflank the nation-state.

Prasad suggests that the notion of infrastructural power is not confined to political institutions. It can also be applied to capitalism, she says (and so perhaps to the other two sources of social power). She is correct but with qualifications. Here we must distinguish two more forms of power, authoritative and diffuse power. So far, I have only used infrastructural power in analyzing authoritative organizations in which decisions are taken at a central point and then implemented downward throughout a zone of control, which states do. Capitalism does have authoritative organizations. They are business corporations in which decisions are taken by a director or board of directors and subordinates are then instructed to implement them. In fact, the business corporation resembles the authoritarian state.

But capitalism has a second realm of activity, the market and this involves diffuse, not authoritative power. Individual actors in a market place may make decisions, but not the market as a whole. Market conditions are not willed by anyone but are the unintended outcome of a myriad of decisions. So is it appropriate to identify the infrastructures of diffused power? In terms of technical infrastructures, clearly yes. The physical media of communication – horses, ships, telephones, literacy, translation, money, etc. – all enabled increasing penetration of the world by market forces, especially in the modern period. There also some social infrastructures of markets, like banks and stock exchanges, which also facilitate market penetration. But other social infrastructure limit the freedom of markets, steering them in certain directions, like monopolies, oligopolies, the Bretton Woods system, or the World Bank. That is why true-believing neoliberals oppose these institutions, on the grounds that they limit market freedom. But in the end, markets dominate actors, not actors markets. I don't think it makes sense to think of this as infrastructural power.

There are similarities to this in ideological power. Some ideologies do have hierarchical organizations. The Catholic Church attempts to dictate how people should live and what is moral and immoral. But other religions are not hierarchical in this way, like Judaism or Islam. The spread of ideologies is usually diffuse, not authoritative, while beliefs are essentially free and uncontrollable. A Catholic may stop believing in Church doctrine and become an apostate or she may simply stop following the Church's instructions on, say, contraception or abortion. Again infrastructural power has only a limited role to play in ideological movements. Military power definitely does have infrastructural power. It resembles capitalism in that the internal structure of armies (not guerillas or terrorists) is high on both despotic and infrastructural power, like the corporation. But its deployment externally also has infrastructures though they are terroristic, arbitrary, sudden, erratic, and lacking routine application. The striking range of an army also greatly exceeds what it can stably control. So the notion of infrastructural power is applicable to varying extents to the other sources of power.

The contemporary state is not all-powerful and it also faces new challenges. The prevalence of the informal or "black" economy and the "sharing economy" both in developing countries and in advanced ones, plus large-scale illegal immigration, tax evasion and tax havens, and attempts to bolster privacy laws are all reactions against intrusive states. People in poor countries often pay no taxes and try to avoid contact with the state. Transnational corporations currently exploit tax loopholes to submit their accounts to countries with low tax rates. Military conscription has been abandoned by most states so that the state only has the power of life or death over paid volunteers, not young male citizens as a whole. Nonetheless, the space for resisting the growth of state infrastructural power in the North has lessened in the post-war period.

As Prasad points out, Hayek, Rueff, and other neoliberals feared this. They believed that the liberation of the price signal would bring more material benefits and freedoms. Most people welcome state powers like compulsory education, social security, and public health provision. Yet some on both the left and the right would agree with Hayek and Rueff that the state has become too intrusive, but they favor cutting back different state infrastructures. Rueff's attack on budget deficits was aimed at expenditure on both the military (he would be appalled by the "deep state") and the welfare state. The left applaud the former attack, conservatives the latter.

But there is a deeper drawback of neoliberalism. It emphasizes the freedom and collective power of largely unregulated markets and equate them with democracy because markets involve many decentralized actors not authoritarian commands. But what neoliberals fail to recognize is that markets are always sites of distributive power. Some market actors have power over others, as capitalists do over workers, or as skilled workers do over unskilled. Capitalists actually own the means of production and left unregulated give themselves more and workers less. The neoliberal surge occurring from the 1970s has widened inequality most where regulations have been removed, as in the Anglophone countries, and where an expanding economy never was much regulated, as in most developing countries. This is the material and moral failure of neoliberalism.

Finally, Prasad concludes that the Great Recession revealed the infrastructural weakness of capitalism. It depends which type of power is being considered. In terms of collective power, she is correct for this was a serious recession, although it might be replied that it is the nature of capitalism to bring slumps as well as booms, and this recession might have been the prelude to another boom. But in the realm of distributive power, the recession proved the strength of capitalists and the ability of a liberated price signal (as desired by neoliberals) to penetrate our lives – but to do us harm. Finance capitalists have paradoxically come out of the crisis very well. They are stronger, we are weaker.

American politics

Two contributors discuss my treatment in Volume 3 of American politics in the first half of the twentieth century. Lilli Riga approves of my general approach but says I barely scratch the surface of American ethnic politics during the first half of the twentieth century. She is right. I do discuss race and I mention that ethnic fragmentation frustrated those who sought to build a united working class movement, but I had not realized the scale of foreign immigration nor the breadth of the Progressives' cultural projects nor of the official Americanization programs aimed at "civilizing" the immigrants. I had not known of the extensive vetting of applicants for citizenship or of how it restrained immigrants' political activity. I did remark the imperfections of American democracy, particularly in the South, and I said that the New Deal would have gone further had all American adults been enfranchised. But I should have added that the scale of immigration left immigrants, much of the male working class population, without citizen rights, including the right to vote. Riga shows that ethnic fragmentation, political exclusion, and widespread deportation of militant workers allowed American employers and governments to repress workers' movements from well before the New Deal period. Yet this was not just a period piece, now gone. It is true again today, now that the United States has returned to the high level of immigration it experienced at the beginning of the twentieth century. If we add the racial black/ white divide onto the native born/ immigrant divide, we have an enlarged version of what I said was the only American exceptionalism, racism. But it is not now exceptional since much of Europe has acquired a racial/ nativist problem too. Riga has made a substantial contribution to scholarship on the American working class and her arguments are applicable to other times and places.

Ed Amenta showers me with praise and a Bob Hope/ Bing Crosby road movie plot. I should first make clear my preference for the most generous welfare state – and so in his movie for Dorothy Lamour. He then gets down to the business of criticism. He is right that I neglect the turn that the New Deal made in 1939 and he makes good points about the tendency of policies to become self-reinforcing. He also says that I treat the development of social policy as a C plotline in a story mainly about empires, revolutions and wars, but I do not accept this. Volume 3 devotes two long chapters to the development of welfare states, and my chapter on neoliberalism in Volume 4 also discusses them. Although I say that countries' social policies were blown in different directions by different wartime experiences, most of my analysis concerns internal national development, though within the context of cultural macro-regions. Like T.H. Marshall, I see welfare states and progressive taxation as mitigating class inequalities and avoiding serious class conflict. I argue that the destiny of the working class was not to overthrow capitalism, as in traditional Marxism, but (with allies) to reform it. Reform included the introduction of welfare states, progressive taxation, and labor union rights.

Nonetheless, Amenta says that I see this mainly as results of outside forces. He agrees with me that progressive taxation in many countries was boosted by the world wars. I add that the Cold War had a regressive impact in the United States since it outlawed communists and socialists and intimidated liberals. Anticommunism was also important within the labor unions, especially visible in their splits which played a large part in their failure to unionize the South in "Operation Dixie." It was followed by the Taft-Hartley Act restricting union rights, and by McCarthyism, which identified radicals as "communists." These were mainly the product of the fear of "Bolshevism" and of the Cold War. Amenta thinks I exaggerate all this. For example, he instances the election of 1942, which produced a Republican majority in Congress which terminated some New Deal programs. This, he says, was a case where the war was not very relevant. Oh, yes it was! Most commentators on that election attribute the unexpected Republican victory to the claim that the Roosevelt administration was skimping in its war preparations, leaving America unprotected.

Since Amenta agrees that the war and Cold War did then have a big impact, it is only a question of emphasis that divides us. I have just instanced cases where a national analysis would not be sufficient to explain the development of social citizenship. But I agree that geopolitical factors were not a sufficient cause either. My domestic analysis often concerns the kinds of developments he also stresses, like the limitations of American democracy and the role of the South. He adds the unbending nature of the Republican Party which I think is right. I agree that domestic considerations were more important up to the outbreak of World War II, but then for a period, the impact of geopolitics predominated before yielding up again to more domestic forces. This was a period in which the structural development of American social relations and the structural development of geopolitics entwined in a rather contingent way. In sociology, the domestic and the international, plus their often contingent interactions, must always be considered, though their relative strengths vary greatly through time and space.

Contingency and rationality

This brings me finally to the role of contingency and irrationality in macro-explanation. Here I used words loosely and so I must clarify what I meant. My stress on contingency in the American case which I just mentioned refers to an interaction between two broad, persistent, structural forces, the inherent development of American society, and geopolitics, especially wars. Each had a certain logic of development and we can produce causal explanations of each. But it was the interaction between them which provided much of the contingency since the causal chains within each were quite different. We often find this kind of conjunctural contingency. The Anglophone countries shared many similarities. None of them had major Marxist or socialist movements. This is why I say that Sombart's famous question "Why is there no socialism in America?" was misplaced, for nor did Britain, Canada, Australia, New Zealand, or Ireland. If we looked at their social citizenship progress in 1938 we would not find major differences between them, except in matters of race. But their war experiences differed and the collision between domestic and the geopolitical causal chains sent them down different paths.

Another example of conjunction is provided by the Bolshevik revolution. The causal chains of severe class conflict differed from the causal chains of Russian involvement in Great Power geopolitics. When Russia got into World War I, the two became intimately entwined. Workers and peasants now experienced severe exploitation as cannon fodder, and they also had weapons in their arms, while defeat in war weakened the cohesion and repressive power of elites. Those contingent connections were the main cause of the Bolshevik Revolution. So conjunction is not pure accident but the collision of two or more orthogonal causal chains. There is a different type of contingency, however (which Heiskala would be the first to point out). It is the interaction between humans and "Mother Nature." River valleys had existed for millennia before humans thought to harness their power. Coal had existed in Britain for millennia before eighteenth century CE Britons thought of burning it in metal devices. Harnessing the wind is a contemporary example. The human side of this contingency is the product of a social causal chain, but the natural side is "just there."

I should also clarify what I mean by "irrationality," which I have argued is common in human societies. John Hall says this is "slightly dangerous talk." But it is common. I give many examples of irrationality among those who wield political power, like the statesmen who led the way into World War I, the failure in the late 1930s of British and French leaders to ally with the Soviet Union to deter further aggression by Hitler, the blind anticommunism of American interventions in Latin America and elsewhere, and the Bush administration's militarism in the Middle East.

The term "irrational" may not have been the best choice, for it has two different senses, "not reasonable or lacking good judgment," and "lacking the power of reason." I meant the former, not the latter. In all four cases just noted, intelligent leaders were thinking hard and fairly systematically about what they should do amid developing crises. But their ideologies and emotions helped define what they thought was reasonable. In the World War I case, their reasoning privileged "national honor" and not "backing down." I said this was analogous to little boys fighting in the playground. The leaders were prepared to risk war but they all thought that the other side, being reasonable men, would back down. They were wrong and a world war engulfed them. They should have acted differently, and had they possessed hindsight they would have acted differently. In the second case, conservative statesmen were driven by anticommunist ideology for they had a greater fear of communism than fascism. Again, they made a mistake, since Hitler was much more dangerous to them than the more defense-minded Stalin. But their decisions were not arbitrary and they are explicable. They were not reasonable and had poor judgment, but they did not lack the power of reason. Perhaps foolish would have been a better term, for these volumes show that folly is a major part of human action. This is one reason why an analysis of human societies in terms of rational action alone (which is currently fashionable) is also folly. Some aspects of human behavior are interpretable in this way, but with human beings there is always the possibility of ideological- and emotional-led disaster – or indeed success. In Volume 4, I instance three current trends which may become disastrous in the future, climate change, nuclear proliferation, and American antipathy to Islam. The odds are that folly will triumph in at least one of them.

References

Barkey, Karen 2008 *Empire of Difference. The Ottomans in Comparative Perspective.* Cambridge: Cambridge University Press.

Blackburn, Robert & Mann, Michael 1975 "The Ideologies of Non-skilled Industrial Workers" in M. Bulmer (ed.) *Workers' Images of Society.* London: Routledge and Kegan Paul, pp. 131–161.

Bockman, Johanna 2014 "*Socialist Globalization and Capitalist Neocolonialism: the Economic Ideas behind the NIEO*", unpublished paper, George Mason University.

Collins, Randall 1994 "Why the Social Sciences won't Become High-consensus, Rapid-discovery Science", *Sociological Forum*, Vol 9, 155–177.

Ikenberry, John 2001 *After Victory: Institutions, Strategic Restraint, and, the Rebuilding of Order After Major Wars.* Princeton, NJ: Princeton University Press.

2011 *Liberal Leviathan. The Origins, Crisis, and Transformation of the American World Order.* Princeton, NJ: Princeton University Press.

Mackinder, Halford 1904 "The Geographical Pivot of History", *The Geographical Journal*, Vol. 23, 421–437

Mann, Michael 1970 "The Social Cohesion of Liberal Democracy", *American Sociological Review*, Vol. 35, 423–439.

2003 *Incoherent Empire*. London: Verso.

2005 *The Dark Side of Democracy*. Cambridge: Cambridge University Press.

2014 "The infrastructural powers of authoritarian states in the Middle East and North Africa" (unpublished, available on my web-site).

Naughton, Barry 2006 *The Chinese Economy: Transitions and Growth.* Boston, MA: M.I.T. Press.

Nee, Victor & Sonja Opper 2007 "On Politicized Capitalism" in *On Capitalism*, Victor Nee and Richard Swedberg (eds.). Stanford, CA: Stanford University Press.

Prasad, Monica 2006 *The Politics of Free Markets: The Rise of Neoliberal Economic Policies in Britain, France, Germany, and the United States.* Chicago, IL: University of Chicago Press.

Priestland, David 2012 *Merchant, Soldier, Sage: A New History of Power.* London: Penguin Books.

Schroeder, Ralph 2007 *Rethinking Science, Technology, and Social Change.* Stanford, CA: Stanford University Press.

Index

Abbott, Andrew, 219
adaptive radiation, 66
Affordable Care Act, 219, 222
After Victory (Ikenberry), 292
agrarian societies/movements
  capitalism's emergence in, 78
  chieftaincy in, 73
  in China, 21–22
  US interventions and, 296
alien labour, 187–188, 190–191, 192–193,
     194–195, 201–202, 203–204. *See*
     also Americanization Movement
Amenta, Edwin
  on American welfare state, 5–6
  Mann's response to, 319–320
  on redistributive policies, 205
American empire. *See also* empire; liberal
     hegemony
  characterisation of, 242–244
  Europe/East Asia and, 266
  geographic insularity and, 265
  globalization and, 165–168
  hegemonic role of, 259–260
  as hierarchical, 260
  as 'informal empire,' 165–166, 242–244
  as last empire, 256–258
  militarism/interventionism, 272–274
  origins of, 262–267
  as post-imperial global power, 257–258
  in post-war world, 275–276
  shift to "international order," 260–262
  support for national movements,
     266–267
  universal principles and, 265–266
American Exceptionalism, 3, 5, 185,
     186–187, 205, 221–222, 319
Americanization Movement. *See also* alien
     labour
  as culturally disciplining project,
     205–206
  ethnic diversity and, 188
  industrial labour and, 188

in nation building, 187
scale of, 189–190
American politics, 318–320
*An Anatomy of Power: The Social Theory of
     Michael Mann* (Hall and Schroeder)
  critical assessment of, 1
  on ideological power, 1–2
  on IEMP framework, 146
  war as topic in, 2
Anderson, Perry, 38, 48, 89
Anglophone countries
  consumer citizenship and, 172–173
  disembedded markets in, 170–171
  global order and, 311
  neoliberalism and, 318
  social citizenship in, 168
Annan, Kofi, 298
Applied Sociology (Runciman), 53
Argentina, 154, 155
Aron, Raymond, 94, 103
artefactual power, 32–33, 288–290. *See also*
     NACEMP model (natural, artefac-
     tual, cultural, economic, military
     and political power sources)
austerity policies, 26–27
Austria-Hungary, 17–18, 128, 309, 310
authoritarian power, 313, 314
authoritative ideologies/system, 144,
     146–147, 154, 284, 316
authoritative power, 12–13, 29–30, 45,
     316–317
Axial Age, 82

Badiou, Alain, 102–103
banks
  after Bretton Woods, 158
  Chinese, 253
  deregulation of, 158–159
  neoliberalism and, 285, 316
  regulation of, 285
Barkey, Karen, 291
Bartov, O., 134, 137

Bayley, Christopher, 2–3, 38
Bell, Daniel, 91
Bendix, Reinhard, 11
Beveridge Plan, 25–26
Billig, M., 132
Binghampton University, 51
Blair, Tony, 96
Bloch, Marc, 56
Bolshevik revolution/Bolshevism, 68, 90,
     137, 192, 300–301, 319, 320–321
Boltanski, L., 156
Bourdieu, P., 155–156
Boutros-Ghali, Boutros, 298
Braudel, Fernand, 38, 56
Brenner, Robert, 110
Bretton-Woods Conference, 22–23, 158, 160
Breuilly, J., 126
Britain/Great Britain
     concentration of capital, 90
     empire of, 243–244, 260–261
     endorsement of Empire, 97–98
     fractured imperialism and, 238–239
     liberal order building of, 270, 271–272
     on liberal-repressive continuum, 186
     neoliberalism and, 151–152, 160
     racism of, 240–241
     rise of nation-state in, 17–18
     state-building and, 266–267
Brunschvicg, Leon, 94
Bryant, Joseph, 149
Burawoy, Michael
     as advocate, 56–57
     in 'big' historical sociology, 38
     biographical/academic context, 43–44
     use of foresight, 57–58
business enterprises, coercive power of, 120

caging concept/effect, 16, 18, 29–30, 31,
     66, 126, 311
capitalism. See also China
     as condition for political decency, 98–99
     cultural embedding in, 187
     dominant ideologies in, 146–147
     flight to globalization, 77–81
     future of, 28
     historic breakthrough of, 74
     life cycle of, 50–51
     militarism, alliance with, 236–237
     organizational principles of, 156–157
     survival of, 54
     transnational, 256, 261, 267, 311
capitalist-industrial nation-state system
     alternative to, 21–22
     consolidation of, 20
     power sources in, 31

Capitalizing on Crisis (Krippner), 111
Carter, Jimmy, 23–24
Castles, Francis, 212
centrifugal ideologisation, 130–131, 135,
     138–139
Chicago School, 51
chieftaincy, 66–67, 68–69, 71–72, 84
China
     agrarian revolution, 21–22
     alternative world-systems and, 22
     capitalism and, 6–7, 28
     economic growth/expansion of, 252–255,
          301–302
     in global-hierarchy of power, 176
     Mann's analysis of, 290–291
     outsourcing to, 79
     totalitarianism and, 76
Chivvis, Christopher, 114–115
Chong, Ian, 266–267
Christianity
     as authoritative ideology, 146–147
     expansion of, 311
     Marxist-Leninist orthodoxy and, 84
     in modern state, 1–2
     role of, 14, 74
class-consciousness, 44, 57, 77–81
classes. See middle-class; working class/
          working middle class
climate change, 171–172, 307–308
coercion
     of alien labour, 191–192
     by banks, 306
     mode of, 47, 48
     by non-state entities, 120
     organizational power and, 119–125,
          129–130, 139–140
     types of, 121–122
Coercion Capital and European States, AD
     990–1990 (Tilly), 42
Coker, C., 124–125
Cold War
     competition for control during, 6–7
     endings/final phase, 250–252
     imperial order in, 165
     liberal analysis of, 146–147
     liberalism in, 262–263
     MAD capability, 24
     origins of, 247–250
     US dominance and, 165
collective power
     analysis of, 12–13
     chieftaincy and, 66–67
     vs. distributive power, 32, 306
     infrastructural power and, 113
     of nation-states, 40

neoliberalism and, 318
of professoriate, 68
recession and, 318
science/technology and, 32, 287, 288
social evolution and, 65–67
Collins, R., 136–137, 146, 170, 287
colonialist globalization, 20–21
Communism. *See also* Cold War; Marxism-
    Leninism
cultural hegemony and, 157
ideological power in, 147, 156
ideology networks in, 146–147
competitive selection, 47
compulsory cooperation, 232–233
connectedness, of communities, 231–232
*Consciousness and Action Among the Western
    Working Class* (Mann), 44, 56
constitutional design, 99–100
consumer citizenship
in Anglophone countries, 172–173
globalizing modernity and, 172–173
Mann on, 286
contingency, role of, 320–322
corvee labour, 15
Crouch, C., 177
cultural diversity. *See also* Americanization
    Movement
nationalism and, 127–128
in nation building, 186–187
socialism and, 206
culturalists/socialists, gap between, 144
cultural power sources, 33. *See also*
    NACEMP model (natural, artefac-
    tual, cultural, economic, military
    and political power sources)
Cultural Revolution, 21–22
cultural selection, 47
cultural turn, excesses of, 143

*The Dark Side of Democracy: Explaining
    Ethnic Cleansing* (Mann), 2, 43, 56,
    90, 133
Darwin, Charles, 46–47, 67, 93–94
Darwin, John, 6, 291–292
decency. *See* political decency
della Porta, D., 135
deregulation
in China, 254
of financial sector, 26, 158–159
globalization and, 79
Great Neoliberal Recession and,
    26–27, 111
Derluguian, Georgi, 4, 283–284
despotic power, 66–67, 108, 109, 113, 114.
    See also chieftaincy

Diamond, Jared, 33–34
diffused power, 12–13, 29–30, 45, 316–317
disembedded markets, 164–165, 169,
    170–171
distributive power, analysis of, 12–13
Does Capitalism Have a Future? (Wallerstein
    et al), 50, 54
Domhoff, William, 213, 216
Durkheim, Emile, 32, 93, 94, 304

Earle, Timothy, 4, 283–284
economic contagion, fear of, 264
economic crisis
influence of, 215–216
neoliberalism and, 6
of 1970s, 158–159
triggers of, 110–111
economic hegemony
cycle of, 50–51
of US, 23, 54
economic power. *See also* IEMP model
    (ideological, economic, military and
    political power sources)
American/US, 167, 297–299
asymmetries of, 168, 176–177
in communist regimes, 156
vs. ideological power, 147
in IEMP model, 14
in institutions, 148
Mann on, 284
state policies and, 316
Eley, Geoff, 143–144
Elias, Norbert, 38
elites
behavior of, 103
in integrated world, 102
empire. *See also* American empire
compulsory cooperation in, 232–233
connectedness of communities in,
    231–232
defeated, 76
definition/scale of, 230
end/breakdown of, 239–240
'fractured imperialism,' 166, 234–235,
    238–239
industrial capitalism and, 236–237
informal empire, 244
logistics and, 230–231
Mann on, 291–292
militarist culture in, 235–236
nationalist movements and, 241–242
origins of, 230
racism, function of, 240–241
reconsolidation, appeal of, 233–234
resurgence of interest in, 229–230

empire (cont.)
  role of, 6
  typology of, 293
  unraveling of, 273
  US as 'incoherent empire,' 23, 24–25
  varieties of, 258–262
environmental challenge, 27, 35. *See also*
    climate change
Esping-Andersen, G., 25, 212, 215, 222
ethnic immigrants. *See* alien labour
European Coal and Steel Union, 20
European empires
  dominance of, 165
  rise and fall of, 19–20, 256
  settler colonialism, 236–237
  social citizenship and, 223
evolutionist theory, 3–4. *See also* social
    evolution
exceptionalism (US). *See* American
    Exceptionalism
exclusion/repression
  of alien labour, 194–195, 196, 203–204
  creation of political consciousness, 103
  political nature of, 202–203
expenditures, on military power, 123
extensive vs. intensive power, 12–13
Eyskens, Mark, 14

fascism
  collapse of, 22, 313
  death toll under, 21
  defeated empires and, 76
  fear of, 321–322
  ideological unity of, 134–135, 137, 310
  rise of, 22, 104–105, 133
  simplified ideologies, 303–304
  state elites and, 213–214
  victory over, 62
Fascists (Mann), 2, 43, 133
Fault Lines (Rajan), 111
Fernand Braudel Center (Binghamton
    University), 51
financialization. *See also* neoliberalism
  disembedded markets and, 171
  Mann's analysis of, 107–108, 109
  Mann's argument for, 110
financial markets
  deregulation of, 158–159
  expansion of, 252
  instabilities of, 165, 179
  power struggles in, 158–159
Foucault, Michel, 3, 30, 31, 154
Fox, Cybelle, 204
'fractured imperialism,' 234–235,
    238–239, 242

Freeden, Michael, 152–154
free trade, 297–299
Freud, Sigmund, 93–94
Fukuyama, Francis, 65, 91

Gallagher, J., 232, 237
GATT (General Agreement on Trade and
    Tariffs), 297–298
Gellner, Ernest, 99–100, 126
gender, analysis of, 34–35
"The Geographical Pivot of History"
    (Mackinder), 300
Germany. *See also* Nazism
  fascism in, 303
  nationalism and, 129
  rise of nation-state in, 17–18
G. I. Bill of Rights, 214
Giddens, Anthony, 12, 38
Global Empires and Revolution (Mann),
    40–41, 42
global history, as historians' focus, 2–3
globalization/globalizations
  American empire and, 165–168
  analysis of Mann's, 165–169
  capitalism's flight to, 77–81
  debates about, 164
  economic power in, 168
  in social theory, 164–165
  sociological treatment of, 2–3
  at transnational/global level, 180
Globalizations (Mann), 41
globalizing modernity
  class relations in, 177–178
  climate change and, 171–172
  consumer citizenship and, 172–173
  core/periphery economic relations in,
    176–177
  cultural change in, 173
  disembedded markets in, 169,
    170–171
  economic inequality in, 169
  geopolitics/geo-economics in, 176
  military power in, 175
  neoliberalism and, 170–171
  political power in, 169–170
  religious fundamentalism and, 170
  social developments and, 174–175
  technoscientific culture and, 171–172
  at transnational/global level, 180
  transnational movements in, 169–170
  Western-centrism and, 173–175
global recession, 26–27. *See also* "Great
    Neoliberal Recession"; Great
    Recession
Goldstone, Jack, 2

Gorbachev, Mikhail. *See also* Soviet Union (USSR)
  nuclear arms reduction treaty, 24
  perestroika's failure, 79
  political leadership of, 96
  reform proposals of, 147, 150–151, 157–158
Gorski, Philip, 146–147
Gramsci, A., 157
Great Depression, 27, 78, 210, 212–213, 218
"Great Neoliberal Recession," 26–27, 111. *See also* neoliberalism
Great Recession
  capitalist bail outs, 81
  Mann's analysis of, 177–178
  Prasad on, 311–312, 318
Great Society legislation, 222
Greenspan, Alan, 110–111
Guevara, Che, 298

Hall, John
  on irrationality, 321
  on liberal regimes, 4
  Mann's response to, 304
Harvey, David, 79
Hayek, Friedrich, 114, 115–116, 152, 317
health care coverage, 6
hegemony. *See* American empire; economic hegemony; liberal hegemony
Heiskala, Risto, 1, 3, 288–290, 314
Hicks, Alexander, 211, 213
higher education. *See* universities
historical sociology
  Bendix on, 11
  Golden Age of, 63, 64–65
  grand syntheses and, 143
  micro-level analyses, 132–133
  post WW II reconstruction, 62–63
  socio-structural approaches, 143–144
Hobsbawn, Eric, 38, 246
Hobson, John, 173–174
Hooks, G., 214
Hopkins, Harry, 216–217
Hopkins, Terence, 53
Huber, E., 210, 213
Hull, Cordell, 24
Hume, David, 91–92
humiliation, dynamics of, 42–43
Huntington, Samuel, 65

identity politics, 28–29
ideological power. *See also* IEMP model (ideological, economic, military and political power sources)
  in Communism, 147, 156

in IEMP model, 13–14
Islamist fundamentalism and, 283, 302–303, 317
Mann's analysis of, 94–95, 283, 302–305
in modern world, 89–90
ideologies
  classification of, 91
  Mann's treatment of, 144–145
  metatheoretical options, 91–94
  morphological approach to, 152–154
  naturalism, 93–94
  of social support, 92–93
ideologisation, centrifugal, 130–131, 135, 138–139
IEMP model (ideological, economic, military and political power sources)
  advancement of, 109
  changes over time, 145, 147–148
  dismissal of, 146
  economic power in, 14
  to explain financial crisis, 111–112
  ideological power in, 13–14
  limits of, 117
  Mann's use of, 15, 215–216, 288–290
  military power in, 14–15
Ikenberry, John
  on benefits of American empire, 6–7, 175
  Mann's response to, 292–300
immanent ideologies, 90, 91
immanent morale, 13–14, 73
imperialism, European, 20
"The Imperialism of Free Trade" (Gallagher and Robinson), 237
inclusion, political consciousness and, 103
incoherent empire, 23, 24–25
Incoherent Empire (Mann), 56, 297
India, Mann's analysis of, 290–291
individualism, 92–93, 143, 147, 148, 160, 304, 305
industrial labour. *See also* alien labour
  Americanization Movement and, 188
  progressivism and, 186–187
industrial revolution, capitalism and, 78
informal empire
  America as, 165–166, 244, 256–257
  economic gains in, 269
  as empire type, 258–259
  gunboat diplomacy and, 295
infrastructural power, 108, 313–318
intellectuals, importance of, 102–103
intensive power, 12–13
internationalist project, 257, 270–271, 272, 275

International Monetary Fund (IMF)
  establishment of, 22–23
  as multilateral institution, 268
  neoliberalism and, 285
  shared dominance through, 297
  under US control, 252
international relations theory, 100–101,
    173–174, 176–177
Iraq, US war in, 128–129, 251, 258, 274,
    294, 297, 307, 315
irrationality, role of, 96, 320–322
Islamism/Islamist fundamentalism
  America and, 297, 321–322
  ideological power and, 283,
    302–303, 317
  in modern state, 1–2
  political change and, 170
  terrorism causes, 297
Italy, 21, 40–41

Janowitz, M., 136
Japan
  colonialism of, 21
  nationalist culture, 134
Jaspers, Karl, 82
Johnson, Lyndon, 222
Johnson, Samuel, 99

Kant, Immanuel, 91–92, 94, 97
Keck, M., 170
Keynes, John Maynard, 22–23,
    94, 99
Keynesianism, 109–110, 167
Khrushchev, Nikita, 150–151, 156,
    157–158, 253
Kiser, E., 133
Kitschelt, Herbert, 156
knowledge, as power, 67–68
Korpi, Walter, 210, 213
Krippner, Greta, 110, 111
Krishnan, A., 124–125

labour, outsourced, 122
labour movement. See also alien labour
  cultural diversity of, 187
  repression of, 185, 186
  weakness of, 185
Lachmann, Richard, 73, 78
Laitin, D., 2
Lamarck, Jean-Baptiste, 67
Latour, Bruno, 3, 32
leading-edge, of power, 41, 42, 112–113
Lenin, Vladimir, on revolution, 21–22
liberal hegemony. See also American empire
  distribution of economic gains, 268–269

integrative tendencies, 267–268
liberal internationalism, 272
shared leadership, 268
tolerance of diversity, 269
Westphalian project, 97, 257, 270–271,
    272, 275
liberal internationalist project, 257,
    270–271, 272, 275
liberalism, balance of political power and,
    90–91
Liberal Leviathan (Ikenberry), 292
"lib-lab welfare regime," 185, 211, 212,
    214–215
Lieberman, Victor, 38
Lieven, Dominic, 38
Linnaeus, Carl, 46–47
Logics of History (Sewell), 154
Long March, 21–22
Lundestad, Geir, 167, 262
Lustick, Ian, 217

Mackinder, Halford, 300
macro-historical frameworks, 64–65, 146,
    154, 156, 161
MAD (mutually assured destruction), 24,
    27–28
Malesevic, Sinisa
  Mann's response to, 303–304, 305–310
  on military force/power, 4–5
Mann, Michael. See also Consciousness
    and Action Among the Western
    Working Class (Mann); The Dark
    Side of Democracy: Explaining Ethnic
    Cleansing (Mann); Fascists (Mann);
    Global Empires and Revolution
    (Mann); Globalizations (Mann);
    IEMP model (ideological, eco-
    nomic, military and political
    power sources); Incoherent Empire
    (Mann); The Sources of Social Power
    (Mann)
  on American welfare state, 5–6
  analytical/theoretical tools of, 29–30, 39
  biographical/academic context, 1, 43–44,
    63–64
  concepts of/conception of power,
    11–12, 31
  contingent explanation, reliance on, 218,
    222–223
  as dedicated empiricist, 43–45
  as examining magistrate, 56, 291
  on free-floating ideology, 2
  on future of capitalism, 28
  on gender, 34–35
  global purview of, 2–3

grand theory, distrust of, 30
on ideologies/ideological power,
    94–95, 283
on infrastructural power, 108, 113
introduction to work of, 1
on 'leading edge' of power, 112–113, 145
micro-level analyses of, 133
on military force/power, 4–5, 63–64, 283
on 1968 protests, 78
as political historian, 19
on political power, 121, 283
on regimes of inequality, 169
on revolution, 21
on role of empire, 6
on role of ideology/culture, 5
on social evolution, 4, 68–69
'track-laying vehicle' conception of, 149
use of foresight, 57–58
use of secondary sources, 216–217
US focus of, 5
Mann, Michael, response to critics
on American empire
    capitalism vs. democracy in, 296
    constitutional institutionalism,
        299–300
    vs. European Union, 293
    as hegemon, 292–293, 300
    military interventions, 293–294, 296
    post-war super powers, 300–302
    trade and treaties, 297–299
    typologies of, 293
on American politics, 318–320
on climate change, 307–308
on contingency and irrationality,
    320–322
on empire, 291–292
on general theory
    consumer citizenship in, 286
    economic power relations, 284–286
    evolutionary psychology in, 290
    gender relations in, 290
    IEMP/NACEMP models, 288–290
    multi-causality in model, 282–283
    neglect of China/India, 284–286
    neglect of human emotion in, 290
    science/technology in, 286
    social evolutionary lens, 283–284
on globalization, 312–313
on ideological power, 302–305
on infrastructural power
    in democratic system, 315
    diffused power and, 316–317
    economic power and, 316
    elite fractionalism and, 314–315
    ideological movements and, 317

informational controls and, 315–316
    of party-states, 313–314
    technological/social structures, 314
on military power
    civil wars and, 307
    coercion in, 306–307
    micro-solidarity and, 309–310
    spending on, 308–309
    in 20th century wars, 309
on nation-states, 310–311
on neoliberalism, 311–312, 318
Mao Zedong, 21–22
markets. See disembedded markets;
    financial markets
Marshall, T. H.
    on class inequalities, 319
    forms of citizenship, 25
    on social citizenship, 286
    on social stratification, 46
    on welfare programs, 211–212
Marwick, Arthur, 214
Marx, Karl
    on decency, 97
    determinist theory of, 104
    'economic' term use, 14
    historical sociology and, 11
    in Mann's conception of power, 13
    on moral unity, 93
    on revolution, 21–22
Marxian-Weberian model, 146, 154, 155,
    156, 157
Marxism-Leninism
    dominant ideologies in, 146–147
    Gorbachev's reforms and, 151
    ideological tensions in, 157
    types of, 149–150, 153
Marxist world-systems theory, 3–4
material structures, 32–33
McClymer, John, 189–190
McFarlane, Alan, 1
McGarry, J., 99–100
McNeill, J. R., 33–34
McNeill, William, 33–34
McQueen, B., 214
Medicare/Medicaid, 222
Merchant, Soldier, Sage (Priestland), 302–303
micro-solidarity, of soldiers, 137–138
middle-class. See also working class/working
    middle class
    push for progressive change, 96
    technological revolution and, 110
    universities and, 67–68
military power. See also chieftaincy; IEMP
    model (ideological, economic, mili-
    tary and political power sources)

military power (cont.)
    American's global reach, 175
    civil wars and, 307
    coercion in, 119–125, 306–307
    in IEMP model, 14–15
    micro-solidarity and, 309–310
    military expenditures, 123
    relevance of, 118–119
    social change and, 4–5
    in social transformations, 118
    sociological engagement with, 2
    spending on, 308–309
    in 20th century wars, 309
Mill, John Stuart, 96
Mises, Ludwig von, 116
modernity. See globalizing modernity
The Modern World-System (Wallerstein),
    49–50
Montesquieu, Charles de, 92, 93
Moore, Barrington
    macro-historical sociology of, 3–4
    Mann and, 56
    on social stratification, 46
    on working class, 44
multinational federations, conditions for,
    99–100
mutually assured destruction (MAD), 24

NACEMP model (natural, artefactual,
        cultural, economic, military and
        political power sources)
    artefactual power, 32–33
    cultural power, 33
    environmental problems analysis, 35
    gender analysis, 34–35
    Mann's response to, 288–290
    natural power, 33–34
nationalism. See also military power
    centrifugal ideologisation, 130–131
    coercive power and, 129–130, 139–140
    cultural diversity and, 127–128
    expansion of, 131–132
    Gellner's theory of, 99–100
    Mann's theory of, 125–127
    within rising powers, 102
National Labor Relations Act, 212
nation building
    cultural diversity in, 187
    redistributive policies in, 205
    social progress in, 186
    working class formation, 204
nation-states
    capitalist-industrial system of, 20,
        21–22, 31
    collective power of, 40

Mann on, 310–311
    as petty empires, 230
    political power in, 169–170
    rise of, 17–18, 39–40
naturalistic view of man, 93
natural power, 33–34, 288–290. See also
        NACEMP model (natural, artefac-
        tual, cultural, economic, military
        and political power sources)
natural selection, 47
Nazism, 20–21, 134, 137–138
Neitzel, S., 137
neoliberalism. See also "Great Neoliberal
        Recession"
    as evolutionary anomaly, 83–84
    of Hayek, 114
    ideological tensions in, 151–152
    infrastructural power and, 113
    Mann's analysis of, 109–110
    power of, 153
    price signals and, 115–116
    responses to, 160
    rise of, 26
    of Rueff, 114–115
    state power and, 112–113
networks of power, 112, 145–146
New Deal
    in exceptionalism debate, 5–6
    Great Depression and, 27
    Mann's analysis of, 217
    as permanent reform, 218
    policy failures of, 219
    social citizenship rights and, 211–212
New Public Management movement,
        26, 159
Nietzsche, Friedrich, 93–94
1968 world wave of protests, 78–79, 80
1989 Eastern European protests, 80
non-state entities, coercive power of, 120

Obama, Barack, 6, 219, 222
O'Leary, B., 99–100
Olson, Mancur, 72
Organisation for Economic Co-operation
        and Development (OECD)
        countries, 22
O'Rourke, K. H., 166
Osterhammel, Jürgen, 2–3, 38

Parker, Geoffrey, 38
Parsons, Talcott, 12, 46, 108
"party-states," 313–314
perpetual peace, 97
persuasion, mode of, 47, 48
Pierson, Paul, 213, 219–220

Piketty, Thomas, 99
Polanyi, Karl
  'double movement' concept of, 285
  'economic' term use, 14
  redistributive economy of, 72
  on rise of market societies, 25
political decency
  conditions for, 98–102
  dangers threatening, 102–104
  Mann's analysis of, 304
  origins of, 95–98
political hegemony, 50–51. *See also*
  American empire; liberal hegemony
political power. *See also* IEMP model
  (ideological, economic, military and
  political power sources)
  in globalizing modernity, 169–170
  liberalism as balance of, 90–91
  Mann on, 283
  in social movements, 131
politics, American, 318–320
Posen, B., 128
post-industrial societies, power networks
  in, 155
power. *See specific types of power*
power crystalizations, 67, 71
power networks
  as bounded, 310–311
  in Communist parties/societies, 91,
    147, 155
  creation of, 48
  globalization and, 286
  importance of, 282
  at the international level, 160–161
  of major social institutions, 281–282
  moral orders in, 156
  sources of power in, 149
power resources
  availability of, 12, 31
  balance of, 24–25
  central accumulation of, 49
  division/distribution of, 16, 34
  economic power and, 289
  social citizenship and, 213
  use of, 12, 46, 53
Prasad, Monica
  on financial crisis of 2008, 4
  on hegemonic America, 79
  Mann's response to, 282–283, 310–312,
    313, 316, 318
price signals, theory of, 115–116
Priestland, David
  on fascism/ethnic cleansing, 89–90
  Mann's response to, 302–303
  on role of ideology/culture, 5, 304

production, mode of, 47, 48
productive intensification, 65–66
Progressive Era
  social protections/reforms in, 185,
    188–189
  weakness of, 185
progressivism
  industrial labour and, 186–187,
    188–189, 196
  labour regulations/legislation in, 191
  protests, world wave of, 78–79, 80

racism
  as American exceptionalism, 319
  in colonial societies, 240–241
  of Europeans, 240
  as harmful, 305
  identity politics and, 29
  of imperialism, 97–98
Rajan, Raghuram, 111
Rawls, John, 46
Reagan, Ronald
  neoliberal turn under, 26
  nuclear arms reduction treaty, 24
recession, 26–27. *See also* "Great Neoliberal
  Recession"; Great Recession
Relative Deprivation and Social Justice
  (Runciman), 45–46, 53
religion. *See also* Christianity; Islamism/
  Islamist fundamentalism
  coercive power of, 120
  evolution in, 82
  as ideological example, 13–14
  in modern state, 1–2
Reno, Will, 4, 283–284
revolution, Mann on, 21
Reykjavik Summit, nuclear arms reduction
  treaty, 24, 27–28
Riga, Liliana
  on ethnic immigrants, 5
  Mann's response to, 318–319
Riley, Dylan, 169
The Rise of Historical Sociology (Smith),
  38, 39
'Rise of the West,' 2, 42, 74
rising powers
  economic affairs and, 101
  nationalism within, 102
  nuclear revolution/threat and, 100–101
Robinson, R., 232, 237
Rodgers, Daniel, 154
Roosevelt, Franklin, 264, 271–272. *See also*
  New Deal
Rousseau, Jean Jacques, 92–93
Rueff, Jacques, 114–115, 317

Runciman, Gary
  Applied Sociology, 53
  comparison with Mann, 291
  'Darwinian' typology of, 46–47
  evolutionist theory of, 3–4
  as heretical insider, 51–53
  Mann on, 53–54
  modes of societal power, 47
  Relative Deprivation and Social Justice,
    45–46, 53
  as reluctant theorist, 45–49
  as scientist, 56
  Treatise of Social Theory, 48, 56
  use of hindsight, 57–58
  Very Different, But Much the Same.
    The Evolution of British Society since
    1714, 56
Russia. *See also* Bolshevik revolution/
    Bolshevism; Soviet Union (USSR)
  as capitalist society, 28
  geopolitical power of, 147–148
  labour repression in, 194–195, 205–206
  revolution in, 21–22
  in super-power conflict, 300–301
  in World War I, 309, 310, 320–321

Sageman, M., 135
Santoro, Carlo Maria, 264–265
Schmidt, Vivien, 153
Schroeder, Ralph
  on infrastructural power, 314
  Mann's response to, 284–288
Schumpeter, J. A., 229
science, 31–32, 286–288. *See also* tech-
    noscience/technoscientific culture
scientific knowledge, in rise of West, 2
secondary sources, use of, 216–217
sectorial globalization, 19–20
selection, competitive, 47
Sewell, William, 143–144, 154, 155, 161
Shils, E. A., 136
Shimazu, N., 137
Shklar, Judith, 195
Sikkink, K., 170
Simmel, G., 136
Skocpol, Theda
  on influences of war, 216
  macro-historical sociology of, 3–4
  political institutional arguments, 210
  revolutions analysis of, 107
  on state elites, 213
Slaughter, A-M., 170
Smith, Adam
  on commercial society, 98, 104
  'economic' term use, 14

  on empires, 231–232
  political rule/economic growth relation-
    ship, 99
  view of human behavior, 93
Smith, Dennis, 1, 3–4, 143, 284, 290
Smith, Philip, 118
Snyder, Jack, 146
social citizenship
  "citizenship rights," 211–212
  development of, 221–222
  European empires and, 223
  Great Depression and, 212–213
  Great Society legislation, 222
  Mann's analysis of, 217–218
  political causes of, 213
  political institutional explanations in,
    220–221
  power resources and, 213
  role of war on, 214–215, 218–219
  slowing of, 213–214
  structural considerations, 222
  veterans' benefits, 214
  voting/electoral requirements, 221
social evolution. *See also* chieftaincy
  Darwinian principles and, 67
  meaning/progression of, 65–67
  middle-class elements and, 96
  neoliberalism and, 83–84
  optimism regarding, 81
  primatological observations, 69–70
  religion and, 82
  stages of, 69
  structural weaknesses, 81–82
  wars/revolution and, 83
social inequality
  historical reversal in, 82
  political decency and, 103
  warfare and, 81
socialism, cultural diversity and, 206
socialist/culturalists, gap between, 144
socialist revolution, 21–22, 54
social movements
  coercive power of, 120, 122
  in collapse of empire, 94
  ideologies and, 303–304
  as macro process, 132
  Mann's exploration of, 133
  nature of regimes and, 103
  in political institutional explanations, 220
  political power of, 131
  in transnational reform, 133, 170
social organisations, coercive nature of,
  119–124, 129–130
social policy (US)
  characteristics of, 209

Great Depression and, 210, 211–216
underdevelopment of, 209
social power
  collective power and, 69
  globalization and, 164–165, 166
  knowledge and, 67–68
  Mann's analysis of, 63, 64
  military power and, 118, 175
  in modern state, 77
  as orthogonal, 178
  sources of, 71
  transcendental ideologies and, 90
  in the West, 75
social science approaches
  advocate, 55
  examining magistrate, 55
  partisan expert witness, 55
  scientist, 55
Social Security Act, 211–212, 217, 220
social selection, 47
societal power, Runciman's modes of,
  47, 48
socio-cultural group, as analytical unit, 157
soldiers
  ideology and, 138–139
  micro-solidarity and, 137–138
  motivations of, 133–137
Sombart, Werner, 186
The Sources of Social Power (Mann)
  historical sociology of, 11
  narrative structure of, 281
  view of human beings in, 56
  Volume I
    agricultural revolution, 16–17
    class struggle, 17
    Mann's analytical tools in, 39
    traditional military powers, 16
  Volume II
    class struggle, 17
    on empires, 258
    nation-state expansion, 39–40
    WW I analysis, 20
  Volume III
    colonialism, 20–21
    empire, 281
    European empires, 40–41
    exceptionalism, 185
    fascism, 20–21
    globalization, 19–20, 164
    Progressivism, 188–189
    socialist revolution, 21–22
    welfare regimes, 25–26
  Volume IV
    Cold War origins, 247–250

economic hegemony, 22–23
exceptionalism, 185
globalization, 22, 164
mutually assured destruction
  (MAD), 24
neoliberalism, 26, 107
welfare regimes, 25–26
Soviet Union (USSR). See also Cold War;
  Gorbachev, Mikhail
  in Afghanistan, 23–24
  alternative world-systems and, 22
  in global system, 257–258
  ideology and, 146–147, 149
  revolution and, 21–22
  Stalinist Terror, 149–150
  totalitarianism and, 76
  weakness of, 251–252
spatial fix, 79, 80–81
Spencer, Herbert, 15
spending, on military power, 123, 308–309
Stalinist Terror, 149–150
Stephens, J. D., 210, 213
Stinchcombe, Arthur L., 219–220
Stouffer, S., 135
structural social history, 143–144
suffrage/voting rights, of alien labour,
  195, 201

Taylor, Charles, 93
technological revolution, 110
technology, as power source, 286–288
technoscience/technoscientific culture,
  164–165, 171–172, 175–176
territorial control/rule, 16, 166
terrorist associations, coercive power
  of, 120
Thatcher, Margaret
  neoliberal turn under, 26
  social inequality and, 103
The Theory of Cultural and Social Selection
  (Runciman), 47
Thompson, E. P., 46
Tilly, Charles
  Coercion Capital and European States, AD
    990–1990, 42
  feudal racketeering concept, 72
  macro-historical sociology of, 144
  on Mann's ideas, 3–4
  on nationalism, 128
  on 1968 protests, 78
  on states and war, 118
Titmuss, Richard, 214
totalitarianism, after WW I, 76
trade and treaties, 297–299

transcendental ideologies, 90, 91
transnational capitalism, 256, 261,
    267, 311
Treatise of Social Theory (Runciman), 48, 56

UNCTAD conference, 298
United States. *See also* American empire;
    Americanization Movement;
    Cold War
  dollar as global currency, 22–23, 54
  economic/cultural hegemony, 23, 54
  as 'incoherent empire,' 23, 24–25
  military budget of, 123
  in world polity, 104
universities
  interstitial situation of, 67–68
  power wielded by, 148

'Varieties of Capitalism' literature, 160
Very Different, But Much the Same.
    The Evolution of British Society since
    1714 (Runciman), 56
veterans, social citizenship of, 214
Viner, Jacob, 264
voting rights/suffrage, of alien labour,
    195, 201

Waal, Frans de, 70
Wallerstein, Immanuel
  biographical/academic context, 49
  comparison with Mann, 291
  Does Capitalism Have a Future? 50
  as global adventurer, 49–51
  as heretical insider, 51–53
  Mann on, 53–54
  The Modern World-System, 49–50
  on 1968 protests, 78
  as partisan expert witness, 56
  use of foresight, 57–58
  world-systems theory of, 3–4, 20, 63, 65
war. *See also* Cold War; World War I; World
    War II
  social change/evolution and, 4–5, 83
  social citizenship and, 214–215, 218–219
  sociological engagement with, 2
War on Poverty, 214–215
The Wealth of Nations (Smith), 104
Weber, Max
  on communities of sacrifice, 136
  cultural pessimism, 91–92
  historical sociology and, 11
  in Mann's conception of power, 13
  on military power, 14
  view of democracy, 93–94

violence, concept of, 121
welfare regimes, development of, 25–26
welfare state, build-up of, 5–6
Welzer, H., 137
West, rise of the, 2, 42, 74
Westad, Arne
  on China, 176
  on Cold War threats, 6–7
  Mann's response to, 296, 300–302
Westphalian project, 97, 257, 270–271,
    272, 275
Why is There No Socialism in the United States
    (Sombart), 186
Wilensky, Harold, 214
Williamson, J.G., 166
Winks, Robin, 273
women
  in Catholic Church, 306–307
  demands of, 18, 29
  gender/biological difference, 34–35
  in guerrilla armies, 75–76
workers. *See* alien labour; labour movement
working class/working middle class. *See also*
    alien labour; Americanization
    Movement
  character/composition of, 186, 196
  collapse of, 110
  ethnic diversity/fragmentation, 188,
    318–319
  as force for change, 44
  formation of, 204
  labour movement and, 185
  neoliberalism and, 160
  as power network, 155
Works Progress Administration, 212
World Bank, 22–23. *See also* International
    Monetary Fund (IMF)
world-system analysis, 3–4, 20, 22, 49–51,
    63, 77
World War I
  attempts to prevent, 27
  dominance/rivalries in, 166–167
  ethnonationalism and, 94–95
  imperial order in, 165
  nationalism and, 127, 128–129
  process leading to, 18, 20
  rise of communism/fascism, 104–105
  rise of totalitarianism, 76
  soldiers' motivations in, 133–134
  US/European dominance and, 165
World War II
  attempts to prevent, 27
  colonialism and, 20
  dominance/rivalries in, 166–167

Great Depression and, 27
impact on social citizenship, 214–215
imperial order in, 165
infrastructural power and, 108
liberal order building after, 271–272
nationalism and, 127, 128–129

post war reconstruction, 62–63
rise of communism/fascism, 104–105
soldiers' motivations in, 133–134
US/European dominance and, 165

Zizek, Slavoj, 102–103

For EU product safety concerns, contact us at Calle de José Abascal, 56–1°, 28003 Madrid, Spain or eugpsr@cambridge.org.

www.ingramcontent.com/pod-product-compliance
Ingram Content Group UK Ltd.
Pitfield, Milton Keynes, MK11 3LW, UK
UKHW020455240426
470322UK00016B/352